Greater New York
GOLF GUIDE

From Montauk to Monticello

Complete Coverage of *all* Public
and Private golf courses of the
Metropolitan area

Esther Kaplan & Debra Wolf
Weathervane Press

Copyright @ 1998 - Weathervane Press

GREATER NEW YORK GOLF GUIDE
Esther Kaplan & Debra Wolf

Published by Weathervane Press

ISBN 0-9645830-3-8

Printed in the United States of America

Library of Congress Cataloging in Publication Data

1. GREATER NEW YORK GOLF GUIDE - Title
2. Golf Guide
3. New York Golf
4. Kaplan, Esther
5. Wolf, Debra

Cover design by Susan Steeg

CONTENTS

Please note: The information in this book was provided by the personnel at the courses and country clubs. Every effort was made to provide accurate data. However, errors may have occurred, and the authors do not claim that every detail is accurate and complete. Information regarding fees, reservation policies and access, is always subject to change without notice and should be verified before planning to play at any of these courses.

Preface

The interest in and fascination with golf have accelerated in recent years for a wide variety of reasons. Most sports require power speed and stamina. Golf, on the other hand, utilizes more subtle skills such as finesse, judgment and coordination so that above average strength and physical endurance are not necessarily the dominant attributes for success. This explains why golf is a sport that is suitable for nearly everyone, witness its soaring popularity. The phenomenon of Tiger Woods has exposed a broader spectrum of our society to the world of golf. To accommodate this growth, many golf courses have been built recently, with many others in various stages of planning and construction. Now, more than ever, women, yougsters and teenagers have discovered what seasoned golfers have known for years; time spent playing golf can delight you, challenge you, introduce you to new friends and places, keep you in touch with nature and help you to stay physically fit.

The Metropolitan area of New York is well known for its many magnificent golf courses. **Bethpage**, a New York State public facility with five courses, has well deserved fame and has been honored for its difficulty by having the Black course chosen to host the US Open in 2002. Well noted private golf clubs such as **Shinnecock Hills, National Golf Links of America, Atlantic National, Winged Foot** and **Saint Andrews** are just some examples of the vast wealth of distinctive layouts that exist in the greater New York area. In addition, New York has some fine courses open to the public such as **Montauk Downs**, the Concord **"Monster"** and **Villa Roma**, the latter two in Sullivan County, an under utilized area with many excellent courses available. We are most intrigued by several new facilities either just opened or opening within the year such as **Centennial** in Carmel, **Hudson National** in Croton-on-Hudson, **Island Green**, (formerly Segalla CC) and **Harbor Links** in Port Washington. As a service to the loyal fans of our first book, **GARDEN STATE GOLF GUIDE**, we have added a New Jersey Update section covering the newest golfing venues. Highlights in the northern part of the State would be **New Jersey National** in Basking Ridge, **Black Bear** and **Ballyowen** in Sussex County and **Roycebrook** in Hillsborough.

Why not take the time to learn about the great golfing opportunities within your reach? New York offers play in the mountains, at the seashore, on wooded former farm and pasture lands and on varied terrain in between. The diversity of golf courses can satisfy the budget minded as well as those looking for beautiful views, challenging experiences and places to spend time in a meaningful and worthwhile way.

In addition to its superlative array of golf facilities, New York has an abundance of natural beauty. With its extensive beaches at the Hamptons and on the south shore of L.I., the rolling hills of Westchester, the Catskill Mouintains, and Long Island's north shore, and their proximity to the dynamic City of New York, there is little doubt that this region has it all. Some of these attractions are well known to tourists and draw many visitors from near and far. However, there are even New York residents who are not aware of the bountiful treasures, sometimes overlooked. including miles of undeveloped rural areas, parks and forests.

This golf guide was initiated after the success of **THE GARDEN STATE GOLF GUIDE.** We knew that the Northeast Region contained some of the finest golf facilities in the world and we discovered many of the less well known as well. How lucky we are to live in such a richly endowed part of the United States.

We personally visited each and every course in this book and it is our hope that our readers use the information that we have gathered to explore new frontiers of golf and enjoy what has given us so much pleasure in researching.

HOW TO USE THIS BOOK

Private and Public Golf Courses

Private means the course is open only to members and their guests. Initiation fees and yearly membership dues vary greatly. To obtain specific information, call the individual club. If you belong to a private club, it is possible for your pro to make arrangements with another club for you to play there.

Various private courses are located within adult communities. These are open only to residents of the community and their guests. If you are considering a move to an adult community, it might be a good idea to inquire about playing a round of golf at their facility.

Public is defined as courses that are open to the public and include the following categories:

1. County or municipally owned and operated courses with special rates and reservation policies

2. Daily fee courses open to the public at daily fee rates

3. Semi-private courses with memberships available at widely varying costs offering reduced or prepaid daily fees and tee time priorities - these clubs also encourage daily fee players

4. Resort courses open to the public with reduced rates for hotel guests

Name, Address and Telephone Number

On each page, we have given the full name of the club and its address. In a few cases, we have abbreviated Country Club as CC. In two cases, counties have been combined (Orange and Rockland, Dutchess and Putnam). For this New York area edition, we have added a special update on the newest courses in New Jersey.

Within each county, the courses are arranged alphabetically, and therefore listed that way at the beginning of each section. An easy way to find an individual course by name is to refer to the **index** for its page number. The numerical dots on the county maps give the **approximate** location of the courses with respect to major highways and towns. Highway designations and their general locations are indicated.

In all cases, the first phone number (or the only one shown) is for the pro shop. The second phone number is either for the clubhouse or tee time reservations.

Course Information

The first paragraph on each course page includes the number of holes on the course, days and months open, types of memberships and reservation policies. Most New York courses that are open all year are dependent on the weather. It is therefore advisable to call in advance for the latest tee time information, as well as for seasonal rate policies. Most private clubs are open six days a week and usually close on Mondays.

Amenities

This box contains a generally self-explanatory check list of the amenities at each course. However, when there are exceptions or clarifications, they are so noted in the text, i.e. Driving Range is checked but practice is limited to irons, or Pull Carts are checked but allowed only during certain hours or days.

Power Carts: Most courses encourage the use of power carts but some do not offer them at all.

Pull Carts: Those courses that permit the use of pull carts may or may not provide them for rent.

Food: When this item is checked, the facility offers anything from a limited snack bar or vending machines to a full-service restaurant and/or bar.

Outings: Many clubs make their facilities available to groups of more than 12 golfers for outings usually sponsored by corporations, charities, townships or club members. Most private clubs encourage outings on the days they are closed to their members (usually Mondays). Semi-private clubs also offer outings and special golf packages.

Caddies: Not offered at public courses.

Soft Spikes: Where required, so noted. Many clubs are now strongly recommending them. Call in advance for policy.

Fees

The fee schedule indicates the prevailing rates. It is recommended, however, that you contact the course to make sure it has not been revised. Published rates are subject to change but generally do not vary greatly from one year to the next.

Weekday: Monday to Friday

Weekend: Saturday, Sunday and holidays - some courses include Friday as part of the weekend

Daily: Greens fee for daily play

Res. with ID: County or township resident with current yearly permit

Twilight: Twilight starting time differs from club to club in off-season - check in advance with club

Cart fees: Generally given for 2 people in a power cart

Course Description

The course description helps you discover what course would be most appropriate and appealing for you. We have discussed degree of difficulty, variety, length and special features. The scorecard shown below each course description gives additional details on course rating, slope and yardages. Whenever possible, information describing what is unique or unusual about these courses has been included; such as, historical, anecdotal or interesting features. These descriptions might offer golfers some clue for course strategy.

Many 9 hole courses have an additional tee box for the second 9 to give the golfer playing 18 holes some added variety. Moreover, courses that have more than two nine hole sets allow combinations of play, i.e. Blue-Red, Blue-White or Red-White.

Course Directions

The first line of directions gives you the course number as indicated on the county map. Directions progress from major to secondary highways to local roads and finally to the club. Care has been taken to alert the driver to landmarks or other helpful navigational features. It is recommended that you bring along a current area map to track your route in more detail as the maps provided herein show only **approximate** location.

Professional Staff

Club Manager: May manage more than just the golf operation

Supt: Superintendent of greens

Pro: Head pro is listed; some courses have assist. pros as well If the pro is PGA affiliated, it is shown following the name.

Architect: The name of the architect(s), year built or redesigned

Estab: Indicates when the club originated

Scorecard

Course Rating is an indication of how difficult the course is to a scratch golfer (one who shoots par or better). The higher the rating, the greater the difficulty.

Slope is useful as a comparison of relative difficulty between courses with the higher slope number indicating the more difficult course.

The categories rated on the scorecard on each page of this book are: **Blue/Championship** or **Professional**, **White/Regular** and **Red/Forward** tees. Many courses are offering additional tee boxes which are indicated on the scorecard. Some tee positions are designated by other colors or names.

Where there is no handicap shown for the forward tees, it is the same as the handicap shown for the regular tees.

NEW YORK CITY

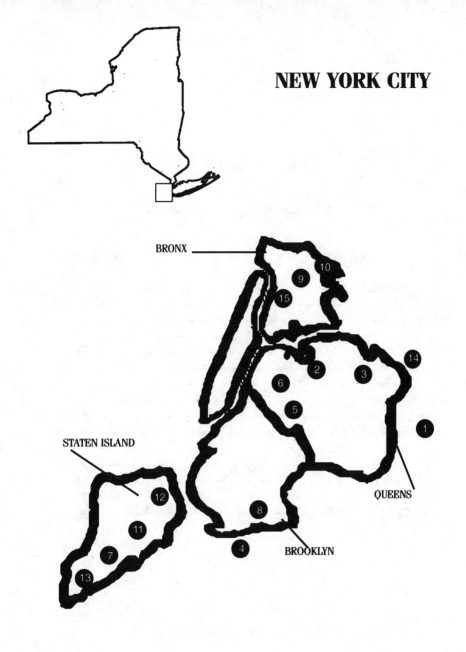

BRONX

STATEN ISLAND

QUEENS

BROOKLYN

NEW YORK CITY

Public Courses appear in *bold italics*

BREEZY POINT GOLF COURSE

Jacob Riis Park, Rockaway, NY 11694   **(718) 474-1623**

Breezy Point is an 18 hole pitch & putt course open 7 days a week from Mar. 15 to Nov. 24. Tee time reservations are not necessary.

Driving Range	Lockers
Practice Green	Showers
Power Carts	• **Food**
•**Pull Carts**	Clubhouse
•**Club Rental**	Outings
Soft Spikes	

Fees	**Weekday**	**Weekend**
Daily Jr.	$5.50	$11
Adults	$8	

Course Description: The Gateway Sports Center runs Breezy Point Golf. There is one par 4 and the rest are par 3's. The drainage is good making it playable soon after a rainfall. This is a fun place to play while the family is at the beach.

Directions: New York City, #1
Belt Pkwy. South over the Marine Parkway bridge; bear left to parking lot; enter and park on right side. Proceed to beach and turn right to golf facility.

Hole	1	2	3	4	5	6	7	8	9	Out	BLUE	Rating
BLUE												Slope
WHITE	67	58	102	103	60	87	93	112	89	771	WHITE	Rating
Par	3	3	3	3	3	3	3	3	3	27		
Handicap	16	18	6	5	17	13	8	3	11			Slope
RED												
Par											RED	Rating
Handicap												Slope

Hole	10	11	12	13	14	15	16	17	18	In		Totals
BLUE											BLUE	
WHITE	90	150	80	89	112	97	140	80	87	925	WHITE	1696
Par	3	4	3	3	3	3	3	3	3	28	Par	55
Handicap	9	1	15	10	4	7	2	14	12			
RED											RED	
Par											Par	
Handicap												

Manager: Rita Lauro   **Pro:** At Driving Range

CLEARVIEW GOLF COURSE

202-12 Willets Point. Blvd. Bayside, NY 11360   (718) 229-2570

Clearview is a public 18 hole course open 7 days a week, all year (weather permitting). For reservations, call (718) 225-GOLF from 8:30AM -2:30PM Mon.-Fri. It is run by American Golf. Golf packages include food & cart.

Driving Range	•Lockers
Practice Green	Showers
•Power Carts	•Food
•Pull Carts	•Clubhouse
•Club Rental	•Outings
Soft Spikes	

Fees	Weekday	Weekend
Daily(6:30-11AM)$51		
Daily (11-1PM)	$49	$56
Daily(1PM...)	$48	$54

Course Description: Clearview is the busiest golf course in the Tri-State area and considered the finest of the Queens layouts. Long and flat with small well-bunkered greens, it is challenging to all levels of play. An errant shot can put you in deep woods or high rough even around the greens. The fourth hole, a par 3 requires a carry over a pond. The signature par 4 17th has a beautiful view of the Throg's Neck Bridge. There is excellent drainage even after a heavy rain.

Directions: New York City #2
LIE to Clearview X-way. (I-295) North toward Throg's Neck Bridge to Willets Point Blvd. Exit #17, (last exit before Throg's Neck Bridge.) At end of ramp, turn left onto Willets Pt. Blvd. to club entrance on left.

Hole	1	2	3	4	5	6	7	8	9	Out	BLUE	Rating
BLUE												Slope
WHITE	356	473	408	190	392	390	140	409	422	3180		
Par	4	5	4	3	4	4	3	4	4	35	WHITE	Rating 69.2
Handicap	14	16	10	12	2	4	7	18	6			Slope 114
RED	310	396	335	138	366	359	105	375	399	2783		
Par	4	5	4	3	4	4	3	4	4	35	RED	Rating 70.4
Handicap	12	4	8	14	2	6	18	16	10			Slope 115
Hole	10	11	12	13	14	15	16	17	18	In		Totals
BLUE												
WHITE	365	343	145	338	442	491	194	386	379	3083	WHITE	6263
Par	4	4	3	4	4	5	3	4	4	35	Par	70
Handicap	11	7	17	15	1	13	3	5	9			
RED	316	313	119	312	413	391	165	345	340	2714	RED	5497
Par	4	4	3	4	4	5	3	4	4	35	Par	70
Handicap	9	13	17	15	1	3	11	7	5			

Manager: Jim Stone   **Pro:** Leo Tabick, PGA   **Supt:** Frank Marra
Architect: Willie Tucker 1925

DOUGLASTON GOLF COURSE

6320 Marathon Pkwy., Douglaston, NY 11363   **(718) 428-1617**

Douglaston is an 18 hole NYC course open all year, 7 days a week, weather permitting. It is run by Leisure Management Corp. Tee times may be reserved 7 days in advance weekdays, & 2 Thursdays prior after 4PM for weekends.

Driving Range	Lockers
•Practice Green	Showers
•Power Carts	•Food
•Pull Carts	•Clubhouse
•Club Rental	Outings

Fees	Weekday	Weekend
Daily(non-res)	$24	$26
Daily(res)	$18	$20
Sr/Jr(res)	$9	$10
Power carts	$24.50	$25.50

Course Description: Douglaston is a challenging rugged city course with rolling hills. Believed to be located at the highest point in Queens, it has a great view of the New York skyline. Formerly called North Hills CC, its beautiful Spanish style cllubhouse is impressive. The signature par 4 11th hole is short and is guarded by three trees in front of the driveable green. There is a pond on the par 3 fifth hole. The greens cannot be cut too low because of the high traffic on the course, therefore they are not particularly fast.

Directions: New York City, #3
LIE to Exit #30 (Douglaston Pkwy.) Stay on service Rd. to Marathon Pkwy, and turn right. Proceed 1/2 mile to club on right.

Hole	1	2	3	4	5	6	7	8	9	Out	BLUE	Rating 66.2
BLUE	381	163	365	431	140	417	505	385	200	2987		Slope 111
WHITE	341	143	332	416	125	367	470	376	170	2740		
Par	4	3	4	4	3	4	5	4	3	34	WHITE	Rating 64.2
Handicap	11	15	5	1	17	3	9	7	13			Slope 107
RED	275	130	320	410	120	355	440	330	150	2530		
Par	4	3	4	4	3	4	5	4	3	34	RED	Rating 66.3
Handicap	11	15	5	1	17	3	9	7	13			Slope 107

Hole	10	11	12	13	14	15	16	17	18	In		Totals
BLUE	324	295	166	390	387	178	175	133	550	2598	BLUE	5585
WHITE	304	275	146	370	377	166	154	113	495	2400	WHITE	5140
Par	4	4	3	4	4	3	3	3	5	33	Par	67
Handicap	8	10	16	6	4	12	14	18	2			
RED	294	205	125	353	360	135	125	95	380	2072	RED	4602
Par	4	4	3	4	4	3	3	3	5	33	Par	67
Handicap	8	10	16	6	4	12	14	18	2			

Manager: Bob Arrowood **Pro:** Helen Finn Gilligan, PGA **Supt:** Mike Procops
Architect: Willie Tucker 1927

DYKER BEACH GOLF COURSE

 PUBLIC

86th & 7th Ave., Brooklyn, NY 11228 (718) 836-9722

Dyker Beach is an 18 hole NYC course, run by American Golf, open 7 days a week, all year, weather permitting. Tee times are made by calling (718) 225-GOLF 11 days in advance. Fees are for residents of NYC with a pass; others add $6.

Driving Range	Lockers
• **Practice Green**	Showers
• **Power Carts**	• **Food**
• **Pull Carts**	• **Clubhouse**
• **Club Rental**	• **Outings**
Soft Spikes	

Fees	Weekday	Weekend
Daily	$18	$20
After 1PM	$16.50	$18.50
Twi	$9	$10
Power carts	$24.50	$25.50

Course Description: Built on 238 acres in a heavily treed park-like setting, Dyker Beach is thoroughly enjoyed by NYC golfers. A relatively flat layout gives golfers (particularly seniors) enjoyment in walking on this well conditioned course. The greens are large, undulating and considered by some to be the best in the Northeast. The signature par 3 #11, 216 yards from the blues, is downhill and quite a challenge. In 1997 the pro shop was greatly improved; bunker renovation is expected in 1998. The Guiness Book of Records shows 116,000 rounds were played one year at this busy course.

Directions: New York City, #4
Belt Pkwy. West to Exit #4(14th Av./Bay 8th St.) Go to 1st light, turn left to next light and turn left again. Bear right to course on 86th St.

Hole	1	2	3	4	5	6	7	8	9	Out	BLUE	Rating 70.5
BLUE	393	163	369	447	427	461	379	211	401	3251		Slope 116
WHITE	376	150	346	438	418	450	365	195	379	3117		
Par	4	3	4	4	4	5	4	3	4	35	WHITE	Rating 69.2
Handicap	9	17	15	1	3	5	7	11	13			Slope 114
RED	350	140	336	418	370	420	320	150	340	2844		
Par	4	3	4	5	4	5	4	3	4	36	RED	Rating 70.4
Handicap	8	18	12	2	7	4	10	15	9			Slope 115
Hole	10	11	12	13	14	15	16	17	18	In		Totals
BLUE	423	201	358	493	423	483	494	374	348	3297	BLUE	6548
WHITE	417	187	338	428	412	170	488	363	340	3143	WHITE	6260
Par	4	3	4	5	4	3	5	4	4	36	Par	71
Handicap	4	18	10	8	2	14	6	16	12			
RED	380	172	290	418	370	152	420	330	320	2852	RED	5676
Par	4	3	4	5	4	3	5	4	4	36	Par	72
Handicap	6	16	13	3	5	17	1	11	14			

Manager: David Nation **Pro:** John Vuono, PGA **Supt:** Michael Stringfellow
Architect: John Van Kleek 1921

FOREST PARK GOLF COURSE

101 Forest Park Drive, Woodhaven, NY 11421   (718) 296-0999

Forest Park is an 18 hole NYC public golf course open all year, 7 days a week. Tee times may made up to 10 days in advance with a credit card. There is a $2 reservation fee.

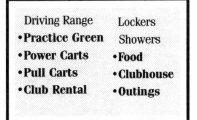

Driving Range	Lockers
•Practice Green	Showers
•Power Carts	•Food
•Pull Carts	•Clubhouse
•Club Rental	•Outings

Fees	Weekday	Weekend
Daily	$23	$25
Twilight	$15	$16
Resident	May deduct $6	
Power carts $24		$24

Course Description: Forest Park Golf Course is short, hilly and abounding in beautiful trees. In this well populated area it is known as a "haven within the city." One can view Manhattan from the 9th green.   Challenge comes from the fast and undulating greens, and the water which comes into play. The 14th, considered the signature hole, is the longest par 4 on the course. There is good drainage here so that play is possible even after a heavy rain. The course had to be shortened when the Interborough Parkway was built. The tees, greens, fairways, clubhouse and pro shop have been modernized.

Directions: New York City, #5
Grand Cent.Pkwy. to Interborough Pkwy. (now called Jackie Robinson Pkwy.) West. Proceed to Forest Park Dr. Exit. Course is directly off the exit.

Hole	1	2	3	4	5	6	7	8	9	Out	BLUE	Rating
BLUE												Slope
WHITE	443	400	123	323	375	171	390	433	414	3072		
Par	4	4	3	4	4	3	4	4	4	34	WHITE	Rating 67.5
Handicap	1	3	17	13	11	15	9	5	7			Slope 111
WHITE	423	381	112	247	362	162	365	415	396	2863		
Par	4	4	3	4	4	3	4	4	4	34	WHITE	Rating 70.4
Handicap	1	3	17	13	11	15	9	5	7			Slope 116
Hole	10	11	12	13	14	15	16	17	18	In		Totals
BLUE											BLUE	
WHITE	196	390	143	319	461	308	349	410	172	2748	WHITE	5820
Par	3	4	3	4	4	4	4	4	3	33	Par	67
Handicap	10	8	16	12	4	18	6	2	14			
WHITE	190	362	137	294	435	293	331	365	161	2568	WHITE	5431
Par	3	4	3	4	4	4	4	4	3	33	Par	67
Handicap	10	8	16	12	4	18	6	2	14			

Manager/Supt: Bob Smith   **Pro:** Paul Giordano, PGA
Architects: Thomas Bendelow, Lindsay Ervin 1896

KISSENA PARK GOLF COURSE

164-15 Booth Memorial Ave., Flushing, NY 11365   **(718) 939-4594**

Kissena Park is an 18 hole NYC public course that is run by Global Golf. It is open 7 days a week all year, weather permitting. There are 8 par 3's and no par 5's. Tee time reservations may be made up to 1 week in advance.

Driving Range	Lockers
•**Practice Green**	Showers
•**Power Carts**	•**Food**
•**Pull Carts**	•**Clubhouse**
•**Club Rental**	•**Outings**
Soft Spikes	

Fees	Weekday	Weekend
Daily	$18	$20
Non ID	$24	$26
Twilight	$9	$10
ID card	$6 (valid for 2 seasons)	

Course Description: Kissena Park, from its highest point has views of the Manhattan skyline. Animals abound here: pheasants, raccoons, hawks etc. The signature par 3 9th is the toughest par 3 in the city; it is uphill 184 yds. from the white tees. The ball rolls back down if you don't make the green. The 7th hole has an elevated green with no room for error. The heights mentioned above result in virtually no flat lies. Very little water comes into play making this short course a great place for iron practice. Chi-Chi Rodriguez played here as well as members of the Mets.

Directions: New York City, #6
LIE to Exit #24 (Kissena Blvd.) Proceed 1 block north to Booth Memorial Ave., turn right. Course is on left just after crossing 164th St.

Hole	1	2	3	4	5	6	7	8	9	Out	BLUE	Rating 61.7
BLUE	330	370	416	122	169	322	162	346	198	2435		Slope 94
WHITE	317	350	371	119	164	314	150	335	184	2304		
Par	4	4	4	3	3	4	3	4	3	32	WHITE	Rating 60.9
Handicap	15	1	5	17	13	11	7	9	3			Slope 93
RED	305	330	338	105	141	275	140	320	168	2122		
Par	4	4	4	3	3	4	3	4	3	32	RED	Rating 63.9
Handicap	15	1	5	17	13	11	7	9	3			Slope 98
Hole	10	11	12	13	14	15	16	17	18	In		Totals
BLUE	117	317	199	331	166	329	124	329	318	2230	BLUE	4665
WHITE	107	302	176	311	156	306	114	306	307	2085	WHITE	4389
Par	3	4	3	4	3	4	3	4	4	32	Par	64
Handicap	16	6	8	14	4	10	18	2	12			
RED	100	295	166	291	148	282	104	289	290	1965	RED	4087
Par	3	4	3	4	3	4	3	4	4	32	Par	64
Handicap	16	6	8	14	4	10	18	2	12			

Manager/Pro: Paul Forest   **Architect:** John Van Kleek 1933

LA TOURETTE GOLF COURSE

 PUBLIC

1001 Richmond Hill Rd., Staten Island NY 10306   (718) 351-1889

La Tourette is an 18 hole NYC public course open all year 7 days a week. Weekday reservations may be made up to 11 days in advance, and for weekends the Wednesday before. It is run by American Golf.

•**Driving Range**	Lockers
•**Practice Green**	Showers
•**Power Carts**	•**Food**
•**Pull Carts**	•**Clubhouse**
•**Club Rental**	•**Outings**
Soft Spikes	

Fees	Weekday	Weekend
Daily (nonres)	$24	$26
Daily(res)	$18	$20
Sr/Jr(res)	$9	$10
Power carts	$24.50	$25.50

Course Description: La Tourette began as a family home built in 1836. The heirs sold the property to NYC in 1928; later it was developed as a golf course keeping the original house. It is a bucolic (nestled in trees in city-like surroundings) and challenging course with spectacular views. The back nine has rolling fairways; the front is flatter. The signature par 5 10th is on top of a hill with a view of the clubhouse from the green. The 15th hole has an undulating fairway and a rolling large green. Water affects play on 3 holes. Good drainage makes it playable soon after a rain.

Directions: New York City, #7
Take the Staten Isl. Exprwy (I-278) Eastbound (from NJ Goethals Br.) to the Bradley Ave. exit. Take first left (crossing Expwy.) Then take first left again and get on service Rd. to Wooley Ave. & turn left. Proceed to Forest Hill Rd. Turn left to club.

Hole	1	2	3	4	5	6	7	8	9	Out	BLUE	Rating 71.3
BLUE	519	325	135	380	438	408	166	370	401	3142		Slope 121
WHITE	509	315	107	370	428	398	152	360	391	3030		
Par	5	4	3	4	4	4	3	4	4	35	WHITE	Rating 69.6
Handicap	13	15	17	7	1	3	11	9	5			Slope 118
RED	434	265	80	330	391	347	141	299	325	2612		
Par	5	4	3	4	4	4	3	4	4	35	RED	Rating 70.9
Handicap	13	15	17	7	1	3	11	9	5			Slope 115
Hole	10	11	12	13	14	15	16	17	18	In		Totals
BLUE	511	382	200	417	354	394	397	497	398	3550	BLUE	6692
WHITE	481	372	137	392	344	384	387	431	364	3292	WHITE	6322
Par	5	4	3	4	4	4	4	5	4	37	Par	72
Handicap	16	14	10	2	18	4	8	12	6			
RED	467	285	131	377	309	317	297	402	296	2881	RED	5493
Par	5	4	3	4	4	4	4	5	4	37	Par	72
Handicap	16	14	10	2	18	4	8	12	6			

Manager: Arnie Muniz   **Pro:** Bill Castner, PGA   **Supt:** Joe Stefanski
Architect: John Van Kleek 1929

MARINE PARK GOLF COURSE

2880 Flatbush Ave., Brooklyn, NY 11234   **(718) 338-7149**

Marine Park is an 18 hole NYC course run by Golf Management Corp.and open all year, 7 days a week, weather permitting. Tee times may be reserved 7 days in advance. To reserve, call (718) 225-GOLF. Residents must show current ID card. Alternate phone # 338-7113.

Driving Range	• Lockers
Practice Green	• Showers
• Power Carts	• Food
• Pull Carts	• Clubhouse
• Club Rental	• Outings

Fees	Weekday	Weekend
Daily-Res	$18	$20
Non-Res	$24	$26
Twi-Res	$9	$10
Cart	$24.50	$25.50

Course Description: Marine Park is a links type wide open course, the longest of the NYC golf facilities. The large greens are undulating and in excellent condition; a few are elevated. There is no water in play. The wind in your face can make play quite difficult. From some places on the course, the Manhattan skyline can be seen. The par 3s are long and the greens are considered difficult to putt. Marine Park is well maintained and has good drainage except after heavy rainstorms. The course is very convenient to reach by car.

Directions: New York City, # 8
From Belt Parkway in Brooklyn, make a right off Exit 11N. Make left turn at second light to course.

Hole	1	2	3	4	5	6	7	8	9	Out	BLUE	Rating 70.5
BLUE	513	447	465	335	186	399	379	183	415	3322		Slope 113
WHITE	498	437	445	328	181	384	359	178	405	3215		
Par	5	4	4	4	3	4	4	3	4	35	WHITE	Rating 70.5
Handicap	2	5	4	13	14	8	12	15	7			Slope 111
RED	430	324	345	264	123	341	268	123	281	2499		
Par	5	4	4	4	3	4	4	3	4	35	RED	Rating
Handicap	2	5	4	13	14	8	12	15	7			Slope

Hole	10	11	12	13	14	15	16	17	18	In		Totals
BLUE	491	381	392	178	516	459	415	182	530	3544	BLUE	6866
WHITE	476	370	369	173	495	431	393	177	510	3394	WHITE	6609
Par	5	4	4	3	5	4	4	3	5	37	Par	72
Handicap	16	9	11	18	3	6	10	17	1			
RED	410	290	298	125	415	371	313	152	450	2824	RED	5323
Par	5	4	4	3	5	4	4	3	5	37	Par	72
Handicap	16	9	11	18	3	6	10	17	1			

Managers: John Annunziata, Neal Barbella   **Pro:** Bob Palmieri, PGA
Supt: Al Huemmer **Architect:** Robert Trent Jones, Jr. 1962

MOSHOLU GOLF COURSE

Jerome & Bainbridge Ave., Bronx, NY 10467   (718) 655-9164

Mosholu Golf is a NYC owned 9 hole course which is leased to Fairway Golf. It is open 7 days a week, all year (weather permitting). Tee times for weekends may be made the Monday prior with a $2 reservation fee.

•**Driving Range**	•**Lockers**
•**Practice Green**	Showers
•**Power Carts**	•**Food**
•**Pull Carts**	•**Clubhouse**
•**Club Rental**	•**Outings**
•**Soft Spikes**	

Fees	Weekday	Weekend
Daily(9)	$15.50	$17.50
Daily(18)	$21	$23
Permit(9)	$9	$13.50
Permit(18)	$17	$18

Course Description: Mosholu is part of Van Cortlandt Park and is one of the few courses that can be reached by subway from NYC (Woodlawn Sta.#4 Lex.line). It is the only city facility that has a driving range (other than LaTourette) and offers grass tees. Narrow fairways and abundant woods are characteristic; golfers may think they are in the country as hardly any buildings are in view. The undulating greens are moderate size and not very fast. The famous frequented Mosholu such as Chi Chi Rodriguez, Elke Sommer and Lou Gehrig.

Directions: New York City, #9
Northbound: I-87 to Exit #13 (East 233rd St.) Turn right at 1st light onto Jerome Ave.to course. Southbound: I-87 to Exit #13, turn right at 2nd light to course.

Hole	1	2	3	4	5	6	7	8	9	Out	BLUE	Rating
BLUE												Slope
WHITE	421	180	248	505	341	380	384	430	230	3119		
Par	4	3	4	5	4	4	4	4	3	35	WHITE	Rating 70.5
Handicap	1	13	17	11	15	3	9	7	5			Slope 124
RED	340	160	238	460	335	330	345	410	220	2838		
Par	4	3	4	5	4	4	4	4	3	35	RED	Rating 76.2
Handicap	1	13	17	11	15	3	9	7	5			Slope 133
Hole	10	11	12	13	14	15	16	17	18	In		Totals
BLUE											BLUE	6382
WHITE	431	194	258	525	354	396	401	465	239	3263		
Par	4	3	4	5	4	4	4	5	3	36	Par	71
Handicap	2	12	18	10	16	4	8	14	6			
RED	340	160	238	460	335	330	345	410	220	2838	RED	5676
Par	4	3	4	5	4	4	4	4	3	35	Par	70
Handicap	2	12	18	10	16	4	8	14	6			

Manager: Norman Tafet   **Pro/Supt:** Paul Giordano, PGA
Architects: John Van Kleek, Stephen Kay **Estab:** 1914

PELHAM/SPLIT ROCK GOLF

870 Shore Rd., Bronx, NY 10464   (718) 885-1258

Pelham/Split Rock is a 36 hole NYC facility operated by American Golf and open all year, 7 days a week. For tee times, ($2 res. fee); call (718) 225-GOLF Tuesdays prior for weekends, 2 weeks prior for weekdays.   Parking fee $2. Early Bird and Senior/Junior discounts. Res.- $6 fee for 2 yr. ID pass.

Driving Range	• Lockers
• Practice Green	Showers
• Power Carts	• Food
• Pull Carts	• Clubhouse
• Club Rental	• Outings

Fees	Weekday	Weekend
Daily-Res	$18	$20
Non-Res	$24	$26
Twilight	$9	$10
Power cart $24.50		$25.50

Course Description: Split Rock is narrow and tree lined with good drainage. On the 17th, water is in play on the second shot to a contoured green. On the 18th, a 365 year old oak tree, with purple blossoms in the summer, is situated on the edge of the putting surface. If the pin is in the back right, the tree overhangs and blocks the shot. The Split Rock Brook meanders through the 1st hole. Pelham is a wide open links style course that is characterized as more forgiving than Split Rock with smaller, undulating greens. Both courses are extremely popular and consequently very busy. Scorecard below is for Split Rock.

Directions: New York City, #10
Take Hutchinson Pkwy. to Orchard Beach(City Island) exit. Go to traffic circle and 3/4 around it onto Shore Rd. Course is 1/4 mile up on the left.

Hole	1	2	3	4	5	6	7	8	9	Out	BLUE	Rating 71.9
BLUE	408	433	180	513	379	349	178	490	416	3346		Slope 125
WHITE	397	418	140	477	358	325	165	475	394	3149		
Par	4	4	3	5	4	4	3	5	4	36	WHITE	Rating 70.3
Handicap	2	8	18	10	6	16	14	12	4			Slope 122
RED	379	378	131	427	328	308	127	427	300	2805		
Par	4	4	3	4	4	4	3	5	4	36	RED	Rating 71.7
Handicap	2	4	18	6	14	8	16	10	12			Slope 122
Hole	10	11	12	13	14	15	16	17	18	In		Totals
BLUE	437	417	407	144	471	220	440	440	392	3368	BLUE	6714
WHITE	423	337	394	115	453	193	420	415	382	3132	WHITE	6218
Par	4	4	4	3	5	3	4	4	4	35	Par	71
Handicap	5	15	9	17	13	7	15	3	11			
RED	365	305	345	110	443	141	333	324	338	2704	RED	5509
Par	4	4	4	3	5	3	4	4	4	35	Par	71
Handicap	3	15	5	17	11	3	7	1	9			

Manager: James Dolan   **Pro:** John Farrell, PGA **Supt:** John Dillon
Architects: Pelham/Lawrence Van Etten 1899   Split Rock/John Van Kleek 1934

RICHMOND COUNTY COUNTRY CLUB `PRIVATE`

1122 Todt Hill Road, Staten Island, NY 10304   **(718) 351-0600**

Richmond County CC is an 18 hole course open 6 days a week all year, weather permitting. Guests may play accompanied by a member. Tee time reservations are necessary on weekends.

> •**Driving Range**   • **Lockers**
> •**Practice Green** •**Showers**
> •**Power Carts**   •**Food**
> Pull Carts   •**Clubhouse**
> •**Club Rental**   •**Outings**
> •**Caddies**   •**Soft Spikes**

Course Description: From the 10th tee at Richmond CC, the highest point on the eastern seaboard, there is a spectacular panoramic view. In the distance Sandy Hook and the Atlantic Highlands are visible. The course is challenging especially for ladies, hence the high slope. The hilly and narrow signature par 3 third hole requires a shot over a pond to a small, fast, severely sloped green. A stream runs the length of the golf course and is in play on 6 holes. This is the only private club entirely in NYC. The horseshoe logo indicates that Richmond had its origins on Staten Island as a riding club.

Directions: New York City, #11
Take I-278 East to Todt Hill Rd.-Slossom Ave. exit. Turn right onto Slossom (will merge into Todt Hill Rd.) Proceed 3.0 miles to club on right.

Hole	1	2	3	4	5	6	7	8	9	Out	BLUE	Rating 72.1
BLUE	330	350	165	326	236	413	498	304	366	2988		Slope 128
WHITE	320	345	122	315	223	400	481	296	348	2850		
Par	4	4	3	4	3	4	5	4	4	35	WHITE	Rating 70.8
Handicap	16	6	18	12	8	2	10	14	4			Slope 126
RED	300	281	101	305	213	390	427	230	251	2498		
Par	4	4	3	4	3	5	5	4	4	36	RED	Rating 73.6
Handicap	14	2	18	6	8	12	10	16	4			Slope 127
Hole	**10**	**11**	**12**	**13**	**14**	**15**	**16**	**17**	**18**	**In**		Totals
BLUE	644	454	326	197	408	408	374	386	434	3631	BLUE	6619
WHITE	620	445	312	182	392	397	350	363	414	3475	WHITE	6325
Par	5	4	4	3	4	4	4	4	4	36	Par	71
Handicap	1	5	17	13	11	7	15	9	3			
RED	458	385	295	175	360	390	275	355	386	3079	RED	5577
Par	5	4	4	3	4	5	4	4	5	38	Par	74
Handicap	3	5	11	17	7	9	15	1	13			

Manager: Kevin Murphy   **Pro:** Bernie Kosinski, PGA   **Supt:** Eric Warchol
Architect: Robert White **Estab:** 1888

SILVER LAKE GOLF COURSE

PUBLIC

915 Victory Blvd., Staten Island, NY 10301   (718) 447-5686

Silver Lake is an 18 hole NYC course open all year, 7 days a week, weather permitting. It is run by American Golf. Tee times may be reserved 7 days in advance weekdays, & 2 Thursdays prior after 4PM for weekends.

Driving Range	•Lockers
•Practice Green	Showers
•Power Carts	•Food
•Pull Carts	•Clubhouse
•Club Rental	•Outings

Fees	Weekday	Weekend
Daily-Res	$18	$20
Non-Res	$24	$26
Twi-Res	$9	$10
Cart	$24.50	$25.50

Course Description: The nines at Silver Lake were switched in 1996 to improve the pace of play. The front side is flatter and the back more hilly. The greens are very fast and contoured with water in play on 2 holes. The course is tight, a "shot makers course". There is only one par 5. The 15th is a 99 yard par 3 with a plateau green and features a new tee box for 1997. The signature par 3 #12 requires a 220 yard shot over a gorge but the ladies tees are being moved up to make the green more reachable on the tee shot.

Directions: New York City, #12
Take the Verrazano Bridge to Staten Island. Take Rte.278West to Clove-Richmond Road Exit. Take service rd. past 2 lights, bear right onto Clove Rd. Go 3 lights and right at Victory Blvd. Club is 1/2 mile ahead on left.

Hole	1	2	3	4	5	6	7	8	9	Out	BLUE	Rating 67.8
BLUE	387	150	406	530	344	332	212	372	418	3151		Slope 110
WHITE	371	137	392	506	327	314	195	360	397	2999		
Par	4	3	4	5	4	4	3	4	4	35	WHITE	Rating 66.1
Handicap	6	17	3	7	12	15	14	10	2			Slope 105
RED	351	128	310	487	310	289	156	330	343	2704		
Par	4	3	4	5	4	4	3	4	4	35	RED	Rating 68.6
Handicap	6	17	3	7	12	15	14	10	2			Slope 119

Hole	10	11	12	13	14	15	16	17	18	In		Totals
BLUE	347	313	233	375	453	110	319	373	376	2899	BLUE	6050
WHITE	326	289	220	364	431	99	309	349	350	2737	WHITE	5736
Par	4	4	3	4	4	3	4	4	4	34	Par	69
Handicap	9	16	11	5	1	18	13	8	4			
RED	296	280	213	319	374	86	264	329	337	2498	RED	5202
Par	4	4	3	4	4	3	4	4	4	34	Par	69
Handicap	9	16	11	5	1	18	13	8	4			

Manager/Pro: Jody Graham, PGA   **Supt:** Charlie Sexton
Architect: John Van Kleek 1929

SOUTH SHORE GOLF COURSE

PUBLIC

200 Huguenot Rd., Staten Island, NY 10312   (718) 984-0101

South Shore is an 18 hole NYC public course run by American Golf and open all year, 7 days a week, weather permitting. Tee times may be reserved 7 days in advance weekdays, & 2 Thursdays prior for weekends by calling the central reservation office at (718) 225-GOLF. Residents must show current year ID card.

• **Driving Range**	Lockers
• **Practice Green**	Showers
• **Power Carts**	• **Food**
• **Pull Carts**	• **Clubhouse**
• **Club Rental**	• **Outings**

Fees	Weekday	Weekend
Daily-Res	$18	$20
Non-Res	$24	$26
Twi-Res	$9	$10
Cart	$24.50	$25.50

Course Description: South Shore is a scenic, relatively flat course with tree lined fairways and no water in play. Although it has some gently rolling hills, it is certainly walkable. The par 5 14th hole is the most difficult and the longest. The par 5 signature #18 is an eye pleasing finishing hole having a pretty pond beside the green. The course is fairly wide open; in some instances, trees will block errant shots. The scorecard below has yardages for "back tees" and "forward tees."

Directions: New York City, #13
From NYC, take Bklyn Battery Tunnel to Gowanus to Verrazano Bridge. Take Rte.278, (S. I. Xpresswy) to Exit 4, Arthur Kill Rd. Turn left, proceed under overpass bearing right at fork to Huguenot Ave. Make 1st right into golf course.

Hole	1	2	3	4	5	6	7	8	9	Out	BLUE	Rating
BLUE												Slope
WHITE	348	411	458	353	161	395	388	221	369	3104		
Par	4	4	5	4	3	4	4	3	4	35	WHITE	Rating 68.6
Handicap	10	5	11	13	15	6	3	9	12			Slope 113
RED	252	338	412	352	157	290	388	184	271	2644		
Par	4	4	5	4	3	4	5	3	4	36	RED	Rating 69.8
Handicap	16	6	2	8	18	12	4	10	14			Slope 114
Hole	10	11	12	13	14	15	16	17	18	In		Totals
BLUE											BLUE	
WHITE	412	465	313	270	573	145	383	162	539	3262	WHITE	6366
Par	4	5	4	4	5	3	4	3	5	37	Par	72
Handicap	2	8	14	18	1	17	7	16	4			
RED	345	367	288	269	454	132	317	161	458	2791	RED	5435
Par	4	4	4	4	5	3	4	3	5	36	Par	72
Handicap	7	9	11	13	1	17	5	15	3			

Manager: Joe Baumbach **Supt:** Jay Long
Architect: Alfred Tull 1927

TOWERS COUNTRY CLUB

PRIVATE

272-86 Grand Cent.Pkwy., Floral Park, NY 11005   **(718) 279-1848**

The Towers is an 18 hole course open 6 days a week from Mar.1 through Dec. 31. Guests may play when accompanied by a member. Tee time reservations are necessary on weekends.

Driving Range	•**Lockers**
•**Practice Green**	•**Showers**
•**Power Carts**	•**Food**
Pull Carts	•**Clubhouse**
•**Club Rental**	•**Outings**
Caddies	Soft Spikes

Course Description: The Towers is a short, (5800 yds.) abundantly treed narrow golf course. It is challenging with well-bunkered undulating greens (some of which play quite fast). Water is in play on only one hole. The signature 3rd hole is a 410 yard par 4 with a very narrow fairway playing to an elevated, difficult green. The first 4 holes actually are in Nassau County and straddle the border of NYC. Originally, built as Glen Oaks CC, that club moved further out on L. I. in 1971. The Towers apartment buildings were built on part of the property, thus reducing the yardage for golf.

Directions: New York City, #14
LIE to Exit #33, Lakeville Rd. Go south over Northern State Pkwy. (also called Grand Central Pkwy.) Turn right at first light after Northern State. Proceed 0.3 miles to club on left (part of the North Shore Tower complex).

Hole	1	2	3	4	5	6	7	8	9	Out	GOLD	Rating 67.2
GOLD	315	175	405	340	335	490	325	135	255	2775		Slope 113
BLUE	290	160	370	320	310	460	305	125	245	2585		
Par	4	3	4	4	4	5	4	3	4	35	BLUE	Rating 65.5
Handicap	11	15	1	7	9	5	3	17	13			Slope 109
RED	265	135	340	305	280	435	265	105	235	2365		
Par	4	3	4	4	4	5	4	3	4	35	RED	Rating 69.7
Handicap	11	15	1	7	9	5	3	17	13			Slope 114
Hole	10	11	12	13	14	15	16	17	18	In		Totals
GOLD	310	375	460	165	335	475	330	240	335	3025	GOLD	5800
BLUE	285	350	450	150	310	460	315	205	305	2830	BLUE	5415
Par	3	4	5	3	4	5	4	3	4	35	Par	70
Handicap	14	4	2	18	8	6	10	16	12			
RED	265	330	400	125	300	425	300	160	280	2585	RED	4950
Par	3	4	5	3	4	5	4	3	4	35	Par	70
Handicap	14	4	2	18	8	6	10	16	12			

Manager: Janice Dellaquilla **Pro:** Robert Guido, PGA   **Supt:** Jim Reidy
Architects: W.H. Follett, Frank Duane **Estab:** 1925

VAN CORTLANDT GOLF COURSE PUBLIC

Van Cortlandt Park S. & Bailey Ave., Bronx, 10471   **(718) 543-3114**

Van Cortlandt is a public 18 hole course, run by American Golf, open 7 days a week, all year. Tee times are made by calling (718) 225-GOLF up to 10 days in advance. Fees are for NYC residents with a pass; others add $6. There are discounts for seniors.

Driving Range	•**Lockers**
Practice Green	•**Showers**
•**Power Carts**	•**Food**
•**Pull Carts**	•**Clubhouse**
•**Club Rental**	•**Outings**

Fees	Weekday	Weekend
Daily	$23	$25
Twilight	$15	$16
Power carts	$24	$25

Course Description: Van Cortlandt is one of the oldest public courses in the US. The first manager here introduced the advanced tee time policy. A group of prominent businessmen tried to make it private calling it Mosholu GC, however, it was considered a public course by the Parks Commission. Because of its proximity to NYC, people can reach here easily by subway. Some famous players include Babe Ruth, Sydney Poitier, Kramer (of Sienfeld fame), Sugar Ray and Willie Nelson. Two par 5s are over 600 yds. long and the well bunkered par 4 signature hole #18, has a dogleg. This truly scenic and unusual city course has been recently renovated.

Directions: New York City, #15
Take I-87 North (Major Deegan) to Van Cortlandt Pkwy., South exit. Proceed around circle 200 ft. Bear left & make a U turn at end of circle. Course is straight ahead.

Hole	1	2	3	4	5	6	7	8	9	Out	BLUE	Rating 68.6
BLUE	370	620	192	393	362	292	229	328	391	3177		Slope 110
WHITE	360	605	172	388	347	283	215	318	381	3069		
Par	4	5	3	4	4	4	3	4	4	35	WHITE	Rating 67.7
Handicap	9	1	17	3	11	15	7	13	5			Slope 108
RED	345	550	142	372	324	268	185	295	370	2851		
Par	4	5	3	4	4	4	3	4	4	35	RED	Rating 68.0
Handicap	9	1	17	3	11	15	7	13	5			Slope 108
Hole	10	11	12	13	14	15	16	17	18	In		Totals
BLUE	490	160	607	160	389	285	310	210	334	2945	BLUE	6122
WHITE	472	150	600	150	360	280	305	200	327	2844	WHITE	5913
Par	5	3	5	3	4	4	4	3	4	35	Par	70
Handicap	4	16	2	18	6	10	14	8	12			
RED	455	130	475	143	330	263	291	163	320	2570	RED	5421
Par	5	3	5	3	4	4	4	3	4	35	Par	70
Handicap	14	16	2	18	6	10	14	8	12			

Manager: James Dolan   **Supt:** Hidalgo Nakashima
Architects: Thomas Bendolow, William Mitchell **Estab:** 1895

Work is for people who don't know how to play golf.

(Glen Cove Golf Course)

Golf is a sport in which the ball usually lies poorly,

but the player well.

(Nassau Country Club)

He who has the fastest cart never has a bad lie.

(South Fork Country Club)

NASSAU COUNTY

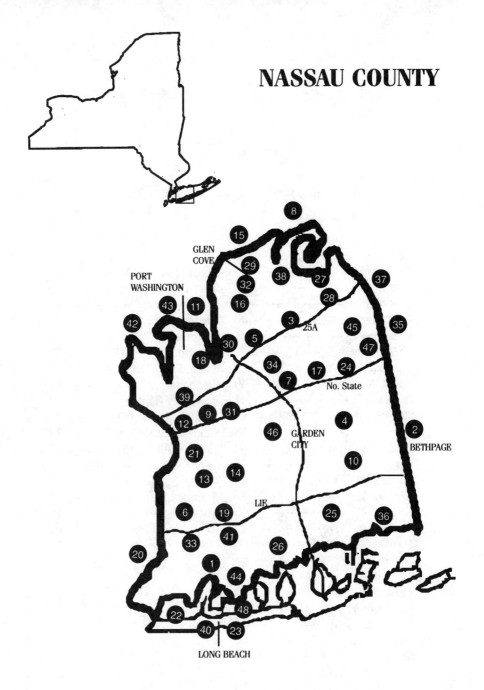

NASSAU COUNTY

Public Courses appear in *bold italics*

BAY PARK GOLF COURSE

Bay Park, East Rockaway, NY 11518   **(516) 571-7244**

Bay Park is a municipal 9 hole course open between March 17 and December 20. It is closed on Wednesdays. Tee time reservations are not necessary.

Driving Range	Lockers
•**Practice Green**	Showers
Power Carts	Food
•**Pull Carts**	Clubhouse
Club Rental	Outings
Soft Spikes	

Fees	Weekday	Weekend
Daily(Res)	$8	$9
Non-Res	$16	$18
Sr.	$4	$9
Power carts $14		

Course Description: Bay Park overlooking Hewlett Bay is a wide open course that is easy to walk and has some gentle undulation. It is a challenging, small executive course that gets ocean breezes most of the time. It is often called "Balmy Bay Park". Water is not a factor here.

Directions: Nassau County, #1
Southern St. Pkwy. to Exit #17S. Bear left on Ocean Ave. all the way to Atlantic Ave. Go right for 2 lights to Rhame Ave. & go left. 2nd Stop is Adams; go left into park..

Hole	1	2	3	4	5	6	7	8	9	Out	BLUE	Rating
BLUE												Slope
WHITE	299	142	163	190	352	190	130	159	331	1956		
Par	4	3	3	3	4	3	3	3	3	30	WHITE	Rating
Handicap	1	6	8	4	2	5	9	7	3			Slope
RED												
Par											RED	Rating
Handicap												Slope

Hole	10	11	12	13	14	15	16	17	18	In		Totals
BLUE											BLUE	
WHITE											WHITE	
Par											Par	
Handicap												
RED											RED	
Par											Par	
Handicap												

Manager: Peggy Van Nostrand   **Supt:** Eddie Contino
Built: 1969

BETHPAGE STATE PARK GC

Powell Ave., Farmingdale, NY 11735 **(516) 249-0701**

Beth Page is a NY State facility with 5 18 hole courses designated by colors Red, Blue, Yellow, Green and Black. Golfers call in advance for tee times. Senior discounts apply Mon- Fri. Twilight rates available. No power carts allowed on the Black course.

•Driving Range	•Lockers
•Practice Green	•Showers
•Power Carts	•Food
•Pull Carts	•Clubhouse
•Club Rental	•Outings

Fees	Weekday	Weekend
4 Colors	$20	$24
9 holes	$11	$13
Black	$25	$30
Power carts	$25	$25

Course Description: In the early 1930s, the 1,386 acre residential estate of Texas oill magnate Benjamin Yoakum was acquired for use as a public park. Part of the now Green course was originally the private Lenox Hills CC. The ensuing construction was done as a Work Relief Project and the new courses were opened in 1935. Excitement at Bethpage is now building in anticipation of the US Open to be held on the Black in 2002. It is an extremely challenging layout, a Tillinghast gem. No power carts are allowed. The 5th has a drive of 225 yards to the tree lined fairway with the green uphill to the left. All of the colorful courses are of high quality and very popular. The Yellow was the last one built. The scorecard below is for the Bethpage Black course.

Directions: Nassau County, #2
LIE to Exit 44S. Take Seaford Oyster Bay Expressway for 3.5 miles to Exit 8. Turn left onto Powell Ave. Follow signs to Golf Course.

Hole	1	2	3	4	5	6	7	8	9	Out	BLUE	Rating 75.4
BLUE	430	371	160	528	446	404	585	195	401	3520		Slope 144
WHITE	423	359	143	481	424	391	514	182	391	3308		
Par	4	4	3	5	4	4	5	3	4	36	WHITE	Rating 73.1
Handicap	7	9	17	5	1	11	3	15	13			Slope 140
RED												
Par											RED	Rating 78.9
Handicap												Slope 146
Hole	10	11	12	13	14	15	16	17	18	In		Totals
BLUE	419	433	480	572	159	438	466	200	378	3545	BLUE	7065
WHITE	387	419	411	497	149	412	436	183	354	3248	WHITE	6556
Par	4	4	4	5	3	4	4	3	4	35	Par	71
Handicap	14	12	6	4	18	2	8	10	16			
RED											RED	
Par											Par	
Handicap												

Dir. of Golf: Chuck Workman, PGA   **Pro:** Joe Rehor, PGA   **Supt:** Dave Catalano
Architects: A. W. Tillinghast, Devereux Emmet, Alfred Tull 1923, 1935, 1958

BROOKVILLE COUNTRY CLUB

PRIVATE

Chicken Valley Rd., Glen Head, NY 11545   **(516) 671-8466**

Brookville is a private 18 hole club open 6 days a week all year, weather permitting. Guests play accompanied by a member. Tee time reservations are not necessary. Pull carts are allowed only at off peak, off season times.

•Driving Range	•Lockers
•Practice Green	•Showers
•Power Carts	•Food
•Pull Carts	•Clubhouse
•Club Rental	•Outings
•Caddies	•Soft Spikes

Course Description: Brookville underwent some major renovations in 1996 to improve the greens and to restore a Seth Raynor flavor. Some yardages were extended to increase the length of this relatively flat contoured course. The form of the greens vary; some are elevated, others severely undulating or somewhat recessed. The signature par 3 3rd is a tough hole on which to make par. It is uphill and long with a two-tiered green guarded by deep bunkers. The ball must land on the pin level to score well. The fairways are generally tree-lined and there is no water in play.

Directions: Nassau County, #3
Take the LIE to Exit 41. Take Rte.107 North. After crossing over Rte.25A(Northern Blvd.), turn right immediately onto Hegeman's Lane. At its end is Chicken Valley Rd. and the club entrance immediately on the right.

Hole	1	2	3	4	5	6	7	8	9	Out	BLUE	Rating 71.8
BLUE	489	353	244	305	369	438	173	399	352	3122		Slope 126
WHITE	482	333	220	298	350	411	165	385	347	2991		
Par	5	4	3	4	4	4	3	4	4	35	WHITE	Rating 70.3
Handicap	9	5	11	7	13	1	17	3	15			Slope 124
RED	450	282	145	267	325	361	155	366	324	2675		
Par	5	4	3	4	4	4	3	4	4	35	RED	Rating 67.2
Handicap	5	9	15	7	11	1	17	3	13			Slope 117

Hole	10	11	12	13	14	15	16	17	18	In		Totals
BLUE	396	146	440	388	523	323	195	465	600	3476	BLUE	6598
WHITE	383	135	427	372	512	312	187	397	577	3302	WHITE	6293
Par	4	3	4	4	5	4	3	4	5	36	Par	71
Handicap	10	18	2	12	4	14	16	8	6			
RED	338	102	398	359	459	292	160	347	486	2941	RED	5616
Par	4	3	5	4	5	4	3	4	5	37	Par	72
Handicap	12	18	8	10	2	14	16	6	4			

Manager: Donald Emery   **Pro:** Douglas Miller, PGA   **Supt:** Will Eifert
Architect: Seth Raynor 1922

CANTIAGUE PARK GOLF COURSE

PUBLIC

West John Street, Hicksville, NY 11801   (516) 571-7062

Cantiague Park is a nine hole executive Nassau county course open 6 days a week (closed Tuesdays) all year. Tee time reservations are not necessary.

- **Driving Range**   Lockers
- **Practice Green**   Showers
- **Power Carts**   Food
- **Pull Carts**   Clubhouse
- **Club Rental**   •**Outings**
- **Soft Spikes**

Fees	Weekday	Weekend
Residents	$8	$9
Non-res	$16	$18
Srs.	$4	$9
Power carts	$14 (9)	

Course Description: Cantiague Park is a flat easily walkable course that is great for beginners and seniors. Lessons are taught at the adjacent driving range which, along with the pro shop, is separate from the county course. There are vending machines for light snacks.

Directions: Nassau County, #4
LIE to Exit 41S onto Rte. 106/107 South 1 mile and make a right on West John St. Course is on right.

Hole	1	2	3	4	5	6	7	8	9	Out	BLUE	Rating
BLUE												Slope
WHITE	259	173	150	200	257	272	157	228	182	1878		
Par	4	3	3	3	4	4	3	3	3	30	WHITE	Rating
Handicap	2	7	9	5	1	3	8	4	6			Slope
RED												
Par											RED	Rating
Handicap												Slope

Hole	10	11	12	13	14	15	16	17	18	In		Totals
BLUE											BLUE	
WHITE											WHITE	
Par											Par	
Handicap												
RED											RED	
Par											Par	
Handicap												

Manager: Steve Teischman   **Pro:** Tom Corrigan, PGA   **Supt:** Eugene Contino
Built: 1968

THE CEDARBROOK CLUB

Oak Lane, Old Brookville, NY 11545   **(516) 759-8447**

The Cedarbrook Club is a private 18 hole course open 6 days a week and closed in February. Guests play accompanied by a member. Tee time reservations are necessary on weekends.

•Driving Range	•Lockers
•Practice Green	•Showers
•Power Carts	•Food
Pull Carts	•Clubhouse
•Club Rental	•Outings
Caddies	•Soft Spikes

Course Description: Cedarbrook is a relatively flat challenging layout with fairly wide, long fairways. The greens are of average size, fast in summer with slight breaks. The course was built on former farmland. The 16th hole, a dogleg left, is quite scenic. From an elevated tee, it requires a long carry to the fairway and has an OB on the right and a pond in front of the green. Earlier in the club's existence, Tommy Bolt was the head Pro.

Directions: Nassau County, #5
Take the LIE to Exit 41. Take Rte.107 north about 5 miles to Chicken Valley Rd and turn right. Go about 1 mile to Oak Lane. Club entrance is on the left.

Hole	1	2	3	4	5	6	7	8	9	Out	BLUE	Rating 72.2
BLUE	400	175	529	452	423	365	404	223	394	3453		Slope 129
WHITE	469	163	513	421	415	346	389	206	389	3311		
Par	5	17	1	11	3	9	7	15	13	36	WHITE	Rating 70.8
Handicap	7	4	9	6	1	2	8	5	3			Slope 126
RED	444	444	475	327	341	330	350	151	300	2862		
Par	5	3	5	4	4	4	4	3	4	36	RED	Rating 72.1
Handicap	4	18	2	8	6	14	12	16	10			Slope 124

Hole	10	11	12	13	14	15	16	17	18	In		Totals
BLUE	423	243	354	160	337	482	394	310	502	3205	BLUE	6658
WHITE	408	196	338	150	327	467	388	298	485	3057	WHITE	6368
Par	4	3	4	3	4	5	4	4	5	36	Par	72
Handicap	4	18	10	16	12	14	2	8	6			
RED	323	151	271	138	317	420	369	285	437	2711	RED	5573
Par	4	3	4	3	4	5	4	4	5	36	Par	72
Handicap	7	15	13	17	9	5	1	11	3			

Manager: Daniel Abitol   **Pro:** June Staton, PGA   **Supt:** Kirk Sedlack
Architect: Albert Zikorus 1960

CHERRY VALLEY CLUB

Rockaway Ave & 3rd St., Garden City, NY 11530   **(516) 741-1980**

Cherry Valley is an 18 hole private club open 6 days a week all year weather permitting. Guests play accompanied by a member. Tee time reservations are necessary on weekends.

•**Driving Range**	•**Lockers**
•**Practice Green**	•**Showers**
•**Power Carts**	•**Food**
Pull Carts	•**Clubhouse**
Club Rental	•**Outings**
•**Caddies**	•**Soft Spikes**

Course Description: Before the present Cherry Valley Club was established, it had a history as the Salisbury Links. The course has water in play on 4 holes and lengthy bunkers bordering a few fairways, which are generally narrow and some have OB. The greens are somewhat sloping, fast in summer and well trapped. The 14th green was redesigned by Tillinghast. Later 3 holes were redone by Frank Duane because part of the course had to be relocated. Various MGA tournaments have been held here.

Directions: Nassau County, #6
Take the LIE to Exit 27. Take Shelter Rock Rd. south. After crossing Rte.25, it becomes Herricks Rd. When it becomes Rockaway Ave, look for club entrance on left.

Hole	1	2	3	4	5	6	7	8	9	Out	BLUE	Rating 72.0
BLUE	280	545	563	418	191	377	451	592	204	3621		Slope 127
WHITE	275	517	536	394	171	356	432	533	191	3405		
Par	4	5	5	4	3	4	4	5	3	37	WHITE	Rating 70.4
Handicap	17	5	7	3	15	11	1	9	13			Slope 123
RED	260	404	457	375	155	323	335	415	177	2901		
Par	4	5	5	4	3	4	4	5	3	37	RED	Rating 72.4
Handicap	15	9	3	1	17	5	7	11	13			Slope 127
Hole	10	11	12	13	14	15	16	17	18	In		Totals
BLUE	501	303	357	232	376	388	418	177	453	3205	BLUE	6826
WHITE	478	280	339	207	364	376	395	150	424	3013	WHITE	6418
Par	5	4	4	3	4	4	4	3	4	35	Par	72
Handicap	12	16	14	10	6	8	2	18	4			
RED	449	263	281	162	349	309	379	128	414	2734	RED	5635
Par	5	4	4	3	4	4	4	3	5	36	Par	73
Handicap	4	14	12	16	6	8	2	18	10			

Manager: Tom Baird   **Pro:** Ed Kelly, PGA   **Supt:** Skip Wade
Architect: Devereux Emmet 1916   **Estab:** 1907

CHRISTOPHER MORLEY PARK GC

Searingtown Road, North Hills, NY 11576   **(516) 571-8120**

Christopher Morley is a 9 hole Nassau County Executive course with mostly par 3s. 80% of the players are seniors. Tee time reservations are not necessary.

Driving Range	Lockers
•**Practice Green**	Showers
Power Carts	•**Food**
•**Pull Carts**	Clubhouse
Club Rental	•**Outings**

Fees	Weekday	Weekend
Daily(res)	$8	$9
Non-res	$16	$18
Sr/Jr	$4	$9
Power carts	$14(9)	$22(18)

Course Description: Christopher Morley Golf Course is a good place to practice your game. It is somewhat hilly with wide fairways and large greens. Considered a good novice course for walkers only, Nassau County residents can use a Leisure Pass to play here.

Directions: Nassau County, #7
LIE to Exit 36. Go North on Searingtown Rd. to course on right.

Hole	1	2	3	4	5	6	7	8	9	Out	BLUE	Rating
BLUE												Slope
WHITE	267	143	153	119	145	152	300	97	144	1520		
Par	4	3	3	3	3	3	4	3	3	29	WHITE	Rating
Handicap	2	7	5	6	3	4	1	9	8			Slope
RED												
Par											RED	Rating
Handicap												Slope

Hole	10	11	12	13	14	15	16	17	18	In		Totals
BLUE											BLUE	
WHITE											WHITE	
Par											Par	
Handicap												
RED											RED	
Par												
Handicap												

Manager: Chris Lucas   **Supt:** Park Commission

THE CREEK

Horse Hollow Rd., Locust Valley, NY 11560   **(516) 671-1001**

The Creek is an 18 hole private course open 7 days a week all year. Guests may play accompanied by a member. Tee time reservations are necessary on weekends.

•**Driving Range**	•**Lockers**
•**Practice Green**	•**Showers**
•**Power Carts**	•**Food**
Pull Carts	•**Clubhouse**
•**Club Rental**	•**Outings**
•**Caddies**	•**Soft Spikes**

Course Description: The first 5 holes at the Creek are tree lined and the rest are links style near the L.I. Sound. The bent grass greens are fast and rather small with considerable break. After a majestic drive approaching the club, a meticulously manicured course comes into view. From the later holes there are breathtaking vistas. The signature 6th hole has a view of Connecticut across the water. The long par 3 #11 has an island green. The water in play on both the 10th and the 11th is the Sound. The Met Open will be held here in 1998. The beach facility here is an attractive amenity for members.

Directions: Nassau County, #8
Take the LIE to Exit 39N (Glen Cove Rd). Bear left at fork onto Rte.107N. go 1.3 miles to Glen Cove Firehouse, turn right onto Brewster St. (becomes Forest Ave.) Go 1.4 mi. to Lattingtown Rd & bear left. At light, turn left onto Horse Hollow Rd. Club on left.

Hole	1	2	3	4	5	6	7	8	9	Out	BLUE	Rating 72.0
BLUE	376	375	382	173	396	453	521	179	420	3275		Slope 131
WHITE	344	349	361	160	368	429	510	167	381	3069		
Par	4	4	4	3	4	4	5	3	4	35	WHITE	Rating 69.9
Handicap	13	11	7	17	9	1	3	15	5			Slope 127
RED	301	304	345	137	343	400	441	130	330	2731		
Par	4	4	4	3	4	4	5	3	4	35	RED	Rating 71.1
Handicap	10	12	16	2	4	14	6	18	8			Slope 126
Hole	10	11	12	13	14	15	16	17	18	In		Totals
BLUE	308	195	357	439	425	357	440	151	455	3127	BLUE	6402
WHITE	305	155	328	428	395	344	385	137	413	2890	WHITE	5959
Par	4	3	4	4	4	4	4	3	5	35	Par	70
Handicap	14	12	16	4	2	10	6	18	8			
RED	303	134	318	367	340	285	312	132	355	2546	RED	5277
Par	4	3	4	4	5	4	4	3	5	36	Par	71
Handicap	10	12	16	2	4	14	6	18	8			

Manager: Robert Stein   **Pro:** John C. Sanges, PGA   **Supt:** Bill Jones
Architects: Charles Blair Macdonald, Seth Raynor 1923

DEEPDALE GOLF CLUB

North Service Road, Manhasset, NY 11030   **(516) 627-7880**

Deepdale Golf Club is a private 18 hole golf course open 6 days a week. Guests may play accompanied by a member. Tee time reservations are not necessary.

•**Driving Range**	•**Lockers**
•**Practice Green**	•**Showers**
•**Power Carts**	•**Food**
Pull Carts	•**Clubhouse**
•**Club Rental**	Outings
•**Caddies**	Soft Spikes

Course Description: Situated on the former Grace estate, Deepdale is an exclusive golf club that is in superb condition; (with few members it does not get overly used). The tree-lined tight fairways are unforgiving. Many celebrities and presidents have belonged here (Eisenhower, Bob Hope, Vic Damone.) Deepdale, which twice hosted the Met Amateur, used to be located where Lake Success Golf Club is now located.

Directions: Nassau County, #9
Take the LIE to Shelter Rock Rd. (Exit #34). Cross over the expressway and get on the service road towards NYC. Course is 400 yards on the right.

Hole	1	2	3	4	5	6	7	8	9	Out	BLUE	Rating 72.6
BLUE	407	527	391	188	420	157	370	408	354	3222		Slope 135
WHITE	395	502	377	177	407	142	355	393	311	3059		
Par	4	5	4	3	4	3	4	4	4	35	WHITE	Rating 71.3
Handicap	5	13	9	11	3	17	7	1	15			Slope 132
RED	365	434	293	130	317	130	300	316	235	2520		
Par	4	5	4	3	4	3	4	4	4	35	RED	Rating 71.5
Handicap	5	13	9	11	3	17	7	1	15			Slope 119

Hole	10	11	12	13	14	15	16	17	18	In		Totals
BLUE	410	451	516	185	397	431	365	224	422	3401	BLUE	6623
WHITE	378	439	505	173	382	411	356	217	402	3263	WHITE	6322
Par	4	4	5	3	4	4	4	3	4	35	Par	70
Handicap	12	2	14	16	8	6	18	10	4			
RED	360	390	465	159	332	363	318	137	347	2871	RED	5391
Par	4	4	5	3	4	4	4	3	4	35	Par	70
Handicap	12	2	14	16	8	6	18	10	4			

Manager: Tom Heaney   **Pro:** Darrell Kestner, PGA   **Supt:** Samuel Murphy
Architect: Dick Wilson 1956

EISENHOWER PARK GOLF COURSE PUBLIC

Hempstead Turnpike, East Meadow, NY 11554   (516) 542-0015

Eisenhower Park is a county course consisting of 54 holes (three 18 hole courses) open 7 days a week, all year. It is the 2nd largest public golf operation (next to Bethpage) in NY. Leisure Pass for Nassau residents is available allowing 7 day advance tee time reservations.

•Driving Range	•Lockers
•Practice Green	•Showers
•Power Carts	•Food
•Pull Carts	•Clubhouse
•Club Rental	•Outings
Soft Spikes	

Fees	Weekday	Weekend
Daily	$28	$32
Resident	$14	$16
Power carts $32		
Discounts for Srs. and Twilight		

Course Description: The variety of play at Eisenhower Park and its scenic views are reason enough to travel here for golf but on certain days, one of the nines is closed for maintenance. A new irrigation system helps keep this busy course in good shape. The Red is the longest and considered the most challenging and (beautiful)with its long par 5 17th, and a green surrounded by bunkers and evergreens. The signature 211 yard par 3 13th is well bunkered with wind playing havoc most of the time. Golf Digest awarded the Red 2 & 1/2 stars in a rating of best courses to play. Scorecard is for the Red course.

Directions: Nassau County, #10
LIE to Exit #38 to Meadow Brook Pkwy. Proceed South to Exit M-4. Stay on service road to 1st intersection & turn left. Proceed to club.

Hole	1	2	3	4	5	6	7	8	9	Out	BLUE	Rating 71.5
BLUE	488	277	451	444	143	430	424	374	338	3369		Slope 121
WHITE	462	266	420	418	130	385	405	336	334	3156		
Par	5	4	4	4	3	4	4	4	4	36	WHITE	Rating 69.7
Handicap	9	15	3	1	17	5	7	11	13			Slope 117
RED	419	252	356	348	116	350	285	260	288	2674		
Par	5	4	4	4	3	4	4	4	4	36	RED	Rating 70.7
Handicap	9	15	3	1	17	5	7	11	13			Slope 111
Hole	10	11	12	13	14	15	16	17	18	In		Totals
BLUE	421	312	493	211	369	450	166	556	447	3425	BLUE	6794
WHITE	405	292	461	193	365	402	150	514	419	3201	WHITE	6357
Par	4	4	5	3	4	4	3	5	4	36	Par	72
Handicap	6	16	14	8	12	4	18	10	2			
RED	385	264	405	176	347	307	136	460	350	2830	RED	5504
Par	4	4	5	3	4	4	3	5	4	36	Par	72
Handicap	6	16	14	8	12	4	18	10	2			

Manager: Robert Kluck **Pro:** Sal Silverstrone, PGA   **Supt:** Gene Contino
Architects: Devereux Emmet, Robert Trent Jones **Estab:** 1917

ENGINEER'S COUNTRY CLUB

Glenwood Road, Roslyn Harbor, NY 11576   **(516) 621-6513**

Engineer's is an 18 hole private course open 6 days a week and closed from Jan. 20 through March 1. Guests may play when accompanied by a member. Tee times are recommended on weekends.

•**Driving Range**	•**Lockers**
•**Practice Green**	•**Showers**
•**Power Carts**	•**Food**
Pull Carts	•**Clubhouse**
•**Club Rental**	•**Outings**
•**Caddies**	•**Soft Spikes**

Course Description: Initially called Roslyn Harbor CC, Engineer's is a relatively short scenic old fashioned course with rolling hills, and multi-tiered, sharply undulating greens. On many holes, greenside bunkers are distanced from the green requiring a long shot out of the sand. The par 4 sixteenth, with a tee below fairway level, requires an accurate drive to avoid the fairway bunkers. A ravine is another obstacle encountered on the way to the green. Originally built by the American Society of Engineers, it later became a private club. The PGA Championship in 1919 and the USGA Amateur in 1920 were played here.

Directions: Nassau County, # 11
LIE to Exit #37; Willis Ave. Go left (North) onto Willis Ave. to 25A. Turn right (East) on Northern Blvd. Take first right-hand exit after bridge & bear right onto Bryant Ave. Then turn right for about 1 mile to Glenwood and make a left; club is 1/2 mile on right.

Hole	1	2	3	4	5	6	7	8	9	Out	BLUE	Rating 71.9
BLUE	389	405	228	493	459	395	292	340	193	3194		Slope 128
WHITE	377	390	193	487	423	385	268	328	180	3031		
Par	4	4	3	5	4	4	4	4	3	35	WHITE	Rating 70.5
Handicap	10	4	16	8	6	2	18	12	14			Slope 125
RED	353	374	139	409	349	281	243	314	159	2621		
Par	4	5	3	5	4	4	4	4	3	36	RED	Rating 73.0
Handicap	10	6	18	2	4	8	14	12	16			Slope 126
Hole	10	11	12	13	14	15	16	17	18	In		Totals
BLUE	551	163	360	355	432	452	365	370	420	3468	BLUE	6662
WHITE	533	150	337	340	407	407	357	363	405	3299	WHITE	6330
Par	5	3	4	4	4	4	4	4	4	36	Par	71
Handicap	3	17	11	15	1	5	9	13	7			
RED	458	139	316	324	386	391	271	282	396	2963	RED	5584
Par	5	3	4	4	5	4	4	4	5	38	Par	74
Handicap	1	17	13	15	5	3	11	9	7			

Manager: David Shaw   **Pro:** Eric Feltman, PGA   **Supt:** Don Szymkowitz
Architects: Herbert Strong, Devereux Emmet, Frank Duane   **Estab:** 1917

FRESH MEADOW COUNTRY CLUB   PRIVATE

255 Lakeville Road, Lake Success, NY 11020   (516) 482-7300

Fresh Meadow is an 18 hole private course open 6 days a week; it closes in Dec. and reopens in April. Guests may play accompanied by a member. Tee time reservations are necessary.

- •Driving Range   •Lockers
- •Practice Green   •Showers
- •Power Carts   •Food
- Pull Carts   •Clubhouse
- Club Rental   •Outings
- •Caddies   •Soft Spikes

Course Description: This well manicured, picturesque championship golf course can be proud of having had such members as Eddie Cantor, Irving Berlin, Babe Ruth and Oscar & Arthur Hammerstein. Its proximity to NYC along with its rolling terrain and manicured fairways makes it very desirable. The sloped greens are well-bunkered and in excellent shape. Water affects play on the 13th hole, a par 3. The new pro-shop is exceptionally beautiful and well-stocked. It used to be called The Lakeville CC. until Met Life bought it in the 1940's. Years ago Gene Sarazen was the pro here.

Directions: Nassau County, #12
Take the LIE to Exit #33 (Lakeville Rd. Great Neck) Turn left (north) on Lakeville Rd. 1/2 mile to club on right.

Hole	1	2	3	4	5	6	7	8	9	Out	BLUE	Rating 72.4
BLUE	459	558	456	171	405	385	165	416	379	3394		Slope 133
WHITE	445	537	436	158	381	375	153	395	369	3249		
Par	4	5	4	3	4	4	3	4	4	35	WHITE	Rating 71.3
Handicap	3	9	1	17	11	5	15	7	13			Slope 130
RED	421	440	395	131	352	360	140	377	357	2973		
Par	5	5	5	3	4	4	3	4	4	37	RED	Rating 74.0
Handicap	3	1	5	15	13	7	17	9	11			Slope 129
Hole	10	11	12	13	14	15	16	17	18	In		Totals
BLUE	586	196	466	190	362	212	542	373	382	3309	BLUE	6703
WHITE	561	183	453	175	351	182	524	359	373	3161	WHITE	6410
Par	5	3	4	3	4	3	5	4	4	35	Par	70
Handicap	4	14	2	18	10	16	6	12	8			
RED	544	167	424	140	325	154	460	316	355	2885	RED	5858
Par	5	3	5	3	4	3	5	4	5	37	Par	74
Handicap	2	14	6	16	10	18	4	12	8			

Manager: Jim Cope   **Pro:** Michael O'Reilly, PGA   **Supt:** Bobby Kamp
Architect: Charles Alison 1924

GARDEN CITY COUNTRY CLUB

206 Stewart Ave., Garden City, NY 11530   **(516) 747-2929**

Garden City CC is a private 18 hole course. It is open 6 days a week all year weather permitting. Guests play accompanied by a member. Tee time reservations are necessary on Saturdays.

•**Driving Range**	•**Lockers**
•**Practice Green**	•**Showers**
•**Power Carts**	•**Food**
Pull Carts	•**Clubhouse**
Club Rental	•**Outings**
•**Caddies**	•**Soft Spikes**

Course Description: Garden City CC property is divided by railroad tracks. Holes 1, 2, 17 & 18 are on the north side, the rest to the south. The golfers go under a trestle between 2 and 3. Strategically placed drives are needed on the fairly open fairways. The well bunkered greens are severly undulating and very fast. The signature par 5 #14 is a 600 yard dogleg right with a big tree guarding the right side of the fairway. On the par 5 twelfth, called Iwo Jima, the green is built up to a plateau. The meticulously maintained course is a long par 70. The MET Amateur Qualifying round was held here in July 1997.

Directions: Nassau County, #13
Take LIE to Exit 34. Go south on New Hyde Park Rd. to Stewart Ave (2nd light after RR) and turn left for 1 mile to club on right.

Hole	1	2	3	4	5	6	7	8	9	Out	BLUE	Rating 72.8
BLUE	377	187	387	400	166	469	404	420	458	3268		Slope 130
WHITE	361	173	360	345	141	436	398	398	435	3047		
Par	4	3	4	4	3	4	4	4	4	34	WHITE	Rating 71.3
Handicap	13	17	7	9	15	1	11	5	3			Slope 127
RED	301	142	283	277	130	403	353	327	355	2571		
Par	4	3	4	4	3	5	4	4	4	35	RED	Rating 71.1
Handicap	7	15	11	13	17	3	18	9	5			Slope 119
Hole	10	11	12	13	14	15	16	17	18	In		Totals
BLUE	341	170	525	203	606	440	512	216	430	3443	BLUE	6711
WHITE	335	142	494	183	583	424	502	203	417	3047	WHITE	6330
Par	4	3	5	3	5	4	5	3	4	36	Par	70
Handicap	14	18	8	16	2	4	10	12	6			
RED	306	125	444	160	513	374	417	214	367	2920	RED	5491
Par	4	3	5	3	5	4	5	4	4	37	Par	72
Handicap	12	18	4	16	2	6	8	14	10			

Manager: Jack Blank   **Pro:** Don Beatty, PGA   **Supt:** Tom McAvoy
Architect: Walter Travis 1916

GARDEN CITY GOLF CLUB

315 Stewart Ave., Garden City, NY 11530   **(516) 747-2880**

Garden City Golf Club is a private 18 hole course   open 6 days a week all year weather permitting.   Guests play accompanied by a member. Tee time reservations are not necessary.

•**Driving Range**	•**Lockers**
•**Practice Green**	•**Showers**
•**Power Carts**	•**Food**
Pull Carts	•**Clubhouse**
•**Club Rental**	Outings
•**Caddies**	•**Soft Spikes**

Course Description: The Scottish influence is apparent in this outstanding layout built in a links style. High native fescue grasses in the unforgiving rough add to the challenge at this contoured natural course; the well manicured fairways flow into the fast and medium size greens. A lake on the 18th is in play for the shot to the well bunkered green. The Walter Travis Invitational, is a major competitive amateur event held here annually in May. In the early part of this century, Walter Travis was a member, a dominant player who influenced the design of the bunkers and tees. Garden City Golf Club is steeped in the tradition and history of golf.

Directions: Nassau County, #14
Take the LIE to Exit 34. Go South on New Hyde Park Rd. to Stewart Ave. (2nd light after RR crossing) and turn left. Go 2 miles and turn left on Cherry Valley Rd. 1 block to club entrance on left.

Hole	1	2	3	4	5	6	7	8	9	Out	BLUE	Rating 73.7
BLUE	302	137	388	523	360	440	550	418	323	3441		Slope 139
WHITE	285	133	366	502	349	411	531	394	296	3267		
Par	4	3	4	5	4	4	5	4	4	37	WHITE	Rating 72.0
Handicap	15	17	9	5	11	3	1	7	13			Slope 135
RED												
Par											RED	Rating
Handicap												Slope
Hole	10	11	12	13	14	15	16	17	18	In		Totals
BLUE	414	416	193	538	343	447	405	495	190	3441	BLUE	6882
WHITE	394	411	172	515	337	405	382	471	152	3239	WHITE	6506
Par	4	4	3	5	4	4	4	5	3	36	Par	73
Handicap	8	6	16	2	14	4	10	12	18			
RED											RED	
Par											Par	
Handicap												

Manager: Jimmy Gilchrist   **Pro:** Gil McNally, PGA   **Supt:** Eddie Butler
Architect: Devereux Emmet 1899

GLEN COVE GOLF COURSE

Lattingtown Rd., Glen Cove, NY 11542 **(516) 676-0550**

Glen Cove is an 18 hole town course with memberships available for out of towners and discounts for Glen Cove residents. It is open 6 days a week. In Jan & Feb: open Fri-Sun. weather permitting. No reservations Tues-Thurs. Lottery system for tee time on weekends. Prices below are for permit holders.

•**Driving Range**	•**Lockers**
•**Practice Green**	•**Showers**
•**Power Carts**	•**Food**
•**Pull Carts**	•**Clubhouse**
•**Club Rental**	•**Outings**

Fees	Weekday	Weekend
Resident	$12	$14
Non-res	$14	$16
Guest	$30	$30
Power carts	$22	

Course Description: Glen Cove is a short (par 66) course. It is flat with tight fairways and spectacular views of the L.I Sound from the 1st and 10th holes. It is an unusual setting for a town course on extremely valuable shoreline property. Water is in play on about 7 holes. The par 3s are challenging. The rather small greens, some elevated, are fairly flat and considered "old style." The par 4 6th signature hole features water on the right, and in front of the green.

Directions: Nassau County, #15
LIE to Exit 39N. Take Glen Cove Rd. 5 mi to fork. Bear left onto Rte107. Turn right at Bridge St. (becomes School St.) then turn right at Forest. Make immediate left onto Dosoris Lane. At Lattingtown Rd, turn right. Go 1/2 mile to club on left.

Hole	1	2	3	4	5	6	7	8	9	Out	BLUE	Rating
BLUE												Slope
WHITE	478	376	157	173	307	357	374	115	187	2524		
Par	5	4	3	3	4	4	4	3	3	33	WHITE	Rating 63.4
Handicap	5	1	15	13	9	7	3	17	11			Slope 108
RED	442	338	141	127	295	281	263	95	162	2144		
Par	5	4	3	3	4	4	4	3	3	33	RED	Rating 62.8
Handicap	1	5	15	13	3	9	7	17	11			Slope 98

Hole	10	11	12	13	14	15	16	17	18	In		Totals
BLUE											BLUE	
WHITE	447	157	212	254	242	326	163	263	227	2291	WHITE	4815
Par	4	3	3	4	4	4	3	4	4	33	Par	66
Handicap	2	16	12	6	10	4	18	8	14			
RED	413	144	152	211	221	226	144	251	202	2004	RED	4148
Par	5	3	3	4	4	4	3	4	4	34	Par	67
Handicap	2	16	18	8	10	6	14	4	12			

Manager: John Simon   **Pro:** Mal Galletta, Jr.   **Supt:** Carmine Gentile
Architect: William Mitchell 1970

GLEN HEAD COUNTRY CLUB

Cedar Swamp Road, Glen Head, NY 11545   **(516) 676-4051**

Glen Head is an 18 hole private course open 6 days a week and closed in Feb. Golf is available all year, weather permitting. Tee time reservations are required on weekends in season.

•**Driving Range**	•**Lockers**
•**Practice Green**	•**Showers**
•**Power Carts**	•**Food**
Pull Carts	•**Clubhouse**
•**Club Rental**	•**Outings**
•**Caddies**	•**Soft Spikes**

Course Description: Glen Head is relatively hilly with undulating fast greens, several of which have tricky breaks. The view from the clubhouse looks out onto nearly the entire front nine. The signature 16th hole is a beautiful par 3 offering a lovely view and a green surrounded by bunkers. It has an elevated tee for the ladies which leads downhill to the green. Three holes have water in play. This course was originally the Women's National Golf Club; built by a group of 350 women who in those early days were not allowed to play at the nearby men's clubs.

Directions: Nassau County, #16
Take the LIE to Exit 39North, Glen Cove Rd. Continue North 4.9 miles. This joins 107 (Cedar Swamp Rd.) at this point. Club is on left.

Hole	1	2	3	4	5	6	7	8	9	Out	BLUE	Rating 71.7
BLUE	445	343	523	206	350	378	220	421	386	3272		Slope 129
WHITE	426	330	511	186	342	361	182	400	375	3113		
Par	4	4	5	3	4	4	3	4	4	35	WHITE	Rating 70.5
Handicap	3	13	5	11	17	7	15	1	9			Slope 126
RED	406	278	436	170	335	353	149	390	361	2878		
Par	5	4	5	3	4	4	3	4	4	36	RED	Rating 74.4
Handicap	7	15	3	13	11	5	17	1	9			Slope 128
Hole	10	11	12	13	14	15	16	17	18	In		Totals
BLUE	368	350	170	349	438	502	138	466	453	3234	BLUE	6506
WHITE	360	340	151	340	428	492	120	449	438	3118	WHITE	6231
Par	4	4	3	4	4	5	3	5	4	35	Par	71
Handicap	14	10	16	8	2	6	18	12	4			
RED	354	331	141	330	422	438	105	406	424	2951	RED	5829
Par	4	4	3	4	5	5	3	5	5	38	Par	74
Handicap	12	14	16	10	6	2	18	4	8			

Manager: Gregory Felle   **Pro:** Scott Hawkins, PGA   **Supt:** Lynn O'Neill
Architect: Devereux Emmet 1924

GLEN OAKS COUNTRY CLUB

PRIVATE

175 Post Road, Old Westbury, NY 11568   (516) 626-0161

Glen Oaks is a 27 hole golf course open 6 days a week, and closed in January & February. Guests may play accompanied by a member. Tee time reservations are not necessary. The course has 3 nines, Red, White and Blue.

•**Driving Range**	•**Lockers**
•**Practice Green**	•**Showers**
•**Power Carts**	•**Food**
Pull Carts	•**Clubhouse**
Club Rental	•**Outings**
•**Caddies**	•**Soft Spikes**

Course Description: Formerly a Vanderbilt estate, Glen Oaks is a long course with rolling hills, tree-lined fairways and some elevated tees & greens. The property was at one time owned by a horticulturist, hence the aged copper and weeping beech speciman trees. The Club, originally in Queens, moved to its present location in the early 1970s. The course is challenging to all levels and there are water hazards on 5 holes. The PGA Met Championship has been held here twice. The scorecard below indicates the Red and White nines.

Directions: Nassau County, #17
Take the LIE to Exit 39S; stay on the service road for 1.9 miles to Post Rd. and turn left. Proceed 0.4 miles to club on right.

Hole	1	2	3	4	5	6	7	8	9	Out	BLUE	Rating 74.7
BLUE	417	384	170	565	432	435	381	152	558	3494		Slope 136
WHITE	402	369	158	545	407	409	361	142	553	3346		
Par	4	4	3	5	4	4	4	3	5	36	WHITE	Rating 73.1
Handicap	9	11	17	5	7	1	13	15	3			Slope 132
RED	345	297	137	460	342	351	310	111	501	2854		
Par	4	4	3	5	4	4	4	3	5	36	RED	Rating 73.6
Handicap	9	13	15	5	7	3	11	17	1			Slope 126
Hole	10	11	12	13	14	15	16	17	18	In		Totals
BLUE	530	223	422	432	434	183	545	361	401	3531	BLUE	7025
WHITE	513	208	392	414	412	156	530	350	391	3366	WHITE	6712
Par	5	3	4	4	4	3	5	4	4	36	Par	72
Handicap	9	15	3	7	1	17	11	13	5			
RED	443	167	330	350	356	138	430	292	339	2845	RED	5699
Par	5	3	4	4	4	3	5	4	4	36	Par	72
Handicap	3	15	13	5	1	17	9	7	11			

Manager: Don Molitor   **Pro:** Tom Joyce, PGA   **Supt:** Richie Struss
Architect: Joe Finger, 1971 **Estab:** 1924

49

HARBOR LINKS GOLF COURSE

Spine Rd., Port Washington, NY 11050

Harbor Links is a Town of North Hempstead public golf course with reduced rates and priority tee times for town residents. There will be a championship 18 hole course 7016 yds. from the back and a full 9 hole executive course with 4 par 4s & 5 par 3s. Information about this course may be obtained from the Town of Hempstead office.

•Driving Range	•Lockers
•Practice Green	•Showers
•Power Carts	•Food
•Pull Carts	•Clubhouse
•Club Rental	•Outings

Fees	Weekday	Weekend
Rates not available at press time		

Course Description: Opening in late spring 1998, Harbor Links is a links type course taking advantage of the existing topography. The wetlands, deep native grasses and the wind are factors in giving it challenge and variety. Originally, this tract of land was mined for sand which was used in the making of concrete for downtown NYC buildings. The course offers 5 sets of tees which gives the improving golfer a chance to move back a tee. Some fairways are two tiered with differing routes to the large subtly contoured greens. Although near the harbor, the land rises up to 200 ft. affording great views of the spectacular layout. The executive course has moguls, pot bunkers and severely contoured greens, truly a quality golf experience.

Directions: Nassau County, #18
Take the LIE to Exit 37. Go North on Willis Ave bearing right onto Old No. Blvd. Make left onto West Shore Rd & left at Roslyn U-turn. Course on right at Spine Rd.

Architect: Michael Hurzdan 1998

HEMPSTEAD GOLF & CC

60 Front St., Hempstead, NY 11550   **(516) 481-7411**

Hempstead is an 18 hole private course open all year 6 days a week. Guests may play accompanied by a member. Tee time reservations are necessary on Sundays between 11AM and 2:30 PM.

- •**Driving Range**
- •**Practice Green**
- •**Power Carts**
- Pull Carts
- •**Club Rental**
- •**Caddies**

- •**Lockers**
- •**Showers**
- •**Food**
- •**Clubhouse**
- •**Outings**
- •**Soft Spikes**

Course Description: Hempstead CC, with its tree-lined fairways, is located in the middle of town. The structure now used as the clubhouse was originally an 18th century farmhouse and has been added onto and modernized. Although no water is in play and fairly flat, the course does have some elevated greens and tees. Stephen Kay has recently done a marvelous job of bunker restoration. The signature par 4 fifth hole is a double dogleg featuring a major sand trap in the fairway and a ridge on the elevated green. This busy course is very well groomed. The Met Junior was held here in 1996 and the L.I. Amateur in 1993.

Directions: Nassau County, #19
Take the So. State Pkwy to Exit 19N (Peninsula Blvd.) Go 1/2 m to President St and turn left. Go 3 lights & turn left at Front. At 1st light turn left and entrance is immediately on the right.

Hole	1	2	3	4	5	6	7	8	9	Out	BLUE	Rating 71.6
BLUE	313	429	485	413	388	441	414	178	328	3389		Slope 126
WHITE	306	420	475	404	380	405	400	168	320	3278		
Par	4	4	5	4	4	4	4	3	4	36	WHITE	Rating 70.8
Handicap	17	1	11	3	7	5	9	15	13			Slope 124
RED	286	410	413	353	310	397	347	133	312	2961		
Par	4	5	5	4	4	5	4	3	4	38	RED	Rating 73.8
Handicap	18	6	4	2	14	10	8	16	12			Slope 127

Hole	10	11	12	13	14	15	16	17	18	In		Totals
BLUE	196	414	317	540	387	525	318	139	370	3206	BLUE	6595
WHITE	187	405	306	530	380	509	309	127	358	3111	WHITE	6389
Par	3	4	4	5	4	5	4	3	4	36	Par	72
Handicap	10	6	16	2	8	4	14	18	12			
RED	180	396	296	475	373	486	301	80	348	2935	RED	5896
Par	3	4	4	5	4	5	4	3	4	36	Par	74
Handicap	9	1	13	7	5	3	15	17	11			

Manager: Michael Thorne   **Pro:** Walter Ostroske, PGA   **Supt:** Joe Tamborski
Architects: A. W. Tillinghast, Peter Lees 1921

INWOOD COUNTRY CLUB

PRIVATE

Peppe Drive, Inwood, NY 11696   **(516) 239-4454**

Inwood is an 18 hole course open 6 days a week all year, weather permitting. Tee times are required on weekends. Guests may play accompanied by a member.

•**Driving Range**	•**Lockers**
•**Practice Green**	•**Showers**
•**Power Carts**	•**Food**
Pull Carts	•**Clubhouse**
Club Rental	•**Outings**
•**Caddies**	•**Soft Spikes**

Course Description: An old fashioned Scottish links type course surrounded by Jamaica Bay, Inwood is close to Kennedy Airport with the Manhattan skyline in the distance. The layout is well known for its lush fairways, many greenside bunkers, irregularly shaped hazards, sharp dropoffs and severe rough. The relatively small greens are undulating and fast at times. Water affects play on 5 holes. Bobby Jones won his first US Open here in 1923 where on the signature par 4 18th he hit the "shot of the century" with a mid iron to the green, putting the ball 6 ft. from the cup and giving him the coveted championship. Walther Hagen won the PGA Championship here in 1921. The former pro, Jack Mackie, was a founding father of the PGA.

Directions: Nassau County, # 20
Southern St. Pkwy. to Exit #19-S(Peninsula Blvd.) Go South 7.2 miles to Rockaway Tpk.; cross over it & go 200 yds. Turn left at light & follow signs to Burnside Ave. Proceed on Burnside (becomes Sheridan); at S turn go straight onto Bayswater Blvd. 3 blocks to Peppe Dr. to club.

Hole	1	2	3	4	5	6	7	8	9	Out	BLUE	Rating 73.1
BLUE	345	362	514	539	512	171	219	415	419	3496		Slope 131
WHITE	332	342	500	527	480	160	207	396	403	3347		
Par	4	4	5	5	5	3	3	4	4	37	WHITE	Rating 71.8
Handicap	13	11	5	1	9	17	15	3	7			Slope 128
RED	316	309	401	482	451	150	141	368	317	2935		
Par	4	4	5	5	5	3	3	4	4	37	RED	Rating 74.5
Handicap	9	11	5	1	7	15	17	3	13			Slope 130
Hole	10	11	12	13	14	15	16	17	18	In		Totals
BLUE	106	433	456	341	155	471	376	405	408	3151	BLUE	6647
WHITE	96	418	437	325	140	463	363	377	398	3017	WHITE	6364
Par	3	4	4	4	3	5	4	4	4	37	Par	74
Handicap	18	4	2	14	16	12	10	8	6			
RED	80	405	365	306	123	447	350	361	335	2772	RED	5707
Par	3	5	4	4	3	5	4	4	4	36	Par	73
Handicap	18	12	4	14	6	2	8	6	10			

Manager: Jeff Plain   **Pro:** Tommy Thomas, PGA   **Supt:** Pete Ruggieri
Architects: Herb Strong, Jack Mackie   **Estab:** 1902

LAKE SUCCESS GOLF CLUB PUBLIC

318 Lakeville Road, Lake Success, NY11020   (516) 482-4012

Lake Success is a semi-private 18 hole course open only to residents of Lake Success and is owned by the town. There are no daily fees; members must pay only for their carts. Tee time reservations are not necessary.

•Driving Range	•Lockers
•Practice Green	•Showers
•Power Carts	•Food
•Pull Carts	•Clubhouse
•Club Rental	Outings
•Soft Spikes	

Fees	Weekday	Weekend
Daily	**Membership Only**	
Twilight		
Sr/Jr		
Power carts		

Course Description: Lake Success is a very narrow heavily bunkered course. The actual lake significantly comes into play on 3 holes especially on the par 3 eighth. The course is fairly short but plays longer than the scorecard indicates. The greens are in great shape but because the fairways are quite moist due to drainage problems, there is not much roll. This course was formerly the location of Deepdale CC; when the LIE was built several holes had to be reconfigured. The US Open local qualifying rounds were held here in 1990, 91, & 92.

Directions: Nassau County, # 21
LIE to Exit #33, Lakeville Rd. Go south on Lakeville Rd. 0.3 miles to club on right.

Hole	1	2	3	4	5	6	7	8	9	Out	BLUE	Rating 70.7
BLUE	467	451	181	337	427	174	454	158	398	3047		Slope 128
WHITE	453	443	163	330	412	162	445	140	378	2926		
Par	5	4	3	4	4	3	5	3	4	35	WHITE	Rating 69.5
Handicap	13	1	17	9	3	11	7	15	5			Slope 126
RED	443	433	151	277	379	146	385	94	325	2633		
Par	5	5	3	4	4	3	5	3	4	36	RED	Rating 72.6
Handicap	5	3	15	13	1	11	7	17	9			Slope 126
Hole	10	11	12	13	14	15	16	17	18	In		Totals
BLUE	421	178	394	531	403	380	346	184	373	3210	BLUE	6257
WHITE	412	162	382	518	398	360	338	175	360	3105	WHITE	6031
Par	4	3	4	5	4	4	4	3	4	35	Par	70
Handicap	2	18	8	4	6	14	16	10	12			
RED	400	146	335	467	403	338	328	130	344	2891	RED	5524
Par	5	3	4	5	5	4	4	3	4	37	Par	73
Handicap	6	16	14	2	4	12	8	18	10			

Manager: Roberta Penchina   **Pro:** Robby Mistretta, PGA   **Supt:** Chuck Santanani
Architects: Orrin Smith, Albert Zikorus   **Estab:** 1957

LAWRENCE VILLAGE COUNTRY CLUB

100 Causeway Rd., Lawrence, NY 11559   **(516) 239-8263**

Lawrence Village CC is an 18 hole course open 6 days a week, and closed in Feb. It is only for Lawrence residents and private members. Guests may play accompanied by a member. Tee time reservations are necessary on weekends.

•Driving Range	•Lockers
•Practice Green	•Showers
•Power Carts	•Food
Pull Carts	•Clubhouse
Club Rental	Outings
•Caddies	•Soft Spikes

Course Description: Lucky the Lawrence residents who can play on this lovely links style course. It faces the Atlantic Beach Bridge and Reynolds Channel. The course is relatively flat with narrow fairways and small well bunkered greens. Sixteen holes either have water or are near water. Wind is always in play. The signature 440 yard par 4 eighteenth has an approach shot requiring a major carry over water to a narrow green with an adjacent creek. Built in the 1920s, it was redesigned by Joe Finger in 1968. The layout is being reconfigured to accommodate a larger driving range.

Directions: Nassau County, # 22
Southern St. Pkwy. to Exit #19S (Peninsula Blvd.) Go 7.2 miles (on Pen. Blvd.) to Rockaway Blvd. (Pass Law. High Sch.) turn left. Go 1.4 mi. (rd. becomes Meadow Lane) to Causeway, turn left. Club immediately on right.

Hole	1	2	3	4	5	6	7	8	9	Out	BLUE	Rating 72.3
BLUE	384	397	465	161	529	354	401	411	205	3307		Slope 123
WHITE	370	383	457	148	505	348	382	405	177	3175		
Par	4	4	4	3	5	4	4	4	3	35	WHITE	Rating 72.4
Handicap	11	9	1	17	5	13	7	3	15			Slope 123
RED	358	310	444	138	443	336	295	340	130	2794		
Par	4	4	5	3	5	4	4	4	3	36	RED	Rating 72.4
Handicap	8	12	4	18	2	10	14	6	16			Slope 123
Hole	10	11	12	13	14	15	16	17	18	In		Totals
BLUE	355	180	392	516	387	377	186	383	445	3221	BLUE	6528
WHITE	340	150	382	498	372	357	172	373	433	3077	WHITE	6252
Par	4	3	4	5	4	4	3	4	4	35	Par	70
Handicap	18	16	6	2	8	12	14	10	4			
RED	320	100	315	450	346	342	160	290	360	2683	RED	5477
Par	4	3	4	5	4	4	3	4	4	35	Par	71
Handicap	13	17	9	1	5	7	15	11	3			

Manager: Frank Argento **Pro**: Craig W. Thomas, PGA **Supt**: Joe Ciaravalo
Architect: Devereux Emmet, 1924

LIDO GOLF COURSE

255 Lido Blvd., Lido Beach, NY 11561   **(516) 889-8181**

Lido is an 18 hole course owned by the Town of Hempstead. It is open all year 7 days a week. The new management, Double Eagle Golf Course at Lido, leases from the town and is doing a major renovation of both the clubhouse and the golf course. Call for tee time reservations.

• Driving Range	• Lockers
• Practice Green	• Showers
• Power Carts	• Food
• Pull Carts	• Clubhouse
• Club Rental	• Outings

Fees	Weekday	Weekend
Res/Hemp	$18	$23
Res/LBeach	$21	$26
Non-res	$30	$33
Power carts	$24	$24

Course Description: A challenging heavily bunkered course, Lido provides its residents with a links type layout bordering Reynolds Channel. In order to be environmentally sensitive, the new management is creating and enhancing the ponds, improving the cart paths and installing natural and native plantings. Water is in play on many of the back holes. The large elevated greens are fast. The signature par 5 16th requires 2 shots over water. Since the wind varies close to the ocean, it affects play. The goal here is to restore this course to its former highly rated quality.

Directions: Nassau County, #23
LIE to Exit 38. Take Meadowbrook Parkway South to Exit M-10. Follow signs to Loop Parkway and go west. It becomes Lido Blvd. and club is 2.5 miles on right.

Hole	1	2	3	4	5	6	7	8	9	Out	BLUE	Rating 73.5
BLUE	452	367	358	378	175	382	214	404	625	3355		Slope 128
WHITE	439	347	315	356	157	346	193	387	552	3092		
Par	4	4	4	4	3	4	3	4	5	35	WHITE	Rating 71.3
Handicap	3	9	5	13	17	11	15	7	1			Slope 124
RED	418	332	261	346	112	315	175	370	490	2819		
Par	5	4	4	4	3	4	3	4	5	36	RED	Rating 71.4
Handicap	9	5	15	7	17	13	11	3	1			Slope 114
Hole	10	11	12	13	14	15	16	17	18	In		Totals
BLUE	420	405	544	436	402	182	487	200	437	3513	BLUE	6868
WHITE	396	385	502	413	376	166	460	189	408	3295	WHITE	6387
Par	4	4	5	4	4	3	5	3	4	36	Par	71
Handicap	8	12	4	6	14	18	2	16	10			
RED	370	365	457	286	351	95	405	150	305	2764	RED	5603
Par	4	4	5	4	4	3	5	3	4	36	Par	72
Handicap	8	10	6	16	4	18	2	14	12			

Manager: John Monteforte   **Pro:** Richard Rizzo, PGA **Supt:** JImmy Vogel
Architect: Robert Trent Jones 1949 **Estab:** 1914

MEADOW BROOK CLUB

Cedar Swamp Road, Jericho, NY 11753   **(516) 822-3354**

Meadow Brook is an 18 hole private course open 6 days a week and closed in Jan. & Feb. Guests may play accompanied by a member. Tee time reservations are not necessary.

•Driving Range	•Lockers
•Practice Green	•Showers
•Power Carts	•Food
Pull Carts	•Clubhouse
•Club Rental	•Outings
•Caddies	•Soft Spikes

Course Description: Originally a nine hole layout in Westbury, Meadow Brook later became 18 holes on entirely different property. The well maintained course has wide open fairways, particularly on the front, and large undulating greens, some of which are multi-tiered. The signature par 5 8th is 617 yards from the back with a double dogleg and three sets of fairway bunkers. The tee shot on the par 3 6th requires negotiating a pond. The back nine has abundant trees in contrast to the front. The Senior PGA Tournament and Northville LI Classic are held here every year.

Directions: Nassau County, #24
LIE to Exit 41N. Take Rte. 106/107 and follow 107. At SUNY Old Westbury, make a U turn and then proceed immediately to club on right.

Hole	1	2	3	4	5	6	7	8	9	Out	BLUE	Rating 74.6
BLUE	520	411	456	432	340	240	418	617	168	3602		Slope 137
RED	506	389	434	412	328	230	401	590	157	3447		
Par	5	4	4	4	4	3	4	5	3	36	RED	Rating 73.0
Handicap	11	7	1	5	15	13	9	3	17			Slope 133
WHITE	453	305	335	315	288	195	345	463	137	2836		
Par	5	4	4	4	4	3	4	5	3	36	WHITE	Rating 73.2
Handicap	11	7	5	9	13	15	3	1	17			Slope 126

Hole	10	11	12	13	14	15	16	17	18	In		Totals
BLUE	549	404	478	212	438	421	184	373	440	3499	BLUE	7101
RED	537	389	463	195	419	367	171	353	417	3311	RED	6758
Par	5	4	5	3	4	4	3	4	4	36	Par	72
Handicap	12	6	16	10	2	8	14	18	4			
WHITE	471	338	396	152	373	330	127	298	343	2828	WHITE	5664
Par	5	4	5	3	4	4	3	4	4	36	Par	72
Handicap	6	10	16	14	2	8	18	12	4			

Manager: Dennis Harrington   **Pro:** Richard Meskell, PGA   **Supt:** John Carlone
Architect: Dick Wilson 1955   **Estab:** 1881

MERRICK PARK GOLF COURSE

2550 Clubhouse Rd., Merrick, NY 11566   **(516) 546-1122**

Merrick Park is a 9 hole town facility operated privately. It is open all year and closed on Wednesdays. Tee time reservations are not necessary.

•**Driving Range**	Lockers
•**Practice Green**	Showers
Power Carts	•**Food**
•**Pull Carts**	•**Clubhouse**
•**Club Rental**	•**Outings**

Fees	Weekday	Weekend
Res	$8	$8
Non-res	$10	$10
Sr-Res	$5	$6

Course Description: Some consider this well maintained waterfront property "the most beautiful 9 hole golf course in creation." There is water in play on some holes. Merrick is a narrow, lightly contoured course with large greens having some break. The 4th is a long par 4 over water. The 1st hole is scenic; water borders the left side and the green has a major dip. The 7th and 9th holes have elevated tees. The eye-pleasing vistas referred to above are of East Bay and Jones Beach. The clubhouse is being renovated.

Directions: Nassau County, #25
Take LIE or No. State to Meadow Brook Pkwy.South. Exit at M-9East. Make 1st right at light to Clubhouse Rd and course.

Hole	1	2	3	4	5	6	7	8	9	Out	BLUE	Rating
BLUE												Slope
WHITE	480	147	351	405	353	487	330	159	403	3115		
Par	5	3	4	4	4	5	4	3	4	36	WHITE	Rating 34.5
Handicap	1	4	3	5	2	6	7	8	9			Slope 108
RED	440	122	326	375	328	452	300	124	378	2845		
Par	5	3	4	4	4	5	4	3	4	36	RED	Rating
Handicap	1	4	3	5	2	6	7	8	9			Slope

Hole	10	11	12	13	14	15	16	17	18	In		Totals
BLUE											BLUE	
WHITE											WHITE	3115
Par											Par	36
Handicap												
RED											RED	2845
Par											Par	36
Handicap												

Manager: Shaun McGarry   **Pro:** Sam Musacchio, PGA   **Supt:** Todd Tarantino
Architect: Frank Duane 1967

MIDDLE BAY COUNTRY CLUB

3600 Skillman Ave., Oceanside, NY 11572   (516) 766-7956

Middle Bay is a private 18 hole course open 6 days a week and closed in Feb. Guests play accompanied by a member. Tee time reservations are necessary Fri-Sun in season.

> • **Driving Range** • **Lockers**
> • **Practice Green** • **Showers**
> • **Power Carts** • **Food**
>   Pull Carts • **Clubhouse**
> • **Club Rental** • **Outings**
> • **Caddies** • **Soft Spikes**

Course Description: Middle Bay is a links style course with many holes along the bay. The wind is a major factor and can blow from different directions on any one day providing variety for players. The greens are small and fast. Some fescue grass grows between holes giving a natural look to a flat, relatively treeless layout. The policy at this well manicured course is to be environmentally aware. Water is in play on 9 holes.

Directions: Nassau County #26
Take So. State Pkwy to Exit 20S (Grand Ave). Go 3.5 miles to Atlantic Ave and turn right. Turn left at Waukena Ave and then left onto Skillman Ave to club.

Hole	1	2	3	4	5	6	7	8	9	Out	BLUE	Rating 73.5
BLUE	533	378	346	187	402	549	200	340	446	3381		Slope 131
WHITE	520	367	331	180	378	537	190	308	437	3248		
Par	5	4	4	3	4	5	3	4	4	36	WHITE	Rating 72.1
Handicap	7	9	11	17	5	1	15	13	3			Slope 129
RED	467	270	271	130	305	455	168	294	352	2712		
Par	5	4	4	3	4	5	3	4	4	36	RED	Rating 72.4
Handicap	3	15	7	17	5	1	13	9	11			Slope 117

Hole	10	11	12	13	14	15	16	17	18	In		Totals
BLUE	344	362	185	413	592	146	422	415	561	3440	BLUE	6821
WHITE	332	356	168	360	553	140	408	387	553	3257	WHITE	6505
Par	4	4	3	4	5	3	4	4	5	36	Par	72
Handicap	14	10	16	12	2	18	4	8	6			
RED	313	314	129	315	444	125	405	312	420	2777	RED	5489
Par	4	4	3	4	5	3	5	4	5	37	Par	73
Handicap	6	10	18	12	2	16	8	14	4			

Manager: Nicholas Batos   **Pro:** Tim Shifflet, PGA   **Supt:** Michael Benz
Architect: Alfred Tull 1955 **Estab:** 1931

MILL RIVER CLUB

Mill River Road, Upper Brookville, NY 11771   (516) 922-3556

The Mill River Club has an 18 hole course that is open 6 days a week all year, weather permitting. Guests may play accompanied by a member. Tee time reservations are recommended on weekends.

- •Driving Range
- •Practice Green
- •Power Carts
- Pull Carts
- •Club Rental
- •Caddies
- •Lockers
- •Showers
- •Food
- •Clubhouse
- •Outings
- •Soft Spikes

Course Description: The gracious and unique Normandy Tudor mansion, known formerly as Appledore, is now used as the clubhouse at the Mill River Club. The tight tree lined hilly fairways on the back nine are completely different from the gently undulating front nine. Characteristic of Mill River are a variety of elevation changes, hazards and natural beauty. Wind blows regularly from the Sound off to the west. The view from the 18th hole makes it one of the the most picturesque finishing holes in existence. The aforementioned clubhouse has been recently renovated.

Directions: Nassau County, #27
LIE to Exit #41N. Go north on Rte.106, 4.2 miles to Northern Blvd(Rte.25A). Turn left to Mill River Rd.(1st traffic light) then turn right to club on left.

Hole	1	2	3	4	5	6	7	8	9	Out	BLUE	Rating 72.3
BLUE	495	355	173	442	527	396	180	391	403	3362		Slope 134
WHITE	473	322	148	411	513	368	156	361	391	3143		
Par	5	4	3	4	5	4	3	4	4	36	WHITE	Rating 70.4
Handicap	11	9	17	1	13	7	15	3	5			Slope 131
RED	425	289	145	370	443	362	150	308	304	2796		
Par	5	4	3	4	5	4	3	4	4	36	RED	Rating 72.1
Handicap	9	13	17	1	7	3	15	5	11			Slope 126
Hole	10	11	12	13	14	15	16	17	18	In		Totals
BLUE	370	415	185	370	497	335	157	514	390	3233	BLUE	6595
WHITE	347	399	183	350	483	330	141	458	360	3051	WHITE	6194
Par	4	4	3	4	5	4	3	5	4	36	Par	72
Handicap	6	2	16	10	8	14	18	4	12			
RED	314	355	178	269	463	300	131	392	315	2717	RED	5513
Par	4	4	3	4	5	4	3	5	4	36	Par	72
Handicap	6	2	16	14	4	8	18	12	10			

Manager: Wayne Russell   **Pro:** Mark Mielke, PGA   **Supt:** Steve Sweet
Architect: Gerald Roby, 1965

THE MUTTONTOWN CLUB

Route 25A, E.Norwich, NY 11732   (516) 922-7500

Muttontown is an 18 hole course open 6 days a week and closed for the month of January. Tee time reservations should be made for weekends. Guests may play accompanied by a member.

•Driving Range	•Lockers
•Practice Green	•Showers
•Power Carts	•Food
Pull Carts	•Clubhouse
•Club Rental	•Outings
•Caddies	•Soft Spikes

Course Description: The beautifully maintained Muttontown Club is a par 71 that offers great variety of play on its rolling, well treed terrain.   It is fairly narrow with sloping, well bunkered greens, some of which are elevated.   Water is in play on the 16th and 18th. The signature 13th looks like a par 3 at Augusta, beautifully flowered and very picturesque. The finishing eighteenth hole needs an accurate drive to avoid fairway bunkers, followed by an approach shot over a pond to the green . The tee positions are changed often adding variety to the holes.

Directions: Nassau County, #28
LIE to Exit #43 (Rtes.106/107) and go north to Rte.25A.   Proceed West (left on 25A) 1 & 1/2 miles to club on right.

Hole	1	2	3	4	5	6	7	8	9	Out	BLUE	Rating 72.4
BLUE												Slope 128
WHITE	420	400	510	435	150	310	160	525	400	3310		
Par	4	4	5	4	3	4	3	5	4	36	WHITE	Rating 70.8
Handicap	11	7	1	5	17	13	15	3	9			Slope 124
RED	375	380	465	405	115	295	125	485	375	3020		
Par	4	4	5	5	3	4	3	5	4	37	RED	Rating 73.3
Handicap	9	3	1	11	17	13	15	7	5			Slope 127
Hole	10	11	12	13	14	15	16	17	18	In		Totals
BLUE											BLUE	
WHITE	330	375	440	205	335	420	140	520	335	3100	WHITE	6410
Par	4	4	4	3	4	4	3	5	4	35	Par	71
Handicap	12	8	4	16	14	6	18	2	10			
RED	310	315	415	165	300	400	120	475	295	2795	RED	5815
Par	4	4	5	3	4	5	3	5	4	37	Par	74
Handicap	12	14	6	16	10	4	18	2	8			

Manager: John Crean   **Pro:** Roger Ginsberg, PGA   **Supt:** Stanley Choinski
Architect: Alfred Tull 1962

NASSAU COUNTRY CLUB

St. Andrews Lane, Glen Cove, NY 11542 **(516) 759-3020**

Nassau CC is a private 18 hole course open all year 6 days a week. Guests may play accompanied by a member. Tee time reservations are not necessary.

```
• Driving Range    • Lockers
• Practice Green   • Showers
• Power Carts      • Food
  Pull Carts       • Clubhouse
• Club Rental      • Outings
• Caddies          • Soft Spikes
```

Course Description: Originally called Queens County Golf Club, it later became Nassau CC with a Herb Strong redesign. This club is well known among Met area golfers as the location of the "Nassau" way of scoring or betting on a match. The fairways here are of mid width and tree lined. The undulating greens are rather small and fast. The signature par 4 7th has an elevated tee with bunkers in play. (A prudent golfer plays safe and goes around them). Nassau has had 4 head pros in 100 years. On many occasions, the Met Open, the Met Amateur and L.I. Open have been played here,

Directions: Nassau County, #29
Take the LIE to Exit 39N (Glen Cove Rd). Go north approx 5 m. to fork and bear right over RR tracks. Then turn right onto Pearsall Ave. Proceed about 1 m. past Glen Cove RR station. Street name changes to St. Andrews Lane. Club is on right.

Hole	1	2	3	4	5	6	7	8	9	Out	BLUE	Rating 72.6
BLUE	403	357	376	386	187	414	424	407	305	3259		Slope 134
WHITE	390	351	341	346	144	388	408	387	286	3041	WHITE	Rating 71.4
Par	4	4	4	4	3	4	4	4	4	35		Slope 131
Handicap	5	11	13	9	17	1	3	7	15			
RED	382	345	306	325	106	330	328	323	253	2698	RED	Rating 72.9
Par	5	4	4	4	3	4	4	4	4	36		Slope 126
Handicap	11	3	13	9	17	1	5	7	15			

Hole	10	11	12	13	14	15	16	17	18	In		Totals
BLUE	195	437	453	385	384	556	175	419	385	3259	BLUE	6648
WHITE	175	426	442	369	362	533	159	396	373	3235	WHITE	6276
Par	3	4	4	4	4	5	3	4	4	35	Par	70
Handicap	16	2	6	8	12	4	18	10	14			
RED	146	355	431	315	317	437	139	371	326	2837	RED	5535
Par	3	4	5	4	4	5	3	4	4	36	Par	72
Handicap	16	2	14	8	12	6	18	4	10			

Manager: Frank Keefe   **Pro:** Harold Kolb, PGA   **Supt:** Lyman Lambert
Architects: Herbert Stong, Seth Raynor, Devereux Emmet **Estab:** 1896

NORTH HEMPSTEAD COUNTRY CLUB PRIVATE

Port Washington Blvd., Port Washington, NY 11050   **(516) 365-7500**

North Hempstead is an 18 hole private course open 6 days a week and closed in February. Guests play accompanied by a member. Tee time reservations are necessary on weekends.

> • **Driving Range**   • **Lockers**
> • **Practice Green** • **Showers**
> • **Power Carts**   • **Food**
>   Pull Carts   • **Clubhouse**
> • **Club Rental**   • **Outings**
> • **Caddies**   • **Soft Spikes**

Course Description: North Hempstead is a short, hilly, par 70 layout featuring narrow, tree lined fairways and high rough. The undulating greens are small and get quite fast in summer. Water is in play on 2 holes. The course has recently been restored by Gil Hanse; work was done on the tees and bunkers. On the par 5 8th hole, the drive must travel through a chute to a rising and rolling fairway. The elevated green is on a plateau with a rock on the right and three deep bunkers in front. The last three holes could be considered the signature; they are all very difficult and challenging.

Directions: Nassau County, #30
Take LIE to Exit 36. Go north on Searingtown Rd crossing over Northern Blvd. It becomes Port Washington Blvd. or Rte.101. Club is on right.

Hole	1	2	3	4	5	6	7	8	9	Out	BLUE	Rating 71.2
BLUE	381	124	336	360	540	184	446	541	169	3081		Slope 132
WHITE	363	117	329	347	504	167	432	520	155	2934		
Par	4	3	4	4	5	3	4	5	3	35	WHITE	Rating 70.0
Handicap	8	18	12	10	4	16	2	6	14			Slope 131
RED	352	112	321	292	424	137	417	443	133	2631		
Par	4	3	4	4	5	3	5	5	3	36	RED	Rating 72.2
Handicap	5	17	9	11	3	15	7	1	13			Slope 126

Hole	10	11	12	13	14	15	16	17	18	In		Totals
BLUE	433	402	367	180	502	298	463	205	470	3320	BLUE	6401
WHITE	419	377	360	168	475	290	427	190	470	3176	WHITE	6110
Par	4	4	4	3	5	4	4	3	4	35	Par	70
Handicap	1	7	11	17	9	15	3	13	5			
RED	402	353	296	143	468	256	338	163	415	2834	RED	5465
Par	5	4	4	3	5	4	4	3	5	37	Par	73
Handicap	10	4	14	18	2	12	6	16	8			

Manager: Joe Carraher   **Pro:** Gregory Hurd, PGA   **Supt:** Tom Cicale
Architects: A. W. Tillinghast, Charles Banks 1916 **Redesign:** Robert Trent Jones 1958

NORTH HILLS COUNTRY CLUB PRIVATE

North Service Rd.,LIE, Manhasset, NY 11030   (516) 627-9100

North Hills is an 18 hole course that is open 6 days a week and closed for the month of Feb. Guests may play accompanied by a member. Tee time reservations are not necessary.

- •Driving Range
- •Practice Green
- •Power Carts
- Pull Carts
- Club Rental
- •Caddies
- • Lockers
- • Showers
- • Food
- • Clubhouse
- • Outings
- •Soft Spikes

Course Description: The difficult and challenging North Hills is hilly and picturesque. measuring 6472 yards from the blue tees, there are hazards of every type to be found putting an emphasis on accuracy. Tricky greens with a lot of break and water affecting play on 5 holes are part of the difficulty here, however drainage is quite good. The long signature 445 yard par 4 10th has a dogleg right with a big tree situated in the right corner. Originally established in 1927 and located where Douglaston Park is now, North Hills moved to Manhasset in 1960. Eddie Ford (son of Whitey Ford) holds the course record of 64.

Directions: Nassau County, # 31
Take the LIE to Exit #35 (Shelter Rock Rd.) At first traffic light, turn left crossing over the LIE. Turn left again onto the Westbound service Rd; club is on right.

Hole	1	2	3	4	5	6	7	8	9	Out	BLUE	Rating 71.6
BLUE	528	419	172	501	363	167	368	423	342	3283		Slope 129
WHITE	484	403	157	475	344	136	352	407	317	3075		
Par	5	4	3	5	4	3	4	4	4	36	WHITE	Rating 69.6
Handicap	5	1	15	7	13	17	9	3	11			Slope 125
RED	465	391	148	436	332	125	340	393	301	2931		
Par	5	4	3	5	4	3	4	4	4	36	RED	Rating 73.0
Handicap	5	1	15	7	13	17	9	3	11			Slope 125
Hole	10	11	12	13	14	15	16	17	18	In		Totals
BLUE	445	497	158	374	472	338	166	387	352	3189	BLUE	6472
WHITE	421	476	126	341	439	321	146	359	335	2964	WHITE	6039
Par	4	5	3	4	5	4	3	4	4	36	Par	72
Handicap	2	4	16	8	12	14	18	6	10			
RED	322	458	98	317	424	312	134	348	319	2732	RED	5663
Par	4	5	3	4	5	4	3	4	4	36	Par	72
Handicap	10	2	18	8	4	14	16	6	12			

Manager: Arthur Russell   **Pro:** Joe Ennis, PGA   **Supt:** Ed Genova
Architect: Robert Trent Jones Jr. 1963   **Estab:** 1927

NORTH SHORE COUNTRY CLUB

Shore Road, Glen Head, NY 12550 **(516) 676-4225**

North Shore is an 18 hole course open 6 days a week and closed for the month of Feb. Guests may play when accompanied by a member. Tee time reservations are not necessary.

```
•Driving Range   •Lockers
•Practice Green  •Showers
•Power Carts     •Food
 Pull Carts      •Clubhouse
 Club Rental     •Outings
•Caddies          Soft Spikes
```

Course Description: This traditional Tillinghast course with its rolling terrain, many uneven lies and severely sloped plateaued small greens is challenging indeed. The golfer must try to land below the cup to get down in two. The #2 handicap par 4 signature eleventh hole, actually considered the most difficult on which to make par, has every hazard possible. The hole has a sharp dogleg right, water, woods and a large tree in the corner. The par 3 5th hole has a huge ravine to traverse.

Directions: Nassau County, # 32
Take the LIE to Exit #39N. Proceed north on Glen Cove Rd. (Guinea Woods Rd.) for 4 miles and go left onto Glen Head Rd. which becomes Glenwood. At end of road, turn right onto Shore Rd; club is ahead on right.

Hole	1	2	3	4	5	6	7	8	9	Out	BLUE	Rating 72.3
BLUE	372	385	489	493	215	406	325	405	184	3274		Slope 130
WHITE	358	354	479	472	200	401	264	335	178	3041		
Par	4	4	5	5	3	4	4	4	3	36	WHITE	Rating 71.2
Handicap	9	11	17	15	5	1	13	3	7			Slope 128
RED	335	296	393	406	176	320	251	322	168	2667		
Par	4	4	5	5	3	4	4	4	3	36	RED	Rating 72.6
Handicap	5	13	9	1	17	11	7	3	15			Slope 125

Hole	10	11	12	13	14	15	16	17	18	In		Totals
BLUE	152	404	350	386	426	376	507	327	415	3343	BLUE	6617
WHITE	144	376	345	369	419	373	501	319	401	3247	WHITE	6288
Par	3	4	4	4	4	4	5	4	4	36	Par	72
Handicap	18	2	8	12	4	14	10	16	6			
RED	127	350	290	351	414	346	398	304	363	2943	RED	5610
Par	3	5	4	4	5	4	5	4	4	38	Par	74
Handicap	18	2	14	12	4	8	6	16	10			

Pro: Bill Burke, PGA   **Supt:** Richard Tacconelli
Architect: A.W. Tillinghast   **Estab:** 1912

NORTH WOODMERE GOLF COURSE PUBLIC

Branch Blvd., N. Woodmere, NY 11581   **(516) 571-7813**

North Woodmere is a 9 hole Executive Nassau County Park course. It is open between Mar. 17 and Dec.20 and closes on Thursdays. Tee time reservations are not necessary; golfers should call to find out the waiting time.

•**Driving Range**	Lockers
•**Practice Green**	Showers
Power Carts	Food
•**Pull Carts**	Clubhouse
•**Club Rental**	Outings
Soft Spikes	

Fees	Weekday	Weekend
Daily(Res)	$8	$9
Non-Res	$16	$18
Sr.	$4	$9

Course Description: An executive type 9 hole course, North Woodmere is flat and easy to walk. There is no water in play. It is near Kennedy Airport and gets quite busy in season, (about 60,000 rounds a year.) There is also a driving range.

Directions: Nassau County, #33
Southern St. Pkwy. to Exit #19. Go south on Peninsula Blvd. for about 6 miles and then go right on Branch Blvd.(6 lights before Rockaway Tpke. in Woodmere). Course is 1 mile on left.

Hole	1	2	3	4	5	6	7	8	9	Out	BLUE	Rating
BLUE												Slope
WHITE	390	395	310	177	167	200	143	360	140	2282		
Par	4	4	4	3	3	3	3	4	3	31	WHITE	Rating
Handicap	2	1	4	6	7	5	8	3	9			Slope
RED												
Par											RED	Rating
Handicap												Slope

Hole	10	11	12	13	14	15	16	17	18	In		Totals
BLUE											BLUE	
WHITE											WHITE	
Par											Par	62
Handicap												
RED											RED	
Par											Par	
Handicap												

Manager: Phyllis La Selva   **Pro:** Tom Berry   **Supt:** Edward Contino
Built: 1974

OLD WESTBURY GOLF & CC

270 Wheatley Rd., Old Westbury, NY 11568   **(516) 626-1810**

Old Westbury is a private 27 hole course open 6 days a week all year weather permitting. The nines are called Woods, Overlook and Blue Grass. Guests play accompanied by a member. Tee time reservations are necessary on Saturdays.

- •**Driving Range**
- •**Practice Green**
- •**Power Carts**
- Pull Carts
- •**Club Rental**
- •**Caddies**

- •**Lockers**
- •**Showers**
- •**Food**
- •**Clubhouse**
- •**Outings**
- •**Soft Spikes**

Course Description: Situated on the estate of Cornelius Vanderbilt Whitney III, Old Westbury is considered an awesome course. The still extant landmark water tower was a windmill on the original property. The greens are generally small and undulating. Fairways, carved from a forest, are heavily wooded with rolling terrain. The Overlook nine is more wide open. Its 7th is a long par 4 tight driving hole; an overlong tee shot may go through the fairway which drops off to the right. In 1983, the Met Open was played here and won by Darrell Kestner. The scorecard below is for Blue Grass and Overlook. The ratings are an average of the three nines.

Directions: Nassau County, #34
Take the LIE to Exit 39S (Glen Cove Rd). Stay on the service road to 2nd left. Make left onto Wheatley Rd. Stay on Wheatley; turn left at "T" to club on left.

Hole	1	2	3	4	5	6	7	8	9	Out	BLUE	Rating 73.8
BLUE	382	522	168	376	521	451	183	421	428	3452		Slope 130
WHITE	372	486	153	334	501	423	160	393	390	3212		
Par	4	5	3	4	5	4	3	4	4	36	WHITE	Rating 71.5
Handicap	7	4	9	6	1	2	8	5	3			Slope 126
RED	342	458	112	304	433	348	137	366	334	2834		
Par	4	5	3	4	5	4	3	4	4	36	RED	Rating 74.2
Handicap	7	1	9	6	2	5	8	4	3			Slope 132
Hole	10	11	12	13	14	15	16	17	18	In		Totals
BLUE	444	441	508	372	178	505	438	189	401	3476	BLUE	6928
WHITE	410	395	479	322	152	461	433	159	377	3188	WHITE	6400
Par	4	4	5	4	3	5	4	3	4	36	Par	72
Handicap	6	4	2	7	8	1	3	9	5			
RED	376	364	450	302	127	435	387	141	344	2926	RED	5760
Par	4	4	5	4	3	5	4	3	4	36	Par	72
Handicap	6	4	2	7	9	1	3	8	5			

Manager: Jurgen Schuman   **Pro:** Jim Andrews, PGA   **Supt:** Phil Anderson
Architect: William Mitchell 1962

OYSTER BAY GOLF COURSE

1 Southwoods Rd., Woodbury, NY 11797

(516) 364-1180

Oyster Bay Town Golf Course & Clubhouse is 18 holes open to the public all year, 6 days a week. The greens are temporary in winter. Tee times are on a first come basis. Residents of Oyster Bay pay reduced fees. Power cart fee is $22.

•Driving Range	Lockers
•Practice Green	Showers
•Power Carts	•Food
•Pull Carts	•Clubhouse
•Club Rental	•Outings

Fees	Weekday	Weekend
Res.mbr	$15	$22
Res.nonmbr	$25	$31
Non-res	$50	$62
Res.mbr.Sr	$10	$22

Course Description: Built on a former Mellon estate of 121 acres, Oyster Bay is a hilly, narrow and wooded course. The undulating bent grass greens are of average size and some are multi-tiered. The par 4 4th hole is the most memorable, with a dogleg and fairway bunkers leading up to an elevated green. 4 ponds affect play on some holes. The last four holes are outstanding. After a heavy rain, there can be a drainage problem.

Directions: Nassau County, 35
Take the LIE to Exit 44N. Go north on Rte.135 to Exit 14E (Rte.25) and turn right. Then turn left onto Southwoods Rd. Club is 1/2 m.on the left.

Hole	1	2	3	4	5	6	7	8	9	Out	BLUE	Rating 71.5
BLUE	348	571	152	415	378	173	387	228	320	2972		Slope 131
WHITE	295	531	130	375	354	147	354	207	281	2692		
Par	4	5	3	4	4	3	4	3	4	34	WHITE	Rating 69.0
Handicap	13	5	17	1	7	15	3	9	11			Slope 126
RED	264	471	100	311	329	117	329	164	273	2367		
Par	4	5	3	4	4	3	4	3	4	34	RED	Rating 70.4
Handicap	13	3	17	1	7	15	5	9	11			Slope 126

Hole	10	11	12	13	14	15	16	17	18	In		Totals
BLUE	365	280	125	394	522	366	439	445	443	3379	BLUE	6351
WHITE	334	250	118	358	470	344	412	426	391	3103	WHITE	5795
Par	4	4	3	4	5	4	4	4	4	36	Par	70
Handicap	14	16	18	8	12	10	4	2	6			
RED	312	230	100	328	421	253	337	401	360	2742	RED	5109
Par	4	4	3	4	5	4	4	4	4	36	Par	70
Handicap	10	16	18	8	12	14	6	2	4			

Manager: Bill Gallo　**Pros:** Pat Morris, Bob Posillico, PGA　**Supt:** Stephen Matuza
Architect: Tom Fazio 1989

PENINSULA GOLF CLUB

50 Nassau Rd., Massepequa, NY 11758   **(516) 798-9776**

Peninsula is a 9 hole course open to the public all year 7 days a week. Golfers do not need to make tee time reservations in advance.

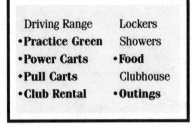

Driving Range   Lockers
- **Practice Green**   Showers
- **Power Carts**   **•Food**
- **Pull Carts**   Clubhouse
- **Club Rental**   **•Outings**

Fees	Weekday	Weekend
Daily	$11/8	$12/8
2nd price is for a 2nd nine		
Power carts $12/$10		

Course Description: Caddies from Inwood and Lawrence CCs got together and bought an abandoned golf course. They worked to clear the high grass and make it playable. On Sundays, it is open just for members until 12:30 PM, and then open to the public. It is a flat, regulation size course with no water in play and easy to walk. Most greens are small except for the fifth hole. The property is surrounded by private homes.

Directions: Nassau County, #36
From Southern State Pkway Exit #44-S (Seaford/Oyster Bay Expressway) and proceed south to Merrick Rd. Turn left and go 2 and 1/2 m. to Unqua Rd and turn right to club at end of road.

Hole	1	2	3	4	5	6	7	8	9	Out	BLUE	Rating
BLUE												Slope
WHITE	460	442	292	334	410	160	383	350	460	3291		
Par	5	4	4	4	4	3	4	4	5	37	WHITE	Rating 71.6
Handicap	7	3	15	13	1	17	9	11	5			Slope 123
RED												
Par											RED	Rating 74.5
Handicap												Slope 127

Hole	10	11	12	13	14	15	16	17	18	In		Totals
BLUE											BLUE	
WHITE											WHITE	6582
Par											Par	74
Handicap												
RED											RED	
Par											Par	
Handicap												

Manager: Larry Maglione   **Pro:** George Tavalaro, PGA   **Supt:** Ennio Lataini
Architect: Maurice McCarthy 1946

PINE HOLLOW COUNTRY CLUB

Northern Blvd., E. Norwich, NY 11732   **(516) 922-0300**

Pine Hollow is an 18 hole private course open 6 days a week and closed in Jan. & Feb. Guests may play accompanied by a member. Tee time reservations are necessary on Fri. Sat. & Sun. in season.

•**Driving Range**	•**Lockers**
•**Practice Green**	•**Showers**
•**Power Carts**	•**Food**
Pull Carts	•**Clubhouse**
Club Rental	•**Outings**
•**Caddies**	•**Soft Spikes**

Course Description: Formerly a Vanderbilt estate, the Normandy mansion was later converted to the clubhouse at Pine Hollow. The well-maintained, somewhat hilly course is challenging, with plenty of deep bunkers. Water comes into play on several holes. The tenth and fifteenth have numerous fairway bunkers which narrow the hitting area. The panoramic view of the clubhouse from the 457 yard signature par 4 #18 is spectacular. The medium size greens have some undulation and are fast in season. Pine Hollow has a relatively young membership.

Directions: Nassau County, #37
Take the LIE to Exit #41N (Rte.106/107). Bear right at fork (106) Proceed 3.5 miles to Rte.25A (Northern Blvd.) and turn right (East); club is 1/2 mile on left.

Hole	1	2	3	4	5	6	7	8	9	Out	BLUE	Rating 72.3
BLACK	529	199	380	544	448	402	345	222	378	3447		Slope 131
WHITE	513	174	371	527	435	374	328	202	355	3279		
Par	5	3	4	5	4	4	4	3	4	36	WHITE	Rating 70.5
Handicap	3	17	7	5	1	9	11	15	13			Slope 129
YELLOW	481	136	349	445	348	334	297	148	321	2859		
Par	5	3	4	5	4	4	4	3	4	36	RED	Rating 71.5
Handicap	1	17	7	3	5	9	13	15	11			Slope 121

Hole	10	11	12	13	14	15	16	17	18	In		Totals
BLACK	381	182	400	570	148	384	370	392	457	3284	BLUE	6731
WHITE	360	153	374	551	133	368	342	365	434	3080	WHITE	6359
Par	4	3	4	5	3	4	4	4	4	35	Par	71
Handicap	14	16	12	2	18	8	10	6	4			
YELLOW	343	107	317	463	121	330	271	306	404	2662	RED	5521
Par	4	3	4	5	3	4	4	4	5	36	Par	72
Handicap	10	18	6	2	16	8	14	12	4			

Manager: Gaspar Klamor   **Pro:** Tom DeBellis, PGA   **Supt:** Jerry Kunkel
Architect: William Mitchell 1955

PIPING ROCK CLUB

Chicken Valley Road, Locust Valley, NY 11560   (516) 676-0460

Piping Rock is an 18 hole private course that is open 6 days a week and closed in the winter, depending on the weather. Guests may play accompanied by a member. Tee time reservations are required on weekends.

```
•Driving Range    •Lockers
•Practice Green   •Showers
•Power Carts      •Food
 Pull Carts       •Clubhouse
•Club Rental      •Outings
•Caddies           Soft Spikes
```

Course Description: Piping Rock is situated on 500 acres of impeccably groomed land. The extremely impressive driving range was formerly a polo field and offers a breathtaking view as you drive up the entrance to the club. Some of the difficulty on this course is caused by the fescue grass in the roughs, the changes in elevation and the deep bunkers. The sloping greens are large with subtle breaks and double tiers. On the most memorable segment, the "amen corner," (#s 14, 15 & 16), the golfer faces a series of formidable challenges. The MET PGA was held here in 1996.

Directions: Nassau County # 38
Take the LIE to Exit #41North (Rte.106/107, toward Glen Cove). Take 107 for 5 miles to Hegeman's Lane (1st right after N.Blvd.) to Chicken Valley Rd. and turn right. Go to 1st light and turn left onto Piping Rock Rd. to club on right.

Hole	1	2	3	4	5	6	7	8	9	Out	BLUE	Rating 71.3
BLUE	402	375	180	400	305	516	430	380	210	3198		Slope 131
WHITE	380	360	170	375	300	430	380	370	185	2950		
Par	4	4	3	4	4	5	4	4	3	35	WHITE	Rating 68.5
Handicap	3	11	15	5	17	7	1	9	13			Slope 125
RED	360	345	160	340	255	420	375	329	180	2764		
Par	4	4	3	4	4	5	4	4	3	35	RED	Rating 72.5
Handicap	3	9	15	5	17	7	1	11	13			Slope 128
Hole	10	11	12	13	14	15	16	17	18	In		Totals
BLUE	495	175	370	295	402	378	370	156	520	3161	BLUE	6359
WHITE	480	155	345	290	380	350	320	145	510	2975	WHITE	5925
Par	5	3	4	4	4	4	4	3	5	36	Par	71
Handicap	10	14	12	16	2	4	8	18	6			
RED	444	145	342	258	340	315	318	125	450	2737	RED	5501
Par	5	3	4	4	4	4	4	3	5	36	Par	71
Handicap	8	14	12	16	2	10	4	18	6			

Manager: Matt Oggero   **Pro:** Iain Mossman, PGA   **Supt:** Rick Spear
Architects: C.B. MacDonald, Pete Dye **Estab:** 1911

PLANDOME COUNTRY CLUB

Stonytown Rd., Plandome, NY 11030 **(516) 627-1273**

Plandome is a private 18 hole course open 6 days a week and closed in January and February. Guests play accompanied by a member. Reservations are necessary for guests.

Driving Range	•**Lockers**
•**Practice Green**	•**Showers**
•**Power Carts**	•**Food**
Pull Carts	•**Clubhouse**
Club Rental	•**Outings**
•**Caddies**	•**Soft Spikes**

Course Description: This well groomed course uses modern design technology while retaining the original character. It is hilly, resulting in many uneven lies, and plays longer because of the uphill holes. Some tees and greens, which are small and undulating, are elevated. The tight layout requires good ball control due to the narrow target areas. Water is in play on the 18th, as part of OB, and also on the 3rd hole. The latter is the signature, a scenic par 3 with a tee shot over a pond to a sloping green. The Met Junior and the Met PGA have been held here.

Directions: Nassau County, #39
Take the LIE to Exit 36. Go north on Searingtown Rd. which becomes Port Washington Blvd. At Stonytown Rd. turn left. Club is ahead on the right.

Hole	1	2	3	4	5	6	7	8	9	Out	BLUE	Rating 71.6
BLUE	430	545	160	360	545	150	345	455	355	3345		Slope 132
WHITE	400	535	150	320	530	145	340	440	320	3180		
Par	4	5	3	4	5	3	4	4	4	36	WHITE	Rating 69.6
Handicap	3	1	15	9	7	17	11	5	13			Slope 127
RED	365	490	110	270	385	130	335	420	235	2740		
Par	5	5	3	4	4	3	4	5	4	37	RED	Rating 71.5
Handicap	5	1	13	11	3	17	7	9	15			Slope 122
Hole	10	11	12	13	14	15	16	17	18	In		Totals
BLUE	310	180	470	420	290	220	425	480	315	3110	BLUE	6455
WHITE	305	150	430	400	285	210	410	475	290	2955	WHITE	6135
Par	4	3	4	4	4	3	4	5	4	35	Par	71
Handicap	14	18	2	4	8	10	6	16	12			
RED	300	130	315	375	230	185	400	470	235	2640	RED	5380
Par	4	3	4	5	4	3	5	5	4	37	Par	74
Handicap	10	14	16	6	8	12	4	2	18			

Manager: Lee Koons   **Pro:** Jim Hundertmark, PGA   **Supt:** Tommy Nelson
Architect: Orrin Smith 1931 **Redesign:** David Postlethwait

ROCKAWAY HUNTING CLUB

PRIVATE

615 Ocean Avenue, Cedarhurst, NY 11516   **(516) 569-3445**

Rockaway Hunting is an 18 hole course open 6 days a week, and closed between Nov. 1 & April 1. Guests may play accompanied by a member. Tee time reservations are required on weekends.

•Driving Range	•Lockers
•Practice Green	•Showers
•Power Carts	•Food
•Pull Carts	•Clubhouse
•Club Rental	•Outings
•Caddies	•Soft Spikes

Course Description: The oldest country club in the US, Rockaway Hunting Club was begun as a venue for fox-hunting and steeplechase racing in 1876. The golf course was added later. Tennis on grass courts, and racquetball are available. Wind and water characteristic of a links style layout, affect play here. The final three holes on the front nine play along Woodmere and Reynold's Channels. The well conditioned small greens are undulating, and some are multi-tiered. Many New Yorkers are members since it is at the first train stop in Nassau out of Wall St. on the LIRR.

Directions: Nassau County, #40
Southern St. Pkwy. to Exit #19-S (Peninsula Blvd.) Go south 6.7 miles to light at Cedarhurst Ave. & turn left. Go 2.5 miles to Ocean Ave. & turn left. Club is 2 miles on right.

Hole	1	2	3	4	5	6	7	8	9	Out	BLUE	Rating 70.9
BLUE	341	368	166	441	159	507	381	320	454	3137		Slope 129
WHITE	335	353	156	424	150	491	365	305	433	3012		
Par	4	4	3	4	3	5	4	4	4	35	WHITE	Rating 69.1
Handicap	11	9	17	1	15	7	5	13	3			Slope 126
RED	326	341	126	390	134	430	342	294	387	2770		
Par	4	4	3	4	3	5	4	4	5	36	RED	Rating 70.4
Handicap	13	5	17	1	15	3	9	11	7			Slope 119
Hole	10	11	12	13	14	15	16	17	18	In		Totals
BLUE	314	348	563	380	200	372	138	424	375	3114	BLUE	6251
WHITE	310	339	472	362	188	323	127	384	356	2854	WHITE	5866
Par	4	4	5	4	3	4	3	4	4	35	Par	70
Handicap	16	14	4	10	6	8	18	2	12			
RED	295	330	407	347	172	313	120	374	335	2693	RED	5463
Par	4	4	5	4	3	4	3	4	4	35	Par	71
Handicap	16	8	2	6	10	14	18	4	12			

Manager: Nick Benvin   **Pro:** Randy Cavanaugh, PGA   **Supt:**Nick Broziak
Architects: Devereux Emmet, A.W. Tillinghast **Estab:** 1878

72

ROCKVILLE LINKS CLUB

Long Beach Rd., Rockville Center, NY 11570 **(516) 766-7446**

Rockville Links is a private 18 hole course open 6 days a week and closed in January. Guests play accompanied by a member. Tee time reservations are not necessary.

•**Driving Range**	•**Lockers**
•**Practice Green**	•**Showers**
•**Power Carts**	•**Food**
Pull Carts	•**Clubhouse**
Club Rental	•**Outings**
•**Caddies**	•**Soft Spikes**

Course Description: Rockville Links began as a 9 hole course with the second nine completed by 1926. The Pro here in the 1930s was the uncle of the present Pro, a member of the well known Turnesa family. The well bunkered course, tucked in amongst 106 acres surrounded by beautiful homes, is rather flat with rough that can get quite thick. Target golf is imperative here. The signature fifth hole is a short par 3, intimidating with water in front and to the left of the green and a bunker on the right.

Directions: Nassau County, #41
Take the Southern State to Exit19S (Peninsula Blvd.) Make immediate left at 1st light onto N. Village Ave. Go 1mile, turn left on DeMott. Then turn left onto Long Beach Rd. Club is ahead on left.

Hole	1	2	3	4	5	6	7	8	9	Out	BLUE	Rating
BLUE												Slope
WHITE	304	360	423	357	124	402	501	500	223	3194		
Par	4	4	4	4	3	4	5	5	3	36	WHITE	Rating 70.3
Handicap	13	7	1	11	15	3	9	5	15			Slope 128
RED	288	320	410	326	100	360	427	429	198	2858		
Par	4	4	5	4	3	4	5	5	3	37	RED	Rating 73.4
Handicap	13	9	3	11	17	7	5	1	15			Slope 127
Hole	10	11	12	13	14	15	16	17	18	In		Totals
BLUE											BLUE	
WHITE	136	496	345	389	350	324	282	181	560	3194	WHITE	6257
Par	3	5	4	4	4	4	4	3	5	36	Par	72
Handicap	18	2	6	8	12	10	14	16	4			
RED	125	480	309	377	341	309	267	165	500	2873	RED	5731
Par	3	5	4	4	4	4	4	3	5	36	Par	73
Handicap	18	2	12	6	8	10	14	16	4			

Manager: John Daskos   **Pro:** Mike Turnesa, Jr PGA   **Supt:** John McPike
Architect: Devereux Emmet 1924

SANDS POINT GOLF CLUB

140 Middle Neck Rd., Sands Point , NY 11050   **(516) 883-3130**

Sands Point is an 18 hole private course open 6 days a week and closed in January. Guests play accompanied by a member. Tee time reservations are not necessary.

> • **Driving Range**   • **Lockers**
> • **Practice Green**   • **Showers**
> • **Power Carts**   • **Food**
>   Pull Carts   • **Clubhouse**
> • **Club Rental**   • **Outings**
> • **Caddies**   Soft Spikes

Course Description: Originally called Harbor Hills and a venue where polo was played, Sands Point is fairly flat with tree lined fairways of medium width. The deeply bunkered small greens are fast and have subtle breaks. The rough is thick and long around the greens. There is no water in play. The signature 14th, a 600 yard par 5, is long and straight with looming fairway bunkers, gentle slopes and OB to provide an additional challenge. The Met Amateur was held here in 1993, the L.I Amateur in 1997.

Directions: Nassau County, #42
Take the LIE to Exit 36 (Searingtown Rd). Go north as road becomes Port Washington Blvd. Go 6.5 miles to club on left.

Hole	1	2	3	4	5	6	7	8	9	Out	BLUE	Rating 72.2
BLUE	509	191	358	409	490	394	161	414	355	3281		Slope 127
WHITE	480	166	338	395	467	386	140	397	342	3111		
Par	5	3	4	4	5	4	3	4	4	36	WHITE	Rating 70.8
Handicap	12	18	8	2	10	4	16	6	14			Slope 124
RED	430	136	320	382	345	318	108	390	322	2751		
Par	5	3	4	4	5	4	3	4	4	36	RED	Rating 73.7
Handicap	5	15	13	1	3	7	17	11	9			Slope 127
Hole	10	11	12	13	14	15	16	17	18	In		Totals
BLUE	382	367	205	371	600	391	401	157	489	3363	BLUE	6644
WHITE	370	352	183	357	581	384	393	151	466	3237	WHITE	6348
Par	4	4	3	4	5	4	4	3	5	36	Par	72
Handicap	7	11	13	9	1	3	5	17	15			
RED	359	300	174	287	516	291	386	128	433	2874	RED	5625
Par	4	4	3	4	5	4	4	3	5	36	Par	72
Handicap	8	14	16	12	2	10	4	18	6			

Manager: Stephan Fischl   **Pro:** Rick Haldas, PGA   **Supt:** Richard Raymond
Architect: A. W. Tillinghast 1927

VILLAGE CLUB OF SANDS POINT

Astor Lane, Sands Point , NY 11050   (516) 944-5022

The Village owns this 9 hole course. Memberships are for residents. Limited memberships available for non residents. It is open all year 7 days a week weather permitting.
Tee time reservations are necessary on weekends.

•Driving Range	•Lockers
•Practice Green	•Showers
•Power Carts	•Food
• Pull Carts	•Clubhouse
Club Rental	•Outings
Caddies	•Soft Spikes

Course Description: This 210 acre property was formerly owned by IBM and used as
a country club and executive training center. Sands Point took it over in 1994.
Originally, it was part of the Isaac Guggenheim estate and the elegant, landmark
mansion remains with a beautiful view of the harbor. The course, on 60 acres, is
relatively flat and wide open with no water in play. The greens are fairly fast and of
average size. The 3rd hole is a dogleg par 5, the 6th a long challenging par 3. The
architect, Tom Doak, is designing a 2nd nine and will refurbish the original nine. He
believes in following the natural contours; some holes will be built along the water
using shorefront property.

Directions: Nassau County, #43
Take the LIE to Exit 36. Go north on Searingtown Rd. until it becomes Port Washington
Rd. Club is ahead on right.

Hole	1	2	3	4	5	6	7	8	9	Out	BLUE	Rating
BLUE												Slope
WHITE	280	128	575	404	353	235	490	120	530	3115		
Par	4	3	5	4	4	3	5	3	5	36	WHITE	Rating 69.1
Handicap	13	17	1	5	9	11	3	15	7			Slope 120
RED	275	115	475	330	344	160	470	115	460	2744		
Par	4	3	5	4	4	3	5	3	5	36	RED	Rating 69.8
Handicap	11	15	1	10	8	13	5	17	3			Slope 116
Hole	10	11	12	13	14	15	16	17	18	In		Totals
BLUE											BLUE	
WHITE	280	115	541	465	365	200	510	140	520	3136	WHITE	6251
Par	4	3	5	4	4	3	5	3	5	36	Par	72
Handicap	14	18	4	2	10	12	6	16	8			
RED	275	110	475	330	344	160	470	135	460	2759	RED	5503
Par	4	3	5	4	4	3	5	3	5	36	Par	72
Handicap	12	18	2	7	9	14	6	16	4			

Manager: Carlos Duarte   **Pro:** Brian Crowell, PGA   **Supt:** Bill Knight
Built: 1924   **Redesign:** Robert Trent Jones 1950s

THE SEAWANE CLUB

Club Drive, Hewlett Harbor, NY 11557   **(516) 374-1110**

Seawane is an 18 hole course open 6 days a week and closed in February. Tee time reservations are required on weekends. Guests may play accompanied by a member.

•**Driving Range**	•**Lockers**
•**Practice Green**	•**Showers**
•**Power Carts**	•**Food**
Pull Carts	•**Clubhouse**
Club Rental	•**Outings**
•**Caddies**	•**Soft Spikes**

Course Description: An extremely flat links style course, Seawane is "sneaky long" with water affecting a few holes. The medium sized greens are undulating, fairly fast and sometimes two tiered. The wide open treeless fairways are windswept by the breezes off the nearby bay. The layout is made more challenging by canals and a myriad of bunkers both in the fairways and protecting the greens. The signature #13 (Eden) runs along a canal and overlooks Reynold's Channel. The clubhouse was recently renovated.

Directions: Nassau County, # 44
Southern St. Pkwy. East to Central Ave. (Exit 13S). Central Ave. becomes Mill Rd.; go to end, turn left onto W. Broadway. Go to fork, bear left onto Broadway. Go 2 blocks, turn right onto E. Rockaway Rd. for 1/2 mile to Schenck Lane, turn right. Go to end, bear right onto Club Rd. to club.

Hole	1	2	3	4	5	6	7	8	9	Out	BLUE	Rating 71.6
BLUE	375	413	353	285	205	496	432	145	508	3212		Slope 127
WHITE	362	399	335	272	182	486	413	121	496	3066		
Par	4	4	4	4	3	5	4	3	5	36	WHITE	Rating 70.1
Handicap	5	3	11	15	13	1	9	17	7			Slope 124
RED	337	339	324	261	141	456	401	113	455	2827		
Par	4	4	4	4	3	5	5	3	5	37	RED	Rating 73.1
Handicap	7	5	11	13	17	1	9	15	3			Slope 124

Hole	10	11	12	13	14	15	16	17	18	In		Totals
BLUE	336	185	331	405	199	551	385	542	385	3319	BLUE	6531
WHITE	321	165	313	387	176	530	356	513	365	3126	WHITE	6192
Par	4	3	4	4	3	5	4	5	4	36	Par	72
Handicap	16	14	18	4	12	2	6	8	10			
RED	294	150	306	303	163	477	322	429	331	2775	RED	5602
Par	4	3	4	4	3	5	4	5	4	36	Par	73
Handicap	8	18	14	12	16	2	4	6	10			

Manager: Eddie Closs   **Pro:** Bob Longo, PGA   **Supt:** David Parsons
Architects: Devereux Emmet, Alfred Tull 1927

THE TAM O'SHANTER CLUB

Fruitledge Road, Brookville, NY 11545　　　**(516) 626-1580**

Tam O'Shanter is an 18 hole private course open 6 days a week and closed in Jan. & Feb. Guests play accompanied by a member. Tee time reservations are necessary on weekends.

- •Driving Range
- •Practice Green
- •Power Carts
- Pull Carts
- •Club Rental
- •Caddies
- •Lockers
- •Showers
- •Food
- •Clubhouse
- •Outings
- •Soft Spikes

Course Description: Tam O'Shanter's long, wide open layout has many doglegs. With heavily bunkered, large sloping greens and treacherous rough, golfers certainly find this layout a challenging experience. The powerful effect of the wind blowing here can surely require 2 extra club lengths at times. Seven holes are affected by water. The memorable par 5 fourth hole is 594 yards from the blues. The clubhouse was rebuilt in the 1970s after a fire destroyed it and overlooks land that was once a potato farm.

Directions: Nassau County, #45
LIE to Exit #41, Rte.106/107 North. At fork of 106/107, take 107(stay left). Turn right on Fruitledge; club entrance is 1 & 1/2 miles on right.

Hole	1	2	3	4	5	6	7	8	9	Out	BLUE	Rating 72.5
BLUE	424	156	374	594	388	388	180	448	537	3489		Slope 131
WHITE	405	138	342	557	363	365	158	430	513	3271		
Par	4	3	4	5	4	4	3	4	5	36	WHITE	Rating 70.7
Handicap	11	17	9	3	7	13	15	1	5			Slope 128
RED	375	118	277	428	261	333	138	338	434	2702		
Par	4	3	4	5	4	4	3	4	5	36	RED	Rating 71.4
Handicap	7	17	11	5	9	13	15	3	1			Slope 120

Hole	10	11	12	13	14	15	16	17	18	In		Totals
BLUE	435	554	410	215	395	435	548	216	375	3583	BLUE	7072
WHITE	408	520	368	190	367	407	530	195	337	3322	WHITE	6593
Par	4	5	4	3	4	4	5	3	4	36	Par	72
Handicap	10	8	4	18	14	2	6	16	12			
RED	290	444	282	160	285	333	456	150	316	2716	RED	5418
Par	4	5	4	3	4	4	5	3	4	36	Par	72
Handicap	14	6	12	18	8	4	2	16	10			

Manager: David Mackrell　　**Pro:** Mark Brown, PGA　　**Supt:** Bob Langhauser
Architects: Steve Christoff, Robert Trent Jones　**Estab:** 1963

WHEATLEY HILLS GOLF CLUB

147 E. Williston Ave., E. Williston, NY 11596   **(516) 747-8822**

Wheatley Hills is an 18 hole private club open all year 6 days a week. Guests play accompanied by a member. Tee time reservations are not necessary.

```
•Driving Range    •Lockers
•Practice Green   •Showers
•Power Carts      •Food
 Pull Carts       •Clubhouse
•Club Rental      •Outings
•Caddies          •Soft Spikes
```

Course Description: Wheatley Hills is a rather unusual layout: it has 3 par 5s on the front nine, as well as 3 par 3s. The parkland course has rolling fairways of average width with many uneven lies. The course utilizes every hill to challenge the golfer. The tees and greens are elevated and no water is in play. Bunkers guard some greens in a most protective way.

Directions: Nassau County, #46
Take the LIE to Exit 39S (Glen Cove Rd.) Go South 1.5 mi. on Guinea Woods Rd and turn right on Rte.25B (E. Williston Ave.) Club is on right.

Hole	1	2	3	4	5	6	7	8	9	Out	BLUE	Rating 73.2
BLUE	340	373	214	576	541	219	545	158	404	3370		Slope 133
WHITE	324	359	179	537	510	182	506	139	389	3125		
Par	4	4	3	5	5	3	5	3	4	36	WHITE	Rating 71.1
Handicap	13	7	9	1	11	15	3	17	5			Slope 128
RED	253	330	162	495	477	142	410	130	348	2747		
Par	4	4	3	5	5	3	5	3	4	36	RED	Rating 71.6
Handicap	13	7	9	1	11	15	3	17	5			Slope 124
Hole	10	11	12	13	14	15	16	17	18	In		Totals
BLUE	210	463	527	335	177	594	350	408	400	3464	BLUE	6834
WHITE	179	431	503	316	155	571	335	393	365	3248	WHITE	6373
Par	3	4	5	4	3	5	4	4	4	36	Par	72
Handicap	12	4	6	16	18	2	14	8	10			
RED	156	350	437	297	131	496	219	353	281	2720	RED	5467
Par	3	4	5	4	3	5	4	4	4	36	Par	72
Handicap	12	4	6	16	18	2	14	8	10			

Manager: Fred Goldman   **Pro:** Mike Reynolds, PGA   **Supt:** Vince Sharkey
Architects: Devereux Emmet, Alfred Tull 1913

THE WOODCREST CLUB

225 Eastwoods Road, Syosset, NY 11791   **(516) 921-1518**

Woodcrest is an 18 hole course open 6 days a week and closed in Jan. & Feb. During March & Nov. it is open 5 days a week. Guests may play accompanied by a member. Tee time reservations may be made in advance for weekends in season.

•Driving Range	•Lockers
•Practice Green	•Showers
•Power Carts	•Food
Pull Carts	•Clubhouse
•Club Rental	•Outings
•Caddies	•Soft Spikes

Course Description: The challenging Woodcrest Club located in a stately, park-like setting, is relatively flat with narrow oak-lined fairways. Many doglegs, ample bunkering and out of bounds affect play here. The eighth and fourteenth are par 3 s each over a pond. The average size well conditioned greens are smooth, undulating and in some cases very tricky. The par 4 18th is considered the signature hole with picturesque views of the brick and stone Georgian clubhouse.

Directions: Nassau County, #47
LIE to Exit #41N. Take Rtes.106-107 to fork, bear right onto Rt.106. Proceed approx. 2 miles to Muttontown Rd. Turn right at stop light and go 1 mile to club on right.

Hole	1	2	3	4	5	6	7	8	9	Out	BLUE	Rating 71.8
BLUE	446	515	162	428	501	341	342	202	365	3302		Slope 130
WHITE	423	502	146	415	488	325	333	182	347	3161		
Par	4	5	3	4	5	4	4	3	4	36	WHITE	Rating 70.5
Handicap	3	9	17	1	5	15	7	13	11			Slope 127
RED	377	472	129	396	476	315	305	129	332	2931		
Par	4	5	3	4	5	4	4	3	4	36	RED	Rating 73.1
Handicap	3	7	17	1	5	11	9	15	13			Slope 123

Hole	10	11	12	13	14	15	16	17	18	In		Totals
BLUE	358	304	421	476	158	360	509	193	398	3177	BLUE	6479
WHITE	331	285	407	464	138	341	496	174	384	3020	WHITE	6181
Par	4	4	4	5	3	4	5	3	4	36	Par	72
Handicap	8	16	2	10	18	12	4	14	6			
RED	302	276	357	431	113	329	465	157	294	2724	RED	5655
Par	4	4	4	5	3	4	5	3	4	36	Par	72
Handicap	10	14	4	6	16	12	2	18	8			

Manager: Arthur Crouch   **Pro:** Jon Kudysch, PGA   **Supt:** Greg Koldinsky
Architect: William F. Mitchell 1963

THE WOODMERE CLUB

PRIVATE

Meadow Drive, Woodmere, NY 11598   **(516) 295-2500**

The Woodmere Club is an 18 hole private course open 6 days a week all year, weather permitting. Tee time reservations are recommended on weekends & holidays. Guests may play accompanied by a member.

•Driving Range	•Lockers
•Practice Green	•Showers
•Power Carts	•Food
Pull Carts	•Clubhouse
Club Rental	•Outings
•Caddies	•Soft Spikes

Course Description: The Woodmere Club is a tight, generally flat course with severely undulating well trapped greens.   The outstanding signature par 3 sixteenth features tricky cross winds and water in front of the green that make landing on the right level a matter of great skill or amazing luck.   The 545 yard par 5 #12 offers difficulty due to both its length and a pond in play on the approach shot.   Scenic views of Reynold's Channel, an outlet to the ocean, abound.   Woodmere has hosted several Met championships and sectional qualifiers for the US Open and LI Open.

Directions: Nassau County, # 48
Southern St. Pkwy. to Exit #19-S (Peninsula Blvd.) Go 6 miles to light at Woodmere Blvd. and turn left. Go to Broadway (2nd light after RR) & turn right.   Proceed to Meadow Dr. at light and go left to club.

Hole	1	2	3	4	5	6	7	8	9	Out	BLUE	Rating 70.7
BLUE	400	390	154	355	516	423	295	351	194	3078		Slope 129
WHITE	395	385	129	352	501	411	285	347	192	2997		
Par	4	4	3	4	5	4	4	4	3	35	WHITE	Rating 69.7
Handicap	5	7	15	11	3	1	17	9	13			Slope 127
RED	380	373	100	337	477	404	274	342	181	2868		
Par	4	4	3	4	5	5	4	4	3	36	RED	Rating 71.6
Handicap	7	5	17	11	1	3	15	9	13			Slope 118

Hole	10	11	12	13	14	15	16	17	18	In		Totals
BLUE	312	175	525	374	362	391	175	361	427	3102	BLUE	6180
WHITE	298	141	512	354	337	381	150	325	417	2915	WHITE	5912
Par	4	3	5	4	4	4	3	4	4	35	Par	70
Handicap	18	14	2	8	12	4	16	10	6			
RED	274	105	426	328	320	351	112	321	333	2570	RED	5438
Par	14	16	2	10	8	4	18	12	6	35	Par	71
Handicap	4	4	15	4	13	4	5	5	14			

Manager: Chad Cutler   **Pro:** Joe Moresco, PGA   **Supt:** R. McGuiness
Architect: Robert Trent Jones 1952 **Estab:** 1910

SUFFOLK COUNTY

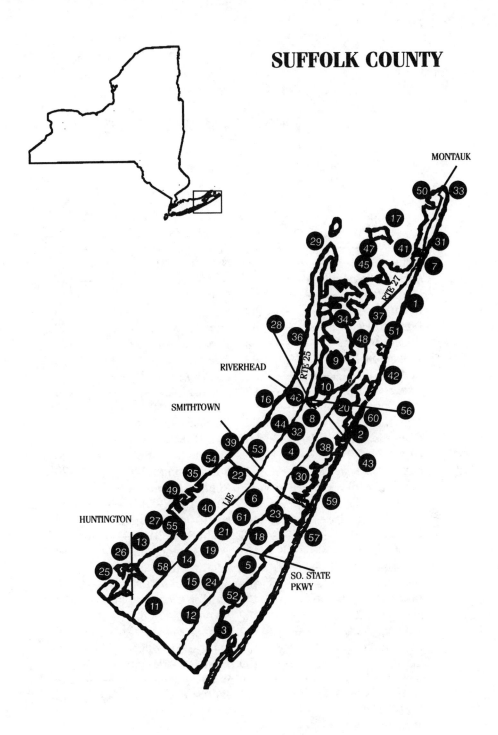

SUFFOLK COUNTY

Public Courses appear in *bold italics*

ATLANTIC GOLF CLUB

Scuttle Hole Rd., Bridgehampton, NY 11932   **(516) 537-1818**

Atlantic is an 18 hole course open all year 7 days a week. Guests play accompanied by a member. Tee time reservations are not necessary.

> • **Driving Range**   • **Lockers**
> • **Practice Green** • **Showers**
> • **Power Carts**   • **Food**
>   Pull Carts   • **Clubhouse**
> • **Club Rental**   • **Outings**
> • **Caddies**   • **Soft Spikes**

Course Description: Meticulously maintained, this outstanding, relatively new links type course was built on interesting contoured former farmland. The greens are fairly fast, medium size with subtle breaks. Moguls and mounds, along with fescue grass in the rough, defy the golfer. On the par 5 6th, there is a pond just off the middle tees. Both the 9th and the 18th have hazards that project into the wildlife preserve. Major environmental requirements had to be met to build here. There is a "Shinnecock" atmosphere at this very long, challenging layout. Atlantic is rated in the top 100 courses in the country.

Directions: Suffolk County, #1
LIE to Exit 70 to Rte.27East. Continue on 27 past Watermill (about 20 miles). Make left onto Scuttle Hole Rd. after Hess Sta. and go about 1 mile. Turn left into club.

Hole	1	2	3	4	5	6	7	8	9	Out	BLUE	Rating 74.0
BLUE	530	428	343	218	455	501	165	348	437	3425		Slope 136
WHITE	465	381	330	171	413	475	133	315	401	3084		
Par	5	4	4	3	4	5	3	4	4	36	WHITE	Rating 72.3
Handicap	7	3	15	11	1	9	17	13	5			Slope 132
RED	395	375	299	130	328	401	107	284	347	2666		
Par	5	4	4	3	4	5	3	4	4	36	RED	Rating 72.4
Handicap	7	1	5	15	9	11	17	13	3			Slope 128

Hole	10	11	12	13	14	15	16	17	18	In		Totals
BLUE	477	127	369	535	409	180	427	382	609	3515	BLUE	6940
WHITE	455	108	311	498	361	160	400	344	549	3186	WHITE	6270
Par	4	3	4	5	4	3	4	4	5	36	Par	72
Handicap	2	18	12	6	8	16	10	14	4			
RED	396	97	272	351	271	124	320	298	501	2630	RED	5296
Par	4	3	4	5	4	3	4	4	5	36	Par	72
Handicap	6	18	12	2	8	16	10	14	4			

Manager: Jim Mathers   **Pro:** Rick Hartman, PGA   **Supt:** Bob Ranum
Architect: Rees Jones 1992

BELLPORT COUNTRY CLUB

So. Country Rd., Bellport, NY 11713   **(516) 286-7206**

Bellport is a private 18 hole course owned by the Village of Bellport. It is open 7 days a week for members only. Guests play accompanied by a member. Tee times may be made up to 2 days ahead for weekends.

Driving Range	•Lockers
•Practice Green	•Showers
•Power Carts	•Food
•Pull Carts	•Clubhouse
•Club Rental	•Outings
Caddies	•Soft Spikes

Course Description: Bellport is an open, flat course where the wind blows in from the Bay. The fairways are narrow and defined by the encroaching rough. The rather small greens are well-maintained and fast, with little break. Water is in play on 7 holes. The 7th hole, a dogleg right, has a beautiful view overlooking the Great South Bay. In the early 1960s, Robert Trent Jones did some redesign on the holes bordering the water. Residents of Bellport are fortunate to have such a lovely golf facility to enjoy.

Directions: Suffolk County, #2
Take the LIE to Exit 64. Take Rte.112S to Montauk Highway and turn left. Go about 3 miles and bear right at fork onto So. Country Rd. Club is 2 miles ahead on the right.

Hole	1	2	3	4	5	6	7	8	9	Out	BLUE	Rating 70.1
BLUE	408	132	312	179	518	192	380	543	363	3027		Slope 118
WHITE	389	119	300	150	506	160	350	533	349	2856		
Par	4	3	4	3	5	3	4	5	4	35	WHITE	Rating 68.9
Handicap	5	17	13	11	1	15	7	3	9			Slope 115
RED	379	102	280	128	423	130	332	433	309	2516		
Par	4	3	4	3	5	3	4	5	4	35	RED	Rating 69.2
Handicap	3	17	9	13	1	15	7	5	11			Slope 112
Hole	10	11	12	13	14	15	16	17	18	In		Totals
BLUE	510	420	319	278	191	276	372	414	427	3207	BLUE	6234
WHITE	497	410	310	262	179	274	365	380	420	3097	WHITE	5953
Par	5	4	4	4	3	4	4	4	4	36	Par	71
Handicap	6	2	14	18	12	16	10	4	8			
RED	368	403	300	236	159	270	291	329	410	2766	RED	5282
Par	5	4	4	4	3	4	4	4	5	37	Par	72
Handicap	8	2	10	18	16	12	14	4	6			

Manager/Pro: Leo McMahon, PGA   **Supt:** Edward Bishop
Architect: Seth Raynor 1916   **Estab:** 1899

BERGEN POINT GOLF CLUB

69 Bergen Avenue, West Babylon, NY 11704   **(516) 661-8282**

Bergen Point is an 18 hole Suffolk County course (privately run by Global Golf). It is open 7 days a week, and closes between 12/15 & 3/15. The Green Key Card is used here by residents of the county. There is a 7 day advance for tee times (516)244-7275.

•**Driving Range** Lockers	
•**Practice Green** Showers	
•**Power Carts** •**Food**	
•**Pull Carts** •**Clubhouse**	
•**Club Rental** •**Outings**	
Soft Spikes	

Fees	Weekday	Weekend
Daily(Res)	$19	$20
Non-res	$28	$32
Twi (4PM)	$8	$13
Power carts	$25	

Course Description: Water and wind affect play at the well maintained Bergen Point. Improved drainage, cart paths, greens & bunkers are the result of a recent renovation. Several holes run along a canal on the back nine. The par 4 18thsignature hole, 436 yards from the blue, has a stadium backdrop and finishes to a picturesque elevated green. This links style course is basically flat and easily walkable with picturesque views of the bay. It gets quite busy in season.

Directions: Suffolk County, #3
Southern State Pkwy. East to Rte.109East. Proceed to Great Eastneck Rd. which becomes Bergen Ave. to club on right.

Hole	1	2	3	4	5	6	7	8	9	Out	BLUE	Rating 71.1
BLUE	348	193	405	513	419	232	404	516	352	3382		Slope 116
WHITE	332	173	395	490	397	185	389	497	327	3185		
Par	4	3	4	5	4	3	4	5	4	36	WHITE	Rating 69.1
Handicap	7	15	5	17	1	11	3	9	13			Slope 112
RED	320	156	373	435	374	164	355	473	302	2952		
Par	4	3	4	5	4	3	4	5	4	36	RED	Rating 71.9
Handicap	7	15	5	17	1	11	3	9	13			Slope 117
Hole	10	11	12	13	14	15	16	17	18	In		Totals
BLUE	418	167	350	481	404	383	383	172	436	3194	BLUE	6576
WHITE	404	155	334	464	380	367	358	143	416	3021	WHITE	6206
Par	4	3	4	5	4	4	4	3	4	35	Par	71
Handicap	2	18	16	8	6	12	10	14	4			
RED	338	136	297	451	350	337	333	134	401	2777	RED	5729
Par	4	3	4	5	4	4	4	3	4	35	Par	71
Handicap	2	18	16	8	6	12	10	14	4			

Manager/Pro: Victor Romano, PGA   **Supt:** Gene Contino
Architect: William Mitchell, 1972

BLUE RIDGE GOLF CLUB

899 Golf Lane, Medford, NY 11763   (516) 698-7575

Blue Ridge is a 9 hole executive course within a private community. The golf is for residents only and is open all year seven days a week, weather permitting. Reservations for tee times are not necessary.

Driving Range	•Lockers
•Practice Green	•Showers
Power Carts	•Food
•Pull Carts	•Clubhouse
•Club Rental	•Outings
Caddies	Soft Spikes

Course Description: With the houses in this private community circling the golf course, the home owners have attractive views to enjoy. The clubhouse has an indoor pool and other amenities. The course itself is tree lined and relatively flat. There are hilly banks on some holes. No water is in play; the greens are small.

Directions: Suffolk County, #4
Take the LIE to Exit 64 and Rte.112N. Make left at Granny Rd. The main entrance is off Granny on the left.

Hole	1	2	3	4	5	6	7	8	9	Out	BLUE	Rating
BLUE												Slope
WHITE	153	149	155	300	139	257	120	96	222	1591		
Par	3	3	3	4	3	4	3	3	4	30	WHITE	Rating 55.0
Handicap	4	6	5	1	7	2	8	9	3			Slope 84
RED	136	139	144	243	132	245	112	87	215	1453		
Par											RED	Rating 55.0
Handicap												Slope 82
Hole	10	11	12	13	14	15	16	17	18	In		Totals
BLUE											BLUE	
WHITE											WHITE	3182
Par											Par	60
Handicap												
RED											RED	2906
Par											Par	60
Handicap												

Manager: Frank Kiefer   **Supt:** Tom Blend
Built: Late 1970s

BRENTWOOD COUNTRY CLUB

 PUBLIC

100 Pennsylvania Ave., Brentwood, NY 11717 **(516) 436-6060**

Brentwood is an 18 hole Town of Islip course. Residents obtain a recreation card for discounted fees. It is closed on Mondays from Dec.1 to March 15. Tee times are necessary on weekends and may be made up to one week in advance.

Driving Range	•Lockers
•Practice Green	•Showers
•Power Carts	•Food
•Pull Carts	•Clubhouse
•Club Rental	•Outings

Fees	Weekday	Weekend
Res	$18	$20
Non-res	$23	$28
Sr/Jr	$10	
Power carts	$25	$25

Course Description: Brentwood in the Pines is a wide open relatively flat tree-lined course that is easily walkable. There is no water in play. Some tees and greens are elevated. The 17th is the signature hole, a very narrow par 5. The course is very busy in the summer. Wednesdays, from 8:30-10AM, is "Ladies Day."

Directions: Suffolk County, #5
Take LIE to Exit 54. Go across Wicks Rd. to Washington and turn right. Course is 1 mile ahead on left.

Hole	1	2	3	4	5	6	7	8	9	Out	BLUE	Rating 69.3
BLUE	489	372	180	497	149	386	369	304	338	3084		Slope 121
WHITE	480	352	169	483	133	375	350	285	303	2930		
Par	5	4	3	5	3	4	4	4	4	36	WHITE	Rating 67.8
Handicap	6	2	14	8	16	4	10	18	12			Slope 118
RED	435	302	142	443	124	345	305	234	278	2608		
Par	5	4	3	5	3	5	4	4	4	37	RED	Rating 68.4
Handicap	4	2	14	6	16	10	8	18	12			Slope 111
Hole	10	11	12	13	14	15	16	17	18	In		Totals
BLUE	357	310	386	326	170	417	277	479	367	3089	BLUE	6173
WHITE	308	284	370	293	158	404	262	467	355	2905	WHITE	5835
Par	4	4	4	4	3	4	4	5	4	36	Par	72
Handicap	13	11	5	9	15	1	17	3	7			
RED	248	230	327	238	145	355	222	390	330	2485	RED	5093
Par	4	4	4	4	3	5	4	5	4	37	Par	74
Handicap	11	7	3	13	15	9	17	1	5			

Pro: Richard Loughlin, PGA   **Supt:** Joe Graham
Architect: Devereux Emmet 1923

BRETTON WOODS COUNTRY CLUB   PRIVATE

1027 Clubhouse Court., Coram, NY 11727   **(516) 736-9704**

Bretton Woods is a private residential community. The 9 hole course is available to residents only. Open 7 days a week, it is closed in the winter. Guests play accompanied by a member. Reservations for tee times are not necessary.

Driving Range	**•Lockers**
•Practice Green	**•Showers**
Power Carts	**•Food**
•Pull Carts	**•Clubhouse**
Club Rental	Outings
Caddies	Soft Spikes

Course Description: Bretton Woods golf course circles the community and ends up at the clubhouse. The layout has par 4s and par 3s. It is somewhat hilly with no water in play. Well bunkered and well maintained, it is an attractive amenity for the residents who also have bowling and indoor and outdoor pools available.

Rating: WHITE 57.8 Slope 91   The scorecard was unavailable at press
Rating: RED   59.7 Slope 92   time.

Directions: Suffolk County, #6
Take LIE to Exit 64. Take Rte.112N for 3.2 miles to Middle Country Rd. (Rte.25). Turn left and make 1st left onto Mooney Pond Rd. 2nd left is entrance to Bretton Woods. Follow to clubhouse.

Pro: Jimmy Batjer
Architect: Schwartz 1970s

THE BRIDGEHAMPTON CLUB

PRIVATE

Ocean Rd., Bridgehampton, NY 11932   **(516) 537-9875**

Bridgehampton is a private 9 hole course open all year 7 days a week. Guests may play accompanied by a member. Tee time reservations are not necessary.

Driving Range	Lockers
•**Practice Green**	Showers
•**Power Carts**	•**Food**
•**Pull Carts**	•**Clubhouse**
Club Rental	Outings
Caddies	Soft Spikes

Course Description: Bridgehampton is a somewhat hilly well maintained course in the heart of the town. The fairways are narrow and the rough is tough. It has small greens that are quite fast. The par 3 #7 signature hole has a sloped green with deep bunkers surrounding it. The golfer is severely penalized when the shot lands above the hole because a downhill putt is liable to end up off the green.

Directions: Suffolk County, #7
In Hamptons, take Rte27 East through Watermill and through Village of Bridgehampton and make right on Ocean Rd. Club is on the left a few blocks down.

Hole	1	2	3	4	5	6	7	8	9	Out	BLUE	Rating
BLUE												Slope
WHITE	306	260	365	373	349	406	170	451	166	2846		
Par	4	4	4	4	4	4	3	5	3	35	WHITE	Rating 67.6
Handicap	13	17	3	7	5	1	11	9	15			Slope 116
RED	303	239	359	364	345	336	150	403	139	2688		
Par	4	4	4	4	4	5	3	5	3	36	RED	Rating 67.6
Handicap	13	17	3	7	5	1	11	9	15			Slope 119
Hole	10	11	12	13	14	15	16	17	18	In		Totals
BLUE											BLUE	
WHITE											WHITE	5692
Par											Par	70
Handicap												
RED											RED	5376
Par											Par	72
Handicap												

Manager: John Bowley   **Supt:** Scott Bertrand
Architect: Willard Wilkinson 1924

89

CALVERTON LINKS

149 Edwards Avenue, Calverton, NY 11933   **(516) 369-5200**

Calverton Links is a 9 hole course open 7 days a week, all year, weather permitting. Tee times may be made up to 1 week in advance. There is a miniature golf course on the premises.

•**Driving Range**	Lockers
•**Practice Green**	Showers
•**Power Carts**	•**Food**
•**Pull Carts**	Clubhouse
•**Club Rental**	•**Outings**
•**Soft Spikes**	

Fees	Weekday	Weekend
Daily (9)	$14	$16
Daily (18)	$24	$26
Power carts	$13(9)	$25(18)

Course Description: Formerly farmland, Calverton Links is a tight course with heavy rough and bent grass tees and greens. It is short but challenging with fast, gently rolling contoured greens. There are private course conditions on the fairways which have a botanical garden look. Hole #s 5,6 &7 have ponds that affect play.

Directions: Suffolk County, # 8
LIE to Exit #71 (Edwards Ave.) Turn left onto Edwards Ave. and proceed 1/2 mile to club on left.

Hole	1	2	3	4	5	6	7	8	9	Out	BLUE	Rating
BLUE	507	222	315	321	341	310	444	338	238	3036		Slope
WHITE	444	191	282	285	311	280	429	275	185	2682		
Par	5	3	4	4	4	4	5	4	3	36	WHITE	Rating 69.4
Handicap	2	3	8	6	1	5	4	7	9			Slope 119
RED	381	163	253	257	226	195	404	200	138	2217		
Par	5	3	4	4	4	4	5	4	3	36	RED	Rating 65.6
Handicap	2	3	8	6	1	5	4	7	9			Slope 108

Hole	10	11	12	13	14	15	16	17	18	In		Totals
BLUE											BLUE	6072
WHITE											WHITE	5364
Par											Par	36
Handicap												
RED											RED	4434
Par											Par	36
Handicap												

Manager: John Schippers   **Pros:**Brian Misiewicz, Danny Malawista, PGA   **Supt:** Bill Nohejl
Architect: Cole Hayes 1994

CEDARS GOLF CLUB

Cases Lane, Cutchogue, NY 11935   **(516) 734-6363**

Cedars is a 9 hole executive par 3 golf course open 7 days a week from April 1 through December 31. Tee time reservations are not necessary.

Driving Range	Lockers
•**Practice Green**	Showers
Power Carts	•**Food**
•**Pull Carts**	Clubhouse
•**Club Rental**	Outings
•**Soft Spikes**	

Fees	Weekday	Weekend
Daily	$5.50	$7.00
2nd round	$3.00	$3.50
Sr/Jr	$5.00	$6.00

Course Description: Situated in the heart of the North Fork of Long Island, Cedars is slightly hilly with trees, vines, shrubs and wildflowers decorating this pretty course. Well bunkered, it has ponds on three holes, and offers a variety of hazards. Easy to walk and good for iron practice, the layout consists of par 3s of differing yardages. The fairways range from flat to hilly and narrow to wide. There is a great deal of wildlife and in the Fall the water hyacinths are lovely.

Directions: Suffolk County, # 9
LIE to Rte. 25 East. Continue on Rte.25 E to Village Green and turn right onto Cases Lane. Follow signs to course ahead.

Hole	1	2	3	4	5	6	7	8	9	Out	BLUE	Rating
BLUE												Slope
WHITE	130	110	120	115	125	175	100	120	125	1120		
Par	3	3	3	3	3	3	3	3	3	27	WHITE	Rating
Handicap	2	8	5	7	3	1	9	6	4			Slope
RED												
Par											RED	Rating
Handicap												Slope

Hole	10	11	12	13	14	15	16	17	18	In		Totals
BLUE											BLUE	
WHITE											WHITE	
Par											Par	
Handicap												
RED											RED	
Par											Par	
Handicap												

Manager/Supt. John Dennison   **Pro:** Russell Case
Architect: Russell Case 1964

CHERRY CREEK GOLF LINKS

PUBLIC

900 Reeves Ave., Riverhead, NY 11901   (516) 369-6500

Cherry Creek is an 18 hole public course open 7 days a week, all year. Golfers may walk during the week and after 2PM weekends. Reservation Club may make tee time 5 days in advance; non-club walk-on or call same day.

•Driving Range	•Lockers
•Practice Green	•Showers
•Power Carts	•Food
•Pull Carts	•Clubhouse
•Club Rental	•Outings
Soft Spikes	

Fees	Weekday	Weekend
Daily	$24	$29
Daily(9)	$15	$19
Power carts	$26/18	$15/9-

Course Description: Privately owned and operated, Cherry Creek is situated on a former potato and sod farm. It is a links style course featuring elevated tees and greens, generous and long fairways and water coming into play on 4 holes. The 18th, a 644 yd. par 6, is a daunting double dogleg finishing hole. The signature #12, a 389 yd. par 4, overlooks a narrow sloping fairway with a pond on the right. The approach shot is to an elevated green guarded by bunkers on both sides. The driving range offers grass tees.

Directions: Suffolk County, #10
LIE East to Exit #73,(becomes Rte.58East). Follow for approx. 4 miles to traffic circle. Go 3/4 around circle & head north on Roanoke Ave. Continue 1 1/2 miles and turn right onto Reeves Ave. Course is 3/4 mile on left.

Hole	1	2	3	4	5	6	7	8	9	Out	BLUE	Rating 73.8
BLUE	446	145	465	623	439	192	352	515	393	3570		Slope 127
WHITE	402	130	411	585	386	163	313	495	371	3256		
Par	4	3	4	5	4	3	4	5	4	36	WHITE	Rating 71.1
Handicap	7	17	5	1	9	15	13	3	11			Slope 121
RED	346	91	356	519	335	130	280	435	316	2808		
Par	4	3	4	5	4	3	4	5	4	36	RED	Rating 72.1
Handicap	7	17	5	1	9	15	13	3	11			Slope 122

Hole	10	11	12	13	14	15	16	17	18	In		Totals
BLUE	419	396	422	224	558	397	387	170	644	3617	BLUE	7187
WHITE	405	370	389	184	521	357	349	154	612	3341	WHITE	6597
Par	4	4	4	3	5	4	4	3	6	37	Par	73
Handicap	6	10	8	16	4	12	14	18	2			
RED	362	344	326	141	468	312	313	110	572	2948	RED	5756
Par	4	4	4	3	5	4	4	3	6	37	Par	73
Handicap	6	10	8	16	4	12	14	18	2			

Manager/Pro: Steve T. Keating, PGA   **Supt:** Joe Ransey
Architects: Charles Jurgens,Sr. Vincent Sasso 1996

COLD SPRING COUNTRY CLUB

East Gate Drive, Cold Spring Harbor, NY 11724   **(516) 692-6550**

Cold Spring CC is open all year 6 days a week. Guests may play accompanied by a member. Tee times may be made for weekends a week in advance.

- •Driving Range
- •Practice Green
- •Power Carts
- Pull Carts
- •Club Rental
- •Caddies
- •Lockers
- •Showers
- •Food
- •Clubhouse
- •Outings
- •Soft Spikes

Course Description: Formerly an Otto Kahn estate, Cold Spring was his private golf course and is considered a historical landmark. His castle is still on the premises and may be the largest private home in the world. Deep bunkers, 30-40 yard wide fairways, and small bent grass greens are characteristic here. An upgrade is under way to make room for a variety of pin placements. The signature par 3 #13, the only hole with water, also has the largest tree on LI (the trunk is 12 feet in diameter).

Directions: Suffolk County, #11
LIE East to Exit #44North (Seaford-Oyster Bay X-way, Rte.135) Proceed 1/2 mile to Rte.25 (Jericho Tpke.) Go 3 miles east to club on left.

Hole	1	2	3	4	5	6	7	8	9	Out	BLUE	Rating 70.1
BLUE	577	348	154	335	418	386	386	325	539	3422		Slope 131
WHITE	563	338	133	310	388	352	378	315	527	3261		
Par	5	4	3	4	4	4	4	4	5	37	WHITE	Rating 70.0
Handicap	3	9	17	11	1	13	7	15	5			Slope129
RED	496	304	116	258	364	325	364	295	480	3002		
Par	5	4	3	4	4	4	4	4	5	37	RED	Rating 73.4
Handicap	1	9	17	15	3	11	7	13	5			Slope 126
Hole	10	11	12	13	14	15	16	17	18	In		Totals
BLUE	322	155	368	184	454	412	488	201	389	2973	BLUE	6395
WHITE	315	145	363	175	442	407	471	198	381	2897	WHITE	6158
Par	4	3	4	3	4	4	5	3	4	34	Par	71
Handicap	12	18	8	16	2	4	10	14	6			
RED	244	115	360	125	427	403	425	191	375	2665	RED	5667
Par	4	3	4	3	5	5	5	5	4	37	Par	73
Handicap	14	8	2	16	10	6	8	12	4			

Manager: Greg Smith   **Pro**: Tom Herzog, PGA   **Supt**: Peter Candelora
Architects: Seth Raynor, Robert Trent Jones 1947 **Estab**: 1923

COLONIAL SPRINGS GOLF COURSE PUBLIC

Long Island Avenue, E. Farmingdale NY 11735   (516) 643-1051

Colonial Springs is a 27 hole course that is open 7 days a week & closed between 10/31 & 4/1 (depending on the weather). Tee time reservations are required (1 wk advance wkdays) and a permanent starting time for weekends may be purchased for the year. Members get preference.

- **Driving Range**
- **Practice Green**
- **Power Carts**
- Pull Carts
- **Club Rental**
- **Soft Spikes**

- **Lockers**
- **Showers**
- **Food**
- **Clubhouse**
- **Outings**

Fees	Weekday	Weekend
Daily(w/card)	$56	$69
Daily (w/o card)	$62	$75
Prices differ on Fridays		
Power carts included		

Course Description: Colonial Springs has been compared to a Myrtle Beach type course featuring pine trees, undulating large greens and rolling hills. There was a great deal of excavating to make the deep valley and the high mounding around the grass driving range. A lake stretches across 11 acres affecting play on the finishing holes of each nine. The fairways are well-bunkered and contoured. The signature par 5 7th on Valley has a Shinnecock type look with fescue grass and heather in the rough. This course was cut out of the pinelands; the only structure in view is the clubhouse with its beautiful restaurant overlooking the water. The scorecard is for the Pines & Valley courses.

Directions: Suffolk County, #12

LIE to Exit 49South. Stay on service road to 3rd traffic light,(Pinelawn Rd.), go right for 2 & 1/2miles then left over RR tracks onto Long Is. Ave. Club is 1/2 mi. on right.

Hole	1	2	3	4	5	6	7	8	9	Out	BLUE	Rating 70.0
BLUE	382	377	154	522	410	363	500	145	390	3243		Slope 120
WHITE	351	358	138	510	395	347	480	127	367	3073		
Par	4	4	3	5	4	4	5	3	4	36	WHITE	Rating 68.2
Handicap	6	5	9	3	4	7	2	8	1			Slope 116
RED	288	307	112	495	373	287	467	110	313	2752		
Par	4	4	3	5	4	4	5	3	4	36	RED	Rating 70.5
Handicap	7	5	9	1	2	6	3	8	4			Slope 119

Hole	10	11	12	13	14	15	16	17	18	In		Totals
BLUE	335	305	405	186	527	401	495	157	379	3190	BLUE	6433
WHITE	310	280	387	167	503	372	471	135	357	2982	WHITE	6055
Par	4	4	4	3	5	4	5	3	4	36	Par	72
Handicap	6	7	5	8	1	3	2	9	4			
RED	292	259	372	115	475	315	455	113	337	2733	RED	5485
Par	4	4	4	3	5	4	5	3	4	36	Par	72
Handicap	7	6	3	8	1	5	2	9	4			

Manager: Pete Misilewich **Pro:** Tom Kelly, PGA **Supt:** Jeff Hemphill
Architect: Arthur Hill, 1995

CRAB MEADOW GOLF COURSE

 PUBLIC

220 Waterside Ave., Northport, NY 11768   (516) 757-8800

Crab Meadow is a Town of Huntington 18 hole course. It is open 7 days a week and closed in January with a restricted schedule until April. Tee times can be reserved by residents with permits. Lockers-men only.

•Driving Range	•Lockers
•Practice Green	•Showers
•Power Carts	•Food
•Pull Carts	•Clubhouse
•Club Rental	•Outings

Fees	Weekday	Weekend
Resident	$17	$17
Non-res	$30	$30
Twi	$11	$11
Power carts	$23.75	

Course Description: This windy, somewhat flat course has water in play on a few holes. The marshlands necessitate environmentally sensitive development of the property. With beautiful views of Long Island Sound, Crab Meadow is a shot making course. The small greens are in good condition and of average speed with some break. One of the most difficult holes is the signature 12th, a par 4.

Directions: Suffolk County, #13
LIE to Exit 53. Take the Sunken Meadow Pkwy.North and turn right onto Exit 25A West. Go 3 miles to Waterside Ave. & turn right. Go 2 miles to a left bend and then bear right. Follow signs to course.

Hole	1	2	3	4	5	6	7	8	9	Out	BLUE	Rating 70.9
BLUE	377	385	222	511	395	330	359	488	166	3233		Slope 118
WHITE	367	378	205	482	373	322	345	457	150	3079		
Par	4	4	3	5	4	4	4	5	3	36	WHITE	Rating 69.7
Handicap	6	8	12	16	4	18	10	2	14			Slope 116
RED	360	308	143	465	355	316	329	436	123	2835		
Par	4	4	3	5	4	4	4	5	3	36	RED	Rating 72.6
Handicap	8	16	18	6	4	12	10	2	14			Slope 120

Hole	10	11	12	13	14	15	16	17	18	In		Totals
BLUE	369	470	427	184	528	404	155	421	422	3380	BLUE	6613
WHITE	358	458	417	175	512	396	127	403	407	3253	WHITE	6332
Par	4	5	4	3	5	4	3	4	4	36	Par	72
Handicap	13	9	3	15	1	7	17	5	11			
RED	331	424	392	144	485	359	127	387	361	3010	RED	5845
Par	4	5	4	3	5	4	3	4	4	36	Par	72
Handicap	13	11	5	15	1	7	17	3	9			

Manager: Perry DiMattia   **Pro:** Sal Silvestrone, PGA   **Supt:** Art Gardner
Architect: William Mitchell 1965

DIX HILLS COUNTRY CLUB

PUBLIC

527 Half Hollow Rd, Dix Hills, NY 11746   **(516) 271-4788**

Dix Hills CC is a 9 hole course open to the public 7 days a week all year weather permitting. A weekend membership is available. Golfers may reserve in person or walk on for tee times.

Driving Range	Lockers
•**Practice Green**	Showers
Power Carts	•**Food**
•**Pull Carts**	Clubhouse
•**Club Rental**	•**Outings**

Fees	Weekday	Weekend
Daily	$13	$15
Sr	$10	

Course Description: Dix Hills is an excellent short regulation course for beginners and those eager to practice their game. It is mostly flat and wide open with no water in play. Two hills on the course provide some elevation but it is generally easy to walk. The 4th hole is short with a downhill target. The greens, which are average in size, have some break.

Directions: Suffolk County, #14
Take LIE to Exit 50. Stay on the service rd. to 2nd light and make left on Half Hollow Rd. Course is 1/2 mile ahead on the right.

Hole	1	2	3	4	5	6	7	8	9	Out	BLUE	Rating
BLUE												Slope
WHITE	475	256	303	90	168	312	261	239	470	2574		
Par	5	4	4	3	3	4	4	3	5	35	WHITE	Rating 60.9
Handicap	1	8	4	9	5	6	7	3	2			Slope 90
RED												
Par											RED	Rating 57.2
Handicap												Slope 83

Hole	10	11	12	13	14	15	16	17	18	In		Totals
BLUE											BLUE	
WHITE											WHITE	
Par											Par	
Handicap												
RED											RED	
Par											Par	
Handicap												

Manager: Mark Bonavita   **Pro:** Bill Lavin, PGA   **Supt:** Noe Cipriano
Built: 1948

DIX HILLS GOLF COURSE

Vanderbilt Parkway, Dix Hills, NY 11746   (516) 499-8005

Dix Hills is a 9 hole Town of Huntington course in Dix Hills Park. It is open 7 days a week and closed in winter. Tee time reservations are not necessary. The driving range is for irons only.

•**Driving Range**	Lockers
•**Practice Green**	Showers
•**Power Carts**	•**Food**
•**Pull Carts**	•**Clubhouse**
•**Club Rental**	•**Outings**

Fees	Weekday	Weekend
Res. w/ID	$8	$11
Sr w/ID	$4.25	
Non-res.	$13	$15.50

Course Description: This 9 hole well-maintained executive course looks easier than it plays. The straight hitting golfer will not find the layout difficult. The fairways are tree lined and two big hills give some variety. There is no water in play. The greens are of moderate size; some are fast and have contour. The course is very busy on weekends.

Directions: Suffolk County, #15
Take LIE to Exit 51. Take Deer Park Ave. North (Rte.231) to Vanderbilt and turn right. Course is ahead on the left.

Hole	1	2	3	4	5	6	7	8	9	Out	BLUE	Rating
BLUE												Slope
WHITE	166	130	275	140	121	265	312	283	248	1930		
Par	3	3	4	3	3	4	4	4	3	31	WHITE	Rating 28.5
Handicap	5	9	5	7	8	2	3	4	1			Slope
RED	166	130	242	140	121	240	312	283	248	1882		
Par	3	3	4	3	3	4	4	4	4	32	RED	Rating
Handicap												Slope
Hole	10	11	12	13	14	15	16	17	18	In		Totals
BLUE											BLUE	
WHITE											WHITE	
Par											Par	62
Handicap												
RED											RED	
Par											Par	64
Handicap												

Manager: Perry DiMattia   **Pro:** Bob Greenstein, PGA   **Supt:** Elliot Rogers
Built: 1965

FOX HILL GOLF & COUNTRY CLUB PUBLIC

100 Fox Hill Drive, Baiting Hollow, NY 11933   (516) 369-4455

Fox Hill Golf & CC has an 18 hole course that is open 7 days a week and closed for the month of Feb. Tee times may be made up to 2 wks. in advance with credit card (516-Fox Hill).

- •Driving Range •Lockers
- •Practice Green •Showers
- •Power Carts •Food
- Pull Carts •Clubhouse
- •Club Rental •Outings
- •Soft Spikes

Fees	Weekday	Weekend
Daily(M-Thur)	$67	$80

Price includes cart & Driving Range

Course Description: The picturesque Fox Hill Golf & Country Club utilizes the GPS system that monitors the course, giving a complete on-screen layout to help speed up the pace of play. Hilly terrain, elevated greens and tees, and open tight fairways are characteristic here. The rough is quite challenging utilizing fescue and other natural grasses. The par 4 16th signature hole, a dogleg left is ranked as one of the most difficult 100 holes in the state by Golf Digest. Water on 6 holes affect play. Qualifying rounds have been played here for the Met, Ike, & US Open.

Directions: Suffolk County, #16
LIE to Exit 71(Edwards Ave.), turn left. Go 4 miles North to Sound Ave. & turn right. Proceed to Oakleigh Ave., turn left (North). Club is 1/2 mi. on right.

Hole	1	2	3	4	5	6	7	8	9	Out	BLUE	Rating 73.7
BLUE	430	155	450	230	375	390	525	401	384	3340		Slope 131
WHITE	388	148	444	202	329	363	500	385	364	3123		
Par	4	3	4	3	4	4	5	4	4	35	WHITE	Rating 71.5
Handicap	6	18	2	14	16	10	8	12	4			Slope 127
RED	332	140	335	171	296	321	411	371	334	2711		
Par	4	3	4	3	4	4	5	4	4	35	RED	Rating 72.5
Handicap	8	18	10	16	12	14	2	6	4			Slope 125
Hole	10	11	12	13	14	15	16	17	18	In		Totals
BLUE	493	172	402	363	493	408	462	187	495	3475	BLUE	6815
WHITE	453	152	380	338	477	391	406	166	478	3241	WHITE	6364
Par	5	3	4	4	5	4	4	3	5	37	Par	72
Handicap	5	17	3	13	11	9	1	15	7			
RED	406	121	364	316	410	330	353	144	383	2827	RED	5538
Par	5	3	4	4	5	4	4	3	5	37	Par	72
Handicap	5	17	11	13	7	9	1	15	3			

Manager: Barry Beil **Pro:** John Hines, PGA   **Supt:** Andrew Rego
Architect: Robert Trent Jones Sr., 1968

GARDINER'S BAY COUNTRY CLUB

12 Dinah Rock Rd., Shelter Island Heights, NY 11965 **(516) 749-1033**

Gardiner's Bay is an 18 hole private course open all year 7 days a week. Guests play accompanied by a member. Tee time reservations are not necessary.

•**Driving Range**	•**Lockers**
•**Practice Green**	•**Showers**
•**Power Carts**	•**Food**
•**Pull Carts**	•**Clubhouse**
•**Club Rental**	•**Outings**
Caddies	•**Soft Spikes**

Course Description: Gardiner's Bay Country Club, situated on a beautiful piece of land, features rolling hills, large trees and scenic views of the water. The prevailing winds are always a factor here. The superb undulating greens are somewhat fast and larger than average. The signature hole is the eye-pleasing par 3 ninth. The 4th requires a tee shot over a pond to a green bounded by sand traps. The fairways are relatively narrow. Over the years, many changes have occurred both in ownership and in the design of the course. The METPGA Senior Championship is played here each year.

Directions: Suffolk County, #17
Take LIE to last Exit (Orient Pt.) Take Rte.25 East to Greenport & follow signs to & take the Shelter Island Ferry. Take Rte.114 to Winthrop Ave on left.

Hole	1	2	3	4	5	6	7	8	9	Out	BLUE	Rating
BLUE	356	521	312	206	398	556	164	393	169	3075		Slope
WHITE	349	511	305	149	388	544	158	371	161	2936		
Par	4	5	4	3	4	5	3	4	3	35	WHITE	Rating 68.1
Handicap	9	5	11	15	1	3	17	7	13			Slope 116
RED	341	412	296	139	314	461	153	327	132	2575		
Par	4	5	4	3	4	5	3	4	3	35	RED	Rating 71.2
Handicap	3	7	11	13	9	1	17	5	15			Slope 117
Hole	10	11	12	13	14	15	16	17	18	In		Totals
BLUE	391	184	385	370	458	490	422	203	381	3284	BLUE	6359
WHITE	386	175	377	363	429	481	414	192	371	3188	WHITE	6124
Par	4	3	4	4	4	5	4	3	4	35	Par	70
Handicap	6	18	10	14	2	12	4	16	8			
RED	344	167	309	299	419	411	372	174	307	2802	RED	5377
Par	4	3	4	4	5	5	4	3	4	36	Par	71
Handicap	4	18	10	14	6	8	2	16	12			

Manager: Kathy Regan   **Pro:** Bob DeStefano, PGA   **Supt:** Mark Lester
Architects: C. A. Fox, Seth Raynor, William Mitchell 1967 **Estab:** 1896

GULL HAVEN GOLF CLUB

Gull Haven Drive, Central Islip, NY 11722   **(516) 436-6059**

Gull Haven is a 9 hole course now owned by the Town of Islip. It is open 7 days a week all year, weather permitting. Tee time reservations are not necessary.

Driving Range	Lockers
•Practice Green	Showers
•Power Carts	•Food
•Pull Carts	Clubhouse
•Club Rental	•Outings

Fees	Weekday	Weekend
Res	$12	$14
Non-res	$15	$18
Sr/Jr	$8	
Power carts	$20/18	

Course Description: This 9 hole facility was recently bought by the Town of Islip and provides reduced rates for residents. It is a relatively flat executive length and style course. The property used to be State Hospital grounds. The psychiatric patients helped in the construction using mounds for tees and greens. It is characterized as "cow pasture design". Ideal for practice and easy to walk, it may be utilized by beginners, seniors and juniors.

Directions: Suffolk County, #18
Take LIE to Exit 56. Go north onto Rte.111. At fork, bear left onto Wheeler which becomes Carleton Ave. Go about 3 miles to Gull Haven Dr. and turn left to course.

Hole	1	2	3	4	5	6	7	8	9	Out	BLUE	Rating
BLUE												Slope
WHITE	290	465	330	140	155	350	355	340	280	2705		
Par	4	4	4	3	3	4	4	4	4	34	WHITE	Rating 66.5
Handicap	11	2	9	16	18	5	3	7	13			Slope 105
RED	290	465	330	140	155	350	280	340	280	2630		
Par	4	5	4	4	3	4	4	4	4	36	RED	Rating 69.8
Handicap	4	4	15	4	13	4	5	5	14			Slope 107
Hole	**10**	**11**	**12**	**13**	**14**	**15**	**16**	**17**	**18**	**In**		Totals
BLUE											BLUE	
WHITE	290	510	330	148	260	350	355	340	280	2863	WHITE	5568
Par	4	5	4	3	4	4	4	4	4	36	Par	70
Handicap	12	1	10	17	15	6	4	8	14			
RED	290	465	330	140	155	350	280	340	280	2630	RED	5260
Par	4	5	4	4	3	4	4	4	4	36	Par	72
Handicap	11	1	5	18	16	9	13	7	14			

Pro: Doug Jansen, PGA   **Supt:** Joe Graham
Built: Early 20th century

HAMLET GOLF & COUNTRY CLUB PRIVATE

Hauppauge Rd., Commack, NY 11725   **(516) 499-5200**

The Hamlet Golf & CC is a private 18 hole course. It is open all year, 6 days a week. Guests play accompanied by a member. Tee times may be made up to 1 week in advance. A residential community of 170 private homes is on the property.

```
• Driving Range    • Lockers
• Practice Green   • Showers
• Power Carts      • Food
  Pull Carts       • Clubhouse
• Club Rental      • Outings
  Caddies          • Soft Spikes
```

Course Description: The Hamlet was formerly the public Commack Hills course. It was closed and redesigned with a beautiful new clubhouse and now is the site of the ATP Hamlet Cup, a well known tennis event. The narrow course features fairways lined with bunkers. The greens are large and undulating. Water is in play on 6 holes. The signature par 3 8th is reminiscent of the 12th at Augusta. The tee shot is over a lake to a picturesque green with pretty flowers planted behind it. Mounding is present alongside some of the fairways; OB is present on many holes.

Directions: Suffolk County, #19
Take the LIE to Exit 52N (Commack Rd.) Proceed to light at Hauppauge Rd. Turn left and go 500 yards to club ahead on left.

Hole	1	2	3	4	5	6	7	8	9	Out	BLUE	Rating 71.1
BLUE	417	362	548	191	390	187	537	165	392	3189		Slope 132
WHITE	408	352	536	165	376	175	526	151	382	3071		
Par	4	4	5	3	4	3	5	3	4	35	WHITE	Rating 70.1
Handicap	5	11	1	17	9	13	3	15	7			Slope 130
RED	346	268	429	115	332	122	444	118	258	2432		
Par	4	4	5	3	4	3	5	3	4	37	RED	Rating 69.3
Handicap	5	11	3	17	7	15	1	13	9			Slope 123
Hole	10	11	12	13	14	15	16	17	18	In		Totals
BLUE	471	200	355	177	416	485	449	203	517	3273	BLUE	6462
WHITE	466	181	340	160	406	475	429	167	508	3132	WHITE	6203
Par	4	3	4	3	4	5	4	3	5	35	Par	70
Handicap	2	16	12	14	8	10	4	18	6			
RED	392	116	302	125	315	429	405	120	445	2649	RED	5081
Par	5	3	4	3	4	5	5	3	5	37	Par	74
Handicap	2	16	12	14	10	6	8	18	4			

Manager: Aage Nielsen   **Pro:** Jim Thompson, PGA   **Supt:** Mike Paquette
Architect: Stephen Kay   **Redesign:** 1994

HAMPTON HILLS GOLF & CC

County Rd. 51 (Box 1087), Riverhead, NY 11901   **(516) 727-6862**

Hampton Hills is a private 18 hole course that is open 7 days a week and closes for the month of Feb. Guests play accompanied by a member. Tee time reservations may be made 1 week in advance for wkends. Club has a Westhampton Beach mailing address.

Driving Range	•**Lockers**
•**Practice Green**	•**Showers**
•**Power Carts**	•**Food**
Pull Carts	•**Clubhouse**
Club Rental	•**Outings**
•**Caddies**	•**Soft Spikes**

Course Description: The variable Westhampton wind is always a factor at the Hampton Hills Golf & CC. The course is quite hilly and plays longer than one expects. It has an interesting layout; elevated greens and tees causing blind shots and uneven lies. The ball should not land above the hole in summer as the greens get very fast. Water affects play on 4 holes. The signature par 4 17th hole has a huge drop from the tee and requires laying up; the approach is a long shot over water.

Directions: Suffolk County, #20
LIE to Exit #70, turn right. Proceed to end of road, turn left onto Rte. 27 East. Go to Exit #63North. Club is on left.

Hole	1	2	3	4	5	6	7	8	9	Out	BLUE	Rating 72.9
BLUE	385	354	212	491	412	335	410	171	429	3199		Slope 134
WHITE	366	342	188	463	384	308	370	147	373	2941		
Par	4	4	3	5	4	4	4	3	4	35	WHITE	Rating 70.7
Handicap	9	13	17	5	7	11	3	15	1			Slope 130
RED	283	278	164	364	251	292	323	97	330	2382		
Par	4	4	3	5	4	4	4	3	4	35	RED	Rating 69.4
Handicap	9	13	17	5	7	11	3	15	1			Slope 118
Hole	10	11	12	13	14	15	16	17	18	In		Totals
BLUE	437	519	234	382	378	413	169	391	512	3435	BLUE	6634
WHITE	412	501	177	347	363	383	162	380	493	3218	WHITE	6159
Par	4	5	3	4	4	4	3	4	5	36	Par	71
Handicap	2	6	14	18	8	10	16	4	12			
RED	379	450	132	214	298	333	139	316	365	2626	RED	5008
Par	4	5	3	4	4	4	3	4	5	36	Par	71
Handicap	2	6	14	18	8	10	16	4	12			

Manager: Mike Askin   **Pro**: Jack McGown, PGA   **Supt**: Frank Franceschini
Architect: Frank Duane, 1964

HAUPPAUGE COUNTRY CLUB

Veterans Memorial Highway, Hauppauge, NY 11788   **(516) 724- 7500**

Hauppauge is an 18 hole semi-private course with memberships for Sat, Sun. and holidays and daily fee rates weekdays. It is open all year, weather permitting, 7 days a week. Credit card reservations with $10 fee available up to 1 week in advance.

•**Driving Range**	•**Lockers**
•**Practice Green**	•**Showers**
•**Power Carts**	•**Food**
•**Pull Carts***	•**Clubhouse**
•**Club Rental**	•**Outings**

Fees	Weekday	Weekend
Daily/car	$55	mbrs only
4/28-5/9	$45	
9/29-10/31	$45	
Off season power carts not req.		

Course Description: Originally built as a private facility, Hauppauge has an impressive clubhouse. It is well maintained and challenging with 5 holes that have water in play. Because daily fee players are not allowed on weekends, there is a private club atmosphere here. The signature 12th hole is a difficult par 4 with out of bounds on the right, trees on the left and a very small green.

Directions: Suffolk County, #21
Exit 57 from LIE. Go north on Rte454 (Veterans Highway) to club on right just past the intersection with Rte.111.

Hole	1	2	3	4	5	6	7	8	9	Out	BLUE	Rating 71.0
BLUE	507	310	134	364	487	192	372	412	366	3144		Slope 122
WHITE	493	300	124	351	474	179	350	400	355	3026		
Par	5	4	3	4	5	3	4	4	4	36	WHITE	Rating 69.9
Handicap	5	15	17	11	9	7	13	1	3			Slope 120
RED	479	290	114	338	460	165	312	388	344	2890		
Par	5	4	3	4	5	3	4	5	4	37	RED	Rating 75.5
Handicap	5	13	17	3	7	15	11	9	1			Slope 131

Hole	10	11	12	13	14	15	16	17	18	In		Totals
BLUE	184	551	417	495	195	370	394	388	387	3381	BLUE	6525
WHITE	173	539	407	473	184	360	370	375	373	3254	WHITE	6280
Par	3	5	4	5	3	4	4	4	4	36	Par	72
Handicap	18	14	2	6	10	16	8	12	4			
RED	162	527	300	452	173	350	350	362	359	3035	RED	5925
Par	3	5	4	5	3	4	4	4	5	37	Par	74
Handicap	18	2	14	8	16	10	4	6	12			

Manager: Bob Behringer   **Pro:** Kevin Beatty, PGA   **Supt:** Tom Cosenza
Built: 1960

HEATHERWOOD GOLF CLUB

303 Arrowhead Lane, Centereach, NY 11720   **(516) 473-9000**

Heatherwood is an 18 hole semi-private club open 7 days a week all year. Special Sr and reserved tee time memberships. Daily fee for public after 11AM Sat & 10AM Sun. For $4 per person, non-members call 3 days in advance for tee times.

Driving Range	•**Lockers**
•**Practice Green**	•**Showers**
•**Power Carts**	•**Food**
•**Pull Carts**	•**Clubhouse**
•**Club Rental**	•**Outings**
	Soft Spikes

Fees	Weekday	Weekend
Daily	$20	$22
After 3 PM	$15	$17
After 5	$10	$11
Power carts	$22	

Course Description: Heatherwood is a par 60 course with 12 par 3s and 6 par 4s. It is set on rolling terrain with large greens having little break. Water is in play on 2 holes. Not very wide open, the layout has some elevated tees and greens and tree-lined fairways. The signature ninth hole, a 148 yard picturesque par 3, has a shot from an elevated tee to a green with bunkers on each side. Although short, Heatherwood is not considered an executive course.

Directions: Suffolk County, # 22
LIE to Exit 62. Take Rte.97North (Nichols Rd.) to Rte.347 and turn right. Course is 2 miles ahead on the right. Route 347 is also called Nesconset Highway.

Hole	1	2	3	4	5	6	7	8	9	Out	BLUE	Rating
BLUE												Slope
WHITE	158	351	200	194	336	161	151	379	148	2078		
Par	3	4	3	3	4	3	3	4	3	30	WHITE	Rating 58.6
Handicap	15	9	1	3	7	11	17	5	13			Slope 95
RED	134	314	161	137	318	126	125	332	100	1747		
Par	3	4	3	3	4	3	3	4	3	30	RED	Rating 58.5
Handicap	13	9	7	3	5	11	15	1	17			Slope 91
Hole	10	11	12	13	14	15	16	17	18	In		Totals
BLUE											BLUE	
WHITE	190	171	119	278	388	135	370	193	167	2011	WHITE	4089
Par	3	3	3	4	4	3	4	3	3	30	Par	60
Handicap	8	14	16	6	2	18	4	14	8			
RED	110	144	103	258	334	112	333	119	135	1648	RED	3395
Par	3	3	3	4	4	3	4	3	3	30	Par	60
Handicap	12	10	16	6	2	18	4	14	8			

Manager/Pro: Bob Freund   **Supt:** John Wolkiewicz
Architect: Charles Jurgens   **Estab:** 1960s

HOLBROOK COUNTRY CLUB

PUBLIC

700 Patchogue-Holbrook Rd. Holbrook, NY 11741   **(516) 467-3417**

Holbrook is a Town of Islip 18 hole course open 7 days a week and closed Dec.15-Mar. 15.   Residents call Monday for weekend tee times, non-res, call Wednesday.

•**Driving Range**	•**Lockers**
•**Practice Green**	•**Showers**
•**Power Carts**	•**Food**
•**Pull Carts**	•**Clubhouse**
Club Rental	•**Outings**

Fees	Weekday	Weekend
Resident	$18	$20
Non-res	$23	$28
Twi	$15	
Power carts	$25	$25

Course Description: Holbrook features narrow, tree lined fairways and large well-bunkered greens, (some elevated.) The latter are medium fast with break. On four holes, the golfer has to deal with water in play. Wind is also a factor. The signature par 3 17th has a sinister 2 tiered green. Tree trouble abounds around the target area which has a severe back to front slope. The course mascot is a dog named Bogey who chases the geese. This busy facility is the most difficult of the Town of Islip courses.

Directions: Suffolk County, #23
Take the LIE to Exit 61. Go south 1 & 1/2 miles. Course is on the right on the Patchogue-Holbrook Rd.

Hole	1	2	3	4	5	6	7	8	9	Out	BLUE	Rating 69.8
BLUE	365	337	143	531	436	322	536	207	380	3257		Slope 128
WHITE	350	321	133	516	420	309	490	192	370	3101		
Par	4	4	3	5	4	4	5	3	4	36	WHITE	Rating 68.5
Handicap	7	13	17	3	1	15	5	11	9			Slope 126
RED	281	246	116	406	323	236	435	148	290	2481		
Par	4	4	3	5	4	4	5	3	4	36	RED	Rating 66.9
Handicap	7	13	17	3	1	15	5	11	9			Slope 119

Hole	10	11	12	13	14	15	16	17	18	In		Totals
BLUE	428	138	393	326	325	397	309	179	500	2995	BLUE	6252
WHITE	423	127	383	311	311	368	300	166	488	2877	WHITE	5978
Par	4	3	4	4	4	4	4	3	5	35	Par	71
Handicap	2	18	4	14	12	8	16	10	6			
RED	335	114	313	235	230	292	242	128	366	2255	RED	4736
Par	4	3	4	4	4	4	4	3	5	35	Par	71
Handicap	2	18	4	14	12	8	16	10	6			

Manager/Pro: Bill Leposa, PGA **Supt:** Greg Meservey
Architect: Ward Associates 1992

HOLLOW HILLS COUNTRY CLUB

PUBLIC

49 Ryder Ave., Dix Hills, NY 11746

(516) 242-0010

Hollow Hills is a 9 hole course, privately owned and open to the public all year 7 days a week. Memberships run from 11/1-10/31. Tee times; Wed after 12 for Sat; Thurs. for Sunday for $3 per pers. On weekend, $2 for weekday reservations.

Driving Range	Lockers
•Practice Green	Showers
•Power Carts	•Food
•Pull Carts	Clubhouse
•Club Rental	•Outings

Fees	Weekday	Weekend
Daily	$12	$15
Senior	$9	
Power carts	$9 pp	

Course Description: Hollow Hills is an executive length course. It is fairly hilly and features one of the largest pot bunkers in the US on the 8th hole. The greens are difficult and fast with a great deal of slope; the golfer needs accurate putting skills. Every hole is tree-lined and no water is in play. The very scenic 4th is the signature, from which one can see the Robert Moses Causeway to the south.

Directions: Suffolk County, #24
Take the LIE to Exit 51S. Take Deer Park Ave (Rte231) one mile south and turn right onto Ryder Ave. Club is 7/8 mile ahead on left.

Hole	1	2	3	4	5	6	7	8	9	Out	BLUE	Rating
BLUE												Slope
WHITE	350	420	115	305	96	225	265	305	240	2341		
Par	4	5	3	4	3	4	4	4	4	35	WHITE	Rating
Handicap	2	1	8	7	9	5	4	3	6			Slope
RED	325	400	110	285	90	210	265	275	220	2180		
Par	4	5	3	4	3	4	4	4	4	35	RED	Rating
Handicap	2	1	5	7	9	8	4	3	6			Slope
Hole	10	11	12	13	14	15	16	17	18	In		Totals
BLUE											BLUE	
WHITE											WHITE	
Par											Par	70
Handicap												
RED											RED	
Par											Par	70
Handicap												

Manager: Allison Denlea   **Supt:** Jeff Denlea
Built: 1972

HUNTINGTON COUNTRY CLUB

Route 25A West, Huntington, NY 11743   **(516) 427-0876**

Huntington is a private 18 hole course open 6 days a week all year weather permitting. Guests play accompanied by a member. Reservations for tee times are necessary on weekends.

- •Driving Range
- •Practice Green
- •Power Carts
- Pull Carts
- •Club Rental
- •Caddies
- •Lockers
- •Showers
- •Food
- •Clubhouse
- •Outings
- •Soft Spikes

Course Description: During the winter months at Huntington CC, the members may enjoy ice skating and hockey on the rink adjacent to the first hole. The course features very small greens, a few 2 tiered, and a links style atmosphere. There is no water in play. Challenging, the layout has a fairly hilly back nine, an abundance of bunkers and high fescue grass in the roughs. The par 3 #12 is the signature hole with a tee shot over a gully to a small green flanked by traps and guarded by a grass bunker in front. Par is not likely if the target is missed. Commemorative trees are planted here to honor deceased members. Opened to the public during the Depression, the fee was $1.00.

Directions: Suffolk County, #25
LIE to Exit 49 and take Rte.110 North. At Rte.25A, turn left. Go west 1 mile to club on right. Road also called W. Main St.

Hole	1	2	3	4	5	6	7	8	9	Out	BLUE	Rating 71.2
BLUE	383	370	184	333	376	420	531	332	212	3141		Slope 133
WHITE	373	355	178	323	367	414	523	330	207	3070		
Par	4	4	3	4	4	4	5	4	3	35	WHITE	Rating 70.5
Handicap	9	7	17	11	5	3	1	13	15			Slope 132
RED	357	313	124	282	321	410	490	319	187	2803		
Par	4	4	3	4	4	5	5	4	3	36	RED	Rating 73.1
Handicap	4	4	15	4	13	4	5	5	14			Slope 126
Hole	10	11	12	13	14	15	16	17	18	In		Totals
BLUE	440	330	140	416	186	474	402	420	408	3216	BLUE	6357
WHITE	428	320	134	407	176	471	395	414	395	3140	WHITE	6210
Par	4	4	3	4	3	5	4	4	4	35	Par	70
Handicap	4	14	18	8	16	6	10	2	12			
RED	420	302	112	401	165	405	332	382	362	2881	RED	5684
Par	5	4	3	5	3	5	4	4	4	37	Par	73
Handicap	6	14	18	8	16	2	10	4	12			

Pro: Jim Smoot, PGA   **Supt:** Glen Creutz
Architect: Devereux Emmet 1910

HUNTINGTON CRESCENT CLUB

Washington Drive & Rte. 25A, Huntington, NY 11743   **(516) 421-5180**

Huntington Crescent is an 18 hole course open all year, 6 days a week. Guests may play accompanied by a member. Tee time reservations are required on weekends in season.

•Driving Range	•Lockers
•Practice Green	•Showers
•Power Carts	•Food
Pull Carts	•Clubhouse
•Club Rental	•Outings
•Caddies	Soft Spikes

Course Description: The parkland setting of Huntington Crescent is unique with its contoured rolling hills, many trees, and small undulating greens. The course was formerly 36 holes but part was sold off in the 1940s. The signature par 5 9th is all uphill with an "S" shaped double dogleg. It measures 571 yards from the blue and is rarely reached in two. There is no water on the course. A great deal of effort has been expended in trying to keep the Devereux Emmet design intact. An estate mansion remains and serves as the clubhouse.

Directions: Suffolk County, #26
LIE to Exit 49N. Proceed north on Rte. 110, for 6.7 miles, then turn right onto 25A (Main St). Go 2 miles to Stop light at Wash. Dr., bear left. Club is 200 yds. on left.

Hole	1	2	3	4	5	6	7	8	9	Out	BLUE	Rating 71.2
BLUE	332	390	147	348	391	163	570	389	571	3301		Slope 131
WHITE	308	370	138	339	386	145	535	379	558	3158		
Par	4	4	3	4	4	3	5	4	5	36	WHITE	Rating 70.0
Handicap	13	11	15	9	3	17	7	5	1			Slope 129
RED	290	330	122	312	305	130	450	332	442	2713		
Par	4	4	3	4	4	3	5	4	5	36	RED	Rating 72.2
Handicap	13	11	17	7	3	15	9	5	1			Slope 126
Hole	10	11	12	13	14	15	16	17	18	In		Totals
BLUE	420	421	405	170	358	431	315	207	375	3102	BLUE	6403
WHITE	410	411	380	150	344	421	305	188	370	2979	WHITE	6137
Par	4	4	4	3	4	4	4	3	4	34	Par	70
Handicap	10	2	8	18	6	4	14	16	12			
RED	360	365	317	113	338	404	294	179	307	2677	RED	5390
Par	4	4	4	3	4	5	4	3	4	35	Par	71
Handicap	12	2	8	18	4	10	6	16	14			

Manager: John Tangorra   **Pro:** John Schob, PGA   **Supt:** Harry Bahrenburg
Architect: Devereux Emmet, 1931

INDIAN HILLS COUNTRY CLUB

21 Breeze Hill Road, Northport, NY 11768   **(516) 757-7718**

Indian Hills is an 18 hole course open 6 days a week and closed from Dec. to March. Guests may play accompanied by a member.   Tee time reservations may be made up to 1 week in advance.

> - **Driving Range**   • **Lockers**
> - **Practice Green**   • **Showers**
> - **Power Carts**   • **Food**
>   Pull Carts   • **Clubhouse**
> - **Club Rental**   • **Outings**
>   Caddies   • **Soft Spikes**

Course Description: Indian Hills is quite hilly as its name implies. It features narrow fairways, uneven lies sloping greens and high rough. The views of Long Island Sound from the par 3 #12 signature hole are wonderful although an errant shot can wind up on the beach.   From the blues one must hit 170 yards over a canyon; a daunting shot. Ponds affect play on seven holes.   Greens are average in size, undulating, fast and sloping toward the water.

Directions: Suffolk County, #27
LIE to Exit #53S; Sagtikos Pkwy. North. Continue to entrance of Sunken Meadow State Park, turn right onto 25A West. Go 2.3 mi. to Fresh Pond Rd. & go right for 2 blocks to Breeze Hill Rd. & turn left. Proceed to club on left at top of hill.

Hole	1	2	3	4	5	6	7	8	9	Out	BLUE	Rating 73.1
BLUE	430	393	195	343	510	163	510	323	380	3247		Slope 135
WHITE	400	378	174	323	487	147	488	302	359	3058		
Par	4	4	3	4	5	3	5	4	4	36	.WHITE	Rating 71.5
Handicap	7	1	13	9	3	17	11	15	5			Slope 132
RED	346	307	116	303	393	135	485	214	322	2621		
Par	4	4	3	4	5	3	5	4	4	36	RED	Rating 71.7
Handicap	11	5	15	7	1	13	3	17	9			Slope 126
Hole	10	11	12	13	14	15	16	17	18	In		Totals
BLUE	549	240	347	320	495	352	185	444	437	3369	BLUE	6616
WHITE	537	207	293	291	480	338	170	421	423	3160	WHITE	6218
Par	5	3	4	4	5	4	3	4	4	37	Par	72
Handicap	4	16	12	18	10	8	14	2	6			
RED	434	141	130	272	460	319	159	401	393	5330	RED	5330
Par	5	3	3	4	5	4	3	4	5	36	Par	72
Handicap	10	16	18	4	2	6	14	12	8			

Manager: Lenny Witowski   **Pro:** Keith Miller, PGA   **Supt:** John Paquette
Architects: Steve Christoff, Charles & Fred Jurgens **Estab:** 1965

INDIAN ISLAND GOLF CLUB

Riverside Drive, Riverhead, NY 11901   (516) 727-7776

Indian Island is an 18 hole Suffolk County course open 7 days a week, and closed between Jan.1 & March 15. For reservations call 244-7275 up to 7 days in advance for residents. Non-res. are on a first come basis.

• Driving Range	• Lockers
• Practice Green	• Showers
• Power Carts	• Food
• Pull Carts	• Clubhouse
• Club Rental	• Outings
• Soft Spikes	

Fees	Weekday	Weekend
Daily(Res)	$19	$20
Non Res	$28	$32
Power carts	$25	

Course Description: Indian Island has tight fairways where an errant shot can cause trouble; the key is to hit straight. Water affects play on holes 5 through 10 adding to the challenge. Wind is always a factor here. The greens are large and fast with considerable break and ever changing pin placement. The par 4 fifth is thought to be the prettiest hole, having a view of the Peconic River, Flanders Bay and boats and seagulls in the distance.

Directions: Suffolk County, #28
LIE to Exit #71. Proceed South on Rte.24 approx. 7 miles to Rte.105 & turn left. Go over bridge to course on right.

Hole	1	2	3	4	5	6	7	8	9	Out	BLUE	Rating 71.0
BLUE	385	354	212	491	412	335	410	171	429	3199		Slope 124
WHITE	366	342	188	463	384	308	370	147	373	2941		
Par	4	4	3	5	4	4	4	3	4	35	WHITE	Rating 69.3
Handicap	9	13	17	5	7	11	3	15	1			Slope 121
RED	283	278	164	364	251	292	323	97	330	2382		
Par	4	4	3	5	4	4	4	3	4	35	RED	Rating 72.8
Handicap	9	13	17	5	7	11	3	15	1			Slope 126

Hole	10	11	12	13	14	15	16	17	18	In		Totals
BLUE	437	519	234	382	378	413	169	391	512	3435	BLUE	6634
WHITE	412	501	177	347	363	383	162	380	493	3218	WHITE	6159
Par	4	5	3	4	4	4	3	4	5	36	Par	71
Handicap	2	6	14	18	8	10	16	4	12			
RED	379	450	132	214	298	333	139	316	365	2626	RED	5008
Par	4	5	3	4	4	4	3	4	5	36	Par	71
Handicap	2	6	14	18	8	10	16	4	12			

Manager/Pro: Bob Fox, PGA   **Supt:** Charles Ryder
Architect: William Mitchell 1973

ISLAND'S END GOLF & CC

Route 25, Greenport, NY 11944   **(516) 477-0777**

Island's End is an 18 hole course that is privately owned and open to the public 7 days a week, all year. Memberships are available. Non-members may call 12 noon on the prior day for tee times.

•**Driving Range**	•**Lockers**
•**Practice Green**	•**Showers**
•**Power Carts**	•**Food**
•**Pull Carts**	•**Clubhouse**
•**Club Rental**	•**Outings**
Soft Spikes	

Fees	Weekday	Weekend
Daily(Spring)	$21	$25
Summer	$26	$30
Power carts	$15PP	

Course Description: Island's End is located on the North Fork of Long Island right on the Sound. Generally flat and open, it is in excellent condition with average-sized plush contoured greens. Wind is a factor; a constant threat of a change of direction affects play. The signature 210 yard par 3 #16, has breathtaking views of the Sound and the shoreline and requires a shot over water. It is sometimes referred to as the "Pebble Beach Hole". The irrigation system has been recently upgraded.

Directions: Suffolk County, #29
LIE to the last exit. Proceed East on County Rd. 58 approx. 3 miles until it joins Rte.25. Go East approx. 19 miles to club on left.

Hole	1	2	3	4	5	6	7	8	9	Out	BLUE	Rating 71.6
BLUE	369	360	163	484	200	407	212	555	375	3125		Slope 118
WHITE	351	335	147	473	180	370	186	540	358	2940		
Par	4	4	3	5	3	4	3	5	4	35	WHITE	Rating 70.6
Handicap	12	8	18	6	14	4	16	2	10			Slope 115
RED	336	225	137	408	121	270	135	445	283	2360		
Par	4	4	3	5	3	4	3	5	4	35	RED	Rating 68.8
Handicap	6	12	8	4	16	14	18	2	10			Slope 116
Hole	10	11	12	13	14	15	16	17	18	In		Totals
BLUE	391	197	515	409	497	304	210	526	465	3514	BLUE	6639
WHITE	382	173	503	389	479	284	170	517	437	3334	WHITE	6274
Par	4	3	5	4	5	4	3	5	4	35	Par	72
Handicap	11	17	5	1	9	15	13	7	3			
RED	300	160	430	308	385	227	116	402	351	2679	RED	5039
Par	4	3	5	4	5	4	3	5	4	35	Par	72
Handicap	11	9	1	13	3	15	17	7	5			

Manager: Board of Trustees   **Pro:** Chris Vedder, PGA   **Supt:** Wayne Mazzaferro
Architects: G. Heron & C. Martin 1961

ISLAND HILLS GOLF CLUB

 PRIVATE

Lakeland Ave., Sayville, NY 11782   **(516) 589-2802**

Island Hills is an 18 hole private course open 6 days a week all year weather permitting. Guests play accompanied by a member. Available weekend times are purchased ahead for the entire season from 5:30-6:45AM.

•**Driving Range**	•**Lockers**
•**Practice Green**	•**Showers**
•**Power Carts**	•**Food**
Pull Carts	•**Clubhouse**
Club Rental	•**Outings**
•**Caddies**	Soft Spikes

Course Description: Island Hills is a narrow tree-lined course with some rolling hills along the fairways. There is not much water in play; 2 holes have ponds. The par 4 432 yard eighth is considered the signature hole. It is a difficult dogleg left uphill to a target that is hard to see for the approach shot. The weather affects the softness of the green and the amount of break to be taken into consideration.

Directions: Suffolk County, #30
Take LIE to Exit 59(Ocean Ave). At split, take Lakeland. After crossing Sunrise Highway, course is just ahead on right.

Hole	1	2	3	4	5	6	7	8	9	Out	BLUE	Rating 71.2
BLUE	425	173	509	544	139	298	354	432	392	3266		Slope 122
WHITE	418	162	500	523	131	286	347	420	382	3169		
Par	4	3	5	5	3	4	4	4	4	36	WHITE	Rating 70.4
Handicap	3	11	5	7	15	17	13	1	9			Slope 120
RED	384	137	420	475	100	222	337	366	310	2751		
Par	4	3	5	5	3	4	4	4	4	36	RED	Rating 71.3
Handicap	7	15	3	1	17	13	9	5	11			Slope 116
Hole	10	11	12	13	14	15	16	17	18	In		Totals
BLUE	352	220	392	475	332	205	445	392	392	3205	BLUE	6471
WHITE	346	210	384	468	318	181	438	387	382	3114	WHITE	6283
Par	4	3	4	5	4	3	4	4	4	35	Par	71
Handicap	16	10	4	14	18	12	2	8	6			
RED	338	135	325	427	290	146	406	366	316	2749	RED	5500
Par	4	3	4	5	4	3	5	4	4	36	Par	72
Handicap	10	18	6	2	14	16	4	8	12			

Pro: Harvey Lannak, PGA   **Supt:** Kevin McManus
Architect: A.W. Tillinghast 1927

MAIDSTONE GOLF CLUB

Old Beach Lane, Easthampton, NY 11937   **(516) 324-5530**

Maidstone is a private 27 hole facility open 7 days a week all year, weather permitting. Guests play accompanied by a member. Tee time reservations are not necessary. The East course is a 9 hole layout, the West 18 holes.

> •**Driving Range** •**Lockers**
> •**Practice Green** •**Showers**
> •**Power Carts** •**Food**
> •**Pull Carts** •**Clubhouse**
> •**Club Rental** •**Outings**
> •**Caddies** Soft Spikes

Course Description: Maidstone is an English links style course running parallel to the Atlantic Ocean with resulting impressive views and blustery wind. The topography is rough and rugged; the nearly treeless terrain follows the natural contours of the land and the dunes are part of the course. The 8th, 9th and 14th run along the coast line; the 8th actually slices into the ocean. The beach is a major sand trap on the right along some fairways. The inland holes have ponds and lakes in play. The greens are rather small with breaks. The scorecard below is for the West course.

Directions: Suffolk County, #31
LIE to Exit 70 and turn right. Go south to the end and turn left onto Rte.27. In Easthampton. bear left remaining on Rte.27, then turn right onto Dunemere Lane. At end, Old Beach Rd. and the club are on the right.

Hole	1	2	3	4	5	6	7	8	9	Out	BLUE	Rating 72.3
BLUE	380	537	408	171	325	403	335	151	402	3112		Slope 132
WHITE	359	512	365	157	294	393	312	133	370	2895		
Par	4	5	4	3	4	4	4	3	4	35	WHITE	Rating 70.8
Handicap	9	1	5	15	13	7	11	17	3			Slope 129
RED	348	497	319	145	285	334	268	120	331	2647		
Par	4	5	4	3	4	4	4	3	4	35	RED	Rating 72.1
Handicap	9	1	7	15	13	5	11	17	3			Slope 128
Hole	10	11	12	13	14	15	16	17	18	In		Totals
BLUE	382	409	179	490	148	493	471	328	378	3278	BLUE	6390
WHITE	362	397	165	452	129	481	466	292	367	3111	WHITE	6006
Par	4	4	3	5	3	5	5	4	4	37	Par	72
Handicap	2	8	16	6	18	4	10	14	12			
RED	311	349	132	441	119	429	463	252	318	2814	RED	5461
Par	4	4	3	5	3	5	5	4	4	37	Par	72
Handicap	2	10	18	8	16	6	4	14	12			

Manager: Bob Gallagher   **Pro:** Eden Foster, PGA   **Supt:** Hook Williams
Architects: Willie Park, Jr., Willie Tucker, Adrian Larkin 1925 **Estab:** 1891

MIDDLE ISLAND COUNTRY CLUB PUBLIC

Middle Island-Yaphank Rd., Middle Island, NY 11953   (516) 924-3000

Middle Island is a public 27 hole course open 7 days a week all year. Golfers may pay for an annual reserved tee time for Sat and Sundays in season. For other tee times there is a computerized system for up to 7 days in advance.

•Driving Range	•Lockers
•Practice Green	•Showers
•Power Carts	•Food
•Pull Carts	•Clubhouse
•Club Rental	•Outings
	Soft Spikes

Fees	Weekday	Weekend
Daily	$25	$28
9 hole	$14	$16
Power carts	$28	

Course Description: Mid Island has 3 distinct nines. The Spruce is the longest and most open with large greens. Dogwood is shorter and features doglegs, elevated tees and greens. Oak is well treed, tight and medium length. Its signature 9th hole is a very narrow long par 5 with OB on both sides and a small well bunkered green. The course has no water in play. The greens have variety due to their contours and size. The scorecard below is for Oak and Spruce.

Directions: Suffolk County, #32
Take the LIE to Exit 66. At end of Exit ramp turn left onto Sills Rd. North. Go about 1 mile to Coram Rd. & bear right. Then turn left onto Yaphank-Mid Island Rd. Club is ahead on right.

Hole	1	2	3	4	5	6	7	8	9	Out	BLUE	Rating 73.4
BLUE	511	484	389	209	370	397	323	227	563	3473		Slope 128
WHITE	487	470	366	198	361	382	300	207	537	3308		
Par	5	5	3	4	3	4	5	5	4	38	WHITE	Rating 71.7
Handicap	3	2	6	8	7	5	9	4	1			Slope 125
RED	415	345	340	188	345	368	276	174	452	2903		
Par	5	4	4	3	4	4	4	3	5	36	RED	Rating 73.4
Handicap	3	2	6	8	7	5	9	4	1			Slope 128
Hole	10	11	12	13	14	15	16	17	18	In		Totals
BLUE	463	369	550	206	409	552	412	178	415	3554	BLUE	7027
WHITE	449	345	529	189	389	530	393	157	392	3373	WHITE	6681
Par	4	4	5	3	4	5	4	3	4	36	Par	74
Handicap	3	7	1	8	4	2	5	9	6			
RED	429	327	453	159	368	430	333	138	366	3003	RED	5906
Par	5	4	5	3	4	5	4	3	4	37	Par	73
Handicap	3	7	1	8	4	2	5	9	6			

Manager: Ryan Mulligan   **Pro:** Vince Gallo, PGA **Supt:** Perry Gallup
Architect: Baier Lustgarten 1965

MONTAUK DOWNS STATE PARK

South Fairview Ave., Montauk, NY 11954   **(516) 668-1100**

Montauk is a NY State 18 hole course open to the public all year 7 days a week. Card holders & NY State residents may call 668-1234 for tee times up to 7 days in advance, others 2 days. Fee for reservation is $3.00.

•Driving Range	•Lockers
•Practice Green	•Showers
•Power Carts	•Food
•Pull Carts	•Clubhouse
•Club Rental	•Outings

Fees	Weekday	Weekend
Daily	$25	$30
Twi	$13	$16
Power carts	$25	$25

Course Description: Montauk Downs was originally a private club. It was taken over by the the State in 1978. This very busy course is beautifully groomed with medium size greens that are absolutely true. The deep rough is punishing; wayward shots can get caught in bramble and trees along the edges. Water affects play on 5 holes: the prevailing winds are also a factor. In many cases, there is considerable carry to the fairway on the tee shot. The signature par 3 #12 requires a long carry from on high to an elevated green. This public course is truly impressive and an excellent golfing experience.

Directions: Suffolk County, #33

LIE to Exit 70 & turn left onto Rte.27East. Take the Montauk Highway through the South Fork through town of Montauk. Look for sign for State Park. Turn left on Westlake Dr. Go 0.3 mi to Fairview, turn left to club.

Hole	1	2	3	4	5	6	7	8	9	Out	BLUE	Rating 73.3
BLUE	394	152	421	423	530	347	508	167	452	3394		Slope 135
WHITE	372	115	374	396	488	326	490	154	435	3150		
Par	4	3	4	4	5	4	5	3	4	36	WHITE	Rating 71.2
Handicap	11	17	9	7	3	13	5	15	1			Slope 130
RED	352	101	335	370	467	301	454	117	398	2895		
Par	4	3	4	4	5	4	5	3	4	36	RED	Rating 74.2
Handicap	11	17	9	7	3	13	5	15	1			Slope 132

Hole	10	11	12	13	14	15	16	17	18	In		Totals
BLUE	499	319	213	494	199	436	377	390	441	3368	BLUE	6762
WHITE	464	289	179	474	185	407	362	362	417	3139	WHITE	6289
Par	5	4	3	5	3	4	4	4	4	36	Par	72
Handicap	2	16	14	4	18	8	12	10	6			
RED	453	274	120	441	159	386	334	351	384	2902	RED	5797
Par	5	4	3	5	3	4	4	4	4	36	Par	72
Handicap	2	16	14	4	18	8	12	10	6			

Manager: Tom Dess   **Pro:** Kevin Smith, PGA   **Supt:** Bob Cosgrove
Architect: Robert Trent Jones 1968 **Estab:** 1927

NATIONAL GOLF LINKS OF AMERICA `PRIVATE`

North Sebonic Inlet Rd., Southampton, NY 11969   (516) 283-0559

National is a private 18 hole course open 7 days a week and closed Nov.1-April 20. Guests play accompanied by a member. Tee time reservations are not necessary.

•Driving Range	•Lockers
•Practice Green	•Showers
•Power Carts	•Food
Pull Carts	•Clubhouse
•Club Rental	•Outings
•Caddies	•Soft Spikes

Course Description: This magnificent links course is adjacent to Shinnecock. It has larger greens, that are contoured and fast. The wind is a major factor here on this rather wide open layout. The windmill that is in view was formerly a water tower to gravity feed the clubhouse. It no longer functions and now is just a landmark. The vista from the signature 17th hole is of Peconic Bay. National has 365 bunkers. The carry for the tee shot on most holes is substantial, making it very difficult for women. A notable feature is that there is no OB, so the golfer plays it as it lies. Bobby Jones played here on the 1st Walker Cup Team in 1922.

Directions: Suffolk County, #34
In Southampton, go east on Rte.27. When it becomes 2 lanes, the 1st left is Sebonic Rd. Turn there and go about 1 and 1/2 m. Sign on left says Sebonic Inlet. Follow road to club on left.

Hole	1	2	3	4	5	6	7	8	9	Out	BLUE	Rating 74.3
BLUE	322	330	426	197	478	141	478	424	540	3336		Slope 141
WHITE	302	270	411	177	466	131	462	404	532	3155		
Par	4	4	4	3	5	3	5	4	5	37	WHITE	Rating 72.7
Handicap	11	15	1	13	9	17	7	3	5			Slope 137
RED	284	240	378	159	451	110	406	286	514	2828		
Par	4	4	4	3	5	3	5	4	5	37	RED	Rating 74.3
Handicap	11	15	1	13	9	17	7	3	5			Slope 133
Hole	10	11	12	13	14	15	16	17	18	In		Totals
BLUE	450	432	435	174	365	397	404	375	502	3534	BLUE	6870
WHITE	429	408	388	161	336	367	381	350	478	3298	WHITE	6453
Par	4	4	4	3	4	4	4	4	5	36	Par	73
Handicap	2	8	4	18	14	12	10	16	6			
RED	391	370	352	147	286	311	360	319	448	2984	RED	5812
Par	4	4	4	3	4	4	4	4	5	36	Par	72
Handicap	2	8	4	18	14	12	10	16	6			

Manager: Randall Herring   **Pro:** Mike Muller   **Supt:** Karl Olsen
Architect: Charles Blair Macdonald 1908

NISSEQUOGUE GOLF CLUB

Moriches Road, St. James, NY 11780   (516) 584-2453

Nissequogue is an 18 hole course that is open 7 days a week, and closed between mid December and March, weather permitting. Guests may play when accompanied by a member. Tee times are necessary on weekends.

•Driving Range	•Lockers
•Practice Green	•Showers
•Power Carts	•Food
Pull Carts	•Clubhouse
•Club Rental	•Outings
Caddies	•Soft Spikes

Course Description: Nissequogue overlooks scenic St. James Bay. With its hilly terrain, well defined slopes, severe drops & elevated tees resulting in many uneven lies, the layout presents a challenge to golfers of all levels. The prevailing wind is a major factor here. Greens are very fast with subtle breaks; several of them are multi-tiered. To reach the island green on the par 3 2nd, (a memorable hole) there is a bridge to cross; it is said by some that it is the most beautiful and frightening hole in the USA. The changes in the tide on this hole presents a danger either in landing in the water or the muddy bottom of the bay.

Directions: Suffolk County, #35

LIE to Exit #53 Sagtikos Pkwy. North (Sunken Meadow Pkwy.) to Rte. 25East (Jericho Tpk). Proceed 4.4 miles, turn left (light at top of hill) onto Edgewood Ave. Go 1 mi. and turn left on Nissequogue River Rd. then right onto Old Mill Rd. for 1.3 mi. to stop sign. Go left to Moriches Rd. to Club on right just before shield of Village Hall, Town Police.

Hole	1	2	3	4	5	6	7	8	9	Out	BLUE	Rating 72.6
BLUE	474	196	399	305	352	197	527	399	320	3169		Slope 135
WHITE	470	134	395	305	350	165	515	360	316	3010		
Par	5	3	4	4	4	3	5	4	4	36	WHITE	Rating 71.2
Handicap	15	3	1	17	11	9	7	5	13			Slope 132
RED	435	86	290	300	275	132	425	318	247	2508		
Par	5	3	4	4	4	3	5	4	4	36	RED	Rating71.3
Handicap	3	17	9	7	13	15	1	5	11			Slope 124
Hole	10	11	12	13	14	15	16	17	18	In		Totals
BLUE	398	556	163	406	309	225	506	416	384	3363	BLUE	6532
WHITE	390	520	151	395	290	197	490	400	377	3210	WHITE	6220
Par	4	5	3	4	4	3	5	4	4	36	Par	72
Handicap	6	2	18	8	16	12	10	4	14			
RED	360	474	147	321	267	145	427	341	327	2809	RED	5317
Par	4	5	3	4	4	3	5	4	4	36	Par	72
Handicap	4	2	16	10	14	18	8	6	12			

Manager: Bob Lehning   **Pro:** John Elwood, PGA   **Supt:** Frank Donroe
Architect: C.K. Martin 1968

NORTH FORK COUNTRY CLUB

Main Rd., Cutchogue, NY 11935　　　　　**(516) 734-7758**

North Fork is an 18 hole private course open 6 days a week, all year. Guests may play accompanied by a member. Tee times are recommended on weekends.

•**Driving Range**	•**Lockers**
•**Practice Green**	•**Showers**
•**Power Carts**	•**Food**
•**Pull Carts**	•**Clubhouse**
Club Rental	Outings
Caddies	Soft Spikes

Course Description: Bent grass greens, water hazards, and scenic views of the Peconic Bay inlet are features of the Donald Ross designed North Fork CC. The course is relatively flat but the 6 holes affected by water require accurate shots. Changing winds are a major factor here especially on the 400 yard signature par 4 3rd which requires a series of shots into strong prevailing winds. The maritime climate allows for play during much of the cold winter months.

Directions: Suffolk County, #36
LIE East to Exit #73 (last exit). Go approx. 3 miles on Rte.58 until it joins Rte.25. Continue 10 miles on Rte.25 to Cutchogue. Club is located on the south side of Rte.25 at the intersection of Moore's Lane.

Hole	1	2	3	4	5	6	7	8	9	Out	BLUE	Rating 69.9
BLUE	306	400	383	309	339	145	244	550	379	3055		Slope 125
WHITE	297	389	376	301	334	132	234	519	358	2940		
Par	4	4	4	4	4	3	3	5	4	35	WHITE	Rating 68.9
Handicap	17	5	1	13	11	15	9	3	7			Slope 123
RED	272	334	320	256	273	100	130	462	276	2423		
Par	4	4	4	4	4	3	3	5	4	35	RED	Rating 68.7
Handicap	7	5	3	9	11	15	17	1	13			Slope 120
Hole	10	11	12	13	14	15	16	17	18	In		Totals
BLUE	213	438	510	153	197	506	281	496	395	3189	BLUE	6244
WHITE	209	430	503	133	189	476	268	476	384	3068	WHITE	6008
Par	3	4	5	3	3	5	4	5	4	36	Par	71
Handicap	14	2	4	18	12	6	16	10	8			
RED	150	385	452	126	130	450	249	408	327	2677	RED	5100
Par	3	5	5	3	3	5	4	5	4	37	Par	72
Handicap	18	12	2	14	16	4	10	6	8			

Manager: Joseph Pfaff　　**Pro**: Peter Cowan, PGA　　**Supt**: Gerard H. Dickerson
Architect: Donald Ross　1912

NOYAC GOLF CLUB

Wildwood Rd., Sag Harbor, NY 11963

(516) 725-1889

Noyac is a private 18 hole course open 7 days a week and closed Nov. 17-March 17. Guests play accompanied by a member. Tee time reservations are not necessary.

- •Driving Range
- •Practice Green
- •Power Carts
- • Pull Carts
- •Club Rental
- Caddies
- •Lockers
- •Showers
- •Food
- •Clubhouse
- •Outings
- •Soft Spikes

Course Description: Noyac is a hilly, rather tight tree-lined course that truly challenges the golfer. The very fast greens are of average size with subtle breaks and the wind is very strong. Water is in play on about 5 holes. The par 3s are very long; the fifth is 235 yards over water against an ever present wind. The 18th is a lengthy par 4 with an extremely narrow landing area and a severely sloped green.

Directions: Suffolk County, #37
Take the LIE to Exit 70 and go south to end. Turn left onto Rte27. Continue east to Southampton and bear left towards Noyac, Shelter Island. At blinking light, bear left onto North Sea Rd. At fork, bear right onto Noyac Rd. Go about 5 miles to Wildwood Rd. and turn right to course on right.

Hole	1	2	3	4	5	6	7	8	9	Out	BLUE	Rating 74.5
BLUE	389	506	397	385	235	387	405	173	502	3379		Slope 136
WHITE	355	478	365	359	213	357	377	153	470	3127		
Par	4	5	4	4	3	4	4	3	5	36	WHITE	Rating 72.1
Handicap	15	1	3	9	7	13	11	17	5			Slope 132
RED	308	418	325	314	145	316	341	119	413	2699		
Par	4	5	4	4	3	4	4	3	5	36	RED	Rating 73.0
Handicap	11	1	5	3	15	13	9	17	7			Slope 125
Hole	10	11	12	13	14	15	16	17	18	In		Totals
BLUE	426	334	218	374	544	445	221	491	454	3507	BLUE	6886
WHITE	407	307	197	348	458	393	181	460	433	3184	WHITE	6311
Par	4	4	3	4	5	4	3	5	4	36	Par	72
Handicap	6	16	10	14	2	12	18	8	4			
RED	366	263	169	318	402	372	171	451	390	2902	RED	5601
Par	4	4	3	4	5	4	3	5	4	36	Par	72
Handicap	6	14	18	12	8	10	16	2	4			

Manager: Ron Garone   **Pro**: David Gosiewski, PGA   **Supt**: George Tiska
Architect: William Mitchell 1964

PINE HILLS COUNTRY CLUB

Wading River Rd., Manorville, NY 11949   **(516) 878-4343**

Pine Hills is an 18 hole semi-private course open 7 days a week all year weather permitting. Weekends: closed to the general public until 2 PM. Reserved starting times may be purchased in advance. For $25 per yr., a 2 days ahead advance is available. Weekday: memberships are available with 3 day advance.

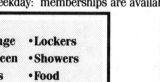

•Driving Range	•Lockers
•Practice Green	•Showers
•Power Carts	•Food
•Pull Carts	•Clubhouse
•Club Rental	•Outings

Fees	Weekday	Weekend
Daily/18	$25	$28
9 (1PM)	$14	$15
Power carts	$28	

Course Description: Pine Hills is always in excellent condition. The wind can affect play; it dies down in the evening. Water on 10 of the holes adds to the challenge. The greens are of average size, fairly fast with some break. The fairways are generous and pace of play is enforced. The signature hole could be considered the downhill par 5 #12, picturesque from the top of that hill. Carts are mandatory on weekends and holidays until after 2PM. A good teaching facility, Pine Hills features a grass driving range, as well as a greenside and a fairway bunker for practice.

Directions: Suffolk County, #38
Take the LIE to Exit 69. Go south on Wading River Rd. Course is about 1 and 1/2 miles down the road on the right.

Hole	1	2	3	4	5	6	7	8	9	Out	BLUE	Rating 72.2
BLUE	400	488	176	402	335	428	451	539	450	3669		Slope 121
WHITE	386	458	143	389	300	379	375	473	426	3329		
Par	4	5	3	4	4	4	4	5	4	37	WHITE	Rating 69.8
Handicap	7	11	17	1	13	5	15	9	3			Slope 117
RED	310	417	126	297	265	295	278	412	314	2714		
Par	4	5	3	4	4	4	4	5	4	37	RED	Rating 71.0
Handicap	9	5	15	11	13	7	17	3	1			Slope 116
Hole	10	11	12	13	14	15	16	17	18	In		Totals
BLUE	393	429	504	305	220	498	396	160	456	3361	BLUE	7030
WHITE	378	406	490	290	180	464	324	142	440	3114	WHITE	6443
Par	4	4	5	4	3	5	4	3	4	36	Par	73
Handicap	6	4	12	18	10	14	8	16	2			
RED	298	310	441	233	125	384	294	119	300	2504	RED	5218
Par	4	4	5	4	3	5	4	3	4	36	Par	73
Handicap	6	2	14	18	8	10	4	16	12			

Manager/Pro: Jimmi Conway, PGA   **Supt:** Marty Ruhter
Architects: Roger Tooker, Anthony Marino 1974

THE PONDS AT LAKE GROVE

New Moriches Rd., Lake Grove, NY 11755   **(516) 737-4649**

The Ponds at Lake Grove is an 18 hole par 60 Executive course open to the public all year 7 days a week. Reserved tee time memberships are available on weekends. Tee times may be made up to 7 days in advance.

•**Driving Range**	Lockers
•**Practice Green**	Showers
•**Power Carts**	•**Food**
•**Pull Carts**	•**Clubhouse**
•**Club Rental**	•**Outings**
	Soft Spikes

Fees	Weekday	Weekend
Daily	$16	$20
Twi	$12	$16
Power carts	$10pp	

Course Description: The Ponds is an excellent course for all levels of players. With gently rolling fairways, there are 12 par 3s and 6 par 4s. Water affects play on six holes and the greens are fast. The signature hole is the par 4 #11, a dogleg requiring careful club selection off the tee plus a pond involved on the approach to the green. It generally takes just a little over 3 hours to play 18 here.

Directions: Suffolk County, #40
Take the LIE to Exit 62N. Then take Rte.347W. to New Moriches Rd. and left into The Ponds just past Smith Haven Mall.

Hole	1	2	3	4	5	6	7	8	9	Out	BLUE	Rating
BLUE												Slope
WHITE	259	101	147	141	259	98	124	152	183	1464		
Par	4	3	3	3	4	3	3	3	3	29	WHITE	Rating 56.9
Handicap	1	15	11	9	5	17	13	7	3			Slope 88
RED	232	80	114	108	229	73	93	118	151	1198		
Par	4	3	3	3	4	3	3	3	3	29	RED	Rating 56.6
Handicap	1	15	11	9	5	17	13	7	3			Slope 85
Hole	10	11	12	13	14	15	16	17	18	In		Totals
BLUE											BLUE	
WHITE	133	264	241	145	118	86	137	264	255	1643	WHITE	3107
Par	3	4	4	3	3	3	3	4	4	31	Par	60
Handicap	14	4	8	12	16	18	10	2	6			
RED	90	235	223	112	90	69	113	235	219	1386	RED	2584
Par	3	4	4	3	3	3	3	4	4	31	Par	60
Handicap	14	4	8	12	16	18	10	2	6			

Manager: Susan Crean   **Supt:** Tom Gordon
Architect: William Buddy Johnson 1995

PORT JEFFERSON COUNTRY CLUB PRIVATE

44 Fairway Drive, Port Jefferson, NY 11777 　　　(516) 473-1464

Port Jefferson is an 18 hole course open 7 days a week and closed from the end of Dec. to April 1, weather permitting. Tee times are necessary for weekends. Guests may play accompanied by a member.

- •Driving Range
- •Practice Green
- •Power Carts
- •Pull Carts
- •Club Rental
- •Caddies
- •Lockers
- •Showers
- •Food
- •Clubhouse
- •Outings
- •Soft Spikes

Course Description: Situated on the contoured rolling hills of the North Shore, Port Jefferson, (formerly Harbor Hills CC), is a tight course with splendid views of LI Sound. The difficulty here comes on the par 5 first which requires a shot over a pond surrounded by high grass to an uphill fairway. On the home hole, a pond again comes into play, this time on the approach shot with a vista of the Sound off in the distance. The signature is the par 4 seventeenth with its interesting bunkers. Accuracy is most important on this challenging course.

Directions: Suffolk County, #39
LIE to Exit #64, then Rte.112 North. Proceed 10 miles to harbor, turn right onto East Broadway. At top of hill, turn left into "Belle Terre." Go left onto Cliff Rd. to Old Homestead Ave. and turn right. Go to end, follow signs to club.

Hole	1	2	3	4	5	6	7	8	9	Out	BLUE	Rating 72.6
BLUE	530	198	375	345	405	455	185	420	525	3438		Slope 130
WHITE	518	173	355	314	393	415	176	410	498	3252		
Par	5	3	4	4	4	4	3	4	5	36	WHITE	Rating 70.6
Handicap	7	9	15	11	5	1	17	3	13			Slope 126
RED	442	152	342	309	351	401	143	336	436	2912		
Par	5	3	4	4	4	5	3	4	5	37	RED	Rating 73.5
Handicap	3	15	11	7	5	13	17	9	1			Slope 127
Hole	10	11	12	13	14	15	16	17	18	In		Totals
BLUE	370	170	540	190	375	455	330	380	515	3325	BLUE	6763
WHITE	365	157	491	177	306	432	327	360	482	3097	WHITE	6349
Par	4	3	5	3	4	4	4	4	5	36	Par	72
Handicap	6	16	8	10	18	2	12	4	14			
RED	365	125	429	152	296	353	316	353	412	2801	RED	5713
Par	4	3	5	3	4	4	4	5	5	37	Par	74
Handicap	2	18	8	14	12	6	10	16	4			

Manager: Jerry Spiliotis　　**Pro**: Ralph Camerlengo, PGA　　**Supt**: Greg Fox
Architects: Alfred Tull, Devereux Emmet　**Estab**: 1924

POXABOGUE GOLF COURSE

3556 Montauk Highway, Bridgehampton, NY 11932   (516) 537-0025

Poxabogue is a 9 hole course open to the public 7 days a week from 3/20-11/30. Tee
time reservations are not necessary. Various specials are available.

•Driving Range	Lockers
•Practice Green	Showers
Power Carts	•Food
•Pull Carts	Clubhouse
•Club Rental	•Outings

Fees	Mon-Thurs	Fri-Sun
Resident	$9	$11
2nd round 1/2 price		

Course Description: Poxabogue is an easily walkable 9 hole layout. No water is in
play. The small to medium sized greens are contoured and of average speed. The
course is wide open with trees throughout the middle of the course. This well bunkered
facility is excellent for beginners and practice for all. The rough is not menacing. The
par 3 #5 signature is a short target hole with several bunkers around the back- to -
front sloping green.

Directions: Suffolk County, #41
In Hamptons, go east on Route 27. Course is located just past the town of
Bridgehampton on the left.

Hole	1	2	3	4	5	6	7	8	9	Out	BLUE	Rating
BLUE												Slope
WHITE	322	135	317	137	63	175	79	320	160	1706		
Par	4	3	4	3	3	3	3	4	3	30	WHITE	Rating
Handicap	3	7	2	8	6	5	4	1	9			Slope
RED												
Par											RED	Rating
												Slope

Hole	10	11	12	13	14	15	16	17	18	In		Totals
BLUE											BLUE	
WHITE											WHITE	1706
Par											Par	30
Handicap												
RED											RED	
Par											Par	
Handicap												

Manager: Rich Walker   **Pro:** Bob Vishno   **Supt:** George Tiska
Architects: Liberty & Treadwell 1962

123

QUOGUE FIELD CLUB

Club Lane, Quogue, NY 11959

(516) 653-9890

Quogue Field Club is a private 9 hole course open 7 days a week and closed 11/1-4/1. Guests play accompanied by a member. Tee time reservations are not necessary. Only a few power carts are available.

- •**Driving Range**   Lockers
- •**Practice Green**   Showers
- •**Power Carts**   •**Food**
- •**Pull Carts**   •**Clubhouse**
- •**Club Rental**   •Outings
-   Caddies   •**Soft Spikes**

Course Description: Originally, the Field Club was 18 holes but lost 9 to stormy weather. Most of the members walk the course for practice and belong to and play at other private clubs. This fairly flat links style layout has high rough. Water affects play but also provides beautiful views. The greens are quite contoured. There are separate sets of tees for the second nine.

Directions: Suffolk County, #42
Take the LIE to Exit 70 and turn right. At end of road, turn left (east) onto Rte27. Proceed to Exit 64, then south onto Montauk Hwy & turn right (west) for 3 miles to fork, bear left onto Quogue St. 2nd left to club.

Hole	1	2	3	4	5	6	7	8	9	Out	BLUE	Rating
BLUE												Slope
WHITE	539	150	273	202	476	305	436	325	530	3236		
Par	5	3	4	3	5	4	4	4	5	37	WHITE	Rating 69.9
Handicap	7	15	17	5	9	13	1	11	3			Slope 123
RED	442	115	250	172	415	240	376	282	485	2777		
Par	5	3	4	3	5	4	4	4	5	37	RED	Rating 70.6
Handicap	7	15	17	5	9	13	1	11	3			Slope 118
Hole	**10**	**11**	**12**	**13**	**14**	**15**	**16**	**17**	**18**	**In**		Totals
BLUE											BLUE	
WHITE	442	168	273	175	476	305	436	325	415	3015	WHITE	6251
Par	5	3	4	3	5	4	4	4	4	37	Par	74
Handicap	10	14	18	8	2	16	4	12	6			
RED	400	130	270	140	415	190	376	315	355	2591	RED	5368
Par	5	3	4	3	5	3	4	4	4	35	Par	72
Handicap	10	14	18	8	2	16	4	12	6			

Manager: William Brown   **Supt**: John Bradley
Architect: R. B Wilson **Redesign**: Stephen Kay   **Estab**: 1887

ROCK HILL GOLF & CC

105 Clancy Rd., Manorville, NY 11949   **(516) 878-2250**

Rock Hill is an 18 hole semi-private course open all year, 7 days a week. There are reserved starting times from April through Oct. for members. Others call up to 7 days in advance for tee times.

•**Driving Range**	•**Lockers**
•**Practice Green**	•**Showers**
•**Power Carts**	•**Food**
•**Pull Carts**	•**Clubhouse**
•**Club Rental**	•**Outings**

Fees	Weekday	Weekend
Daily	$46	$50
Twi	$33	$36
Power carts are included.		

Course Description: The front nine at Rock Hill is quite hilly and challenging with greens that are large and fast. The course is windy, sometimes howling. Originally, the present relatively flat back nine was the front. Later, the architect, Frank Duane, came along and expanded Rock Hill to 18 making it a much more interesting course. Water is in play on 4 holes. The signature par 4 #5 is uphill to a hard to hold back to front sloping green. One feature of note is that the locations of the restrooms on the course are marked on the scorecard.

Directions: Suffolk County, #43
Take the LIE to Exit 70. Go south on Rte.111. Turn right at light by 7-11 onto Chapman Blvd. Go 2 miles. At fork, bear left onto Clancy Rd. to course on left.

Hole	1	2	3	4	5	6	7	8	9	Out	BLUE	Rating 73.4
BLUE	415	555	350	200	420	390	180	390	435	3335		Slope 131
WHITE	375	530	330	160	360	360	150	365	405	3035		
Par	4	5	4	3	4	4	3	4	4	35	WHITE	Rating 70.7
Handicap	5	7	17	11	1	13	15	9	3			Slope 126
RED	300	430	305	125	275	330	125	280	325	2495		
Par	4	5	4	3	4	4	3	4	4	35	RED	Rating 71.4
Handicap	9	1	11	17	3	5	15	13	7			Slope 121

Hole	10	11	12	13	14	15	16	17	18	In		Totals
BLUE	455	390	570	195	390	585	475	205	450	3715	BLUE	7050
WHITE	425	360	535	165	365	550	435	170	425	3430	WHITE	6465
Par	4	4	5	3	4	5	4	3	4	36	Par	71
Handicap	8	18	4	12	16	10	6	14	2			
RED	385	250	430	135	330	460	430	135	340	2895	RED	5390
Par	4	4	5	3	4	5	5	3	4	37	Par	72
Handicap	8	12	4	16	14	2	6	18	10			

President: Ernie Vigliotta   **Pro:** George Cosgrove, PGA **Supt:** Jeff Papp
Architect: Frank Duane 1966 **Estab:** 1960

ROLLING OAKS COUNTRY CLUB

181 Route 25A, Rocky Point, NY 11778 **(516) 744-3200**

Rolling Oaks is an 18 hole public course that is open 7 days a week all year, weather permitting. Weekend tee times may be made 1 week in advance for a $3 fee.

Driving Range   Lockers
- **Practice Green**   Showers
- **Power Carts**   • **Food**
- **Pull Carts**   • **Clubhouse**
- **Club Rental**   • **Outings**
Soft Spikes

Fees	Weekday	Weekend
Daily	$22	$25
Twi(3PM)	$14	
Power carts	$16PP	$28 /2

Course Description Originally called Tall Tree prior to 1996, this well maintained course then became Rolling Oaks. It has postage stamp sized greens and narrow tree-lined fairways. Hitting straight off the tee to keep out of the relatively deep rough and an accurate short game are imperative for a good score. The new ownership has spent over 2 million dollars to improve the clubhouse and pro shop. The drainage is good so that play can start soon after a rain. There are cart paths throughout the course.

Directions: Suffolk County, #44
LIE to Exit #63. Take 83North to Rte.25A and turn right heading east. Course is 3 miles on left.

Hole	1	2	3	4	5	6	7	8	9	Out	BLUE	Rating
BLUE	305	160	335	115	160	470	150	375	185	2255		Slope
WHITE	278	156	319	109	153	408	144	355	180	2102		
Par	4	3	4	3	3	5	3	4	3	32	WHITE	Rating 63.0
Handicap	7	11	5	17	13	1	15	3	9			Slope 105
RED	268	94	254	90	135	278	132	328	123	1702		
Par	4	3	4	3	3	5	3	4	3	32	RED	Rating 67.0
Handicap	7	11	5	17	13	1	15	3	9			Slope 111
Hole	10	11	12	13	14	15	16	17	18	In		Totals
BLUE	160	175	420	320	130	148	310	345	475	2483	BLUE	4738
WHITE	150	161	366	283	129	138	266	308	445	2246	WHITE	4348
Par	3	3	4	4	3	3	4	4	5	33	Par	65
Handicap	14	12	2	10	18	16	8	6	4			
RED	125	147	343	268	110	112	229	264	308	3608	RED	3608
Par	3	3	4	4	3	3	4	4	5	33	Par	65
Handicap	14	12	2	10	18	16	8	6	4			

Manager/Pro: James Haughey, PGA   **Supt:** Chris Vene
Architect: Arthur Colocci, 1961

SAG HARBOR GOLF CLUB

PUBLIC

1 Barcelona Neck Rd., Sag Harbor, NY 11963　　(516) 725-2503

Sag Harbor is a 9 hole course open to the public 7 days a week all year. Memberships are available. Tee time reservations are not necessary.

Driving Range	Lockers
•**Practice Green**	Showers
•**Power Carts**	•**Food**
•**Pull Carts**	Clubhouse
•**Club Rental**	Outings
•**Soft Spikes**	

Fees	Weekday	Weekend
Non-Mbr	$10	$15

Course Description: Sag Harbor Golf Club is located within a NY State wildlife preserve. Wide open and fairly flat, it has small undulating greens and no water hazards. The sixth hole, a dogleg right, it is the toughest and plays the longest on the course. Years ago the Grumman Corporation owned this property.

Directions: Suffolk County, #45
Take Route 27East in the Hamptons to Rte.114. Watch for sign on right to Barcelona Neck Preserve. Make that right and follow road to course on left. Entrance on right.

Hole	1	2	3	4	5	6	7	8	9	Out	BLUE	Rating
BLUE												Slope
WHITE	320	306	145	281	302	349	404	197	357	2661		
Par	4	4	3	4	4	4	5	3	4	35	WHITE	Rating 65.8
Handicap	10	12	8	16	14	2	18	6	4			Slope 115
RED	287	259	134	206	259	297	313	127	320	2202		
Par	4	4	3	4	4	4	5	3	4	35	RED	Rating 62.0
Handicap	10	12	8	16	14	2	18	6	4			Slope 104
Hole	10	11	12	13	14	15	16	17	18	In		Totals
BLUE											BLUE	
WHITE	322	326	160	291	302	357	410	203	361	2732	WHITE	5393
Par	4	4	3	4	4	4	5	3	4	35	Par	70
Handicap	9	11	7	15	13	1	17	5	3			
RED	320	306	145	281	302	349	404	197	357	2661	RED	4863
Par	4	4	3	4	4	4	5	3	4	35	Par	70
Handicap	9	11	7	15	13	1	17	5	3			

Manager: William Boeklen　　**Supt:** Bruce Hulse
Built: 1919

ST. GEORGE'S GOLF & COUNTRY CLUB

134 Lower Sheep Pasture, Setauket, NY 11733   (516) 751-0585

St. George's has an 18 hole golf course open 7 days a week and closed in Jan. & Feb. Guests may play accompanied by a member. Tee time reservations are not necessary.

- •Driving Range
- •Practice Green
- •Power Carts
- •Pull Carts
- Club Rental
- •Caddies
- •Lockers
- •Showers
- •Food
- •Clubhouse
- •Outings
- •Soft Spikes

Course Description: Typical of North Shore courses is St. George's, with its rolling hills, scenic views and traditional greens. It was built in a links style and is now being restored to its original state with added high rough and fescue grass. The small fast greens have a lot of break and are flanked by grass faced deep bunkers. It plays longer than its yardages indicate with water affecting play on holes 14 & 16. The 450 yard par 4 13th signature hole, called the Knoll, is long and beautiful; it sinks down to a low undulating fairway, considered quite difficult even by low handicappers.

Directions: Suffolk County, #46
LIE to Exit #62 (Nichols Rd.) Go North approx. 10 miles and just before RR overpass, turn right on Sheep Pasture Rd. to club on right.

Hole	1	2	3	4	5	6	7	8	9	Out	BLUE	Rating
BLUE												Slope
WHITE	374	574	408	360	356	465	181	382	147	3247		
Par	4	5	4	4	4	5	3	4	3	36	WHITE	Rating 70.4
Handicap	9	1	7	5	13	11	15	3	17			Slope 128
RED	353	468	340	340	339	447	154	375	134	2950		
Par	4	5	4	4	4	5	3	4	3	36	RED	Rating 71.4
Handicap	9	1	13	3	11	7	15	5	17			Slope 124
Hole	10	11	12	13	14	15	16	17	18	In		Totals
BLUE											BLUE	
WHITE	380	194	420	450	388	164	318	122	535	2971	WHITE	6218
Par	4	3	4	4	4	3	4	3	5	34	Par	70
Handicap	10	14	4	2	6	16	12	18	8			
RED	336	149	295	437	292	137	258	107	496	2507	RED	5457
Par	4	3	4	5	4	3	4	3	5	35	Par	71
Handicap	6	18	10	2	8	16	12	14	4			

Manager: Larry King   **Pro:** Rod Heller, PGA   **Supt:** Gary Baumann
Architect: Devereux Emmet, 1917

SANDY POND GOLF COURSE

 PUBLIC

Roanoke Ave. Riverhead, NY, 11901 **(516) 727-0909**

Sandy Pond is a par 3 executive course that is open all year 7 days a week. Tee time reservations are not necessary. Annual memberships are available.

Driving Range	Lockers
•**Practice Green**	Showers
Power Carts	Food
•**Pull Carts**	Clubhouse
•**Club Rental**	Outings
Soft Spikes	

Fees	Weekday	Weekend
Daily(9)	$4.50	$5.50
Sr.	$3.50	$4.50

Course Description: Sandy Pond has moderately rolling hills yet the course is easily walkable making it a good layout for practice. The 6th is over a pond and the 2nd & 3rd have water running alongside the hole. Some of the tees and greens are slightly elevated. The 5th green is steeply sloped, and the 7th hole is on a fairly high hill. The course gets quite busy in summer.

Directions: Suffolk County, #46
Take the LIE East to Exit #73 (last exit). Continue east on Rte.25. Make a left on Roanoke Ave. to club on left.

Hole	1	2	3	4	5	6	7	8	9	Out	BLUE	Rating
BLUE												Slope
WHITE	105	110	120	85	120	160	120	160	90	1070		
Par	3	3	3	3	3	3	3	3	3	27	WHITE	Rating
Handicap												Slope
RED	105	110	120	70	120	90	120	110	90	935		
Par											RED	Rating
Handicap												Slope
Hole	10	11	12	13	14	15	16	17	18	In		Totals
BLUE											BLUE	
WHITE											WHITE	
Par											Par	
Handicap												
RED											RED	
Par											Par	
Handicap												

Manager/Supt: Keith Watson
Built: 1970

SHELTER ISLAND COUNTRY CLUB

26 Sunnyside Ave., Shelter Island Heights, NY 11965   **(516) 749-0416**

Shelter Island is a 9 hole course open to the public all year 7 days a week. Tee time reservations are not necessary. Memberships are available.

•**Driving Range**	Lockers
•**Practice Green**	Showers
•**Power Carts**	•**Food**
•**Pull Carts**	•**Clubhouse**
•**Club Rental**	•**Outings**

Fees	Weekday &	Weekend
9 holes	$10	$10
18 holes	$16	$16
Power carts	$10/9	
" "	$16/18	

Course Description: The clubhouse sits on a high hill from which there are views of Dering Harbor and Shelter Island Sound. The course's nickname isGoat Hill, no doubt inspired by the rugged terrain and the aforementioned height. Uneven lies abound and there are many elevated tees and greens; only 2 greens can be seen from the tee boxes. The layout follows the contours of the hilly topography. The greens are small, hard to read and fairly fast, but considered very true.

Directions: Suffolk County, #48
Cross on ferry to Shelter Island. From <u>South</u>, take Rte.114 up toward No. Ferry and make left onto NY Ave., then right onto Tower Hill and bear left onto Sunnyside to course. From <u>North</u>, go South on Rte.114 and right onto NY Ave and continue as above.

Hole	1	2	3	4	5	6	7	8	9	Out	BLUE	Rating
BLUE												Slope
WHITE	350	407	305	226	157	183	380	303	201	2512		
Par	4	4	4	4	3	3	4	4	3	33	WHITE	Rating 63.8
Handicap	9	3	13	17	7	11	1	15	5			Slope 107
RED	299	396	232	180	138	183	323	240	112	2103		
Par	4	5	4	4	3	3	4	4	3	34	RED	Rating 63.5
Handicap	9	3	13	17	7	11	1	15	5			Slope 105

Hole	10	11	12	13	14	15	16	17	18	In		Totals
BLUE											BLUE	
WHITE											WHITE	5024
Par											Par	66
Handicap												
RED											RED	4206
Par											Par	68
Handicap												

Manager: Bob Clark   **Supt:** George Blados
Architects: Flynn & Mc Donald 1902   **Estab:** 1898

SHINNECOCK HILLS GOLF CLUB

Tuckahoe Rd., Southampton, NY 11969   **(516) 283-3525**

Shinnecock Hills is an 18 hole private course open 7 days a week and closed from Oct. 31-April 1. Guests play accompanied by a member. Reservations for tee times are not necessary.

•**Driving Range**	•**Lockers**
•**Practice Green**	•**Showers**
•**Power Carts**	•**Food**
Pull Carts	•**Clubhouse**
Club Rental	•**Outings**
•**Caddies**	Soft Spikes

Course Description: Shinnecock is one of the original USGA courses. It is very long, challenging and hilly. Several of the early golf course architects had a part in the creation of this famous landmark. Site of a number of US Opens when the yardage is even longer, Golf Digest rates it as #3 in America. The views are breathtaking from the clubhouse overlooking the magnificent expanse. From the elevated 1st tee, the golfer looks out at a rolling layout designed to test every golfing skill. The sixth hole catches water if the drive is missed. Robert Trent Jones has been quoted as saying "There is a sweep and majesty to Shinnecock."

Directions: Suffolk County, #49
LIE to Exit 70, then right to Rte.27E. Travel 16 miles on Rte 27. In Southampton, make left onto Tuckahoe Rd., cross over RR tracks and course is ahead on left.

Hole	1	2	3	4	5	6	7	8	9	Out	BLUE	Rating 74.6
BLUE	391	221	456	409	529	456	184	361	411	3418		Slope 145
WHITE	380	193	422	373	487	415	173	319	373	3135		
Par	4	3	4	4	5	4	3	4	4	35	WHITE	Rating 72.1
Handicap	11	17	3	7	9	1	15	13	5			Slope 135
RED	366	146	395	303	413	368	133	281	307	2712		
Par											RED	Rating 72.1
Handicap												Slope 124
Hole	10	11	12	13	14	15	16	17	18	In		Totals
BLUE	412	158	469	372	447	408	542	169	426	3395	BLUE	6813
WHITE	402	150	427	354	436	357	464	149	374	3113	WHITE	6248
Par	4	3	4	4	4	4	5	3	4	35	Par	70
Handicap	4	16	2	12	6	14	8	18	10			
RED	337	121	396	325	361	288	406	140	289	2663	RED	5375
Par											Par	70
Handicap												

Manager: Henry Nichols   **Pro:** Don McDougall, PGA   **Supt:** Peter Smith
Architects: Toomey & Flynn 1931 **Estab:** 1891

SMITHTOWN LANDING CC

Landing Road, Smithtown, NY 11787   **(516) 360-7618**

Smithtown Landing is an 18 hole public course open 6 days a week all year, weather permitting. On weekends, only residents may play. Tee times are not necessary on weekdays.

•Driving Range	Lockers
•Practice Green	Showers
•Power Carts	**•Food**
•Pull Carts	Clubhouse
Club Rental	**•Outings**
Soft Spikes	

Fees	Weekday	Weekend
Daily(res)	$18	$20
Daily(non-res)	$26	
Sr/Jr(res)	$10	$20
Power carts	$24	

Course Description: Formerly a private club called Merrywood, Smithtown Landing has that kind of atmosphere. It was taken over by the town in the 1970s. There are large fairways lined with big beautiful oak and maple trees. Fairly hilly, it has small greens, (some elevated), that get fast in summer. Downhill, sidehill and uphill lies are prevalent. The Nissequogue River can be seen from the signature par 4 18th hole which has a 2 tiered green surrounded by traps. There is also a par three course on the facility which is great for practicing the short game. Smithtown Landing is one of the top public courses in the region.

Directions: Suffolk County, #50

LIE to Exit #53N Sagtikos Pkwy.(aka/Sunken Meadow Pkwy). to Rte.25A East and go 2 miles. After 5th light, 25A makes a sharp right DO NOT TAKE IT. Go straight onto Rose Ave. 4 blocks to club.

Hole	1	2	3	4	5	6	7	8	9	Out	BLUE	Rating 69.4
BLUE	362	155	275	590	370	465	165	320	370	3072		Slope 129
WHITE	352	145	260	580	357	450	160	300	360	2964		
Par	4	3	4	5	4	5	3	4	4	36	WHITE	Rating 68.3
Handicap	5	15	17	1	3	7	13	11	9			Slope 127
RED	287	115	245	545	300	356	150	270	340	2608		
Par	4	3	4	5	4	5	3	4	4	36	RED	Rating 70.1
Handicap	5	17	15	1	3	7	13	11	9			Slope 126

Hole	10	11	12	13	14	15	16	17	18	In		Totals
BLUE	293	155	485	374	475	330	190	350	390	3042	BLUE	6114
WHITE	273	145	469	362	465	320	180	320	360	2894	WHITE	5858
Par	4	3	5	4	5	4	3	4	4	36	Par	72
Handicap	16	18	6	10	2	14	4	12	8			
RED	257	130	446	346	450	290	120	280	336	2655	RED	5263
Par	4	3	5	4	5	4	3	4	4	36	Par	72
Handicap	16	18	4	8	2	10	12	14	6			

Manager/Supt: Chris Heslin   **Pro:** Michael Hebron, PGA
Architect: Arthur Poole 1971

SOUTH FORK COUNTRY CLUB

PRIVATE

Abraham's Landing Rd., Amagansett, NY 11930   (516) 267-6827

South Fork is a private 9 hole golf course open all year 7 days a week. Guests play accompanied by a member. Reservations for tee times are not necessary.

Driving Range	Lockers
•**Practice Green**	Showers
•**Power Carts**	•**Food**
Pull Carts	•**Clubhouse**
•**Club Rental**	Outings
Caddies	•**Soft Spikes**

Course Description: South Fork is a short nine hole course featuring elevated small difficult greens that are fast and undulating and in some cases crowned. Water is in play on 3 holes. The fairways are narrow; fairly deep rough is along the edges. A big hill runningacross the middle of the layout comes into play from both directions. The signature par 4 #8 is narrow with a green guarded by bunkers. An attempt to avoid them with an extra long approach shot, could result in an encounter with a pond. Those unfamiliar with play here usually have higher scores than they would expect due to the challenging greens.

Directions: Suffolk County, #51
Take Route 27 East into Amagansett. Then go straight at fork over RR tracks to course on left.

Hole	1	2	3	4	5	6	7	8	9	Out	BLUE	Rating
BLUE												Slope
WHITE	281	252	166	519	350	150	516	313	292	2839		
Par	4	4	3	5	4	3	5	4	4	36	WHITE	Rating 68.7
Handicap	8	10	16	4	6	18	2	12	14			Slope 126
RED	272	237	100	348	301	142	444	313	267	2424		
Par	4	4	3	5	4	3	5	4	4	36	RED	Rating 68.5
Handicap	12	14	18	8	6	16	2	4	10			Slope 117
Hole	10	11	12	13	14	15	16	17	18	In		Totals
BLUE											BLUE	
WHITE	286	264	154	531	354	213	527	345	302	2976	WHITE	5815
Par	4	4	3	5	4	3	5	4	4	36	Par	72
Handicap	9	11	17	3	5	7	1	13	15			
RED	281	211	146	348	341	170	444	257	255	2453	RED	4877
Par	4	4	3	5	4	3	5	4	4	36	Par	72
Handicap	7	17	13	5	3	15	1	11	9			

Manager: Anthony Sales   **Pro**: Jon Eisen, PGA   **Supt**: Marshall Garypie
Architect: Frank Duane 1948 **Estab**: 1920s

SOUTHAMPTON GOLF CLUB

1005 County Rd #39., Southampton, NY 11968   (516) 283-0623

Southampton is a private 18 hole course open 7 days a week and closed 10/31-4/1. Guests play accompanied by a member. Tee time reservations are not necessary.

- •Driving Range
- •Practice Green
- •Power Carts
- •Pull Carts
- •Club Rental
- Caddies
- •Lockers
- •Showers
- •Food
- •Clubhouse
- Outings
- •Soft Spikes

Course Description: Adjacent to Shinnecock Golf Club, the links-style front nine at Southampton is quite different from the country like setting of the back. In general, the terrain is gently rolling, and, as at some of the other East End courses, the fescue grass in the rough is punishing. Water is in play on a few holes. The 2nd is a par 3 with a tee shot over water. The medium sized greens are moderately fast and undulating. The sixth is alongside Shinnecock's 12th hole.

Directions: Suffolk County, #52
Take LIE to Exit 70 and turn right. At end of road, turn left onto Rte.27. In Southampton, make a left onto Tuckahoe Rd. and then a right onto Rte.39. Watch for club entrance on the left opposite a driving range.

Hole	1	2	3	4	5	6	7	8	9	Out	BLUE	Rating 71.3
BLUE	392	137	410	413	280	377	201	435	393	3038		Slope 129
WHITE	383	126	404	369	273	362	172	392	379	2860		
Par	4	3	4	4	4	4	3	4	4	34	WHITE	Rating 69.8
Handicap	11	17	5	1	15	7	13	3	9			Slope 126
RED	339	105	398	343	263	347	141	379	359	2674		
Par	4	3	5	4	4	4	3	4	4	35	RED	Rating 72.1
Handicap	11	17	5	1	15	7	13	3	9			Slope 124
Hole	10	11	12	13	14	15	16	17	18	In		Totals
BLUE	153	351	513	381	203	429	334	493	392	3249	BLUE	6287
WHITE	147	331	493	372	195	417	314	464	372	3105	WHITE	5965
Par	3	4	5	4	3	4	4	5	4	36	Par	70
Handicap	16	14	4	8	10	2	18	12	6			
RED	144	262	471	327	148	374	279	451	316	2772	RED	5446
Par	3	4	5	4	3	4	4	5	4	36	Par	71
Handicap	14	12	2	10	16	4	18	6	8			

Manager: Craig Ruhling   **Pro:** Tim Garvin, PGA   **Supt:** Elton Etheredge
Architects: Seth Raynor, Charles Banks 1925

SOUTHWARD HO COUNTRY CLUB

Montauk Highway - Rte 27A, Bay Shore, NY 11760   **(516) 665-1753**

Southward Ho is an 18 hole private club open 6 days a week all year, weather permitting. Guests may play accompanied by a member. Reservations for tee times are not necessary.

- **•Driving Range**
- **•Practice Green**
- **•Power Carts**
- Pull Carts
- **•Club Rental**
- **•Caddies**
- **•Lockers**
- **•Showers**
- **•Food**
- **•Clubhouse**
- **•Outings**
- Soft Spikes

Course Description: Southward Ho is a links-type shot maker's course of mediium length. Relatively flat, water is in play on 5 holes. The signature par 3 14th is long with a small green surrounded by bunkers, and difficult to par if the tee shot is errant. The predominant south wind off the bay was a major consideration in designing the course. The north wind makes the course play longer. The greens are well maintained and #8 is two tiered. Bunkers throughout and deep rough are part of what makes this a challenging layout. The landmark windmill that was blown down in 1996 has been reconstructed.

Directions: Suffolk County, #53
Take the LIE to Exit 44. Go South to So. State Pkwy East to Exit 40S. Go to Montauk Hwy. (Rte.27A). Proceed 1 & 1/2 miles to club on left.

Hole	1	2	3	4	5	6	7	8	9	Out	BLUE	Rating 71.8
BLUE	362	515	413	149	378	382	411	365	164	3139		Slope 131
WHITE	350	476	398	132	340	337	394	350	147	2924	WHITE	Rating 70.2
Par	4	5	4	3	4	4	4	4	3	35		
Handicap	10	14	2	18	8	12	4	6	16			Slope 128
RED	329	455	401	115	321	310	355	311	91	2688	RED	Rating 72.6
Par	4	5	5	3	4	4	4	4	3	36		
Handicap	8	2	10	16	12	14	6	4	18			Slope 120
Hole	10	11	12	13	14	15	16	17	18	In		Totals
BLUE	546	559	327	380	222	357	419	214	419	3443	BLUE	6582
WHITE	531	543	295	349	205	340	395	197	403	3528	WHITE	6182
Par	5	5	4	4	3	4	4	3	4	36	Par	71
Handicap	7	1	17	15	11	9	3	13	5			
RED	429	470	275	329	153	321	374	180	386	2917	RED	5605
Par	5	5	4	4	3	4	4	3	4	36	Par	72
Handicap	9	1	13	11	17	7	3	15	5			

Manager: Helen Wells   **Pro:** Michael Darrell, PGA   **Supt:** William Bodemer
Architect: A. W. Tillinghast 1923

SPRING LAKE GOLF CLUB

30 E. Bartlett Rd., Middle Island, NY 11953   **(516) 924-5115**

Spring Lake is public 27 hole course open all year 7 days a week, weather permitting. Reserved seasonal starting times for weekends 4/1-10/31 are available. Tee times may be made up to one week in advance.

•Driving Range	•Lockers
•Practice Green	•Showers
•Power Carts	•Food
•Pull Carts	•Clubhouse
•Club Rental	•Outings

Fees	Weekday	Weekend
Daily	$28	$32
9 hole	$14	$16
Twi	$20	
Power carts	$26	

Course Description: Spring Lake is a well-conditioned championship calibre course with large greens. The Sandpiper nine, played as a separate course, was the last to be built and is easier than the other two nines, although its first hole is all water. The Thunderbird 18 has water in play on several holes. The signature par 3 third features water on both sides of the fairway. The 17th is considered by Newsday to be one of the toughest holes on Long Island. Spring Lake has a well stocked pro shop.

Directions: Suffolk County, #54
Take the LIE to Exit 64. Take Rte.112N to Rte.25 and turn right. Go about 3 miles to sign and Bartlett Rd. and turn right to course entrance.

Hole	1	2	3	4	5	6	7	8	9	Out	BLUE	Rating 73.2
BLUE	456	382	212	557	381	178	452	431	534	3583		Slope 130
WHITE	436	340	180	507	339	154	420	381	504	3261		
Par	4	4	3	5	4	3	4	4	5	36	WHITE	Rating 72.4
Handicap	7	11	15	1	13	17	9	3	5			Slope 123
RED	400	300	130	457	310	120	380	340	464	2901		
Par	4	4	3	5	4	3	4	4	5	36	RED	Rating 70.0
Handicap	7	11	15	1	13	17	9	3	5			Slope 122

Hole	10	11	12	13	14	15	16	17	18	In		Totals
BLUE	332	525	360	214	456	362	170	475	571	3465	BLUE	7048
WHITE	315	500	340	173	410	333	155	427	541	3194	WHITE	6455
Par	4	5	4	3	4	4	3	4	5	36	Par	72
Handicap	12	4	14	16	6	10	18	2	8			
RED	297	450	280	120	372	303	125	384	500	2831	RED	5732
Par	4	5	4	3	4	4	3	4	5	36	Par	72
Handicap	12	4	14	16	6	10	18	2	8			

Manager: Rick Jurgens   **Pro:** Loring Hawkins, PGA   **Supt:** Don Amsler
Architects: Charles & Fred Jurgens 1966

SUNKEN MEADOW STATE PARK GC | PUBLIC

Kings Park, NY 11754   (516) 269-3838

Sunken Meadow is a NY State owned & operated course open 7 days a week all year, (weather permitting.) It closes Mon. & Tues. in winter. There is an 18 & a 9 hole course here. There is a 7 day advance tee time reservation policy for card holders & 4 day for non-card holders.

•**Driving Range**	Lockers
•**Practice Green**	Showers
•**Power Carts**	•**Food**
•**Pull Carts**	Clubhouse
•**Club Rental**	•**Outings**
Soft Spikes	

Fees	Weekday	Weekend
Daily	$18	$22
9 hole	$9	$11
Srs	Discounts avail.	
Power carts	$25	

Course Description: Sunken Meadow has recently changed to 3 nines on which play is rotated every few days. The courses are short. well designed and each has its own unique character. The Blue is the signature nine; a hilly par 35. The Red is slightly shorter (par 36) and less difficult. The 155 yard par 3 #8 on the Red is straight uphill and plays deceptively long. The Green nine is relatively flat with some difficult par threes and 2 par fives. Its greens are undulating and relatively slow. No water is in play here. The greatest view is from the driving range which overlooks the Sound; you can see Connecticut in the distance. The scorecard below shows one set of yardages for each nine.

Directions: Suffolk County, #55
LIE to Exit #53 to Sunken Meadow Pkwy. North (also called Sagtikos Pkwy.) Continue on Pkwy. to end. Club on left **after entering** Park.

Hole	1	2	3	4	5	6	7	8	9	Out	Red /Blue	Rating 68.2
RED	305	300	130	410	375	345	505	155	515	3040		Slope 112
Par	4	4	3	4	4	4	5	3	5	36		
Handicap	7	6	9	3	4	5	2	8	1		Green/Blue	Rating 68.7
												Slope 111
BLUE	333	393	137	507	413	190	360	380	347	3060		
Par	4	4	3	5	4	3	4	4	4	35	Green/Red	Rating 68.5
Handicap	7	6	9	1	2	8	4	3	5			Slope 112

Hole	10	11	12	13	14	15	16	17	18	In		Totals
GREEN	350	385	395	175	340	145	470	485	380	3125	RED	3040
Par	4	4	4	3	4	3	5	5	4	36	BLUE	3060
Handicap	7	4	2	8	6	9	3	1	5		GREEN	3125

Manager: Doug Bolander   **Pro:** Vincent Cirino Sr., PGA   **Supt:** Buddy Betts
Architect: Alfred Tull, 1968

SWAN LAKE GOLF CLUB

373 River Road Manorville, NY 11949   **(516) 369-1818**

Swan Lake is a semi-private 18 hole course open all year, 7 days a week, weather permitting. Tee times may be made by members for weekends and 1 week in advance weekdays for the public. There is a $25 fee to reserve a foursome.

Driving Range	•**Lockers**
•**Practice Green**	•**Showers**
•**Power Carts**	•**Food**
•**Pull Carts**	•**Clubhouse**
•**Club Rental**	•**Outings**
Soft Spikes (rec)	

Fees	Weekday	Weekend
Daily	$27	$30
Daily (9)	$15	$18
Power carts	$26 (18)	$13 (9)

Course Description: Although it is easily walkable, Swan Lake is a challenging long course, over 7,000 yards from the blue tees. The back nine is more difficult and longer than the front with water affecting play on 12 holes. Characterized by gently rolling hills and thick rough, rye grass is used throughout. The large greens are undulating, tricky and of medium speed. The swans present a pleasant atmosphere. Swan Lake gets quite busy in summer.

Directions: Suffolk County, #56
LIE to Exit #70 and at end of ramp go left. Go 0.3 miles to end of road, turn right onto Ryerson St.; go to STOP sign, turn right onto North St. Bear left at fork to River Rd., turn right and go 1 mile to club on left.

Hole	1	2	3	4	5	6	7	8	9	Out	BLUE	Rating 72.5
BLUE	407	417	521	337	247	507	188	394	373	3391		Slope 121
WHITE	357	370	481	307	177	467	153	354	343	3009		
Par	4	4	5	4	3	5	3	4	4	36	WHITE	Rating 69.5
Handicap	4	8	10	18	12	14	16	6	2			Slope 115
RED	312	310	436	232	157	377	108	289	305	2526		
Par	4	4	5	4	3	5	3	4	4	36	RED	Rating 69.0
Handicap	4	8	10	18	12	14	16	6	2			Slope 112

Hole	10	11	12	13	14	15	16	17	18	In		Totals
BLUE	418	577	466	222	393	537	150	433	424	3620	BLUE	7011
WHITE	383	547	431	177	373	507	124	393	394	3329	WHITE	6338
Par	4	5	4	3	4	5	3	4	4	36	Par	72
Handicap	5	3	1	15	13	7	17	11	9			
RED	308	407	281	127	333	467	94	348	354	2719	RED	5245
Par	4	5	4	3	4	5	3	4	4	36	Par	72
Handicap	5	3	1	15	13	7	17	11	9			

Manager: Sam Panasci   **Supt:** Don Jurgens
Architects: Charles & Fred Jurgens 1979

TIMBER POINT COUNTRY CLUB

Great River Rd., Great River, NY 11739   **(516) 581-2401**

Timber Point is one of Suffolk County's public courses. It is 27 holes and open 7 days a week, closed mid-Jan to mid March. Residents obtain green key and for $3 may reserve by calling 244-7275 up to 7 days in advance. Some walk-on space available.

•Driving Range	•Lockers
•Practice Green	•Showers
•Power Carts	•Food
•Pull Carts	•Clubhouse
•Club Rental	•Outings
	•Soft Spikes

Fees	Weekday	Weekend
Res.	$19	$20
Non-res	$28	$32
Twi/res	$13	
Power carts	$25	$25

Course Description: Originally, this sea front property was a private course for the residents who summered nearby. The wind here is a major factor at this basically flat wide open seashore layout. The Blue is the most prestigious, difficult and beautiful. As it is located along the water, it can get saturated and needs to be closed after a heavy rainfall. Its signature hole is the par 3 5th, called Gibraltar, requiring an uphill battle against the howling wind to an island green. In the early 1970s, 9 holes were added. Very busy in season, about 60,000 rounds are played here each year. The scorecard below is for the Red and the Blue courses.

Directions: Suffolk County, #57
Take Southern State Parkway to end. Exit (Heckscher Park) and bear right. Go east on Timber Point Rd. Club is 1 1/2 mile on right.

Hole	1	2	3	4	5	6	7	8	9	Out	BLUE	Rating 72.9
BLUE	313	172	491	455	194	388	528	424	314	3279		Slope 121
WHITE	298	147	450	425	172	358	482	400	287	3019		
Par	4	3	5	4	3	4	5	4	4	36	WHITE	Rating 70.8
Handicap	8	7	5	2	6	4	3	1	9			Slope 117
RED	278	113	388	400	151	299	447	380	267	2723		
Par	4	3	5	4	3	4	5	4	4	36	RED	Rating 72.5
Handicap	8	7	4	3	6	5	1	2	9			Slope 119

Hole	10	11	12	13	14	15	16	17	18	In		Totals
BLUE	488	146	381	435	208	366	422	490	427	3363	BLUE	6642
WHITE	458	133	368	417	188	343	388	468	405	3168	WHITE	6187
Par	5	3	4	4	3	4	4	5	4	36	Par	72
Handicap	7	9	6	1	5	4	2	8	3			
RED	401	110	303	378	140	298	312	409	381	2732	RED	5455
Par	5	3	4	4	3	4	4	5	4	36	Par	72
Handicap	2	9	6	1	7	8	4	5	3			

Manager/Pro: Andy Carracino, PGA **Supt:** Bill Maxwell
Architects: Colt & Allison 1923   William Mitchell 1971

VETERAN'S HOSPITAL GOLF COURSE

79 Middleville Rd. Northport, NY 11768   **(516) 261-8000**

Veteran's Hosp.is a 9 hole par 34 public golf course run by Global Golf.   It is open 7 days a week, between Mar.15 and Dec.15. Tee time reservations are not necessary.

Driving Range	Lockers
Practice Green	Showers
Power Carts	Food
•**Pull Carts**	Clubhouse
•**Club Rental**	Outings
Soft Spikes	

Fees	Weekday	Weekend
Daily	$9	$11
Sr.	$5	
Hosp.Pers.	$6	$6
All others	$11	$11

Course Description: VA Hospital golf course is a good practice facility for beginners and seniors. It is wide open, flat and short; it doesn't get too busy. The ninth is the only water hole, golfers can take the opportunity to play two nine hole rounds. Motorized carts are not available.

Directions: Suffolk County, #58
LIE to Sunken Meadow Pkwy. (no last exit before tolls). Go West on 25A for 3 miles and left on Rinaldo Rd. Go straight to course in the VA complex.

Hole	1	2	3	4	5	6	7	8	9	Out	BLUE	Rating
BLUE												Slope
WHITE	245	205	240	422	340	370	145	240	140	2347		
Par	4	3	4	5	4	4	3	4	3	34	WHITE	Rating
Handicap	7	6	4	1	3	2	9	5	8			Slope
RED												
Par											RED	Rating
Handicap												Slope
Hole	10	11	12	13	14	15	16	17	18	In		Totals
BLUE											BLUE	
WHITE											WHITE	
Par											Par	
Handicap												
RED											RED	
Par											Par	
Handicap												

Manager: Ron Helkowski

WESTHAMPTON COUNTRY CLUB

Potunk Lane, Westhampton Beach, NY 11978   (516) 288-1110

Westhampton is an 18 hole private course open 7 days a week all year. Guests may play accompanied by a member. Tee time reservations are necessary on weekends. Pull carts are allowed after 3PM.

> - **Driving Range**   • **Lockers**
> - **Practice Green**   • **Showers**
> - **Power Carts**   • **Food**
> - **Pull Carts**   • **Clubhouse**
>   Club Rental   • **Outings**
> - **Caddies**   • **Soft Spikes**

Course Description: Westhampton CC is classic East End golf. The course is half parkland, half bayside, and flat. The greens are small, fast and contain subtle breaks. Water is in play on about half the holes and deep rough also provides challenge. The signature par 3 third has a saucer-like punch bowl green with numerous bunkers and fearsome rough surrounding it. This country club is one of the first 100 in the U.S.

Directions: Suffolk County, #60
LIE to Exit 70. Go south on Rte.111 to Rte.27 and turn left. Continue east to Exit 63-S (County Rd. 31). Take Rte.31 south about 4 miles to course on right.

Hole	1	2	3	4	5	6	7	8	9	Out	BLUE	Rating 72.7
BLUE	307	327	169	447	545	417	187	418	442	3259		Slope 132
WHITE	300	313	165	425	537	400	180	399	430	3149		
Par	4	4	3	4	5	4	3	4	4	35	WHITE	Rating 71.6
Handicap	11	13	17	1	3	7	15	9	5			Slope 130
RED	231	281	118	382	477	374	165	332	399	2759		
Par	4	4	3	4	5	4	3	4	5	36	RED	Rating 71.7
Handicap	13	11	18	1	5	3	15	9	7			Slope 126
Hole	10	11	12	13	14	15	16	17	18	In		Totals
BLUE	440	166	404	322	503	400	335	230	398	3198	BLUE	6457
WHITE	429	147	393	308	492	390	327	221	373	3080	WHITE	6229
Par	4	3	4	4	5	4	4	3	4	35	Par	70
Handicap	2	18	6	16	4	8	12	14	10			
RED	398	104	335	264	399	355	291	156	310	2612	RED	5371
Par	5	3	4	4	5	4	4	3	4	36	Par	72
Handicap	6	17	12	14	4	2	10	16	8			

Manager: Ray Daleo   **Pro:** Bobby Jenkins, PGA   **Supt:** Mike Rewinski
Architect: Seth Raynor 1922   **Estab:** 1890

WEST SAYVILLE COUNTRY CLUB

Montauk Highway, W. Sayville, NY 11796   **(516) 567-1704**

W. Sayville is one of 4 Suffolk County courses. It is open 7 days a week and closed in winter. Suffolk Cty. residents obtain a Green Key. Non-res must have a Tourist Access Key. Call 244-PARK (7275) for reservations up to 7 days in advance, non-res 3 days.

•**Driving Range**	**Lockers**
•**Practice Green**	•**Soft Spikes**
•**Power Carts**	•**Showers**
•**Pull Carts**	•**Food**
•**Club Rental**	•**Clubhouse**
	•**Outings**

Fees	Weekday	Weekend
Res	$19	$20
Tourist	$32	$40
Sr	$11	$20
Power carts	$25	

Course Description: The beautiful landmark clubhouse was built by Isaac Green in 1909 as a summer estate. It was purchased by the county from Florence Bourne in the 1960s. Wetland considerations were dealt with in the subsequent course construction. It is well maintained; the bunkers were recently redone and a new irrigation system has been installed. Many seniors play here and it is comfortably walkable. The signature par 3 8th requires a tee shot over water to a green surrounded by bunkers. Water affects play on holes 8, 11, 16 and 17. Beautiful views of the Bay along with the strong breezes, refreshing in summer, add to the ambience here.

Directions: Suffolk County, #59
LIE to Exit 57 and turn right onto Vet. Mem. Hwy. Go 4.5 mi. to Lakeland Ave & turn right. Go to end of the road and turn right (west) onto Montauk Hwy (Rte.27A). Club is about 1 mile ahead on left.

Hole	1	2	3	4	5	6	7	8	9	Out	BLUE	Rating 72.1
BLUE	515	178	365	402	505	405	395	195	426	3386		Slope 127
WHITE	485	143	317	372	475	367	370	165	398	3092		
Par	5	3	4	4	5	4	4	3	4	36	WHITE	Rating 69.5
Handicap	9	17	11	1	13	5	7	15	3			Slope 122
RED	430	118	297	342	425	333	340	135	358	2778		
Par	5	3	4	4	5	4	4	3	4	36	RED	Rating 70.1
Handicap	2	18	14	10	4	8	12	16	6			Slope 120

Hole	10	11	12	13	14	15	16	17	18	In		Totals
BLUE	385	502	195	401	500	403	392	175	376	3329	BLUE	6715
WHITE	355	472	170	372	473	363	367	123	343	3038	WHITE	6130
Par	4	5	3	4	5	4	4	3	4	36	Par	72
Handicap	10	12	16	2	14	4	6	18	8			
RED	300	417	140	307	413	333	313	93	293	2609	RED	5387
Par	4	5	3	4	5	4	4	3	4	36	Par	72
Handicap	13	1	15	7	3	5	9	17	11			

Manager/Pro: Fred Gipp, PGA   **Supt:** Paul Berner
Architect: William Mitchell 1969

HAMLET WIND WATCH GOLF CLUB

1715 Vanderbilt Motor Pkwy., Hauppauge, NY 11788   (516) 232-9850

Hamlet Wind Watch is open 7 days a week all year weather permitting, Members & Marriott guests may make advanced bookings & have reduced greens fees. Wind Watch has electric pull carts to rent for walkers.

•Driving Range	•Lockers
•Practice Green	•Showers
•Power Carts	•Food
•Electric Pull	•Clubhouse
•Club Rental	•Outings
	•Soft Spikes

Fees	Weekday	Weekend
Daily	$62	$72
Twi /9holes	$29	$39
Fees vary for off season		
Fees incl. cart		

Course Description: Wind Watch is a Florida style relatively flat course featuring small undulating greens bunkered with white sand. Water is in play on 10 holes in the form of man made lakes. Extensive renovations have resulted in a significant upgrade of this meticulously maintained bent grass layout. The signature 16th hole is a short par 4 with water on both sides necessitating a strong carry on the tee shot and great accuracy on the approach to the green. Wind Watch is the site of a John Jacobs Golf School.

Directions: Suffolk County, #61
Take the LIE to Exit #57. Make a left on Vanderbilt Motor Parkway. Course is 1 and 1/2 miles ahead on the left.

Hole	1	2	3	4	5	6	7	8	9	Out	BLUE	Rating 71.0
BLUE	353	550	349	396	495	186	435	190	406	2971		Slope 128
WHITE	348	512	337	380	478	179	424	169	391	2823		
Par	4	5	4	4	5	3	4	3	4	36	WHITE	Rating 69.7
Handicap	11	7	17	5	9	15	1	13	3			Slope 125
RED	338	413	282	331	410	144	356	142	312	2233		
Par	4	5	4	4	5	3	4	3	4	36	RED	Rating 68.6
Handicap	9	11	17	7	15	3	5	13	1			Slope 118
Hole	10	11	12	13	14	15	16	17	18	In		Totals
BLUE	340	342	155	399	245	556	338	395	382	3541	BLUE	6512
WHITE	324	306	150	387	222	545	329	379	362	3399	WHITE	6222
Par	4	4	3	4	3	5	4	4	4	35	Par	71
Handicap	16	14	18	10	8	2	4	12	6			
RED	288	257	122	313	140	453	206	326	313	2913	RED	5146
Par	4	4	3	4	3	5	4	4	4	35	Par	72
Handicap	8	12	18	6	14	2	16	10	4			

Manager/ Pro: Pat Dill, PGA   **Supt**: Frank Galasso
Architect: Joe Lee 1990   **Redesign**: Stephen Kay

The Game of a Lifetime

You don't stop playing because you grow old, you grow old because you stop playing.

(Mohansic)

WESTCHESTER
COUNTY

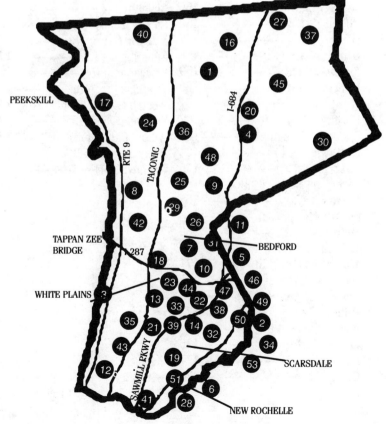

PEEKSKILL

RTE 9

TACONIC

I-684

TAPPAN ZEE
BRIDGE

I-287

BEDFORD

WHITE PLAINS

SAWMILL PKWY

SCARSDALE

NEW ROCHELLE

WESTCHESTER COUNTY

Public Courses appear in *bold italics*

ANGLEBROOK GOLF CLUB

100 Route 202, Lincolndale, NY 10540   **(914) 245-4921**

Anglebrook is a private 18 hole course with corporate memberships. It is open 6 days a week and closed 11/30-4/1. Guests play accompanied by a member. Tee times may be made up to 1 month in advance. Outings are limited to those member sponsored.

> •Driving Range   •Lockers
> •Practice Green   •Showers
> •Power Carts   •Food
> Pull Carts   •Clubhouse
> •Club Rental   •Outings
> Caddies   •Soft Spikes

Course Description: The 250 acres of a farm formerly owned by the Lincoln Hall School provide a magnificent natural setting for an environmentally friendly and safe 18 hole layout. The course is interesting and playable for all levels. From the two high points of the 6th and 15th holes there are beautiful views of the surrounding mountains. The clubhouse is centrally located in their midpoint. From some elevated tees, the contour of the entire hole can be seen. The fairways are more open than other Westchester courses with wildlife in abundance and wooden bridges over wetland areas to get to the greens. The irrigation system is high tech using recycled water.

Directions: Westchester County, #1
Take I-684N to Exit 4. Go left on Rte.139 to Rte.100N junction. Stay on 100/139 and bear left onto 139 again. Follow about 3 1/2 m to 202/139. Watch for club sign & entrance.

Hole	1	2	3	4	5	6	7	8	9	Out	BLUE	Rating 73.8
BLUE	454	521	427	602	183	305	397	195	384	3468		Slope 125
WHITE	425	498	399	582	166	290	365	173	376	3274		
Par	4	5	4	5	3	4	4	3	4	36	WHITE	Rating 71.6
Handicap	3	9	5	1	13	17	7	11	15			Slope 120
RED	318	365	358	392	91	231	207	90	270	2322		
Par	4	5	4	5	3	4	4	3	4	36	RED	Rating 67.2
Handicap	5	7	3	1	9	15	13	17	11			Slope 107

Hole	10	11	12	13	14	15	16	17	18	In		Totals
BLUE	514	431	412	193	430	335	507	202	455	3479	BLUE	6947
WHITE	464	413	388	161	409	318	484	141	414	3192	WHITE	6466
Par	5	4	4	3	4	4	5	3	4	36	Par	72
Handicap	18	4	8	16	6	14	10	12	2			
RED	382	288	327	102	353	125	388	98	321	2384	RED	4706
Par	5	4	4	3	4	3	5	3	4	35	Par	71
Handicap	8	4	12	10	6	14	16	18	2			

Manager: Shigehito Suzuki   **Pro:** John Kirchner, PGA   **Supt:** Lou Quick
Architect: Robert Trent Jones, Sr. 1997

APAWAMIS CLUB

Club Rd., Rye, NY 10580

(914) 967-2100

Apawamis is a private 18 hole course open 6 days a week all year, weather permitting. Guests play accompanied by a member. Tee times are necessary on weekends.

•Driving Range	•Lockers
•Practice Green	•Showers
•Power Carts	•Food
Pull Carts	•Clubhouse
•Club Rental	•Outings
•Caddies	•Soft Spikes

Course Description: Although this layout is not very long, it is difficult, narrow and tree lined. Apawamis has rugged terrain and small fast greens with considerable break. Ben Hogan has been quoted as saying this is the hardest short course he has ever played. Blind shots abound to elevated greens. Water is in play on a few holes. The signature hole is the par 4 4th, called "Eleanor's Teeth", named for the former first lady. The elevated ultimate target area is fronted by 13 bunkers that look like teeth and guard a most severe green. Apawamis has hosted the Met Amateur and the Westchester Classic.

Directions: Westchester County, #2
Take the Hutchinson River Pkwy to Exit 25(North St). Go uphill to light and turn left onto Polly Park Rd. Go 2 - 3 miles to Purchase St (Rte.120) and turn right. Go straight 1.7 miles to STOP at Highland Ave & club entrance on right.

Hole	1	2	3	4	5	6	7	8	9	Out	BLUE	Rating 72.1
BLUE	356	343	347	324	149	319	409	362	582	3191		Slope 131
WHITE	356	334	312	302	138	300	401	343	551	3037		
Par	4	4	4	4	3	4	4	4	5	36	WHITE	Rating 70.5
Handicap	9	7	11	5	17	13	1	15	3			Slope 128
RED	351	281	265	294	115	291	383	320	493	2793		
Par	4	4	4	4	3	4	4	4	5	36	RED	Rating 74.2
Handicap	5	13	11	7	17	9	3	15	1			Slope 133
Hole	10	11	12	13	14	15	16	17	18	In		Totals
BLUE	513	358	203	346	446	412	180	501	321	3280	BLUE	6471
WHITE	493	343	171	324	381	401	177	491	297	3078	WHITE	6115
Par	5	4	3	4	4	4	3	5	4	36	Par	72
Handicap	6	10	14	12	2	4	16	8	18			
RED	472	307	156	296	446	398	150	456	285	2966	RED	5759
Par	5	4	3	4	5	4	3	5	4	37	Par	73
Handicap	4	10	16	8	6	2	18	12	14			

Manager: Sam Nerses   **Pro:** Mike Summa, PGA   **Supt:** Bill Perlee
Architects: Willie Dunn & Maturin Ballou   **Estab:** 1890

ARDSLEY COUNTRY CLUB

N. Mountain Ave., Ardsley, NY 10503   **(914) 591-8403**

Ardsley is an 18 hole private course open six days a week and closed in January and February. Guests play accompanied by a member. Tee time reservations are necessary on weekends.

•Driving Range	•Lockers
•Practice Green	•Showers
•Power Carts	•Food
Pull Carts	•Clubhouse
•Club Rental	•Outings
•Caddies	•Soft Spikes

Course Description: Ardsley, situated 4 miles south of the Tappan Zee Bridge, is one of the most picturesque courses in the U. S with its spectacular panoramic views of the New Jersey Palisades and the Hudson River. The property has some flat sections, some elevated tees and small, well bunkered greens. Creeks cross the fairways and are along the sides. The signature par 4 first hole features a 135 ft. drop to the fairway and a pond in front of the green. Renovations were undertaken by Allister Mackenzie and later by Robert Trent Jones. The Women's US Open was held here in 1898.

Directions: Westchester County, #3
Take the Saw Mill River PkwyN to Dobbs Ferry/Ardsley Exit. Go left over bridge onto Ashford Ave. Turn right at light onto Washington Ave. Turn right onto Sherman and then left on Osceola. Make 1st right onto N. Mountain Drive to club at end of the road.

Hole	1	2	3	4	5	6	7	8	9	Out	BLUE	Rating 72.5
BLUE	381	248	403	536	508	411	338	157	442	3424		Slope 131
WHITE	304	228	357	522	490	397	335	139	430	3202		
Par	4	3	4	5	5	4	4	3	4	36	WHITE	Rating 70.8
Handicap	11	13	7	9	3	5	15	17	1			Slope 128
RED	285	210	280	459	481	317	332	121	410	2895		
Par	4	3	4	5	5	4	4	3	5	37	RED	Rating 73.5
Handicap	11	13	15	3	1	9	5	17	7			Slope 125
Hole	10	11	12	13	14	15	16	17	18	In		Totals
BLUE	356	466	383	170	387	329	427	162	482	3162	BLUE	6586
WHITE	350	444	373	163	358	318	399	138	473	3016	WHITE	6218
Par	4	5	4	3	4	4	4	3	5	36	Par	72
Handicap	10	8	12	14	4	18	2	16	6			
RED	310	372	337	145	337	304	389	121	443	2758	RED	5653
Par	4	4	4	3	4	4	4	3	5	35	Par	72
Handicap	10	2	12	16	8	14	4	18	6			

Manager: Cliff Cable   **Pro:** Jim Bender, PGA   **Supt:** George Pierpoint III
Architects: Willie Dunn 1895 Donald Ross **Redesign:** Robert Trent Jones

BEDFORD GOLF & TENNIS CLUB

 PRIVATE

Route 22, Bedford, NY 10506 **(914) 234-3325**

Bedford is an 18 hole private golf course open 6 days a week and closed from Nov 1 to April 1. Guests play accompanied by a member. Tee time reservations are not necessary.

- •Driving Range •Lockers
- •Practice Green •Showers
- •Power Carts •Food
- •Pull Carts •Clubhouse
- Club Rental Outings
- •Caddies •Soft Spikes

Course Description: Bedford Golf & Tennis Club is located in historic Bedford, the site of a Revolutionary War battle. The hilly and scenic course was redesigned by Emmet and Tull and has tight tree lined fairways. The small greens are fairly slow with water in play on several holes. The par 3 10th requires a tee shot over a pond to a well trapped green. Doglegs on 7 holes ,as well as the severe contour, give the course variety and difficulty.

Directions: Westchester County, #4
Take the Hutchinson Pkwy. to I-684N to Exit 4 (Mt. Kisco-Bedford, Rte.172) and turn right. At end of road, turn left (north) onto Rte.22. Go 1.8 miles to club on left.

Hole	1	2	3	4	5	6	7	8	9	Out	BLUE	Rating 71.4
BLUE	338	400	205	482	188	362	390	411	515	3291		Slope 134
WHITE	316	392	193	475	178	355	382	400	488	3179		
Par	4	4	3	5	3	4	4	4	5	36	WHITE	Rating 70.8
Handicap	17	3	7	13	15	11	1	5	9			Slope 133
RED	276	342	185	438	145	306	381	393	432	2898		
Par	4	4	3	5	3	4	5	4	5	37	RED	Rating 74.1
Handicap	17	3	7	11	15	13	9	1	5			Slope 130

Hole	10	11	12	13	14	15	16	17	18	In		Totals
BLUE	157	383	185	430	350	411	523	327	317	3083	BLUE	6374
WHITE	151	380	180	425	344	406	517	320	312	3035	WHITE	6214
Par	3	4	3	4	4	4	5	4	4	35	Par	71
Handicap	16	6	10	2	12	4	8	14	18			
RED	117	310	171	381	342	407	446	274	297	2745	RED	5643
Par	3	4	3	4	4	5	5	4	4	36	Par	73
Handicap	18	10	14	2	6	12	4	16	8			

Manager: Bill Burke   **Pro:** Tony Chateauvert, PGA   **Supt:** Robert Nielson
Architect: Devereux Emmet 1927 **Estab:** 1896

BLIND BROOK CLUB

PRIVATE

Anderson Hill Rd., Purchase, NY 10577   **(914) 939-1450**

Blind Brook is a private 18 hole course open 6 days a week from mid April to Nov. 1. Guests play accompanied by a member. Tee time reservations are not necessary.

> • **Driving Range**   • **Lockers**
> • **Practice Green**   • **Showers**
> • **Power Carts**   • **Food**
>   Pull Carts   • **Clubhouse**
>   Club Rental   • **Outings**
> • **Caddies**   • **Soft Spikes**

Course Description: Blind Brook property used to be a polo grounds. The course is fairly hilly and meticulously maintained. Some tees and greens are elevated. Several holes have water in play. The course is noted for wide gently contoured fairways and large greens that are sloping and difficult, some multi-tiered. This moderate length layout makes for an enjoyable walk with a caddie, challenging but not too strenuous. The USGA "Super Seniors" Championships have been played here.

Directions: Westchester County, #5
Take the Hutchinson River Pkwy to Exit 30 (King St). Go west on King St. (towards Armonk.) Go 1 mile and turn left onto Anderson Hill Rd. Club entrance on the left.

Hole	1	2	3	4	5	6	7	8	9	Out	BLUE	Rating 70.5
BLUE	478	405	187	383	276	525	159	418	418	3249		Slope 120
WHITE	475	382	177	377	258	516	154	415	410	3164		
Par	5	4	3	4	4	5	3	4	4	36	WHITE	Rating 69.7
Handicap	11	5	13	9	15	3	17	7	1			Slope 118
RED	435	347	165	371	238	456	137	377	372	2898		
Par	5	4	3	4	4	5	3	4	4	36	RED	Rating 67.1
Handicap	11	5	13	9	15	3	17	7	1			Slope
Hole	10	11	12	13	14	15	16	17	18	In		Totals
BLUE	214	419	230	502	529	152	330	364	396	3136	BLUE	6385
WHITE	202	416	223	486	526	121	326	358	392	3050	WHITE	6214
Par	3	4	3	5	5	3	4	4	4	35	Par	71
Handicap	16	4	14	8	2	18	12	10	6			
RED	184	376	193	456	467	121	325	328	357	2807	RED	5705
Par	3	4	3	5	5	3	4	4	4	35	Par	71
Handicap	16	4	14	8	2	18	12	10	6			

Manager: John Bladt   **Supt:** Chubby Autorino
Architects: Charles Blair Macdonald & Seth Raynor 1917

BONNIE BRIAR COUNTRY CLUB

808 Weaver St., Larchmont, NY 10538   **(914) 834-1627**

Bonnie Briar is an 18 hole private golf course open six days a week all year weather permitting. Guests play accompanied by a member. Reservations for tee times are necessary on weekends.

- •Driving Range
- •Practice Green
- •Power Carts
- Pull Carts
- •Club Rental
- •Caddies
- •Lockers
- •Showers
- •Food
- •Clubhouse
- •Outings
- •Soft Spikes

Course Description: Bonnie Briar, a short, flat, "old type" Westchester golf course, is distinguished by rock outcroppings throughout the layout. It features heavily tree-lined tight fairways and relatively small greens, a few with severe breaks. The signature par 4 13th is a difficult driving hole with water in front of the green causing many golfers to lay up. Branches of the Sheldrake River affect play on 7 holes. Qualifying rounds for the US Amateur and for the Westchester Classic have been held here. The scorecard does not give yardages from the middle tees.

Directions: Westchester County, #6
Take the Hutchinson Pkwy North to Weaver St. Exit 21(Rte.125). Turn left on Weaver Street. Club is 1 mile ahead on the left.

Hole	1	2	3	4	5	6	7	8	9	Out	BLUE	Rating 70.3
BLUE	463	341	168	334	156	403	310	373	482	3030		Slope 124
WHITE												
Par	4	4	3	4	3	4	4	4	5	35	WHITE	Rating 69.5
Handicap	4	12	18	10	16	2	14	8	6			Slope 123
RED	437	320	150	313	123	374	290	349	455	2811		
Par	5	4	3	4	3	4	4	4	5	36	RED	Rating 74.1
Handicap	6	10	16	14	18	2	12	8	4			Slope 132
Hole	10	11	12	13	14	15	16	17	18	In		Totals
BLUE	202	429	329	422	318	132	525	480	304	3141	BLUE	6171
WHITE											WHITE	6004
Par	3	4	4	4	4	3	5	5	4	36	Par	71
Handicap	11	3	15	1	9	17	5	7	13			
RED	186	416	307	404	300	123	471	421	285	2913	RED	5724
Par	3	5	4	5	4	3	5	5	4	38	Par	74
Handicap	15	9	11	3	7	17	1	5	13			

Manager: Neal Rubin   **Pro:** Sharon Nolletti, PGA   **Supt:** Mike Medonis
Architect: Devereux Emmet 1921

BRAE BURN COUNTRY CLUB

Brae Burn Drive, Purchase, NY 10577   **(914) 328-8478**

Brae Burn CC is a private 18 hole course open 6 days a week from Mar. 1 to Dec. 15. Guests may play accompanied by a member. Tee time reservations are required on weekends.

•**Driving Range**	•**Lockers**
•**Practice Green**	•**Showers**
•**Power Carts**	•**Food**
Pull Carts	•**Clubhouse**
•**Club Rental**	•**Outings**
•**Caddies**	•**Soft Spikes**

Course Description: Brae Burn is characterized by large undulating greens, elevated tees and beautiful scenic views. The trees are maturing along the hilly terrain. Brooks and ponds affect play on four holes. At the signature downhill par 5 15th there is a steep drop in the drive area, out of bounds on the left and a tall tree in front of the elevated tee on the right. Quite a picturesque effect is reflected in the two ponds on either side of the green. The course is meticulously maintained; a new irrigation system is part of the recent upgrade.

Directions: Westchester County, #7
Hutchinson River Pkwy. to Exit #27 (Purchase St.-Rte.120). Turn left off the ramp for 2.3 miles and another left on Barnes Lane then left on Brae Burn Lane to club on left.

Hole	1	2	3	4	5	6	7	8	9	Out	BLUE	Rating 72.2
BLUE	412	510	375	322	145	377	405	190	500	3236		Slope 130
WHITE	399	500	365	314	127	373	390	156	486	3110		
Par	4	5	4	4	3	4	4	3	5	36	WHITE	Rating 71.0
Handicap	3	7	11	15	17	5	1	13	9			Slope 128
RED	379	440	349	298	112	317	379	126	436	2836		
Par	4	5	4	4	3	4	4	3	5	36	RED	Rating 74.6
Handicap	5	3	11	9	17	13	1	15	7			Slope 134
Hole	10	11	12	13	14	15	16	17	18	In		Totals
BLUE	369	190	432	344	409	493	150	410	485	3282	BLUE	6518
WHITE	357	168	417	335	390	467	140	400	471	3145	WHITE	6255
Par	4	3	4	4	4	5	3	4	5	36	Par	72
Handicap	12	16	4	14	6	8	18	2	10			
RED	331	151	404	322	377	460	125	375	427	2972	RED	5808
Par	4	3	5	4	4	5	3	5	5	38	Par	74
Handicap	10	18	14	8	4	2	16	6	12			

Manager: Mike Galluzzo   **Pro:** Kelley Moser, PGA   **Supt:** Dennis Flynn
Architect: Frank Duane, 1965

BRIAR HALL COUNTRY CLUB

 PRIVATE

Pine Rd., Briarcliff Manor, NY 10510   **(914) 941-0965**

Briar Hall is an 18 hole course open 6 days a week from April 4 to November 30. Guests play accompanied by a member. Reservations for tee times are necessary on weekends.

- •**Driving Range** •**Lockers**
- •**Practice Green** •**Showers**
- •**Power Carts** •**Food**
- Pull Carts •**Clubhouse**
- •**Club Rental** •**Outings**
- •**Caddies** •**Soft Spikes**

Course Description: Briar Hall, nestled in the woods of upper Westchester, features small, undulating well bunkered greens and rolling hills. On much of the layout, the golfer cannot see the next hole. The signature par 3 17th requires a shot over a pond, one of three holes where water is in play. After its construction in the 1920s, the course has had multiple enhancements over the ensuing years. It actually became known as Briar Hall in 1948. A number of well known sports and entertainment figures are members here.

Directions: Westchester County, #8
Take Taconic Parkway North to Pleasantville Rd. Exit. Travel on Pleasantville to the end & turn left. Then take an immediate right at the fork up the hill onto Elm Rd. Take the first right onto Pine Rd. Continue uphill through golf course to entrance on right.

Hole	1	2	3	4	5	6	7	8	9	Out	BLUE	Rating 71.0
BLUE	311	276	356	223	444	399	469	153	353	2984		Slope 129
WHITE	302	263	342	210	430	377	463	147	343	2877		
Par	4	4	4	3	4	4	5	3	4	35	WHITE	Rating 70.1
Handicap	15	13	9	11	1	5	3	17	7			Slope 127
RED	294	249	306	181	367	310	450	139	327	2623		
Par	4	4	4	3	4	4	5	3	5	36	RED	Rating 72.0
Handicap	13	11	7	15	5	9	1	17	3			Slope 122
Hole	10	11	12	13	14	15	16	17	18	In		Totals
BLUE	422	542	497	355	407	178	357	193	378	3329	BLUE	6313
WHITE	412	530	486	341	397	166	347	187	361	3227	WHITE	6104
Par	4	4	5	4	4	3	4	3	4	36	Par	71
Handicap	8	2	6	12	4	18	14	16	10			
RED	369	478	441	309	380	140	332	127	389	2915	RED	5538
	4	5	5	4	5	3	4	3	5	38	Par	74
Handicap	10	2	4	14	8	18	12	16	6			

Manager: Carolyn Kepcher   **Pro:** Frank Graniero, PGA   **Supt:** Daniel Breton
Architect: Devereux Emmet 1922   **Estab:** 1948

CANYON CLUB

568 Bedford Rd., Armonk, NY 10504 — (914) 273-9300

Canyon Club is an 18 hole private course open 6 days a week and closed from Dec. 15 to March 15th. Guests play accompanied by a member. Reservations for tee times are necessary on weekends.

• Driving Range	• Lockers
• Practice Green	• Showers
• Power Carts	• Food
Pull Carts	• Clubhouse
• Club Rental	• Outings
Caddies	Soft Spikes

Course Description: Canyon Club was originally called Bel Air CC, then later Greenwoods. The hilly terrain produces many uneven lies and great views. The greens are fairly generous in size and of comfortable speed. The par 3s are very difficult from the blue tees. The 8th requires a tee shot over water. Water can also be found on the 3rd, 15th and 17th. The course was redesigned by Doug Hansen in 1994. Members at Canyon come from NYC as well as from the surrounding Westchester towns.

Directions: Westchester County, #9
Take Hutchinson River Pkwy and stay in left lane onto I-684N. Go to Exit 3North. Then proceed onto Rte.22(Bedford Rd.) Go approx. 2 & 1/2 miles to club on left.

Hole	1	2	3	4	5	6	7	8	9	Out	BLUE	Rating 71.5
BLUE	391	363	522	428	441	193	393	216	441	3388		Slope 131
WHITE	369	332	503	391	408	178	376	182	346	3085		
Par	4	4	5	4	4	3	4	3	4	35	WHITE	Rating 69.4
Handicap	11	13	9	5	1	17	3	15	7			Slope 126
RED	314	262	400	328	344	128	323	165	309	2573		
Par	4	4	5	4	4	3	4	3	4	35	RED	Rating 69.7
Handicap	11	17	13	7	1	15	3	5	9			Slope 122

Hole	10	11	12	13	14	15	16	17	18	In		Totals
BLUE	210	350	172	352	332	400	175	500	477	2968	BLUE	6356
WHITE	190	338	161	330	293	360	155	457	460	2744	WHITE	5829
Par	3	4	3	4	4	4	3	5	5	35	Par	70
Handicap	14	10	18	8	12	4	16	2	6			
RED	160	273	143	301	250	327	122	410	383	2369	RED	4942
Par	3	4	3	4	4	4	3	5	5	35	Par	70
Handicap	14	10	16	8	12	6	18	2	4			

Manager: Martin Badinelli, Sr.   **Pro:** Doug Hansen, PGA   **Supt:** Paul Gonzalez
Architect: Al Zikorus 1963

CENTURY COUNTRY CLUB

Anderson Hill Road, Purchase NY 10577   (914) 761-0400

Century CC is an 18 hole course open 6 days a week from April 1 to November 1. Guests may play accompanied by a member. Tee time reservations are not necessary.

```
•Driving Range   •Lockers
•Practice Green  •Showers
•Power Carts     •Food
 Pull Carts      •Clubhouse
•Club Rental     •Outings
•Caddies          Soft Spikes
```

Course Description: Century is well known for the condition of its greens; they could be ranked the best in the Met area. Originally built in a links style, a new architect has been hired to restore its layout. The course is tight due to the growth of trees along the fairways. Some consider the par 4 3rd the signature hole; it is tight with a severe back to front green and steep faced bunkers. The first is a long par 4, a very difficult start to a round. The 13th is reminiscent of the 12th at Augusta, picturesque with water in front and bunkers in back of the green. Ben Hogan was the assistant pro here in the late 30s and head pro in 1940.

Directions: Westchester County, #10
Hutchinson Pkwy. North to Exit#27 (Purchase St., Rte.120). Turn left , then go 1 mile on Purchase St., turn left onto Anderson Hill Rd. (at light) and club is 1/2 mile on right.

Hole	1	2	3	4	5	6	7	8	9	Out	BLUE	Rating 73.0
BLUE	444	378	359	173	451	430	165	490	406	3296		Slope 130
WHITE	433	368	343	167	435	422	157	479	396	3200		
Par	4	4	4	3	4	4	3	5	4	35	WHITE	Rating 71.6
Handicap	3	13	9	15	1	5	17	11	7			Slope 127
GOLD	417	353	317	155	407	403	131	446	366	2995		
Par	4	4	4	3	4	4	3	5	4	35	GOLD	Rating 69.2
Handicap	3	13	9	15	1	5	17	11	7			Slope 120
Hole	10	11	12	13	14	15	16	17	18	In		Totals
BLUE	414	563	357	152	448	510	450	234	385	3513	BLUE	6809
WHITE	387	539	346	127	405	493	438	221	366	3322	WHITE	6522
Par	4	5	4	3	4	5	4	3	4	36	Par	71
Handicap	10	6	12	18	4	14	2	16	8			
GOLD	335	468	330	112	391	462	432	198	355	3083	GOLD	6078
Par	4	5	4	3	4	5	4	3	4	36	Par	71
Handicap	10	6	12	18	4	14	2	16	8			

Manager: Burt Ward   **Pro:** Nelson Long, Jr., PGA   **Supt:** J.C. Fulwider
Architects: C.H. Allison, H.S. Colt 1920's   **Estab.** 1898

DORAL GOLF CLUB

Anderson Hill Rd., Rye Brook, NY 10573   (914) 939-2479

The Doral Golf Club of Westchester is a 9 hole regulation length course open 7 days a week to Doral Hotel guests and to private memberships. Hotel guests can reserve tee times in advance when they reserve a room. Members call Tuesday for the weekend.

•Driving Range	•Lockers
•Practice Green	•Showers
•Power Carts	•Food
Pull Carts	•Clubhouse
•Club Rental	•Outings

Fees	Weekday	Weekend
Hotel Guest	$54/9	$58/9
18 holes	$86	$96
Fee includes cart		

Course Description: The Doral at Arrowwood is a challenging 9 hole layout, narrow with large, firm greens of moderate speed. There are many mounds and moguls in the rough that add challenge and demand accuracy at this breezy course. Water is in play on 7 of the holes. The 8th hole is a par 5 that requires the golfer to bear left on the tee shot, lay up on the 2nd, and hit the approach over water to a green with traps on the left and water on the right. Golf is an amenity of the Hotel Conference Center. Overlooking the 9th hole outside of the Pro Shop is Mulligans, the longest outdoor bar & grill in Westchester.

Directions: Westchester County, #11
Take the Hutchinson Pkwy. to Exit 30 (King St). Go west on King towards Armonk for about 1 mile. Turn left onto Anderson Hill Rd. Entrance on right.

Hole	1	2	3	4	5	6	7	8	9	Out	BLUE	Rating 71.6
BLUE	377	221	422	145	503	345	180	450	373	3016		Slope 136
WHITE	352	195	391	138	481	313	160	410	336	2731		
Par	4	3	4	3	5	4	3	5	4	35	WHITE	Rating 68
Handicap	11	13	1	17	5	9	15	3	7			Slope 128
RED	275	125	304	128	425	268	150	395	283	2353		
Par	4	3	4	3	5	4	3	5	4	35	RED	Rating 68.1
Handicap	11	13	1	17	5	9	15	3	7			Slope 122

Hole	10	11	12	13	14	15	16	17	18	In		Totals
BLUE											BLUE	6032
WHITE											WHITE	5462
Par											Par	70
Handicap												
RED											RED	4706
Par											Par	70
Handicap												

Manager: Ed Burns   **Pro:** Chris Caulfield, PGA   **Supt:** Dominick Italiano
Architect: Robert Von Hagge 1992

DUNWOODIE GOLF COURSE

PUBLIC

Wasylenko Lane, Yonkers, NY 10701   **(914) 968-2771**

Dunwoodie is an 18 hole County course open 7 days a week from Apr. 1st to Dec. 15th. County residents with a park pass may reserve up to 7 days in advance, non- res. up to 4 days. For automated tee times, call (914) 593-4653.

•Driving Range	•Lockers
•Practice Green	•Showers
•Power Carts	•Food
•Pull Carts	•Clubhouse
•Club Rental	•Outings

Fees	Weekday	Weekend
Daily w/pass	$14	$17
Sr/Twi "	$9	
Non res.	$37	$42
Power carts	$22	

Course Description: Dunwoodie is a relatively short course having a rather tight wooded front nine needing very accurate shot making skills. The back nine is wider, flatter and more forgiving. The course has no water in play but lots of woods and out of bounds for errant shots. The greens are well maintained. Dunwoodie has one par 3 on the front and four on the back. The signature par 4 fourth is an uphill hole with a narrow landing area and a large bunker in front of the green. The scenic 15th is a long, tough par 4 offering a great view of Manhattan and requiring an adept approach shot to a target green.

Directions: Westchester County, #12
From Saw Mill River Parkway take Exit 5 (Yonkers Ave.) At end of exit, turn left and then make an immediate left onto Wasylenko Lane to course.

Hole	1	2	3	4	5	6	7	8	9	Out	BLUE	
BLUE												
WHITE	275	339	369	392	332	504	175	389	239	3014		
Par	4	4	4	4	4	5	3	4	4	36	WHITE	Rating 68.3
Handicap	13	9	7	1	5	11	17	3	15			Slope 117
RED	201	312	277	288	302	430	159	328	198	2495		
Par	4	4	4	4	4	5	3	5	4	37	RED	Rating 71.5
Handicap												Slope 121
Hole	10	11	12	13	14	15	16	17	18	In		Totals
BLUE											BLUE	
WHITE	176	494	135	325	173	407	516	410	165	2801	WHITE	5815
Par	3	5	3	4	3	4	5	4	3	34	Par	70
Handicap	14	8	16	6	12	4	10	2	18			
RED	121	339	103	203	119	324	399	300	108	2016	RED	4511
Par	3	5	3	4	3	5	5	4	3	35	Par	72
Handicap												

Manager: Gary Metz   **Pro:** Eric & Paul Kellerman, PGA   **Supt:** Doug Hall
Built: 1905

ELMWOOD COUNTRY CLUB

850 Dobbs Ferry Rd., White Plains, NY 10607   **(914) 592-6600**

Elmwood is an 18 hole private course open 6 days a week and closed in February. Guests play accompanied by a member. Tee time reservations must be made in advance.

- **Driving Range**
- **Practice Green**
- **Power Carts**
- Pull Carts
- **Club Rental**
- **Caddies**
- **Lockers**
- **Showers**
- **Food**
- **Clubhouse**
- **Outings**
- **Soft Spikes**

Course Description: Elmwood has recently been redesigned by Ken Dye. Many of the bunkers have been restored and the 9th green was rebuilt. The course maintains the original Tillinghast style with magnificent tree lined, gently rolling fairways, small greens and those deep bunkers. There is water in play on one hole; the course has excellent drainage. The clubhouse recently installed new wood panelled lockers. The fortunate Elmwood members also have a Fitness Center for their use. PGA Sectional and Senior Tournaments have been held here.

Directions: Westchester County, #13
From GWBridge or NYC, take Henry Hudson Pkwy to Saw Mill Pkwy. Exit at Ashford Ave., Dobbs Ferry. Turn right off exit, then left at light onto Saw Mill River Rd. Go 1.5 miles & turn right onto Rte.100B. Proceed about 1 mile to club on left.

Hole	1	2	3	4	5	6	7	8	9	Out	BLUE	Rating 71.8
BLUE	388	130	415	377	195	345	425	430	493	3198		Slope 129
WHITE	378	122	393	357	168	332	415	417	475	3057		
Par	4	3	4	4	3	4	4	4	5	35	WHITE	Rating 70.5
Handicap	11	17	7	5	15	13	1	3	9			Slope 126
RED	372	103	384	343	153	320	405	338	405	2823		
Par	4	3	4	4	3	4	5	4	5	36	RED	Rating 73.3
Handicap	7	17	9	1	15	13	5	11	3			Slope 122
Hole	10	11	12	13	14	15	16	17	18	In		Totals
BLUE	415	385	410	188	480	425	155	330	501	3289	BLUE	6487
WHITE	400	373	383	175	467	415	147	303	493	3156	WHITE	6213
Par	4	4	4	3	5	4	3	4	5	36	Par	71
Handicap	6	12	4	16	10	2	18	14	8			
RED	370	360	376	164	447	401	143	289	397	2947	RED	5770
Par	4	4	4	3	5	5	3	4	5	37	Par	73
Handicap	8	12	2	16	6	10	18	14	4			

Manager: Peter Maguire   **Pro:** David Bakyta, PGA   **Supt:** Scott Tretera
Architect: A. W. Tillinghast 1924

FENWAY GOLF CLUB

Old Mamaroneck Rd., Scarsdale, NY 10583   **(914) 723-1095**

Fenway is an 18 hole private course open 6 days a week from Apr. 1 - Oct. 31. Members may play in the winter months, weather permitting. Guests play accompanied by a member. Tee time reservations are necessary on weekends.

•Driving Range	•Lockers
•Practice Green	•Showers
•Power Carts	•Food
Pull Carts	•Clubhouse
•Club Rental	•Outings
•Caddies	•Soft Spikes

Course Description: Fenway is considered sneaky long or "the little green monster." A good test of golf, an excellent short game is needed here. The emphasis is on the approach shot. The small greens are very undulating, slick and well bunkered. The course abounds with scenic views. The 5th is a very long par 4, #1 handicap for the men. Bunkers catch errant drives and plague the golfer at the green as well. The clubhouse has recently been redone.

Directions: Westchester County, #14
Take the Hutchinson Pkwy to Exit 23 (Mamaroneck Ave.) Go 1.5 miles to light at Ridgeway Ave and turn left. Go 1 mile and turn left onto Old Mamaroneck Rd. Club is about 500 yards ahead on right.

Hole	1	2	3	4	5	6	7	8	9	Out	BLUE	Rating 72.0
BLUE	263	381	493	130	446	217	381	341	388	3040		Slope 128
WHITE	257	374	486	123	439	187	358	277	319	2820		
Par	4	4	5	3	4	3	4	4	4	35	WHITE	Rating 70.9
Handicap	15	9	3	17	1	11	7	13	5			Slope 125
RED	250	367	479	115	431	180	354	273	313	2762		
Par	4	4	5	3	5	3	4	4	4	36	RED	Rating 74.3
Handicap	15	5	1	17	3	13	9	11	7			Slope 130
Hole	10	11	12	13	14	15	16	17	18	In		Totals
BLUE	442	170	445	397	370	290	419	166	509	3208	BLUE	6248
WHITE	418	154	383	336	362	276	384	114	486	2913	WHITE	5733
Par	4	3	4	4	4	4	4	3	5	35	Par	70
Handicap	2	16	4	6	12	14	10	18	8			
RED	414	147	422	331	353	273	378	111	483	2912	RED	5674
Par	5	3	5	4	4	4	4	3	5	37	Par	73
Handicap	2	16	6	10	12	14	8	18	4			

Manager: Steve Arias   **Pro:** Jeff Fox, PGA   **Supt:** Scott Stark
Architect: A.W. Tillinghast 1922

HAMPSHIRE COUNTRY CLUB

Cove Rd., Mamaroneck, NY 10543 **(914) 698-4610**

Hampshire Country Club is an 18 hole private course open 6 days a week and all year weather permitting. Guests play accompanied by a member. Reservations for tee times are necessary on weekends.

•**Driving Range**	•**Lockers**
•**Practice Green**	•**Showers**
•**Power Carts**	•**Food**
Pull Carts	•**Clubhouse**
Club Rental	•**Outings**
•**Caddies**	•**Soft Spikes**

Course Description: Hampshire CC is a narrow, relatively flat golf course in excellent condition. The greens are small and of average speed. As the course is 8 ft. below sea level, the L.I. Sound causes it to flood after heavy rains. Creeks, with stone embankments, run throughout the layout and are a factor in play. Two par 3s are over 210 yds from the men's tee and are quite lengthy for women as well. The signature par 4 12th is a dogleg right that plays longer than the yardage indicates. The course demands pinpoint driving. A qualifying round for the Buick Classic was held here.

Directions: Westchester County, #15
From Hutchinson Pkwy.N Exit 21 (Weaver St.) make left onto Weaver. After crossing Rte.1 (Boston Post Rd.) bear left around school. Then bear left at Stop sign onto Hommocks Rd. with golf course on left. Proceed 1/2 mile to clubhouse.

Hole	1	2	3	4	5	6	7	8	9	Out	BLUE	
BLUE												
WHITE	462	145	372	476	361	357	230	316	216	2935		
Par	5	3	4	5	4	4	3	4	3	35	WHITE	Rating 70.1
Handicap	4	18	8	2	6	10	14	12	16			Slope 128
RED	379	135	350	403	321	320	192	290	170	2560		
Par	5	3	4	5	4	4	3	4	3	35	RED	Rating 73.9
Handicap	4	18	10	2	6	8	16	12	14			Slope 132

Hole	10	11	12	13	14	15	16	17	18	In		Totals
BLUE											BLUE	
WHITE	333	191	435	338	395	353	518	401	364	3328	WHITE	6263
Par	4	3	4	4	4	4	5	4	4	36	Par	71
Handicap	13	17	1	15	7	9	5	3	11			
RED	323	184	321	326	363	265	482	324	340	2928	RED	5488
Par	4	3	4	4	5	4	5	4	4	37	Par	72
Handicap	7	17	13	5	11	15	1	3	9			

Manager: Charles Torrance **Pro:** Phil Rusnack, PGA **Supt:** Will Heintz
Architects: Devereux Emmet & Alfred Tull 1944

HERITAGE HILLS COUNTRY CLUB | PRIVATE

1000 West Hill Dr., Somers, NY 10589   (914) 276-2169

West Hill at private Heritage Hills is 18 holes, East Hill is a 9 hole course. They are open 6 days a week and closed from 12/15-3/1. Guests play accompanied by a member. Tee time reservations are up to a week in advance. Phone # at East Hill is 276-2828

- •Driving Range
- •Practice Green
- •Power Carts
- •Pull Carts
- •Club Rental
- Caddies
- •Lockers
- •Showers
- •Food
- •Clubhouse
- •Outings
- •Soft Spikes

Course Description: The 18 hole West course is short, tight, very hilly and uneven lies abound. The narrow fairways are either tree or condo lined. There are many elevated tees and ffairly fast greens. The signature par 3 #3 requires a shot over a pond to a crown shaped green with a swamp on the right and condos on the left. Water is in play on 8 holes. The 9 hole course was built in 1972 and is a challenging golf experience. The signature is the par 3 9th featuring an elevated tee with a severe drop to the green, a scenic view for a finishing hole. The scorecard below is for West Hill.

Directions: Westchester County, #16
I-684North to Exit 7. Take Rte.116W to end and make left on Rte.202West. Go about 1 mile. Main entrance on right. Follow signs to golf course.

Hole	1	2	3	4	5	6	7	8	9	Out	BLUE	Rating 71.0
BLUE	365	530	200	373	563	311	296	177	379	3194		Slope 126
WHITE	356	522	188	358	553	291	286	166	370	3090		
Par	4	5	3	4	5	4	4	3	4	36	WHITE	Rating 69.9
Handicap	17	3	9	7	1	15	13	11	5			Slope 124
RED	329	435	139	251	479	242	243	117	297	2532		
Par	4	5	3	4	5	4	4	3	4	36	RED	Rating 69.2
Handicap	11	3	13	15	1	7	9	17	5			Slope 118
Hole	10	11	12	13	14	15	16	17	18	In		Totals
BLUE	287	472	389	154	351	501	425	189	322	3090	BLUE	6284
WHITE	272	460	375	139	337	486	413	167	311	2960	WHITE	6050
Par	4	5	4	3	4	5	4	3	4	36	Par	72
Handicap	14	6	10	16	8	4	2	18	12			
RED	225	274	366	126	279	441	332	140	257	2440	RED	4972
Par	4	4	4	3	4	5	4	3	4	35	Par	71
Handicap	18	10	8	14	6	2	4	16	12			

Manager: Wes LaBay   **Pro:** Joe Cipriano, PGA   **Supt:** Todd Polidor
Architect: Geoffrey Cornish 1987 (West Hill)

HUDSON NATIONAL GOLF CLUB

227 Prickly Pear Hill Rd., Croton-on-Hudson, NY10520   **(914) 271-7600**

Hudson National is an 18 hole private golf course open 6 days a week and closed Dec 1 to March 15. Guests play accompanied by a member. Reservations for tee times are not necessary.

•**Driving Range**	•**Lockers**
•**Practice Green**	•**Showers**
•**Power Carts**	•**Food**
Pull Carts	•**Clubhouse**
•**Club Rental**	•**Outings**
•**Caddies**	•**Soft Spikes**

Course Description: Hudson National is a recently opened course on land that is the highest point in Croton, overlooking the Hudson River. At one time, the property was the 9 hole Hessian Hills CC built in the 1920s. The clubhouse, a stone mansion, dates from 1911 and is being renovated. The course features wooded fairways, hilly, uneven lies and intricate bunkers. The splendid terrain contains specimen trees, some brooks and 2 tiered greens. From the 16th hole, Manhattan may be seen in the distance and the Bear Mountain Bridge is visible from the elevated 5th tee. This exquisite and impressive course is a welcome addition to Upper Westchester.

Directions: Westchester County, #17
Take Taconic Pkwy North to Route 9A/Rte 100 Exit. Take Rte.9A about 6 miles to Rte. 9North. Exit at Senesqua Rd. Turn left on North Riverside and go 1 mile to Arrowcrest Rd. Turn right and proceed to clubhouse.

Hole	1	2	3	4	5	6	7	8	9	Out	BLUE	Rating 72.8
BLUE	460	163	421	387	421	570	371	249	522	3564		Slope 131
WHITE	445	163	407	382	388	559	362	165	500	3371		
Par	4	3	4	4	4	5	4	3	5	36	WHITE	Rating 70.0
Handicap	3	15	5	7	13	1	11	17	9			Slope 125
RED	373	97	378	259	366	393	245	118	408	2637		
Par											RED	Rating 75.2
Handicap												Slope 131
Hole	10	11	12	13	14	15	16	17	18	In		Totals
BLUE	395	175	474	187	534	434	249	328	465	3241	BLUE	6805
WHITE	369	142	504	178	524	403	222	320	434	3371	WHITE	6467
Par	4	3	5	3	5	4	3	4	4	36	Par	71
Handicap	12	18	10	16	6	2	4	14	8			
RED	318	88	448	126	454	335	170	256	335	2530	RED	5167
Par											Par	71
Handicap												

Manager: Peter Stanley   **Pro:** Kent Cayce, PGA   **Supt:** Gregg Stanley
Architect: Tom Fazio 1996

KNOLLWOOD COUNTRY CLUB

200 Knollwood Rd., Elmsford, NY 10523 **(914) 592-6182**

Knollwood is a private 19 hole course open 6 days a week all year, weather permitting. Guests play accompanied by a member. Reservations for tee times are necessary on weekends.

- •Driving Range
- •Practice Green
- •Power Carts
- Pull Carts
- Club Rental
- •Caddies
- •Lockers
- •Showers
- •Food
- •Clubhouse
- •Outings
- •Soft Spikes

Course Description: Knollwood is a typical Westchester course, narrow and tree lined with small, fast and undulating greens. The signature par 4 18th requires a long uphill approach shot over water to the green. What is unique here is the actual 19th hole, a par 3 nicknamed the "Bye". It is played for fun downhill with water and bunkers in play. The ball can land on the road or the parking lot and the local rule is play it as it lies. Bobby Jones played here all the time and thought this special hole was a great idea. The course has recently been redesigned by Stephen Kay. On the scorecard, the back tees are gold and the men's regulation tees are blue.

Directions: Westchester County, #18
Take Rte287(Cross Westchester Xpressway) to Exit 4. Go North on Rte.100A. Course is 2nd left, 300 yards from the Exit.

Hole	1	2	3	4	5	6	7	8	9	Out	BLUE	Rating 71.7
BLUE	373	394	128	401	537	437	382	196	511	3359		Slope 132
WHITE	365	390	117	401	537	420	373	196	507	3306		
Par	4	4	3	4	5	4	4	3	5	36	WHITE	Rating 71.2
Handicap	13	5	18	7	3	1	9	11	15			Slope 131
RED	293	356	107	345	444	403	333	165	432	2878		
Par	4	4	3	4	5	5	4	3	5	37	RED	Rating 74.9
Handicap	13	3	17	7	1	5	11	15	9			Slope 131

Hole	10	11	12	13	14	15	16	17	18	In		Totals
BLUE	386	215	333	364	289	394	191	541	444	3157	BLUE	6516
WHITE	373	215	330	348	289	391	184	537	437	3104	WHITE	6410
Par	4	3	4	4	4	4	3	5	4	35	Par	71
Handicap	8	16	10	12	17	4	14	5	2			
RED	353	199	307	304	266	333	158	488	428	2836	RED	5714
Par	4	3	4	4	4	4	3	5	5	36	Par	73
Handicap	4	16	10	12	14	8	18	2	6			

Manager: Mike Lopez **Pro:** Bob Miller, Jr., PGA **Supt:** Tim Moore
Architects: Charles Banks, Seth Raynor, Lawrence Van Etten **Estab:** 1894

LAKE ISLE COUNTRY CLUB

White Plains Road, Eastchester, NY 10707   (914) 337-9645

Lake Isle is an 18 hole course owned by the town of Eastchester. Open to the public 6 days a week, it is closed in December. Only permit holders may make tee times in advance. Tues. for Fri. etc. For reservations, call (914) 961-1905.

Driving Range	Lockers
•**Practice Green**	Showers
•**Power Carts**	•**Food**
•**Pull Carts**	•**Clubhouse**
Club Rental	•**Outings**

Fees	**Weekday**	**Weekend**
Non.Res.	$30	$40
Permit holders	Reduced Rates	

Course Description: Originally private as the Mount Vernon Country Club and later Vernon Hills, the course was bought in 1980 by the Town of Eastchester. It is one of the few golf courses in Westchester that is neither private nor county owned. It is relatively short, picturesque and not too hilly.

Directions: Westchester County, #19
Take the Hutchinson Pkwy to Exit 17. Turn left off ramp onto North Ave. Bear left at 1st light onto Mill Rd. Go 1/2 mile to light & turn right onto California Rd. Go 1 mile and turn right at light onto White Plains Rd. Club is ahead on right.

Hole	1	2	3	4	5	6	7	8	9	Out	BLUE	Rating 69.9
BLUE	300	315	153	425	400	449	150	482	230	2904		Slope 120
WHITE	290	305	133	417	380	425	135	470	220	2775		
Par	4	4	3	4	4	4	3	5	3	34	WHITE	Rating 67.9
Handicap	16	12	18	4	8	2	14	6	10			Slope 118
RED	280	296	126	412	360	360	118	387	210	2549		
Par	4	4	3	5	5	4	3	5	3	35	RED	Rating 70.9
Handicap	15	11	17	3	1	9	13	7	5			Slope 120

Hole	10	11	12	13	14	15	16	17	18	In		Totals
BLUE	300	208	477	345	198	398	396	503	280	3105	BLUE	6009
WHITE	285	202	460	310	192	388	390	498	270	2995	WHITE	5770
Par	4	3	5	4	3	4	4	5	4	36	Par	70
Handicap	17	9	3	11	13	7	1	5	15			
RED	280	194	450	295	167	382	382	468	262	2880	RED	5429
Par	4	3	5	4	3	4	5	5	4	37	Par	72
Handicap	16	10	4	12	18	8	6	2	14			

Manager: Alan Kimmel   **Pro**: Dave Stevenson, PGA   **Supt**: Larry Grasso
Architect: Devereux Emmet 1926

LAKEOVER NATIONAL GOLF CLUB PRIVATE

234 Old Bedford Center Rd., Bedford Hills, NY 10507 **(914) 328-8478**

Lakeover National is a private 18 hole course open 6 days a week all year, weather permitting. Tee time reservations are not necessary. Guests may play accompanied by a member.

•**Driving Range**	•**Lockers**
•**Practice Green**	•**Showers**
•**Power Carts**	•**Food**
Pull Carts	•**Clubhouse**
Club Rental	Outings
•**Caddies**	•**Soft Spikes**

Course Description: Lakeover is aptly named; lakes (one being seven acres) affect play on 8 holes. Formerly Lakeover Estate, the rolling terrain, elevated tees and greens, gentle mounding and deep bunkers add to its challenge. The middle holes lie in a basin and the rest are on the fringe of the property.

Directions: Westchester County, #20
I-287 (Cross Westchester X-Way) OR Hutchinson Pkwy.to I-684 North to Exit#4. Turn right (Rte.172). Proceed to end of road, turn left onto Rte.22 for 2.3 miles to fork in road and bear left toward Bedford Hills onto Bedford Center Rd. to club on right.

Hole	1	2	3	4	5	6	7	8	9	Out	BLUE	Rating 71.4
BLUE	473	370	175	394	478	373	342	206	322	3133		Slope 131
WHITE	448	323	163	360	453	344	332	196	301	2920		
Par	5	4	3	4	5	4	4	3	4	36	WHITE	Rating 70.0
Handicap												Slope 128
RED												
Par											RED	Rating
Handicap												Slope
Hole	10	11	12	13	14	15	16	17	18	In		Totals
BLUE	366	131	517	373	353	357	527	327	187	3138	BLUE	6271
WHITE	340	116	507	355	341	344	512	317	177	3009	WHITE	5929
Par	4	3	5	4	4	4	5	4	3	36	Par	72
Handicap												
RED											RED	
Par											Par	
Handicap												

Manager/Pro: Dennis Petruzzelli, PGA
Architect: Albert Zikorus 1965 **Redesign:** Gary Player 1990

LEEWOOD GOLF CLUB

1 Leewood Dr., Eastchester, NY 10707   (914) 793-5821

Leewood is an 18 hole private course open 6 days a week and closed in Jan. and Feb. Guests play accompanied by a member. Reservations for tee times are not necessary.

```
Driving Range      •Lockers
•Practice Green    •Showers
•Power Carts       •Food
 Pull Carts        •Clubhouse
•Club Rental       •Outings
•Caddies           •Soft Spikes
```

Course Description: Leewood has narrow, sloping, tree lined fairways with many uneven lies. The greens are small, fast and undulating, often guarded by deep bunkers. The course is considered long and difficult for women. The signature par 4 13th is straight uphill; the hole slopes to the right yet feels like it is going left. The Met PGA and various Senior Westchester tournaments have been held here. At the ninth hole, there is a halfway house.

Directions: Westchester County, #21
Take Hutchinson Pkwy.N to Exit 17 (North Ave). Turn left from ramp onto North Ave. Bear left onto Mill Rd. Go 1/2 mile to right at California Rd. Go 1 mile to left at White Plains Rd. Turn right at Leewood Dr. Proceed 1 mile to club entrance on right.

Hole	1	2	3	4	5	6	7	8	9	Out	BLUE	Rating 70.1
BLUE	379	298	338	394	503	178	319	373	180	2962		Slope 127
WHITE	369	290	333	383	488	173	308	363	167	2874		
Par	4	4	4	4	5	3	4	4	3	35	WHITE	Rating 69.2
Handicap	4	16	8	6	2	10	15	12	14			Slope 125
RED	359	237	324	371	457	138	292	337	141	2656		
Par	4	4	4	4	5	3	4	4	3	35	RED	Rating 73.7
Handicap	3	17	9	5	1	11	13	7	15			Slope 134

Hole	10	11	12	13	14	15	16	17	18	In		Totals
BLUE	417	114	474	416	305	498	437	151	410	3222	BLUE	6184
WHITE	363	112	465	403	298	488	427	134	402	3092	WHITE	5966
Par	4	3	5	4	4	5	4	3	4	36	Par	71
Handicap	5	18	11	1	13	9	3	17	7			
RED	352	106	439	358	289	473	412	120	385	2934	RED	5590
Par	4	3	5	4	4	5	5	3	4	37	Par	72
Handicap	2	18	10	4	14	6	12	16	8			

Manager: Michael Sussman   **Pro:** Tim Nevin, PGA   **Supt:** Peter Dirollo
Architect: Devereux Emmet 1922

MAPLE MOOR GOLF COURSE

1128 North St., White Plains, NY 10605 **(914) 949-6752**

Maple Moor is an 18 hole Westchester County course open 7 days a week and closed 12/15-4/1. Residents obtain a Park Pass and call automated system at 242-4653 up to 1 week in advance for tee times.

Driving Range	•Lockers
•Practice Green	•Showers
•Power Carts	•Food
•Pull Carts	•Clubhouse
•Club Rental	•Outings

Fees	Weekday	Weekend
Res/pass	$16	$19
NoPass	$39	$49
Twi	$11	$11
Power carts	$24	$24

Course Description: Maple Moor is a fairly flat course. The front nine is tight and long, the back more wide open. This busy facility, not overly demanding, is a good test for high handicappers. The regulation size greens are of moderate break and speed. Some water challenges the golfer on several holes. The signature par 4 14th requires a good drive and then the player is faced with a creek to play over for the approach shot.

Directions: Westchester County, #22
Take the Hutchinson River Parkway to Exit 25W, towards White Plains. Proceed west then go right into entrance of golf course.

Hole	1	2	3	4	5	6	7	8	9	Out	BLUE	Rating
BLUE												Slope
WHITE	354	188	560	353	408	486	200	376	436	3361		
Par	4	3	5	4	4	5	3	4	4	36	WHITE	Rating 68.8
Handicap	13	17	2	10	3	7	16	9	1			Slope 110
RED	312	144	499	295	376	455	175	331	388	2975		
Par	4	3	5	4	4	5	3	4	5	37	RED	Rating 71.9
Handicap	13	17	2	10	3	7	16	9	1			Slope 116
Hole	10	11	12	13	14	15	16	17	18	In		Totals
BLUE											BLUE	
WHITE	444	145	478	266	407	191	340	344	395	3361	WHITE	6371
Par	4	3	5	4	4	3	4	4	4	35	Par	71
Handicap	5	18	8	14	6	15	12	11	4			
RED	410	114	420	244	366	165	317	327	372	2735	RED	5710
Par	5	3	5	4	4	3	4	4	5	37	Par	74
Handicap	5	18	8	14	6	15	12	11	4			

Manager: John Sackel **Pro:** Rich Paonessa, PGA **Supt:** Kevin Duffy
Architect: Tom Winton 1923

METROPOLIS COUNTRY CLUB

287 Dobbs Ferry Rd., White Plains, NY 10607   **(914) 946-8814**

Metropolis is an 18 hole private course open 6 days a week and closed Jan & Feb. Guests play accompanied by a member. Reservations for tee times are necessary during the summer months.

•**Driving Range**	•**Lockers**
•**Practice Green**	•**Showers**
•**Power Carts**	•**Food**
Pull Carts	•**Clubhouse**
•**Club Rental**	•**Outings**
•**Caddies**	•**Soft Spikes**

Course Description: Extremely well maintained and formerly the venue of Century CC, Metropolis is a difficult course to play. On each nine there are descending and ascending holes with tight doglegs. The par 4, #1 handicap, signature sixth is a downhill dogleg left challenging the golfer to bear right on the tee shot to avoid the fairway bunkers. The approach is to a small 2 tiered green guarded by a sand trap. Water affects play on the 2nd and 14th. The greens are well kept and true. Metropolis has hosted every major Met Championship; this includes the MetPGA, Met Open, the Senior Open and the Westchester Amateur.

Directions: Westchester County, #23
Take I-87N (NYThruway) to Exit 5. Stay on service road to Rte.100 N. Go 1/2 mile to Sprain Brook PkwyN. Proceed about 5 miles to Rte.100B and turn left. Club is ahead on right.

Hole	1	2	3	4	5	6	7	8	9	Out	BLUE	Rating 72.2
BLUE	537	369	405	188	382	409	425	366	165	3246		Slope 134
WHITE	523	362	395	174	375	400	418	352	137	3136		
Par	5	4	4	3	4	4	4	4	3	35	WHITE	Rating 71.2
Handicap	11	13	3	15	7	1	5	9	17			Slope 131
RED	476	330	401	170	332	390	405	293	134	2931		
Par	5	4	5	3	4	4	5	4	3	37	RED	Rating 74.6
Handicap	3	11	5	15	7	1	13	9	17			Slope 134
Hole	10	11	12	13	14	15	16	17	18	In		Totals
BLUE	453	587	445	183	408	147	411	350	398	3382	BLUE	6628
WHITE	444	573	438	173	400	131	362	343	387	3251	WHITE	6387
Par	4	5	4	3	4	3	4	4	4	35	Par	70
Handicap	2	4	8	16	6	18	12	14	10			
RED	361	481	439	114	321	131	362	275	348	2832	RED	5763
Par	4	5	5	3	4	3	4	4	4	36	Par	73
Handicap	12	2	10	18	8	16	4	14	6			

Manager: Max Sands   **Pro:** Gene Borek, PGA **Supt:** Anthony Grasso
Architects: Herbert Strong 1904, A.W. Tillinghast **Estab:** 1922

MOHANSIC GOLF COURSE

Baldwin Rd., Yorktown Heights, NY 10598   **(914) 962-4049**

Mohansic is an 18 hole County course open 7 days a week from Apr. 1st to Dec.15th. County residents with a park pass may reserve up to 7 days in advance, non res. up to 4 days. For automated tee times, call (914) 593-4653.

•**Driving Range**	•**Lockers**
•**Practice Green**	Showers
•**Power Carts**	•**Food**
•**Pull Carts**	•**Clubhouse**
•**Club Rental**	•**Outings**

Fees	Weekday	Weekend
Daily w/pass	$14	$17
Senior/Twi "	$9	
Non res.	$37	$42
Power carts	$24	$24

Course Description: The sloping terrain provides the challenge at Mohansic. The golfer can't see the landing area on many tee shots because of the hills. The par 3 7th is the only water hole; the tee shot must carry over a pond. The 4th, a lengthy par 4, is an uphill dogleg left with an approach shot to a long narrow and elevated green that slopes back to front. This county course is very busy; over 56,000 rounds are played here in a year.

Directions: Westchester County, #24
From Taconic Parkway, take the Baldwin Rd. Exit in Yorktown Hts. Going North, cross left over parkway to entrance on right.

Hole	1	2	3	4	5	6	7	8	9	Out	BLUE	
BLUE												
WHITE	344	373	417	433	123	375	140	333	575	3113		
Par	4	4	4	4	3	4	3	4	5	35	WHITE	Rating 69.9
Handicap	14	10	5	3	18	7	17	12	1			Slope 120
RED	324	357	407	363	118	340	96	276	453	2734		
Par	4	4	5	5	3	4	3	4	5	37	RED	Rating 71.6
Handicap	7	1	11	15	13	5	17	9	3			Slope 119
Hole	10	11	12	13	14	15	16	17	18	In		Totals
BLUE											BLUE	
WHITE	512	403	387	172	417	363	387	402	173	3216	WHITE	3125
Par	5	4	4	3	4	4	4	4	3	35	Par	70
Handicap	9	2	15	13	4	6	11	8	16			
RED	433	393	327	147	402	283	323	383	169	2860	RED	5594
Par	5	5	4	3	5	4	4	5	3	38	Par	75
Handicap	8	10	14	6	18	2	4	16	12			

Manager: Tom Racioppo   **Pro:** John Paonessa, PGA   **Supt:** Rocco Massaro
Architect: Tom Winton 1925

MOUNT KISCO COUNTRY CLUB

10 Taylor Rd., Mt. Kisco, NY 10549 **(914) 666-7300**

Mount Kisco is an 18 hole private course open 6 days a week and closed in January and February. Guests play accompanied by a member. Reservations for tee times are necessary on weekends.

Driving Range	•Lockers
•Practice Green	•Showers
•Power Carts	•Food
Pull Carts	•Clubhouse
•Club Rental	•Outings
•Caddies	•Soft Spikes

Course Description: Formerly known as Lawrence Farms, Mt. Kisco CC is an extremely well maintained heavily treed course. It is fairly hilly with small greens, some elevated and of average break. The side hill lies on the fairways, and streams in play on many holes help to give the course interest and challenge. The signature par 4 5th is very difficult due to its length, uphill terrain and a green severely sloped from back to front. The approach shot must land below the hole for even a chance at one-pitting. The course has been somewhat modified since its founding and original design by Tom Winton.

Directions: Westchester County, #25
Take Hutchinson River Pkwy. North to I-684 to Mt. Kisco-Bedford exit #4. Turn left onto Rte.172 and then right onto Rte.117South. Go 1.1 miles to Old Bedford Rd. and turn right. Proceed 100 yards to Taylor Rd & turn left. Club is ahead on right.

Hole	1	2	3	4	5	6	7	8	9	Out	BLUE	Rating 71.1
BLUE	327	337	372	189	453	342	367	208	549	3144		Slope 129
WHITE	318	333	343	180	420	333	351	200	530	3008		
Par	4	4	4	3	4	4	4	3	5	35	WHITE	Rating 70.0
Handicap	17	7	13	15	1	11	5	9	3			Slope 126
RED	310	297	312	152	370	309	296	179	460	2685		
Par	4	4	4	3	5	4	4	3	5	36	RED	Rating 71.9
Handicap	13	9	7	17	3	11	5	15	1			Slope 123
Hole	10	11	12	13	14	15	16	17	18	In		Totals
BLUE	201	349	446	156	490	376	466	531	347	3362	BLUE	6506
WHITE	173	345	440	150	482	358	422	522	340	3232	WHITE	6240
Par	3	4	4	3	5	4	4	5	4	36	Par	71
Handicap	16	12	2	18	6	8	4	10	14			
RED	129	332	397	120	402	293	372	421	315	2781	RED	5466
Par	3	4	5	3	5	4	4	5	4	37	Par	73
Handicap	18	8	12	16	6	14	2	4	10			

Manager: Hussein Ali   **Pro:** Nick Manolios, PGA   **Supt:** Fred Scheyhing
Architect: Tom Winton 1928

OLD OAKS COUNTRY CLUB

 PRIVATE

Purchase St., Purchase, NY 10577   **(914) 948-8284**

Old Oaks is a private 18 hole course open 6 days a week and closed 1/12-3/6. Guests play accompanied by a member. Tee time reservations are necessary.

•**Driving Range**	•**Lockers**
•**Practice Green**	•**Showers**
•**Power Carts**	•**Food**
Pull Carts	•**Clubhouse**
•**Club Rental**	•**Outings**
•**Caddies**	•**Soft Spikes**

Course Description: Old Oaks is a very difficult par 70 golf course, a 141 slope from the blues! The severely breaking, rather small and lightning fast greens are part of the challenge. The ball must land below the hole for a chance to get down in two. The par 3 12th is uphill all the way, OB on the right, to a 2 tiered green protected by a bunker in front. The best miss is short left. A pond confronts the golfer on the par 4 6th hole and a brook wanders throughout the course. For Rte.684 construction, the State took the property where an additional 9 holes were located. The Met Open and Met PGA Championships were played here as well as US Open Qualifying rounds.

Directions: Westchester County, #26
Hutchinson PkwyN to Exit 27 (Purchase St, Rte.120). Make left onto Purchase St. Pass Manhattanville College. After passing Anderson Hill Rd, club is ahead on the left.

Hole	1	2	3	4	5	6	7	8	9	Out	BLUE	Rating 72.3
BLUE	388	532	189	383	431	373	183	438	387	3304		Slope 141
WHITE	377	518	182	371	409	355	160	425	372	3169		
Par	4	5	3	4	4	4	3	4	4	35	WHITE	Rating 71.1
Handicap	11	7	15	9	3	13	17	1	5			Slope 138
RED	360	502	121	345	304	318	132	413	363	2858		
Par	4	5	3	4	4	4	3	5	4	36	RED	Rating 73.9
Handicap	7	1	17	9	13	11	15	5	3			Slope 132
Hole	10	11	12	13	14	15	16	17	18	In		Totals
BLUE	377	311	216	416	364	391	164	420	552	3211	BLUE	6515
WHITE	370	309	194	404	355	376	152	397	536	3093	WHITE	6262
Par	4	4	3	4	4	4	3	4	5	35	Par	70
Handicap	10	16	12	4	14	6	18	2	8			
RED	357	300	152	400	340	349	140	323	446	2801	RED	5659
Par	4	4	3	5	4	4	3	4	5	36	Par	72
Handicap	10	14	18	2	8	12	16	6	4			

Manager: Scott Burne   **Pro:** Bobby Heins, PGA   **Supt:** Mark Millett
Architects: A.W. Tillinghast, Charles Alison 1925

PEHQUENAKONCK COUNTRY CLUB PUBLIC

Peach Lake, North Salem, NY 10560   (914) 669-9380

Pehquenakonck is a 9 hole public course that is open 7 days a week and closed between Dec. 1 and April 1. Annual memberships are available. Tee time reservations are not necessary.

Driving Range	•Lockers
•Practice Green	•Showers
•Power Carts	•Food
•Pull Carts	•Clubhouse
Club Rental	•Outings
Soft Spikes	

Fees	Weekday	Weekend
Daily	$16	$20
Twi(4PM)	$12	$15
Sr/Jr	Specials available	
Power carts $22 (Members $16)		

Course Description: Pehquenakonck is a hilly course that is probably the shortest layout in Westchester county. Many of the members own property around Peach Lake and enjoy playing here. The 4th, a par 3 that is considered one of the most difficult 115 yarders around, is uphill and nicknamed Mt. Kilimanjaro. Its green sits atop a large mound; golfers must hit this tiny putting surface or face the problem of landing short into rocks, left down a steep cliff or long into one of the four bunkers guarding the rear. The club has recently extended the first hole to make a 218 yard par 4 (not reflected in the scorecard.)

Directions: Westchester County #27
Hutchinson Pky. or I-287 to Rte. 684N to Exit 8, (Hardscrabble Rd.). Turn right (East) for 3 miles to Rte.124. At fork turn left for 3 mi. and go right on Bloomer Rd. Club is on left.

Hole	1	2	3	4	5	6	7	8	9	Out	BLUE	Rating
BLUE												Slope
WHITE	184	323	291	115	150	263	433	280	160	2199		
Par	3	4	4	3	3	4	5	4	3	33	WHITE	Rating 62.0
Handicap	11	1	3	9	13	17	5	7	15			Slope 99
RED	184	323	225	165	145	250	433	210	160	2095		
Par	4	4	4	4	3	4	5	4	4	36	RED	Rating 64.7
Handicap	11	1	3	9	13	17	5	7	15			Slope 102
Hole	10	11	12	13	14	15	16	17	18	In		Totals
BLUE											BLUE	
WHITE	160	352	291	130	175	258	433	290	180	2269	WHITE	4468
Par	3	4	4	3	3	4	5	4	3	33	Par	66
Handicap	12	2	4	10	14	18	6	8	16			
RED	155	255	291	180	175	230	400	280	180	2146	RED	4241
Par	4	4	4	4	3	4	5	4	4	36	Par	72
Handicap	12	2	4	10	14	18	6	8	16			

Manager: Michael Silvestri   **Supt:** Robert Barbieri
Architect: Malcus Knapp 1923

PELHAM COUNTRY CLUB

940 Wynnewood Rd., Pelham Manor, NY 10803   **(914) 738-5074**

Pelham is an 18 hole private course open 6 days a week. It is open all year, but only on weekends in January and February. Guests play accompanied by a member. Reservations for tee times are necessary on weekends.

> •**Driving Range**   •**Lockers**
> •**Practice Green**   •**Showers**
> •**Power Carts**   •**Food**
> Pull Carts   •**Clubhouse**
> •**Club Rental**   •**Outings**
> •**Caddies**   •**Soft Spikes**

Course Description: Pelham CC is the private club closest to Manhattan, (about 15 minutes away). It features small, fast greens and is a very narrow, difficult course that requires target golf. The signature par 4 9th is rather hilly; Mt. Tom on the right of the green gives slope to the hole. Originally this property was a tennis club. When the New England Thruway took away some of the property in the 1950s, Alfred Tull was called in to do some major redesign. The PGA Championship was played here in 1923. In 1996, the MET-PGA Pro Championship took place at Pelham.

Directions: Westchester County, #28
Rte 1-95North to Exit 15. Turn left onto Rte.1 South. Go 1/2 mile to Wynnewood Rd. Turn left and proceed to Club.

Hole	1	2	3	4	5	6	7	8	9	Out	BLUE	Rating 70.7
BLUE	468	209	527	330	181	430	324	142	402	3013		Slope 128
WHITE	447	200	509	294	158	394	316	133	385	2836		
Par	5	3	5	4	3	4	4	3	4	35	WHITE	Rating 69.4
Handicap	8	10	4	12	16	6	14	18	2			Slope 125
RED	445	197	469	292	143	378	265	128	382	2699		
Par	5	3	5	4	3	4	4	3	5	36	RED	Rating 73.5
Handicap	4	10	6	12	18	8	14	16	2			Slope 132
Hole	10	11	12	13	14	15	16	17	18	In		Totals
BLUE	129	502	382	451	514	400	403	436	187	3404	BLUE	6417
WHITE	124	488	361	431	497	382	386	381	146	3196	WHITE	6032
Par	3	5	4	4	5	4	4	4	3	36	Par	71
Handicap	17	7	13	1	3	9	11	5	15			
RED	122	485	359	369	465	380	384	335	110	3009	RED	5708
Par	3	5	4	4	5	4	4	4	3	36	Par	72
Handicap	17	3	11	9	1	7	5	15	13			

Manager: Dan Saalman   **Pro:** Mike Diffley, PGA   **Supt:** Jeff Wentworth
Architect: Devereux Emmet 1921 **Estab:** 1898

PLEASANTVILLE COUNTRY CLUB

PRIVATE

110 Nannahagen Rd., Pleasantville, NY 10570   **(914) 769-2809**

The Country Club at Pleasantville is a 9 hole private course open 7 days a week. The course is closed in the heart of winter. The homeowners in the surrounding private community are automatic members. Outside memberships are available. Tee time reservations are necessary on weekends.

Driving Range	•Lockers
•Practice Green	•Showers
•Power Carts	•Food
•Pull Carts	•Clubhouse
•Club Rental	•Outings
Caddies	Soft Spikes

Course Description: The Pleasantville property was originally owned by the Mannville family. The housing development was built around the existing course. With bunkers, narrow rolling fairways and water in play on several holes, target golf is the challenge here. The greens are small and fast; many are elevated with considerable break. The blind tee shot on the par 4 signature 3rd is to a downhill landing area. The golfer must then hit the approach to an elevated sloped green guarded by a creek and a tree. Pleasantville CC is meticulously maintained.

Directions: Westchester County, #29
From the South, take the Saw Mill River Pkwy to Exit 27 (Marble Ave). Make a right under the trestle to 1st light. Turn left onto Broadway. Go 7/10 mile. Club on left.

Hole	1	2	3	4	5	6	7	8	9	Out	BLUE	
BLUE												
WHITE	291	175	332	114	330	306	111	332	97	2088		
Par	4	3	4	3	4	4	3	4	3	32	WHITE	Rating 61.2
Handicap	10	11	2	13	7	5	15	3	8			Slope 109
RED	307	125	360	105	330	306	127	332	108	2100		
Par	4	4	5	4	3	4	5	5	4	37	RED	Rating 64.7
Handicap	9	14	1	16	8	6	12	4	17			Slope 111
Hole	**10**	**11**	**12**	**13**	**14**	**15**	**16**	**17**	**18**	**In**		Totals
BLUE											BLUE	
WHITE											WHITE	2088
Par											Par	32
Handicap												
RED											RED	2100
Par											Par	32
Handicap												

Mgr/Pro: Todd Barker, PGA   **Supt:** Dominick DiMarzo
Architect: A. W. Tillinghast 1920

POUND RIDGE GOLF CLUB

High Ridge Rd., Pound Ridge, NY 10576 **(914) 764-5771**

Pound Ridge is a semi-private 9 hole course open 7 days a week and closed January and February. Memberships are available with preferred tee times. The course opens to the public on weekends at 1PM. Otherwise, tee time reservations are not necessary. Carts are mandatory on weekends.

- •Driving Range
- •Practice Green
- •Power Carts
- •Pull Carts
- •Club Rental
- •Lockers
- •Showers
- •Food
- •Clubhouse
- •Outings

Fees	Weekday	Weekend
9 Hole	$17	$25
18 hole	$23	$40
Power Carts $22		

Course Description: Pound Ridge is relatively flat with some side hill lies. There is no water to affect play. The tee boxes are small as are the well bunkered and deep elevated greens. The property, so close to Connecticut, is substantial enough to fit the in-progress expansion to 18 holes which will make this a more impressive and full regulation course. At that time, the greens fees will be raised. A new clubhouse will be built as well.

Directions: Westchester County, #30
Take the Hutchinson River Pkwy. to the Merritt Pkway to Exit #35. Go north onto High Ridge Rd. for about 5 miles to club on the left just over the NY State border.

Hole	1	2	3	4	5	6	7	8	9	Out	BLUE	Rating 67.3
BLUE	300	500	149	425	287	178	390	390	387	3006		Slope 113
WHITE	290	487	139	410	277	168	380	372	377	2900		
Par	4	5	3	4	4	3	4	4	4	35	WHITE	Rating 68.3
Handicap	15	3	17	4	11	13	1	7	9			Slope 115
RED	280	335	131	387	270	156	369	346	315	2589		
Par	4	5	3	4	4	3	4	4	4	35	RED	Rating 69.0
Handicap	15	7	13	3	17	11	1	5	9			Slope 114

Hole	10	11	12	13	14	15	16	17	18	In		Totals
BLUE	300	412	149	425	287	178	390	390	387	2918	BLUE	5924
WHITE	290	397	139	410	277	168	380	372	377	2810	WHITE	5710
Par	4	4	3	4	4	3	4	4	4	34	Par	69
Handicap	16	4	18	6	12	14	2	8	10			
RED											RED	2589
Par	4	4	3	4	4	3	5	4	4	35	Par	70
Handicap	16	8	14	4	18	12	2	6	10			

Manager/Pro: Mike DiBuono, PGA **Supt:** Pete Kearny
Architects: Albert Zikorus, Mike DiBuono 1951 **Estab:** 1920s

COUNTRY CLUB OF PURCHASE

10 Country Club Drive, Purchase, NY 10577   **(914) 328-5047**

The CC of Purchase is a private 18 hole course open 6 days a week and closed in the winter. Guests play accompanied by a member. Tee time reservations are not necessary.

- •**Driving Range**
- •**Practice Green**
- •**Power Carts**
- Pull Carts
- •**Club Rental**
- •**Caddies**
- •**Lockers**
- •**Showers**
- •**Food**
- •**Clubhouse**
- •**Outings**
- •**Soft Spikes**

Course Description: On a former farm in the town of Purchase lies this distinctive golf club designed by Jack Nicklaus. The property also contains magnificent new estate homes. The picturesque course is characterized by tight treed fairways, stone outcroppings, many species of wildlife and regular encounters with the wetlands, a natural part of the terrain. Doglegs, water in play and long forced carries add to the challenge here.

Directions: Westchester County, #31
Take the Hutch. Pkwy North to Exit 27 (Purchase St.-Rte.120) and turn left. Pass light at Anderson Hill Rd. and continue approx. 1 mile to club on right.

Hole	1	2	3	4	5	6	7	8	9	Out	BLUE	Rating 73.5
BLUE	422	159	486	459	372	160	539	409	335	3341		Slope 136
WHITE	384	122	472	422	325	122	479	329	305	2960		
Par	4	3	5	4	4	3	5	4	4	36	WHITE	Rating 69.1
Handicap	3	17	11	1	9	15	5	7	13			Slope 127
RED	353	103	428	410	265	109	402	282	287	2639		
Par	4	3	5	4	4	3	5	4	4	36	RED	Rating 70.7
Handicap	3	17	11	1	9	15	5	7	13			Slope 126
Hole	10	11	12	13	14	15	16	17	18	In		Totals
BLUE	429	418	518	436	198	516	456	146	418	3535	BLUE	6876
WHITE	343	354	462	333	128	491	362	103	351	2927	WHITE	6400
Par	4	4	5	4	3	5	4	3	4	36	Par	72
Handicap	6	12	14	8	16	10	2	18	4			
RED	316	321	426	303	101	408	327	97	329	2628	RED	5267
Par	4	4	5	4	3	5	4	3	4	36	Par	72
Handicap	6	12	14	8	16	10	2	18	4			

Manager: John Wash   **Pro:** Michael J. Downey, PGA   **Supt:** Bob Miller
Architect: Jack Nicklaus 1996

QUAKER RIDGE GOLF CLUB

 PRIVATE

Griffen Ave., Scarsdale, NY 10583 **(914) 723-3701**

Quaker Ridge is an 18 hole private golf course open 6 days a week all year, weather permitting. Guests play accompanied by a member. Reservations for tee times are necessary on weekends.

> Driving Range   •**Lockers**
> •**Practice Green**   •**Showers**
> •**Power Carts**   •**Food**
> Pull Carts   •**Clubhouse**
> •**Club Rental**   •**Outings**
> •**Caddies**   •**Soft Spikes**

Course Description: The long, narrow Quaker Ridge Golf Club is a par 70, gently contoured and with average size undulating well bunkered, fast greens. Eight par 4s are over 425 yards. A. W. Tillinghast designed in an era when the sand wedge was not yet used so it placed a premium on the approach shot to the subtle and intriguing putting surfaces. Local area golf pros talk about the difficulty of this beautifully groomed course. Met Opens and Met Amateurs have been held here. The Walker Cup was hosted by Quaker Ridge in August 1997.

Directions: Westchester County, #32
Take the Hutchinson Pkwy. to Exit 22 (Mamaroneck Road) and turn left. Proceed on Mamaroneck Rd. to Griffen Ave. and turn right. Pass tennis courts, entrance on right.

Hole	1	2	3	4	5	6	7	8	9	Out	BLUE	Rating 74.1
BLUE	527	425	441	430	185	446	431	359	164	3408		Slope 142
WHITE	510	405	413	384	151	434	419	335	143	3194		
Par	5	4	4	4	3	4	4	4	3	35	WHITE	Rating 72.3
Handicap	7	5	9	11	17	1	3	13	15			Slope 138
RED	442	359	404	363	113	414	368	316	127	2906		
Par	5	4	5	4	3	5	4	4	3	37	RED	Rating 75.0
Handicap	3	7	11	9	17	5	1	13	15			Slope 137

Hole	10	11	12	13	14	15	16	17	18	In		Totals
BLUE	201	387	437	234	545	394	427	362	440	3427	BLUE	6835
WHITE	186	372	398	209	508	375	417	344	410	3219	WHITE	6413
Par	3	4	4	3	5	4	4	4	4	35	Par	70
Handicap	18	10	4	14	8	12	2	16	6			
RED	130	288	350	190	432	360	408	330	354	2842	RED	5748
Par	3	4	4	3	5	4	5	4	4	36	Par	73
Handicap	18	8	6	16	2	12	10	14	4			

Manager: Bill Kotiades   **Pro:** Rick Vershure, PGA   **Supt:** Tony Savone
Architect: A. W. Tillinghast 1916

RIDGEWAY COUNTRY CLUB

Ridgeway Ave., White Plains, NY 10605   **(914) 946-0681**

Ridgeway is an 18 hole private club open six days a week all year weather permitting. The Pro shop is closed in Jan. & Feb. Guests play accompanied by a member. Tee time reservations are necessary on weekends.

•Driving Range	•Lockers
•Practice Green	•Showers
•Power Carts	•Food
Pull Carts	•Clubhouse
Club Rental	•Outings
•Caddies	•Soft Spikes

Course Description: Ridgeway is deceptively diffiicult; its narrow fairways have OB on 16 of the 18. Originally, the course was 9 holes and known as Gedney Farms, becoming Ridgeway in 1952. The greens are small, fast and hard to read. The par 3s are long and very well trapped. The 8th, a par 5 dogleg left, has a tee shot of 190 yards over a lake. The long par 3 signature 10th features a tee shot to a small green with bunkers and rough bordering it. A qualifying round for the Buick Classic is held here as well as the Women's Met Open.

Directions: Westchester County, #33
Take Hutchinson River Pkwy. to Exit 23. Make right onto Mamaroneck Ave. Turn right at Ridgeway Ave. Club is about a mile up on the left.

Hole	1	2	3	4	5	6	7	8	9	Out	BLUE	Rating 71.9
BLUE	418	378	381	355	456	268	195	525	341	3317		Slope 127
WHITE	403	370	349	348	450	261	155	515	337	3188		
Par	4	4	4	4	4	4	3	5	4	36	WHITE	Rating 70.8
Handicap	3	7	9	11	1	15	17	5	13			Slope 125
RED	380	332	299	341	434	254	123	426	289	2878		
Par	4	4	4	4	5	4	3	5	4	37	RED	Rating 72.6
Handicap	5	7	11	9	1	13	17	3	15			Slope 121
Hole	10	11	12	13	14	15	16	17	18	In		Totals
BLUE	228	321	435	488	380	157	382	476	193	3060	BLUE	6377
WHITE	222	313	430	484	373	151	374	469	188	3004	WHITE	6192
Par	3	4	4	5	4	3	4	5	3	35	Par	71
Handicap	12	16	2	8	4	18	6	10	14			
RED	213	305	362	417	301	130	356	351	184	2619	RED	5497
Par	4	4	4	5	4	3	4	4	3	35	Par	72
Handicap	18	12	2	8	10	16	6	4	14			

Manager: Ed Norian   **Pro:** Pete Donnelly, PGA   **Supt:** Earl Millett
Architect: Pete Clark 1922

RYE GOLF CLUB

330 Boston Post Rd., Rye, NY 10580   **(914) 835-3281**

Rye Golf Club is open 7 days a week all year weather permitting. Guests may play accompanied by a member. Tee time reservations are necessary on weekends.

Driving Range	•**Lockers**
•**Practice Green**	•**Showers**
•**Power Carts**	•**Food**
•**Pull Carts**	•**Clubhouse**
•**Club Rental**	•**Outings**
Caddies	Soft Spikes

Course Description: Rye Golf Club is located on a harbor overlooking Long Island Sound. The course is hilly and very tight with small greens and some elevated tees. There are several blind holes where the green is not visible from the approach shot. Water is in play on three holes. The par 4 signature #7 is very difficult; it is a slight dogleg left and then uphill to a hidden green. The people of the Town of Rye are very fortunate to have a private golf club available to them at a reasonable cost. The Club has a very active Swim Team program.

Directions: Westchester County, #34
Take I-95 (New England Thruway) to Exit 19, Playland Pkwy. Stay right to Rye-Harrison Exit. Turn left at Stop sign and right at next Stop. This road becomes Rte.1 or Boston Post Rd. Continue 1/2 mile to club on left.

Hole	1	2	3	4	5	6	7	8	9	Out	BLUE	Rating 70.3
BLUE	414	478	132	392	395	358	457	349	336	3311		Slope 123
WHITE	404	437	128	388	390	354	452	282	293	3128		
Par	4	5	3	4	4	4	4	4	4	36	WHITE	Rating 69.1
Handicap	7	5	17	11	3	13	1	9	15			Slope 120
RED	374	395	117	342	378	323	425	277	226	2857		
Par	4	5	3	4	4	4	5	4	4	37	RED	Rating 71.7
Handicap	3	7	17	9	1	11	5	13	15			Slope 124
Hole	10	11	12	13	14	15	16	17	18	In		Totals
BLUE	169	567	310	403	124	347	430	163	471	2984	BLUE	6295
WHITE	164	562	304	400	117	342	420	150	459	2918	WHITE	6046
Par	3	5	4	4	3	4	4	3	5	35	Par	71
Handicap	16	2	14	6	18	10	4	12	8			
RED	143	495	297	395	101	300	354	124	427	2636	RED	5493
Par	3	5	4	5	3	4	4	3	5	36	Par	73
Handicap	14	2	12	10	18	8	4	16	6			

Manager: Terri Silverman-Jessen   **Pro:** Dick Santucci, PGA   **Supt:** Dick Gonyea
Architect: Devereux Emmet 1921

SAINT ANDREWS GOLF CLUB

10 Old Jackson Ave., Hastings-on-Hudson, NY 10706 (914) 478-3500

St. Andrews is an 18 hole private course open 6 days a week all year with temporary greens in the winter. Guests play accompanied by a member. Reservations for tee times are not necessary. The handicaps on scorecard may change due to new ratings.

- •Driving Range
- •Practice Green
- •Power Carts
- Pull Carts
- •Club Rental
- •Caddies
- •Lockers
- •Showers
- •Food
- •Clubhouse
- •Outings
- •Soft Spikes

Course Description: Saint Andrews has the oldest original clubhouse in the US. Now, a golfing community of townhouses are part of the property. In the early 1980s, Jack Nicklaus' organization was called in for a redesign. Part of the layout was rerouted or rebuilt with the par 3 #16 Jack's signature hole. This excellently maintained course is beautiful with vistas of the NYC skyline in the distance. It is characterized by elevated tees and small, fast, undulating, tiered greens. There are numerous creeks crossing the contoured fairways and many uneven lies. The challenge here is to hit long and put the ball in the right place for the next shot, a daunting task given the doglegs, difficult rough, hazards and contoured terrain. The new forward yardages will be rated in 1998.

Directions: Westchester County, #35
From NYC, take Henry Hudson Pkwy. to Saw Mill River Pkwy and Exit 13. Make left at light onto Saw Mill River Rd. Turn right at light. Go approx 1 m. to entrance on left.

Hole	1	2	3	4	5	6	7	8	9	Out	BLUE	Rating 73.9
BLUE	341	340	179	414	196	423	547	457	574	3471		Slope 144
WHITE	306	326	165	399	173	401	516	422	547	3253		
Par	4	4	3	4	3	4	5	4	5	36	WHITE	Rating 71.7
Handicap	11	15	17	1	13	9	7	5	3			Slope 139
RED	228	302	132	327	114	351	453	343	408	2668		
Par	4	4	3	4	3	4	5	4	5	36	RED	Rating 70.3
Handicap	11	13	15	5	17	7	1	9	3			Slope 125

Hole	10	11	12	13	14	15	16	17	18	In		Totals
BLUE	219	413	566	209	414	397	176	525	443	3362	BLUE	6833
WHITE	177	386	543	196	394	384	148	483	381	3094	WHITE	6347
Par	3	4	5	3	4	4	3	5	4	35	Par	71
Handicap	12	4	8	14	6	2	10	16	18			
RED	132	297	467	146	344	334	130	447	338	2627	RED	2314
Par	3	4	5	3	4	4	3	5	4	35	Par	71
Handicap	16	4	6	14	2	8	10	12	18			

Manager: Elinor Francis   **Pro:** Charles Hicks, PGA   **Supt:** Jay Regan
Architects: William Tucker. Sr., Harry Talmadge Jack Nicklaus **Redesign:** 1984
Estab: 1888

SALEM GOLF CLUB

Bloomer Road, North Salem, NY 10560 **(914) 667-5551**

Salem Golf Club is an 18 hole course open 6 days a week, and closed from Dec. 1 to March 15. Guests may play accompanied by a member. Tee time reservations are not required.

> •**Driving Range** •**Lockers**
> •**Practice Green** •**Showers**
> •**Power Carts** •**Food**
> •**Pull Carts** •**Clubhouse**
> •**Club Rental** •**Outings**
> •**Caddies** •**Soft Spikes**

Course Description: Salem golf course is very well-maintained offering spectacular views of North Salem. The trickier back nine has elevated tees, large undulating greens and five separate ponds that affect play on more than 7 holes. From the tee at the par 5 14th, considered the signature and prettiest hole, the golfer views a beautiful scene of hills and farms. The approach shot requires a carry over a stream and a pond with a lovely mountain in view. The clubhouse is quaint and Victorian and was formerly owned by the Lawrence family.

Directions: Westchester County, #36
Hutch.Pkwy. or I-287 to I-684 North to Exit #8 (Hardscrabble Rd.) Turn right(East)and go 3 miles. At fork, Rte.124, turn left. As you pass the high school on the left, turn right onto Bloomer Rd. Club is 1 mile ahead on right.

Hole	1	2	3	4	5	6	7	8	9	Out	BLUE	Rating 73.2
BLUE	414	178	531	182	378	323	512	382	429	3329		Slope 133
WHITE	400	167	503	163	362	313	497	377	418	3200		
Par	4	3	5	3	4	4	5	4	4	36	WHITE	Rating 71.9
Handicap	3	15	1	17	7	13	11	9	5			Slope 130
RED	348	142	447	136	301	267	402	332	409	2784		
Par	4	3	5	3	4	4	5	4	5	37	RED	Rating 73.4
Handicap	3	15	1	17	11	13	5	7	9			Slope 129
Hole	10	11	12	13	14	15	16	17	18	In		Totals
BLUE	179	360	158	406	591	365	432	372	568	3431	BLUE	6760
WHITE	162	342	137	385	565	357	420	337	553	3258	WHITE	6458
Par	3	4	3	4	5	4	4	4	5	36	Par	72
Handicap	16	10	18	4	8	12	2	14	6			
RED	154	323	127	325	491	262	415	300	499	2896	RED	5680
Par	3	4	3	4	5	4	5	4	5	37	Par	74
Handicap	16	8	18	6	2	14	12	10	4			

Manager: Robert F. Caeners **Pro:** Kammy Maxfeldt, PGA **Supt:** Justin McFarland
Architect: Edward C. Ryder 1966

THE SANCTUARY COUNTRY CLUB

Route 118, Yorktown Heights, NY 10598   **(914) 962-8050**

The Sanctuary is an 18 hole course open to the public 7 days a week all year, weather permitting. Power carts only on weekends. Reserved starting times for the season may be purchased. Other tee time reservations are not necessary.

Driving Range	Lockers
•Practice Green	Showers
•Power Carts	•Food
•Pull Carts	Clubhouse
•Club Rental	•Outings

Fees	Weekday	Weekend
Daily/cart	$30	$35
9 holes/cart	$20	
Pull cart/18	$20	
9 holes	$16	

Course Description: Formerly called Loch Ledge Golf Club, the nines here have been reversed. The new back nine is being renovated to re-route 8 holes out of the nine. Of course, a new rating and slope will be designated for 1998. The well treed property is hidden by woods from the road. The course features small, relatively slow greens that have subtle breaks. The Sanctuary is hilly on the back; the front is longer with sidehill lies. The signature par 3 #14 has an elevated tee with a shot over a pond to a green with a back to front slope.

Directions: Westchester County, #37
From Taconic Pkwy, take Millwood exit. At T, make left onto Rte.100N. Go about 3 miles over reservoir. At light, make turn onto Rte.118. Go about 1 & 1/2 miles & continue on 118 (bear right). Entrance on left. (Stone pillars).

Hole	1	2	3	4	5	6	7	8	9	Out	BLUE	Rating
BLUE	298	501	155	250	158	363	440	295	197	2657		Slope
WHITE	275	468	145	240	133	348	420	282	186	2497		
Par	4	5	3	4	3	4	4	4	4	35	WHITE	Rating 66.6
Handicap	14	2	10	16	18	4	6	8	12			Slope 114
RED	252	440	135	230	103	333	327	269	175	2265		
Par	4	5	3	4	3	4	4	4	4	35	RED	Rating 68.6
Handicap	11	9	5	13	15	7	17	3	1			Slope 116

Hole	10	11	12	13	14	15	16	17	18	In		Totals
BLUE	483	193	284	262	208	501	424	515	283	3153	BLUE	5810
WHITE	468	178	270	247	189	471	407	505	271	3006	WHITE	5503
Par	5	3	4	4	3	5	4	5	4	37	Par	72
Handicap	3	17	11	9	13	1	7	5	15			
RED	453	163	260	232	170	441	390	492	259	2860	RED	5125
Par	5	3	4	4	3	5	5	5	4	38	Par	73
Handicap	8	2	18	4	12	14	16	6	10			

Manager/Pro: Orlando Fiore, PGA
Architects: Nat Squire, Harry Lewis & Pete Donnelly 1966

SAXON WOODS GOLF COURSE

Mamaroneck Rd., Scarsdale, NY 10583   **(914) 725-3814**

Saxon Woods is a Westchester County 18 hole public course. It is open 7 days a week and closed 12/1-4/1. For tee times, call 242-GOLF to an automated system up to 7 days in advance. Residents obtain a Park Pass.

Driving Range	•Lockers
•Practice Green	•Showers
•Power Carts	•Food
•Pull Carts	•Clubhouse
•Club Rental	•Outings

Fees	Weekday	Weekend
Res/pass	$15	$19
Non-res	$39	$44
Twi	$11	$11
Power Carts	$23.50	

Course Description: Saxon Woods has recently been renovated. The rather small greens are of moderate speed with not much break. This very busy tree-lined course is fairly flat but has a lot of character. It is necessary to think carefully about where to place one's shots.

Directions: Westchester County, #38
Take the Hutchinson River Pkwy. to Exit 22. Make a right and then right to course.

Hole	1	2	3	4	5	6	7	8	9	Out	BLUE	Rating 70.8
BLUE												Slope 122
WHITE	307	292	517	160	413	330	168	520	372	3079		
Par	4	4	5	3	4	4	3	5	4	36	WHITE	Rating 70.2
Handicap	11	9	3	17	1	13	15	5	7			Slope 119
RED	283	234	457	118	361	267	125	456	322	2623		
Par	4	4	5	3	5	4	3	5	4	37	RED	Rating 71.2
Handicap	11	9	3	17	1	13	15	5	7			Slope 120

Hole	10	11	12	13	14	15	16	17	18	In		Totals
BLUE											BLUE	
WHITE	456	312	394	468	381	391	167	425	355	3349	WHITE	6428
Par	4	4	4	5	4	4	3	4	4	36	Par	72
	4	14	8	6	12	10	18	2	16			
RED	397	251	340	417	289	334	145	347	287	2807	RED	5430
Par	5	4	4	5	4	4	3	4	4	37	Par	74
Handicap	4	14	8	6	12	10	18	2	16			

Manager: Don Whitman   **Pro:** Tony Masciola, PGA   **Supt:** Larry Don Francesco
Architect: Tom Winton 1931

SCARSDALE GOLF CLUB

Club Way, Hartsdale, NY 10530 **(914) 723-5202**

Scarsdale is an 18 hole private course open 6 days a week and closed from Oct. 15 to Apr. 12th. Guests play accompanied by a member. Reservations are necessary for weekend tee times.

•**Driving Range**	•**Lockers**
•**Practice Green**	•**Showers**
•**Power Carts**	•**Food**
Pull Carts	•**Clubhouse**
•**Club Rental**	•**Outings**
•**Caddies**	•**Soft Spikes**

Course Description: Scarsdale Country Club course is a classic Tillinghast design. With heavily tree lined narrow fairways, well contoured terrain and fast, undulating and tiered greens, it is challenging and enjoyable. There are blind shots due to some elevated tees and greens. Water is in play on three holes. The entire mountain on the golf course drains into a lake that feeds into the Bronx River. The par 5 signature 18th is a picturesque finishing hole.

Directions: Westchester County, #39
From NYC, take Bronx River PkwyN to Exit 15 Fenimore Rd. Turn left over 2 bridges and straight ahead to Club Way (do not turn into village) to club entrance.

Hole	1	2	3	4	5	6	7	8	9	Out	BLUE	Rating 71.2
BLUE	360	175	335	375	135	510	515	465	325	3195		Slope 130
WHITE	350	163	322	359	117	495	510	446	302	3064		
Par	4	3	4	4	3	5	5	4	4	36	WHITE	Rating 70.1
Handicap	11	15	9	7	17	3	15	5	13			Slope 128
RED	345	135	300	350	105	475	445	420	280	2855		
Par	4	3	4	4	3	4	5	5	4	37	RED	Rating 73.6
Handicap	9	15	7	5	17	1	3	11	13			Slope 128
Hole	10	11	12	13	14	15	16	17	18	In		Totals
BLUE	475	160	350	290	455	130	375	365	527	3127	BLUE	6322
WHITE	455	150	340	288	451	120	368	355	502	3029	WHITE	6093
Par	5	3	4	4	4	3	4	4	5	36	Par	72
Handicap	6	16	8	14	2	18	4	12	10			
RED	440	130	330	236	435	100	350	340	477	2838	RED	5693
Par	5	3	4	4	5	3	4	4	5	37	Par	74
Handicap	4	16	2	14	6	18	8	12	10			

Manager: Douglas Rapp   **Pro:** Bill Smittle, PGA   **Supt:** Herbert Waterous
Architect: A. W. Tillinghast 1898

SHADOW CREEK GOLF COURSE

Route 6, Jefferson Valley, NY 10535   **(914) 962-0302**

Shadow Creek is a 9 hole par 3 course open 7 days a week and closed December through March. Tee time reservations are not necessary.

Driving Range	Lockers
Practice Green	Showers
Power Carts	•**Food**
•**Pull Carts**	•**Clubhouse**
•**Club Rental**	•**Outings**

Fees	M-Thurs	Fri-Sun
9 holes	$10	$14
18 holes	$15	$21

Course Description: Originally known as Indian Valley Par 3, Shadow Creek is flat, easy to walk and good for practice. A creek runs along this wooded short layout. The course is very beautiful, especially in the Fall. Many brides and grooms come here after a wedding to have pictures taken. No power carts are available. In the past several years, there have been some renovations made by the new owners.

Directions: Westchester County, #40
Take the Taconic Parkway. As you take Exit for Route 6 in Shrub Oak, course can be found immediately on the right.

Hole	1	2	3	4	5	6	7	8	9	Out	BLUE	Rating
BLUE												Slope
WHITE	193	149	130	137	181	105	119	110	112	1236		
Par	3	3	3	3	3	3	3	3	3	27	WHITE	Rating
Handicap	2	3	5	4	1	8	6	9	7			Slope
RED												
Par											RED	Rating
Handicap												Slope

Hole	10	11	12	13	14	15	16	17	18	In		Totals
BLUE											BLUE	
WHITE											WHITE	1236
Par											Par	27
Handicap												
RED											RED	
Par											Par	
Handicap												

Manager: Vinnie Vesce   **Owner:** Cary Fields   **Supt:** Ted Brown
Built: 1950s

SIWANOY COUNTRY CLUB

Pondfield Rd., Bronxville, NY 10708   **(914) 337-8858**

Siwanoy is an 18 hole course open six days a week all year, weather permitting. Guests play accompanied by a member. Tee time reservations are necessary for weekends.

- •**Driving Range**
- •**Practice Green**
- •**Power Carts**
- Pull Carts
- •**Club Rental**
- •**Caddies**
- •**Lockers**
- •**Showers**
- •**Food**
- •**Clubhouse**
- •**Outings**
- •**Soft Spikes**

Course Description: Siwanoy is a narrow, difficult well maintained course with small severely bunkered contoured greens. Initially designed by Donald Ross, Robert Trent Jones did a major redesign in the 1950's. Siwanoy has recently gone through an extensive renovation by Arthur Hills to return the course to the Ross style. New lakes have been installed that will affect play on two of the holes. The signature hole will be either the 12th or the 16th, because of the water. From the elevated tees, beautiful scenery is in view. In 1916, the first PGA Championship was played here.

Directions: Westchester County, #41
Take Hutchinson River Parkway to Exit 14. Go left onto New Rochelle Rd. for about 1 mile uphill, crossing over Cross Cty Pkwy, to club on right.

Hole	1	2	3	4	5	6	7	8	9	Out	BLUE	Rating 71.4
BLUE	373	392	206	507	511	166	371	342	293	3161		Slope 136
WHITE	366	385	197	500	486	146	366	331	287	3064		
Par	4	4	3	5	5	3	4	4	4	36	WHITE	Rating 70.4
Handicap	9	1	15	5	3	17	11	7	13			Slope 134
RED	332	303	145	408	421	126	320	260	227	2542		
Par	4	4	3	5	5	3	4	4	4	36	RED	Rating 65.5
Handicap	7	5	15	1	3	17	11	9	13			Slope 125
Hole	10	11	12	13	14	15	16	17	18	In		Totals
BLUE	362	197	358	188	384	441	378	376	531	3215	BLUE	6376
WHITE	348	178	353	169	365	425	356	353	521	3068	WHITE	6132
Par	4	3	4	3	4	4	4	4	5	35	Par	71
Handicap	14	18	6	16	4	2	8	12	10			
RED	314	150	287	105	301	302	290	292	426	2467	RED	5009
Par	4	3	4	3	4	4	4	4	5	35	Par	71
Handicap	14	18	4	16	10	8	2	12	16			

Manager: Robert Kasara   **Pro:** Grant Turner, PGA   **Supt:** Dave Mahoney
Architect: Donald Ross 1913   **Estab:** 1901

SLEEPY HOLLOW COUNTRY CLUB

PRIVATE

777 Albany Post Rd., Scarborough on Hudson, NY10510   **(914) 941-3062**

Sleepy Hollow is a 27 hole private course open 6 days a week and closed January and February. Guests play accompanied by a member. Tee time reservations for weekends are necessary.

•Driving Range	•Lockers
•Practice Green	•Showers
•Power Carts	•Food
Pull Carts	•Clubhouse
•Club Rental	•Outings
•Caddies	•Soft Spikes

Course Description: Spectacular vistas of the Hudson River are a landmark of the wide and hilly Sleepy Hollow. The greens are large, firm and undulating; not much water is in play. The par 3 # 16 signature hole is aptly named "Panorama" due to its elevated tee and memorable view. In the late 19th century, the land that makes up Sleepy Hollow Country Club was purchased by Colonel Eliot F. Shepard. The future clubhouse was originally constructed as his home in 1893 designed by the architect, Stanford White of McKim, Mead & White. Later, William Rockefeller helped make the purchase of the entire property and the golf course was built in 1911.

Directions: Westchester County, #42
Take the NY Thruway (via the Major Deegan or the Saw Mill Pkwy Exit 20) to Exit 9 in Tarrytown. Make right off ramp & left onto Rte.119 & then right onto Rte.9 north for approx. 4.4 miles to club on right. Entrance is through large stone gates.

Hole	1	2	3	4	5	6	7	8	9	Out	BLUE	Rating 71.7
BLUE	419	320	160	422	440	457	208	448	375	3249		Slope 133
WHITE	406	317	153	409	420	447	193	435	365	3145		
Par	4	4	3	4	4	5	3	4	4	35	WHITE	Rating 70.7
Handicap	8	14	18	6	4	10	16	2	12			Slope 130
RED	397	296	146	396	383	412	174	426	358	2988		
Par	4	4	3	4	5	5	3	5	4	37	RED	Rating 74.6
Handicap	3	13	15	5	11	1	17	7	9			Slope 134
Hole	10	11	12	13	14	15	16	17	18	In		Totals
BLUE	168	385	437	392	386	523	156	446	405	3298	BLUE	6547
WHITE	156	368	419	387	378	514	150	438	393	3203	WHITE	6348
Par	3	4	4	4	4	5	3	4	4	35	Par	70
Handicap	15	7	1	3	13	11	17	9	5			
RED	121	318	331	300	358	431	134	434	387	2814	RED	5802
Par	3	4	4	4	4	5	3	5	5	37	Par	74
Handicap	18	12	10	14	6	2	16	8	4			

Manager: Marshall Beraton   **Pro:** Jim O'Mara, PGA   **Supt:** Joel Camborada
Architects: Charles Blair Macdonald, A. W. Tillinghast 1911

SPRAIN LAKE GOLF COURSE

290 East Grassy Sprain Rd. Yonkers, NY 10710 **(914) 779-5180**

Sprain Lake is an 18 hole Westchester County course open 7 days a week from Apr. 1st to Dec. 15th. County residents with a park pass may reserve tee times up to 7 days in advance, non res. up to 4 days ahead. For automated tee times, call (914) 593-4653.

Driving Range	•Lockers
•Practice Green	•Showers
•Power Carts	•Food
•Pull Carts	•Clubhouse
•Club Rental	•Outings

Fees	Weekday	Weekend
Daily w/pass	$14	$17
Senior/Twi	$9	
Non res.	$37	$42
Power carts	$24	

Course Description: Sprain Lake is a very picturesque and hilly layout that requires exacting shots. With lakes, creeks and ponds, water is in play on 10 holes and adds to the difficulty. The golfer is hardly aware of the nearby parkways because of the heavily treed property. There are many uneven lies on the fairways on this short golf course but the fast greens are relatively flat. The signature 15th is a long par 4 which requires a carry over a creek on the approach shot to the green.

Directions: Westchester County, #43
Take Sprain Brook Parkway North to Jackson Ave Exit. Make right onto E. Grassy Sprain Rd. and go 1/2 mile to entrance on right.

Hole	1	2	3	4	5	6	7	8	9	Out	BLUE	
BLUE												
WHITE	361	389	362	138	309	335	418	354	164	2830		
Par	4	4	4	3	4	4	4	4	3	34	WHITE	Rating 68.6
Handicap	10	4	12	16	14	8	2	6	18			Slope 114
RED	338	360	329	121	288	300	381	326	140	2583		
Par	4	4	4	3	4	4	5	4	3	35	RED	Rating 70.2
Handicap	10	4	12	16	14	8	2	6	18			Slope 115

Hole	10	11	12	13	14	15	16	17	18	In		Totals
BLUE											BLUE	
WHITE	524	342	386	187	308	420	173	465	436	3241	WHITE	6071
Par	5	4	4	3	4	4	3	5	4	36	Par	70
Handicap	1	11	7	13	17	5	15	9	3			
RED	491	326	367	168	289	390	145	448	413	2583	RED	5620
Par	5	4	5	3	4	5	3	5	5	35	Par	74
Handicap	1	11	7	13	17	5	15	9	3			

Manager: Joseph Falcone   **Pro:** Thomas Avezzano, PGA   **Supt:** David Emma
Built: 1928

SUNNINGDALE COUNTRY CLUB

 PRIVATE

300 Underhill Rd., Scarsdale, NY 10583 **(914) 472-6972**

Sunningdale is an 18 hole private course open 6 days a week from April 1 to Nov. 1. Guests play accompanied by a member. Reservations for tee times are necessary only for early morning twosomes on weekends.

- •Driving Range
- •Practice Green
- •Power Carts
- Pull Carts
- •Club Rental
- •Caddies

- •Lockers
- •Showers
- •Food
- •Clubhouse
- •Outings
- •Soft Spikes

Course Description: Sunningdale, a sporty Tillinghast layout, has variety in length and style on the par 4s. It features target greens and uneven lies. The signature par 3 17th has an elevated tee box nestled in the trees requiring a shot to a well-bunkered green with water in front. The original Sunningdale Club was actually founded in 1913 on other property. Tillinghast made changes some time after the relocation. The course has recently been renovated by architect Stephen Kay. The bunkers have been improved and the course is more interesting than ever.

Directions: Westchester County, #44
Take the Sawmill Pkwy North to Ashford Ave. (Dobbs Ferry-Ardsley). Go east on Ashford and left on Sprain Rd to Underhill. Turn right, go over Sprain Pkwy & left into club.

Hole	1	2	3	4	5	6	7	8	9	Out	BLUE	Rating 71.6
BLUE	491	389	212	338	332	367	490	192	437	3248		Slope 128
WHITE	477	373	200	328	322	353	480	187	424	3144		
Par	5	4	3	4	4	4	5	3	4	36	WHITE	Rating 70.8
Handicap	9	7	11	5	15	13	3	17	1			Slope 126
RED	473	324	140	323	303	293	442	183	415	2896		
Par	5	4	3	4	4	4	5	3	5	37	RED	Rating 74.9
Handicap	5	11	17	3	9	13	1	15	7			Slope 136

Hole	10	11	12	13	14	15	16	17	18	In		Totals
BLUE	434	307	160	433	404	380	411	177	507	3213	BLUE	6461
WHITE	430	299	153	418	397	373	405	152	498	3125	WHITE	6269
Par	4	4	3	4	4	4	4	3	5	35	Par	71
Handicap	4	14	16	2	6	10	8	18	12			
RED	428	288	139	404	376	369	379	129	448	2960	RED	5856
Par	5	4	3	5	4	4	4	3	5	37	Par	74
Handicap	12	14	18	10	2	4	8	16	6			

Manager: Armand Ausserlechner   **Pro:** Bill Greenleaf, PGA   **Supt:** Dom DiMarzo
Architect: A. W. Tillinghast 1918

WACCABUC COUNTRY CLUB

Mead St., Waccabuc, NY 10597   **(914) 763-8410**

Waccabuc is a private 18 hole course open 6 days a week and closed 12/1-4/1. Guests play accompanied by a member. Reservations for tee times are not necessary.

•Driving Range	•Lockers
•Practice Green	•Showers
•Power Carts	•Food
•Pull Carts	•Clubhouse
•Club Rental	•Outings
•Caddies	•Soft Spikes

Course Description: Waccabuc comes from an Algonquian Indian word which meant Long Pond. Originally it was a 9 hole layout, but expanded to 18 in 1923. The course is in excellent condition; new bunkers have been installed along the fairways and beside the greens. The par 3 9th is long with OB on the right and over the green. The par 4 3rd is considered the toughest hole, a dogleg left with both a sloping fairway and green. The course has hosted qualifying rounds for the US Open, the Buick Classic and the US Amateur.

Directions: Westchester County, #45
Take I-684 North to Exit 6. Go east by turning right onto Rte.35. Go about 5 miles to Mead St. and turn left. Club is about 2 miles ahead on the left.

Hole	1	2	3	4	5	6	7	8	9	Out	BLUE	Rating 70.9
BLUE	320	420	410	357	198	527	160	379	229	3000		Slope 127
WHITE	310	412	408	347	187	520	130	370	221	2905		
Par	4	4	4	4	3	5	3	4	3	34	WHITE	Rating 70.2
Handicap	15	5	1	9	13	3	17	7	11			Slope 124
RED	295	404	400	298	160	480	118	280	229	2664		
Par	4	5	5	4	3	5	3	4	4	37	RED	Rating 72.7
Handicap	7	5	3	9	11	1	17	13	15			Slope 123

Hole	10	11	12	13	14	15	16	17	18	In		Totals
BLUE	480	435	207	455	544	149	363	410	387	3430	BLUE	6430
WHITE	471	430	185	447	536	141	355	400	370	3335	WHITE	6240
Par	5	4	3	4	5	3	4	4	4	36	Par	70
Handicap	14	2	16	4	6	18	12	10	8			
RED	446	353	135	424	462	135	309	356	364	2984	RED	5648
Par	5	4	3	5	5	3	4	4	4	37	Par	74
Handicap	4	8	18	6	2	16	14	12	10			

Manager: John Assumma   **Pro:** John McPhee, PGA   **Supt:** Edward Binsse
Architects: Alfred Tull, Fred Studwell **Estab:** 1912

WESTCHESTER COUNTRY CLUB

North St., Rye, NY 10580   **(914) 967-6000**

Westchester is a private club with 2 18 hole courses open 6 days a week. The South course is open all year. Guests play accompanied by a member. For Sat. & Sun. tee times there is a computerized arrangement. Members call in advance for weekdays.

•**Driving Range**	•**Lockers**
•**Practice Green**	•**Showers**
•**Power Carts**	•**Food**
Pull Carts	•**Clubhouse**
•**Club Rental**	•**Outings**
•**Caddies**	•**Soft Spikes**

Course Description: Westchester CC offers two difficult 18 hole courses that follow the contour of the hilly landscape. The tee shots require considerable carry to the fairway. Women have very little advantage. The Buick Classic is held here every year in June on the West course. The nines are reversed for that event. The signature 450 Yard par 4 17th is a sharp dogleg left with a potentially long second shot over a lake. Many tees and greens are elevated. Due to the thick rough, doglegs and hilly terrain, the course is not forgiving of an errant drive. The Pro Shop is well stocked for the busiest private club in the Northeast. The scorecard below is for the West Course.

Directions: Westchester County, #46
Take the Hutchinson River Pkwy to Exit 25 (North St.). Go east toward Harrison about 1 mile to club on left.

Hole	1	2	3	4	5	6	7	8	9	Out	BLUE	Rating 73.2
BLUE	314	442	473	379	154	462	204	374	526	3328		Slope 136
WHITE	296	424	451	368	136	430	190	350	511	3156		
Par	4	4	5	4	3	4	3	4	5	36	WHITE	Rating 71.6
Handicap	15	3	9	5	17	1	13	11	7			Slope 134
RED	285	414	431	357	136	415	171	336	503	3048		
Par	4	5	5	4	3	5	3	4	5	38	RED	Rating 77.5
Handicap	13	1	9	7	17	3	15	11	5			Slope 145
Hole	10	11	12	13	14	15	16	17	18	In		Totals
BLUE	190	384	408	419	565	133	326	464	505	3394	BLUE	6722
WHITE	180	367	398	410	545	123	316	421	460	3220	WHITE	6376
Par	3	4	4	4	5	3	4	4	5	36	Par	72
Handicap	16	14	6	2	8	18	12	4	10			
RED	170	345	371	386	531	123	307	400	440	3073	RED	6121
Par	3	4	4	4	5	3	4	5	5	37	Par	75
Handicap	16	12	2	6	4	18	14	10	8			

Manager: Bob James   **Pro:** John Kennedy, PGA   **Supt:** Joe Alonzi
Architect: Walter Travis 1922

WESTCHESTER HILLS GOLF CLUB

Ridgeway Ave., White Plains, NY 10605   **(914) 761-7639**

Westchester Hills is a private 18 hole course open 6 days a week. Guests may play accompanied by a member. Tee time reservations are necessary on weekends.

Driving Range	•**Lockers**
•**Practice Green**	•**Showers**
•**Power Carts**	•**Food**
Pull Carts	•**Clubhouse**
•**Club Rental**	•**Outings**
•**Caddies**	Soft Spikes

Course Description: Westchester Hills, originally operated under the name Gedney Farm Country Club, is a typical old fashioned design. It is characterized by tight tree-lined fairways and small, firm and extremely fast greens. This well maintained course is relatively flat; a few holes have some contour. Ponds and streams affect play on two holes. Accuracy is very important here; length itself is not a factor. An LPGA tournament was held here in the 1980s.

Directions: Westchester County, #47
Take the Hutchinson River Pkwy. to Exit 23. Make right onto Mamaroneck Ave. to Ridgeway Ave & turn right. Course is ahead on right.

Hole	1	2	3	4	5	6	7	8	9	Out	BLUE	Rating
BLUE	382	522	168	376	521	451	183	421	428	3452		Slope
WHITE	354	423	160	435	206	512	335	465	287	3177		
Par	4	4	3	4	3	5	4	5	4	36	WHITE	Rating 70.2
Handicap	9	3	15	1	13	7	5	11	17			Slope 127
RED	330	370	153	425	185	445	307	445	250	2910		
Par	4	4	3	5	3	5	4	5	4	37	RED	Rating 72.8
Handicap	9	7	17	5	15	1	11	3	13			Slope 125
Hole	**10**	**11**	**12**	**13**	**14**	**15**	**16**	**17**	**18**	**In**		Totals
BLUE	444	441	508	372	178	505	438	189	401	3476	BLUE	6928
WHITE	407	402	218	391	175	408	149	484	306	2940	WHITE	6117
Par	4	4	3	4	3	4	3	5	4	34	Par	70
Handicap	2	8	12	6	14	4	18	10	16			
RED	385	370	213	369	119	388	128	440	230	2642	RED	5552
Par	5	4	3	5	3	5	3	5	4	37	Par	74
Handicap	8	10	14	2	16	6	18	4	12			

Manager: Drew Bollard   **Pro:** Kevin Morris, PGA   **Supt:** Peter Waterous
Architect: Pete Clark 1913

WHIPPOORWILL CLUB

150 Whippoorwill Rd., Armonk NY 10504   **(914) 273-3059**

Whippoorwill is an 18 hole course open 10 months a year, 6 days a week. Guests play accompanied by a member. Tee times are necessary on weekends.

- •**Driving Range**   •**Lockers**
- •**Practice Green**   •**Showers**
- •**Power Carts**   •**Food**
- Pull Carts   •**Clubhouse**
- •**Club Rental**   •**Outings**
- •**Caddies**   •**Soft Spikes**

Course Description: Whippoorwill's nines are distinguishable; one is more tree-lined with only one hole visible at a time. The other nine is more open and the holes are closer together. On a clear day, Manhattan can be seen from the 9th green, probably the highest point in Westchester. The greens are fast and in excellent shape. The 7th, a long par 4 signature hole, features a carry over a lake on the tee shot and a fairly sharp dogleg left. A long iron approach is necessary to an elevated green. The club has recently installed a practice facility at the driving range where members chip, putt and use the sand traps. A US Open regional qualifying round was held here in 1996.

Directions: Westchester County, #48
From NYC, take I-87(NYThruway) to Rte287 East to I-684North to Exit 3S (Armonk). Then take Rte.22 South to 3rd light and turn right on Rte.120N. Bear right onto Whippoorwill Rd and go for about 3 miles. Club entry gate on right,

Hole	1	2	3	4	5	6	7	8	9	Out	BLUE	Rating 72.7
BLUE	377	346	477	159	453	556	423	226	373	3390		Slope 134
WHITE	370	320	467	140	378	512	413	215	365	3180		
Par	4	4	5	3	4	5	4	3	4	36	WHITE	Rating 71.2
Handicap	7	15	13	17	3	9	1	11	5			Slope 132
RED	327	313	433	133	353	450	370	205	278	2862		
Par	4	4	5	4	3	4	5	5	4	36	RED	Rating 74.1
Handicap	7	15	5	17	3	9	1	11	13			Slope 136
Hole	10	11	12	13	14	15	16	17	18	In		Totals
BLUE	405	186	422	336	450	372	546	158	432	3307	BLUE	6697
WHITE	377	180	405	320	442	350	540	153	425	3192	WHITE	6372
Par	4	3	4	4	4	4	5	3	4	35	Par	71
Handicap	10	16	4	14	2	12	6	18	8			
RED	355	146	330	298	398	306	471	148	383	2835	RED	5697
Par	4	3	4	4	5	4	5	3	5	37	Par	73
Handicap	8	16	4	14	6	10	2	18	12			

Manager: Ray Gradale   **Pro:** Bob Moro, PGA   **Supt:** Chuck Martineau
Architects: Donald Ross, Charles Banks   **Estab:**1928

WILLOW RIDGE COUNTRY CLUB

North St., Harrison, NY 10528   (914) 967-6161

Willow Ridge is a private 18 hole golf course open 6 days a week and closed in February. Guests play accompanied by a member. Tee time reservations are necessary Wed- Sun.

- •Driving Range
- •Practice Green
- •Power Carts
- Pull Carts
- •Club Rental
- •Caddies
- •Lockers
- •Showers
- •Food
- •Clubhouse
- •Outings
- •Soft Spikes

Course Description: Willow Ridge is fairly hilly and deceptively difficult. There are willow trees in abundance; hence, the name.   This very pretty course features tree lined narrow fairways and small moderately fast greens with considerable break. The signature 14th requires a shot from a ridge to the green. Streams cross and are alongside the 6th and 15th holes.   To land many shots most advantageously, local knowledge is helpful. Willow Ridge hosted a local qualifying round for the US Open in May 1997.

Directions: Westchester County, #49
Take the Hutchinson River Pkwy to Exit 25(North St). Go East towards Harrison 1 mile to light. At fork, bear left; club entrance is on the left.

Hole	1	2	3	4	5	6	7	8	9	Out	BLUE	Rating 70.9
BLUE	123	522	168	376	521	451	183	421	428	3452		Slope 135
WHITE	372	486	153	334	501	423	160	393	390	3212		
Par	4	5	3	4	5	4	3	4	4	36	WHITE	Rating 70.0
Handicap	7	4	9	6	1	2	8	5	3			Slope 133
RED	342	458	112	304	433	348	137	366	334	2834		
Par	4	5	3	4	5	4	3	4	4	36	RED	Rating 72.8
Handicap	7	1	9	6	2	5	8	4	3			Slope 128
Hole	10	11	12	13	14	15	16	17	18	In		Totals
BLUE	444	441	508	372	178	505	438	189	401	3476	BLUE	6928
WHITE	410	395	479	322	152	461	433	159	377	3188	WHITE	6400
Par	4	4	5	4	3	5	4	3	4	36	Par	72
Handicap	6	4	2	7	8	1	3	9	5			
RED	376	364	450	302	127	435	387	141	344	2926	RED	5760
Par	4	4	5	4	3	5	4	3	4	36	Par	72
Handicap	6	4	2	7	9	1	3	8	5			

Manager: Barry Chudzikiewicz   **Pro:** James Jond, PGA   **Supt:** Bert Dickinson
Architect: Maurice McCarthy 1917

WINGED FOOT GOLF CLUB

Fenimore Rd., Mamaroneck, NY 10543   **(914) 381-5821**

Winged Foot has 36 holes and is open all year, weather permitting, 6 days a week. Guests play accompanied by a member. Tee time reservations are necessary for weekends.

- •**Driving Range**
- •**Practice Green**
- •**Power Carts**
- Pull Carts
- •**Club Rental**
- •**Caddies**
- •**Lockers**
- •**Showers**
- •**Food**
- •**Clubhouse**
- •**Outings**
- Soft Spikes

Course Description: Both courses at Winged Foot are rated in the top 30 in the U.S. and have hosted many important tournaments including 4 US Opens. In designing these spectacular layouts, A. W. Tillinghast followed the natural terrain resulting in rolling fairways and undulating, fast and well-bunkered greens. The West Course is difficult, more open and longer with many lengthy par 4s. The East is tighter featuring tree lined fairways and deep sand traps. The signature par 3 tenth called the "pulpit"on the West Course is 190 yards with an elevated green pitched back to front. The whole property is filled with magnificent trees of great variety. The 1997 PGA was held here in August. The scorecard below is for the West Course.

Directions: Westchester County, #50
Take the Hutchinson Pkwy to Exit 22 (Mamaroneck Rd.). Make a left off the exit ramp and go approximately 1 mile to back entrance of club on right.

Hole	1	2	3	4	5	6	7	8	9	Out	BLUE	Rating 75.2
BLUE	446	411	216	453	515	324	166	442	471	3444		Slope 140
WHITE	421	385	185	403	493	318	151	427	462	3245		
Par	4	4	3	4	5	4	3	4	5	36	WHITE	Rating 73.2
Handicap	3	9	11	7	5	13	17	1	15			Slope 138
RED	386	348	166	370	470	296	133	381	435	2985		
Par	4	4	3	4	5	4	3	4	5	36	RED	Rating 75.9
Handicap	3	9	15	7	1	13	17	5	11			Slope 134
Hole	10	11	12	13	14	15	16	17	18	In		Totals
BLUE	190	386	535	212	418	417	457	449	448	3512	BLUE	6956
WHITE	183	383	475	204	376	398	444	435	417	3315	WHITE	6560
Par	3	4	5	3	4	4	5	4	4	36	Par	72
Handicap	14	12	6	16	10	4	18	2	8			
RED	159	312	432	178	350	364	413	416	379	3003	RED	5988
Par	3	4	5	3	4	4	5	5	4	37	Par	73
Handicap	16	14	2	18	12	8	10	6	4			

Manager: Colin Burns   **Pro:** Tom Nieporte, PGA   **Supt:** Bob Alonzi
Architect: A. W. Tillinghast 1923

WYKAGYL COUNTRY CLUB

1195 North Ave, New Rochelle, NY 10804   **(914) 632-2359**

Wykagyl is a private 18 hole course open 6 days a week and closed January and February. Guests play accompanied by a member. Tee time reservations are not necessary.

•**Driving Range**	•**Lockers**
•**Practice Green**	•**Showers**
•**Power Carts**	•**Food**
Pull Carts	•**Clubhouse**
•**Club Rental**	•**Outings**
	•**Soft Spikes**

Course Description: The grass and rough are very thick at Wykagyl and the course offers panoramic views from greens to tees. Water affects play on 13 holes. The fast greens are small with lots of break. New tee boxes and bunkers have been installed in the most recent renovation by Arthur Hills. Earlier in this century Donald Ross, and later A. W. Tillinghast had performed architectural redos. The signature 17th has 2 gigantic oak trees overhanging the rough and fairway on the left. The 16th green is sloped back to front. The golfer must land below the hole to have any chance to get down in two. The LPGA JAL Big Apple Classic is played here in July; it is a very difficult layout for the average woman golfer.

Directions: Westchester County, #51
From NYC, take Henry Hudson Pkwy North to the Cross County Pkwy. Bear left onto Hutchison River Pkwy North and take Exit 16, Webster Ave. Take 1st left onto Disbrow Lane up hill to North Ave. Club is across the street.

Hole	1	2	3	4	5	6	7	8	9	Out	BLUE	Rating 72.6
BLUE	517	164	496	210	407	362	226	374	377	3133		Slope 137
WHITE	505	160	482	203	389	342	222	365	359	3027		
Par	5	3	5	3	4	4	3	4	4	35	WHITE	Rating 71.5
Handicap	3	17	5	15	1	11	13	9	7			Slope 135
RED	451	144	463	194	331	322	219	354	272	2750		
Par	5	3	5	3	4	4	4	4	5	36	RED	Rating 75.0
Handicap	3	17	1	11	5	9	15	7	13			Slope 138
Hole	10	11	12	13	14	15	16	17	18	In		Totals
BLUE	540	399	431	147	400	528	172	452	500	3569	BLUE	6702
WHITE	520	389	417	139	387	497	164	439	481	3433	WHITE	6460
Par	5	4	4	3	4	5	3	4	5	37	Par	72
Handicap	12	10	2	18	4	8	16	6	14			
RED	446	363	390	122	374	432	154	401	413	3095	RED	5813
Par	4	4	5	4	3	4	5	5	4	37	Par	73
Handicap	4	14	10	18	6	2	16	12	8			

Manager: Ken Korrel **Pro:** Mark Wanser, PGA **Supt:** Steve Renzetti
Architect: Lawrence Van Etten 1905 **Estab:** 1898

Proof of a Golfer

The proof of the pudding is eating they say

But the proof of a golfer is not

The number of strokes he takes in a day

Or the skill he puts into a shot.

There's more to the game than the score which you make

Here's a truth which all golfers endorse;

You don't prove your worth by the shots

that you make,

But the care which you take of the course.

(Vail's Grove)

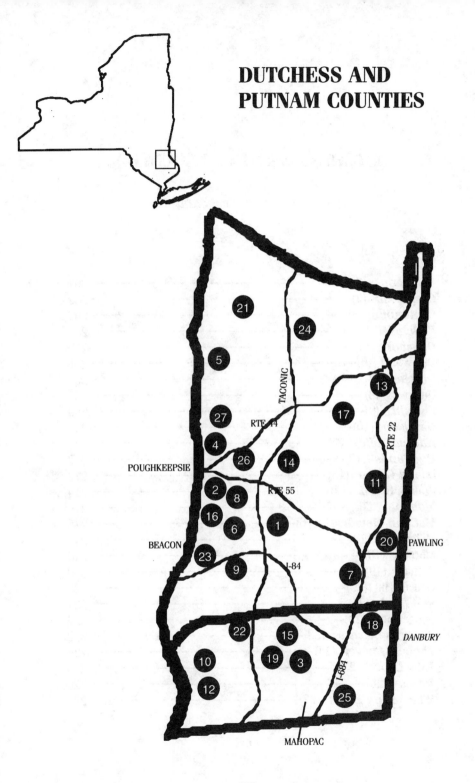

DUTCHESS AND PUTNAM COUNTIES

21

24

5

TACONIC

13

27 RTE 44

17

4

RTE 22

26 14

POUGHKEEPSIE

11

2 RTE 55

8

16

6 1

20 PAWLING

BEACON

23

9 I-84

7

18

DANBURY

22 15

10 19 3

I-684

12

25

MAHOPAC

DUTCHESS & PUTNAM COUNTIES

Public Courses appear in *bold italics*

BEEKMAN COUNTRY CLUB

11 Country Club Rd., Hopewell Junction, NY 12533   **(914) 226-7700**

Beekman has 3 nine hole courses open 7 days a week and closed in winter. Carts are mandatory until 2PM. Weekday memberships are available. Tee times may be reserved up to 7 days in advance. Second fee below is with cart when optional.

•**Driving Range**	•**Lockers**
•**Practice Green**	•**Showers**
•**Power Carts**	•**Food**
•**Pull Carts**	•**Clubhouse**
•**Club Rental**	•**Outings**

Fees	**Weekday**	**Weekend**
Daily/cart	$36	$45
After 1PM	$18/31	$25/35
Senior, lunch & 9 hole specials		
available		

Course Description: Beekman has been doing some major upgrades of its facilities over the last few years. These include installing a full irrigation system, improving the sand traps and constructing new holes in addition to renovating tee boxes on several holes. The Taconic course is considered the most difficult and somewhat hilly; the other two are relatively flat. The greens are fairly fast with subtle breaks. The 9th hole on the Valley features an elevated tee with a shot over a large pond. The layouts provide wide fairways, some doglegs and scenic country views. The scorecard below is for the Highland and Taconic nines.

Directions: Dutchess County, #1
Take the Taconic Pkwy North to Beekman Rd. Exit. Go left onto Beekman Rd. and over pkwy about 1 mile to club on right.

Hole	1	2	3	4	5	6	7	8	9	Out	BLUE	Rating 71.4
BLUE	355	316	134	561	477	330	402	165	410	3150		Slope 126
WHITE	340	305	124	545	460	315	390	150	400	3029		
Par	4	4	3	5	4	4	4	3	4	35	WHITE	Rating 69.3
Handicap	9	13	17	3	1	11	5	15	7			Slope 123
RED	300	267	119	490	410	300	327	136	345	2694		
Par	4	4	3	5	5	4	4	3	4	36	RED	Rating 72.6
Handicap	9	15	13	1	3	11	7	17	5			Slope 128

Hole	10	11	12	13	14	15	16	17	18	In		Totals
BLUE	170	478	397	167	495	477	315	350	388	3237	BLUE	6387
WHITE	160	464	387	160	428	457	305	340	378	3079	WHITE	6108
Par	3	5	4	3	4	5	4	4	4	36	Par	71
Handicap	7	4	5	9	1	3	8	6	2			
RED	150	403	365	155	372	400	280	328	360	2813	RED	5507
Par	3	5	4	3	4	5	4	4	4	36	Par	72
Handicap	7	4	5	9	1	3	8	6	2			

Manager: James Hoffman   **Pro:** Ben McCoy, PGA   **Supt:** Bob Steinman
Architect: Phillip Shatz 1964

CASPERKILL COUNTRY CLUB

575 South Road, Poughkeepsie, NY 12601   **(914) 433-2222**

Casperkill is an 18 hole course open 7 days a week, and closed between Dec. 23 & Mar. 15. Tee times may be made on Wed. eve at 7:30PM for weekends and 6:45AM the day before weekdays. Club memberships are available.

•**Driving Range**	•**Lockers**
•**Practice Green**	•**Showers**
•**Power Carts**	•**Food**
•**Pull Carts**	•**Clubhouse**
•**Club Rental**	•**Outings**
•**Soft Spikes**	

Fees	Weekday	Weekend
Daily(Member)	$18	$20
Daily(Non-Mem)	$40	$40
Twi(5PM)	$12	$19
Power carts	$24	

Course Description: Formerly a private IBM golf course, Casperkill, named for the stream that runs through the property, is under new management in 1997. Utilizing the natural landscape, the course features rolling hills, some deep woods and many doglegs. Strategic bunkers along the relatively tight fairways add to the challenge. The signature par 3 3rd hole requires a tee shot over a pond. The medium sized greens are fairly fast. The golfer is treated to magnificent views from the elevated tees. Even a wild turkey might be seen here reminding us how close to nature we are. The 1977 Dutchess County Amateur was held here.

Directions: Dutchess County, #2
I-287(Cross West. X-way) to I-684 North to I-84 West (or Taconic Pkwy. North to I-84 West) to Rte. 9 North. Proceed 11.2 miles north on Rte. 9 to club on right.

Hole	1	2	3	4	5	6	7	8	9	Out	BLUE	Rating 72.4
BLUE	508	416	204	331	536	338	396	179	353	3261		Slope 130
WHITE	478	387	168	321	495	305	367	159	332	3012		
Par	5	4	3	4	5	4	4	3	4	36	WHITE	Rating 69.9
Handicap	11	1	9	13	15	17	3	7	5			Slope 125
RED	422	279	83	238	410	274	313	92	260	2371		
Par	5	4	3	4	5	4	4	3	4	36	RED	Rating 67.9
Handicap	1	7	15	9	3	13	5	17	11			Slope 117
Hole	10	11	12	13	14	15	16	17	18	In		Totals
BLUE	511	445	208	417	357	393	182	425	491	3429	BLUE	6690
WHITE	474	412	150	375	328	366	156	410	470	3141	WHITE	6153
Par	5	4	3	4	4	4	3	4	5	36	Par	72
Handicap	6	2	14	8	16	12	18	4	10			
RED	367	333	98	274	285	296	134	335	375	2497	RED	4868
Par	5	4	3	4	4	4	3	4	5	36	Par	72
Handicap	4	2	16	8	12	14	18	6	10			

Manager/Pro: Rhett M. Myers, PGA   **Supt:** Clark Bartholomew
Architect: Robert Trent Jones, Sr. 1944

CENTENNIAL GOLF CLUB

Simpson Rd., Carmel, NY 10512   **(914) 225-5700**

Centennial is a 27 hole facility opening in the Spring of 1998. It is open 7 days a week and closed 4/1-11/30. The GPS system is on the power carts. Tee time reservations: up to 1 week in advance. The driving range has grass tees.

•**Driving Range**	•**Lockers**
•**Practice Green**	Showers
•**Power Carts**	•**Food**
Pull Carts	•**Clubhouse**
•**Club Rental**	•**Outings**

Fees	Weekday	Weekend
Daily w/cart	$65	$85

Course Description: On 450 acres of a former horse farm, the Centennial Golf Club is an excellent new facility for play and learning. It has a substantial teaching component with practice areas for bunker and chip shots. The construction takes advantage of the heavily wooded topography with tremendous elevation changes and 4 or 5 tees on every hole. The greens are large and reasonably contoured. Creeks and ponds run through the property that overlooks the reservoir system. The intention here is to make the courses, The Lakes, The Fairways, and The Meadows, playable for every level of golfer and a sorely needed up-scale daily fee golfing club. The yardages below are approximate. The actual scorecard and ratings are not available at press time.

Directions: Putnam County, #3
Take the Hutchinson Pkwy to I-684N to Rte.84West to Exit 19. Make right onto Rte.6 and make a right over reservoir. Then take 1st right onto Simpson Rd. Course on left.

Hole	1	2	3	4	5	6	7	8	9	Out	BLUE	Rating
BLUE	610	370	220	416	185	420	402	347	525	3495		Slope
WHITE												
Par	5	4	3	4	3	4	4	4	5	36	WHITE	Rating
Handicap												Slope
RED												
Par											RED	Rating
Handicap												Slope

Hole	10	11	12	13	14	15	16	17	18	In		Totals
BLUE	585	390	230	434	219	385	575	380	425	3623	BLUE	7118
WHITE											WHITE	
Par	5	4	3	4	3	4	5	4	4	36	Par	72
Handicap												
RED											RED	
Par											Par	
Handicap												

Supt: Frank Polizzi
Architect: Larry Nelson 1998

COLLEGE HILL GOLF COURSE

PUBLIC

N. Clinton Street, Poughkeepsie, NY 12602 **(914) 486-9112**

College Hill is a 9 hole Town of Poughkeepsie municipal course open 7 days a week, from Apr. 1 to Dec. 1. Only season pass players can play 18 holes on weekends. Tee time reservations are not necessary.

Driving Range	Lockers
•**Practice Green**	•**Showers**
•**Power Carts**	•**Food**
•**Pull Carts**	Clubhouse
•**Club Rental**	•**Outings**
Soft Spikes	

Fees	Weekday	Weekend
Daily (9)	$7	$8
Jr.(17 & under)	$3	$7
Power carts	$11(9)	

Course Description: Originally called Alexander Caven Memorial Golf Course, College Hill has the highest elevation in the area with scenic views of Poughkeepsie. The signature par 4 8th has a major ascent, referred to as "Cardiac Hill". That green has a back to front slope and the smart play is to stay below the hole. The par 4 #4 hole overlooks Morgan Lake. and is considered another signature hole. The medium sized greens are fast in summer and have a little break. The fairways are open yet many are tree lined.

Directions: Dutchess County, #4
Take Rte. 9 North of the Mid-Hudson Bridge to Rte. 44/55 East for 1/2 mile to light at Clinton St. Make a left, go through 5 lights and course is on right.

Hole	1	2	3	4	5	6	7	8	9	Out	BLUE	Rating
BLUE												Slope
WHITE	304	321	196	319	462	320	185	286	163	2556		
Par	4	4	3	4	5	4	3	4	3	34	WHITE	Rating 64.3
Handicap	8	7	5	1	2	6	4	3	9			Slope 111
RED												
Par											RED	Rating 68.6
Handicap												Slope 116
Hole	10	11	12	13	14	15	16	17	18	In		Totals
BLUE											BLUE	
WHITE											WHITE	5112
Par											Par	68
Handicap												
RED											RED	
Par											Par	
Handicap												

Manager: Bob Paquet   **Pro:** Bruce Flesland, PGA   **Supt:** Eric Jappen
Built: 1933

DINSMORE GOLF COURSE

PUBLIC

Mills Norrie St. Park, Old Post Rd., Staatsburg NY 12580 **(914) 889-4071**

Dinsmore is an 18 hole NYState operated course open 7 days a week, between April 11 & November 30. Tee time reservations may be made Thurs. for the weekend by calling 889-3126.

Driving Range	•Lockers
•Practice Green	•Showers
•Power Carts	•Food
•Pull Carts	•Clubhouse
•Club Rental	•Outings
• Soft Spikes	

Fees	Weekday	Weekend
Daily	$16	$19
Sr/Jr	$9	
9 holes	$8	$10
Power carts	$22	

Course Description: Scenic Dinsmore offers panoramic views of the Hudson River, the Catskills, and historic Hyde Park. It is the second oldest golf course in the country and was originally built for Mr. Dinsmore as a private 9 hole course. The back nine is harder and hillier than the front with a nearly 1,000 yard difference in length between them. The ascending par 3 sixth is known as "Cardiac Hill." Postage stamp greens are prevalent on the front nine and larger more contoured greens on the back. No water in is in play on the course. It is in a 988 acre historic park with hiking trails, a marina and camping facilities available.

Directions: Dutchess County, #5
NYThruway, Exit #18, Kingston. Take Rte.199 East over bridge to Rte.9G South which becomes Rte.9South through Rhinebeck to Staatsburg. Follow signs to club.

Hole	1	2	3	4	5	6	7	8	9	Out	WHITE	Rating 66.7
WHITE	460	137	369	120	301	90	460	181	371	2489		Slope 107
RED	400	137	300	120	220	90	400	150	275	2092		
Par	5	3	4	3	4	3	5	3	4	34	RED	Rating 66.7
Handicap	6	8	3	7	4	9	5	2	1			Slope 107
GOLD	375	137	300	120	220	90	370	150	250	2012		
Par	5	3	4	3	4	3	5	3	4	34	GOLD	Rating 65.3
Handicap	6	8	3	7	4	9	5	2	1			Slope 103
Hole	10	11	12	13	14	15	16	17	18	In		Totals
WHITE	401	354	539	325	120	422	548	198	323	3230	WHITE	5719
RED	300	275	360	275	120	350	400	145	250	2475	RED	4567
Par	4	4	5	4	3	4	5	3	4	36	Par	70
Handicap	4	3	6	8	9	1	5	2	7			
GOLD	300	250	360	275	120	320	375	145	250	2395	GOLD	4407
Par	4	4	5	4	3	4	5	3	4	36	Par	70
Handicap	4	3	6	8	9	1	5	2	7			

Supt: Alan Smith   **Built:** 1890s

DOGWOOD GOLF CENTER

 PUBLIC

Route 376, Hopewell Junction, NY 12533 **(914) 226-7317**

Dogwood is a 9 hole facility open 7 days a week and closed in winter. Season passes are available as well as lunch specials. Tee time reservations are necessary for Saturdays.

Driving Range	Lockers
•**Practice Green**	Showers
•**Power Carts**	•**Food**
•**Pull Carts**	Clubhouse
•**Club Rental**	•**Outings**

Fees	Weekday	Weekend
9 hole	$8	$10
18	$13	$15
Power carts	$14/9	$22/18

Course Description: New ownership in 1996 changed the name of this course from Dogwood Knolls. A noticeable result is improved irrigation on the greens and tees, work on the cart paths and upgrading of the course. The 2nd and 3rd holes go up a hill; the signature par 3 8th is downward with trouble lurking all around it. The small greens are relatively slow but with considerable break. The course is generally wide open. It is the longest 9 hole course in Dutchess County.

Directions: Dutchess County, #6
Take the Taconic Pkwy north to Rte.52. Go west 1 mile to Rte.376. Turn right and proceed about 4 miles to course on right.

Hole	1	2	3	4	5	6	7	8	9	Out	BLUE	Rating
BLUE												Slope
WHITE	482	126	391	378	289	411	473	171	384	3106		
Par	5	3	4	4	4	4	5	3	4	36	WHITE	Rating 69.0
Handicap	9	15	2	8	18	5	17	10	6			Slope 122
RED	477	110	372	354	267	395	400	171	366	2936		
Par	5	3	4	4	4	4	5	3	4	36	RED	Rating 73.6
Handicap	9	15	2	8	18	5	17	10	6			Slope 112

Hole	10	11	12	13	14	15	16	17	18	In		Totals
BLUE											BLUE	
WHITE	467	135	424	385	300	432	496	186	440	3265	WHITE	6371
Par	5	3	4	4	4	4	5	3	4	36	Par	72
Handicap	14	12	1	7	16	4	11	13	3			
RED	482	126	391	378	289	411	473	171	384	3106	RED	6041
Par	5	3	4	4	4	4	5	3	4	36	Par	72
Handicap	14	12	1	7	16	4	11	13	3			

Manager: William Brady **Supt:** Craig Hinney
Built: 1930s

THE DUTCHER GOLF COURSE

PUBLIC

135 East Main St., Pawling, NY 12564   **(914) 855-9845**

Dutcher is a 9 hole course open to the public 7 days a week and closed Nov. 1-April 1. It is a Town of Pawling facility. Tee time reservations are not necessary.

Driving Range   Lockers
- **Practice Green**   Showers
- **Power Carts**   •**Food**
- **Pull Carts**   Clubhouse
- **Club Rental**   •**Outings**

Fees	Weekday	Weekend
Resident	$10	$12
Non-res	$13	$15
Sr.	$9	$11
Power carts	$15/18	$10/9

Course Description: Originally built by John Dutcher, the Mayor of Pawling, the course was attached to his hotel. Much later, the Dutcher family donated this land to the town to be forevermore a golf course. When first built, clubs didn't hit as long, nor balls go as far, consequently, the layout is fairly short. However, it is challenging with well groomed average sized greens that are fast and true. No water is in play. Stone walls cut across the fairway and surround the perimeter (OB). The par 3 #3 is a very difficult hole featuring the aforementioned stone wall throughout it and trees in front of the green.

Directions: Dutchess County, #7
Take I-684North which become Rte.22 to Brewster and continue <u>OR</u> take Rte.55 (from Poughkeepsie) to 22North. On Rte.22 in Pawling, exit on E. Main St. to club on left.

Hole	1	2	3	4	5	6	7	8	9	Out	BLUE	Rating
BLUE												Slope
WHITE	235	230	193	361	230	175	165	355	375	2319		
Par	4	4	3	4	4	3	3	4	5	34	WHITE	Rating 61.7
Handicap	7	11	13	1	9	15	17	3	5			Slope 95
RED												
Par											RED	Rating 65.6
Handicap												Slope 101

Hole	10	11	12	13	14	15	16	17	18	In		Totals
BLUE											BLUE	
WHITE	240	207	150	355	220	120	150	335	375	2152	WHITE	4471
Par	4	4	3	4	4	3	3	4	5	34	Par	68
Handicap	8	12	14	2	10	16	18	4	6			
RED											RED	
Par											Par	
Handicap												

Manager: Delores Golisano   **Pro:** Salvatore Golisano, PGA **Supt:** Fred Lattrell
Built: James Dutcher 1890

DUTCHESS GOLF & COUNTRY CLUB   PRIVATE

421 South Road, Poughkeepsie, NY 12603   **(914) 452-5403**

Dutchess Golf & CC is an 18 hole private course open 7 days a week all year, weather permitting. Tee time reservations may be made on weekends in season. Guests may play accompanied by a member.

•**Driving Range**	•**Lockers**
•**Practice Green**	•**Showers**
•**Power Carts**	•**Food**
•**Pull Carts**	•**Clubhouse**
Club Rental	•**Outings**
Caddies	•**Soft Spikes**

Course Description: Dutchess County is a difficult, hilly, tight course. The greens are relatively small and undulating. The signature par 4 14th is a dogleg with a large pond in play on the approach shot. The terrain produces many uneven lies; rarely a flat lie throughout. An accurate drive is important here; the rough can be punishing. The NYState Men's Amateur was held here in '97. NY State Jr. & Ladies Amateur Tournaments have been held at Dutchess as well.

Directions: Dutchess County, #8
I-287 (Cross West. X-way) to I-684 North. Go to I-84 west (or Taconic Pkwy. North to I-84 West) to Rte.9 North. Proceed 11.2 miles north on Rte. 9 to club on right.

Hole	1	2	3	4	5	6	7	8	9	Out	BLUE	Rating 71.3
BLUE	390	298	411	442	567	194	437	159	389	3287		Slope 125
WHITE	387	296	395	400	566	190	420	136	384	3174		
Par	4	4	4	4	5	3	4	3	4	35	WHITE	Rating 70.3
Handicap	11	15	13	5	3	1	17	7				Slope 123
RED	387	296	383	346	494	168	413	118	369	2974		
Par	4	4	4	4	5	3	5	3	4	36	RED	Rating 73.1
Handicap	5	15	9	11	1	13	3	17	7			Slope 123
Hole	10	11	12	13	14	15	16	17	18	In		Totals
BLUE	370	450	552	92	416	171	412	406	319	3188	BLUE	6475
WHITE	367	450	510	90	414	168	410	398	297	3104	WHITE	6278
Par	4	4	5	3	4	3	4	4	4	35	Par	70
Handicap	8	4	10	18	2	14	6	12	16			
RED	290	402	457	90	370	151	357	365	284	2766	RED	5740
Par	4	5	5	3	4	3	4	4	4	36	Par	72
Handicap	12	8	2	18	4	14	6	10	16			

Manager: Thomas Behnke   **Pro:** Fred Lux Jr., PGA   **Supt:** Steven Humphreys
Built: Members 1897

FISHKILL GOLF COURSE

Route 9 P.O. Box 594, Fishkill, NY 12524   **(914) 896-5220**

Fishkill is a 9 hole executive course open 7 days a week and closed Dec. - March. Tee time reservations are not necessary.

•**Driving Range**	Lockers
•**Practice Green**	Showers
Power Carts	•**Food**
•**Pull Carts**	•**Soft Spikes**
•**Club Rental**	•**Outings**

Fees	Weekday	Weekend
9 hole	$7	$7
18 hole	$12	$12

Course Description: This executive layout is fairlyflat and in very good condition with a pond and a creek in play. The greens are average size and speed with some break. The facility is excellent for working on the short game. The driving range has both grass and mats. There are areas for chipping, putting and sand practice.

Directions: Dutchess County, #9
From Exit 13 on Rte.84, go South on Rte.9 to course on right just after shopping center.

Hole	1	2	3	4	5	6	7	8	9	Out	BLUE	Rating
BLUE												Slope
WHITE	280	101	146	164	130	80	170	110	340	1521		
Par	4	3	3	3	3	3	3	3	4	29	WHITE	Rating
Handicap	9	4	5	2	6	8	3	7	1			Slope
RED												
Par											RED	Rating
Handicap												Slope

Hole	10	11	12	13	14	15	16	17	18	In		Totals
BLUE											BLUE	
WHITE											WHITE	1521
Par											Par	29
Handicap												
RED											RED	
Par											Par	
Handicap												

Manager/Supt: Jack Villeto   **Pro:** Joe Garnott, PGA
Architect: Wilton Villetto 1988

GARRISON GOLF CLUB

Route 9, P.O. Box 167, Garrison, NY 10524   (914) 424-3605

Garrison is an 18 hole course open to the public 7 days a week and closed in winter. Carts are mandatory on weekends. Memberships are available with 7-8AM tee time privileges. For tee times, call up to 7 days in advance. Fees below include power cart.

- •Driving Range
- •Practice Green
- •Power Carts
- •Pull Carts
- •Club Rental
- •Lockers
- •Showers
- •Food
- •Clubhouse
- •Outings

Fees	Weekday	Weekend
Daily	$42	$73
12-3PM	$42	$61
After 3PM	$27	$36
Sr	$32/cart	

Course Description: Garrison is a hilly, challenging course with many uneven lies. It is very wooded; streams and a pond affect play. The greens are small, fast and very true. The 2nd has a spectacular downhill tee shot off a severe vertical drop over vegetation, then a narrow chute to the landing area. From the 10th & 11th, West Point across the Hudson can be seen. On many holes, an errant shot means a lost ball. The pond on the right on the signature par 3 14th requires an accurate carry because the green has a stream behind it. The wooden bar at the restaurant has each hole carved with yardages and other features so that the 19 holers can replay their round.

Directions: Putnam County, #10
Take GW Bridge to Pal Pkwy north. At end, cross over Bear Mtn. Bridge and left on Rte.9D. Proceed about 5 miles to Rte.403 and turn right. Make left onto Rte.9 to club.

Hole	1	2	3	4	5	6	7	8	9	Out	BLUE	Rating 71.3
BLUE	398	378	176	525	390	410	452	201	348	3278		Slope 130
WHITE	388	370	166	505	367	387	439	193	338	3153		
Par	4	4	3	5	4	4	5	3	4	36	WHITE	Rating 70.0
Handicap	7	5	17	9	3	1	13	11	15			Slope 128
RED	365	113	125	425	282	310	329	143	325	2417		
Par	4	3	3	5	4	4	4	3	4	34	RED	Rating 69.3
Handicap	5	15	7	9	3	1	7	13	11			Slope 122

Hole	10	11	12	13	14	15	16	17	18	In		Totals
BLUE	490	433	324	370	215	342	293	200	525	3192	BLUE	6470
WHITE	477	421	312	356	156	332	273	185	505	3017	WHITE	6170
Par	5	4	4	4	3	4	5	3	5	36	Par	72
Handicap	6	2	16	4	12	10	18	14	8			
RED	425	391	287	334	112	255	253	127	440	2624	RED	5041
Par	5	4	4	4	3	4	5	3	5	36	Par	70
Handicap	8	2	16	4	12	10	18	14	6			

Manager/Pro: Tim Campbell, PGA   **Supt:** Richie Brown
Architect: Dick Wilson 1963

HARLEM VALLEY GOLF CLUB

PUBLIC

Wheeler Rd., Wingdale, NY 12594   **(914) 832-9957**

Harlem Valley is a 9 hole course on the grounds of the Harlem Valley State Hospital. It is open 7 days a week and closed in the winter. Tee times are available only for members until 11AM on weekends. Otherwise tee time reservations are not necessary.

Driving Range	•Lockers
•Practice Green	•Showers
•Power Carts	•Food
•Pull Carts	•Clubhouse
Club Rental	•Outings

Fees	Weekday	Weekend
9 holes	$8.50	$11
18	$15	$18
Senior discounts		
Power carts $11.50/9	$20/18	

Course Description: Harlem Valley has a quaint little clubhouse in the valley. The hilly tree-lined course has 18 different tees and nice views of the Hudson Valley. The greens are slow to average, and well bunkered; the rough is uniform. The 3rd is considered a very difficult par 3. The 8th and 9th holes have water in play. Although the course is relatively easy to walk, about one half of the golfers ride.

Directions: Dutchess County, #11
Take Rte.684 to end (becomes Rte22)to town of Wingdale. Make left at light (hospital) to course.

Hole	1	2	3	4	5	6	7	8	9	Out	BLUE	Rating 71.0
BLUE												Slope 122
WHITE	406	392	148	309	384	334	364	541	129	3007		
Par	4	4	3	4	4	4	4	5	3	35	WHITE	Rating 68.9
Handicap	1	5	15	9	7	3	11	13	17			Slope 116
RED	351	392	65	218	300	250	339	445	93	2453		
Par	5	5	3	4	4	4	4	5	3	37	RED	Rating 68.6
Handicap	5	3	13	15	11	7	9	1	17			Slope 114
Hole	10	11	12	13	14	15	16	17	18	In		Totals
BLUE											BLUE	
WHITE	351	417	159	297	363	316	339	587	147	2976	WHITE	5983
Par	4	4	3	4	4	4	4	5	3	35	Par	70
Handicap	10	8	4	12	14	6	16	2	18			
RED	351	320	135	297	363	250	290	425	50	2481	RED	4934
Par	5	4	3	4	4	4	4	5	3	36	Par	73
Handicap	6	14	4	16	10	8	12	2	18			

Manager: Al & Alice Towle   **Supt:** Don Anderson
Built: 1939

HIGHLANDS COUNTRY CLUB

Route 9D, Garrison, NY 10524   **(914) 424-3727**

Highlands is a 9 hole course open to the public only during the week in season. Memberships necessary for weekends from Memorial Day to Labor Day. It operates 7 days a week and closes 11/1-4/1. Tee time reservations are not required.

Driving Range	• Lockers
• Practice Green	• Showers
• Power Carts	• Food
• Pull Carts	• Clubhouse
• Club Rental	• Outings

Fees	Weekday	Weekend
Daily	$17	$19
Senior	$12	
Power carts	$16	$18

Course Description: Highlands is well maintained with a private club atmosphere. A pond affects play on the 5th and 6th and a brook can cause trouble on the third hole. The course is fairly short, tight and tree-lined. The small greens are soft with some break. From some spots, spectacular views of the Hudson and West Point across the river can be seen.

Directions: Putnam County, #12
From NJ, take the Pal Pkwy North to the Bear Mtn Bridge. Cross the Hudson and make an immediate left on Rte.9D to Garrison. Club is on left near intersection of Rte.403.

Hole	1	2	3	4	5	6	7	8	9	Out	BLUE	Rating
BLUE												Slope
WHITE	265	272	359	119	279	100	117	467	250	2228		
Par	4	4	4	3	4	3	3	5	4	34	WHITE	Rating 62.5
Handicap	6	11	4	18	8	15	17	2	14			Slope 105
RED	265	272	298	119	279	100	117	467	250	2112		
Par	4	4	4	3	4	3	3	5	4	34	RED	Rating 65.2
Handicap	6	11	4	18	8	15	17	2	14			Slope 105
Hole	10	11	12	13	14	15	16	17	18	In		Totals
BLUE											BLUE	
WHITE	285	272	359	126	279	149	123	467	250	2310	WHITE	4538
Par	4	4	4	3	4	3	3	5	4	34	Par	68
Handicap	5	11	3	12	7	9	16	1	13			
RED	285	272	359	126	279	108	123	467	250	2215	RED	4327
Par	4	4	5	4	3	4	5	5	4	34	Par	68
Handicap	5	11	3	12	7	9	16	1	13			

Manager: Jim Delmar   **Pro:** Joe Cristello   **Supt:** Steve Burke
Built: 1898

ISLAND GREEN COUNTRY CLUB

Route 22, Amenia, NY 12501 (914) 373-9200

Island Green, formerly Segalla CC, is an 18 hole course open to the public 7 days a week and closed 11/30-4/15. Carts are required until 4PM. Tee time reservations may be made up to 6 days in advance. The complex is presently adding 9 new holes. The course is now under new ownership.

•**Driving Range**	Lockers
•**Practice Green**	•**Showers**
•**Power Carts**	•**Food**
•**Pull Carts**	•**Clubhouse**
•**Club Rental**	•**Outings**

Fees	Weekday	Weekend
Daily	$23	$29
After 4PM	$10/9	$10/9
Jr/Sr M-Th	$16	
Power Carts	$22	

Course Description: Island Green, a beautifully maintained quite busy course, offers breathtaking views of the surrounding mountains. Seven ponds affect play on several holes. The bent grass greens are fairly large, medium fast and somewhat sloped. With many elevated tees and greens, there are few possibilities to bump and run. The dogleg right par 4 15th features a shot from an elevated tee over a ravine. The open fairways are contoured, some sloping from one side to the other so that strategic drive placement will help the golfer's play. The newly designated signature hole will be chosen by creating an *island green* on an existing pond, (hence the new name). A large, impressive clubhouse adds to the attraction here.

Directions: Dutchess County, #13
Take I-684North toward Brewster (becomes Rte.22). Continue on Rte.22 about 30 minutes to course on left.

Hole	1	2	3	4	5	6	7	8	9	Out	BLUE	Rating 72.0
BLUE	550	379	180	511	366	350	380	185	368	3269		Slope 133
WHITE	535	366	166	488	346	330	362	168	342	3103		
Par	5	4	3	5	4	4	4	3	4	36	WHITE	Rating 70.3
Handicap	1	5	17	3	11	13	9	15	7			Slope 129
RED	494	295	145	439	323	307	329	149	300	2781		
Par	5	4	3	5	4	4	4	3	4	36	RED	Rating 72.3
Handicap	1	13	17	3	7	9	5	15	11			Slope 129
Hole	10	11	12	13	14	15	16	17	18	In		Totals
BLUE	520	375	204	343	332	433	193	564	384	3348	BLUE	6617
WHITE	509	352	172	315	307	396	170	540	362	3123	WHITE	6226
Par	5	4	3	4	4	4	3	5	4	36	Par	72
Handicap	6	10	14	12	18	2	16	4	8			
RED	457	286	151	297	284	358	136	521	330	2820	RED	5601
Par	5	4	3	4	4	4	3	5	4	36	Par	72
Handicap	4	12	16	10	14	6	18	2	8			

Dir. of Golf: Cart Bates   **Supt:** Willie Moriarity
Architect: Albert Zikorus 1992

JAMES BAIRD STATE PARK GOLF COURSE

PUBLIC

Freedom Plains Road, Pleasant Valley, NY 12569 (914) 473-1052

James Baird is an 18 hole NY State owned public course open 7 days a week, from April 1 to Dec. 15. Tee times may be made 10 days in advance between 2 & 4 PM by calling (914) 485-7358.

•**Driving Range** •**Lockers**
•**Practice Green** •**Showers**
•**Power Carts** •**Food**
•**Pull Carts** •**Clubhouse**
•**Club Rental** •**Outings**
Soft Spikes

Fees	Weekday	Weekend
Daily	$17	$20
Power carts	$23/2	
	$15/1	

Course Description: James Baird is a challenging course with some elevated greens that are well trapped and medium in size. The front nine is more open and forgiving than the back, which is tighter. On the par 5 13th signature hole, an accurate tee shot is imperative because the chute fairway has a "humpback". The par 3 15th requires a shot over a large pond and a substantial uphill carry to the green. Several other holes have water in play.

Directions: Dutchess County, #14
Taconic Pkwy. North to the exit 1 mile north of Rte.55. Look for James Baird State Park. (approx. 15 miles North of the I-84 Interchange).

Hole	1	2	3	4	5	6	7	8	9	Out	BLUE	Rating 71.3
BLUE	382	393	117	443	213	529	461	159	361	3058		Slope 124
WHITE	345	383	109	426	202	464	381	159	355	2824		
Par	4	4	3	4	3	5	4	3	4	34	WHITE	Rating 69.5
Handicap	12	8	18	4	10	6	2	16	14			Slope 120
RED	245	373	101	407	190	427	340	159	348	2590		
Par	4	4	3	5	4	5	4	3	4	36	RED	Rating 70.9
Handicap	8	6	18	4	14	2	10	16	12			Slope 122
Hole	10	11	12	13	14	15	16	17	18	In		Totals
BLUE	537	398	216	560	360	214	487	397	389	3558	BLUE	6616
WHITE	515	387	204	526	353	170	480	386	356	3377	WHITE	6201
Par	5	4	3	5	4	3	5	4	4	37	Par	71
Handicap	7	11	5	1	15	9	17	13	3			
RED	412	368	127	406	297	126	473	375	331	2951	RED	5541
Par	6	4	3	5	4	3	5	4	4	38	Par	74
Handicap	1	9	15	3	11	17	5	7	13			

Manager: Jim Gell **Pro:** Brad Davis, PGA **Supt:** Larry Salvatore
Architect: Robert Trent Jones, 1953

MAHOPAC GOLF CLUB

PRIVATE

601 N. Lake Blvd., Mahopac, NY 10541   **(914) 628-8090**

Mahopac is a private 18 hole club open 6 days a week and closed from mid Nov. to mid April. Guests play accompanied by a member. Tee time reservations are necessary on weekends only.

•**Driving Range**	•**Lockers**
•**Practice Green**	•**Showers**
•**Power Carts**	•**Food**
•**Pull Carts**	•**Clubhouse**
•**Club Rental**	•**Outings**
•**Caddies**	•**Soft Spikes**

Course Description: Overlooking Lake Mahopac lies one of the oldest NY area golf clubs. The original course began as a nine holer and was later increased to 18 holes. The rolling hills offer a challenging layout with not much water in play. There are thick trees bordering the lush fairways. The small greens are deceptively fast and well trapped. The golf course is conveniently located in Putnam County, not far from I-684.

Directions: Putnam County, #15
Take the Taconic Pkwy to Rte.6. Go right approx. 7 mi into Mahopac and at light at E. Lake Blvd turn left. In about 1 mi, make left onto N. Lake Blvd. Club is on right.

Hole	1	2	3	4	5	6	7	8	9	Out	BLUE	Rating 70.4
BLUE	380	438	159	373	475	190	601	163	380	3159		Slope 120
WHITE	360	430	150	368	463	183	591	157	352	3054		
Par	4	4	3	4	5	3	5	3	4	35	WHITE	Rating 69.3
Handicap	13	1	17	11	7	9	3	15	5			Slope 117
RED	337	383	145	343	368	175	438	151	288	2628		
Par	4	5	3	4	5	3	5	3	4	36	RED	Rating 71.4
Handicap	7	3	17	9	5	13	1	15	11			Slope 116
Hole	10	11	12	13	14	15	16	17	18	In		Totals
BLUE	430	371	190	385	204	338	436	404	483	3241	BLUE	6400
WHITE	425	351	180	375	197	305	412	397	465	3107	WHITE	6161
Par	4	4	3	4	3	4	4	4	5	35	Par	70
Handicap	8	10	18	2	14	16	6	14	12			
RED	405	254	170	283	147	274	400	375	431	2739	RED	5367
Par	4	4	3	4	3	4	5	4	5	36	Par	72
Handicap	6	12	16	10	18	14	8	2	4			

Manager: Howard Kelly   **Pro:** Todd Heyda, PGA   **Supt:** Scott Ferguson
Architect: Tom Bendelow **Estab:** 1898

McCANN MEMORIAL GOLF COURSE

155 Wilbur Blvd., Poughkeepsie, NY 12603　　(914) 471-3917

McCann Memorial is an 18 hole municipal course open 7 days a week between April 1 and Dec. 1. Tee times may be made 1 week in advance for weekends (call Sundays at 2PM•• 454-1968) and are not necessary during the week. Memberships are available.

•**Driving Range**	Lockers
•**Practice Green**	Showers
•**Power Carts**	•**Food**
•**Pull Carts**	•**Clubhouse**
•**Club Rental**	•**Outings**
Soft Spikes	

Fees	Weekday	Weekend
Daily(Town Res)	$11	$15
County Res.	$15	$18
Non-Res	$25	$30
Power carts	$22	

Course Description: McCann is an easy course to walk with gentle hills and narrow tree-lined fairways. It is known to have the largest greens and tees in the area, many of which are elevated. Water is in play on 7 holes. The signature #18 is a long par 4, dogleg right and is considered by some as the best finishing hole in Dutchess County. Jim McCann, a Poughkeepsie merchant who funded various sporting, educational, and recreational endeavors, originally wanted the city to benefit by having a wonderful course with discounted rates. Many qualifying rounds for state tournaments have been played here.

Directions: Dutchess County, #16
I-684North to Rte.84 to Exit 13. Take Rte. 9 North. Turn right at Spackenbill Rd. & left at 2nd light on Wilbur Blvd. Course is ahead on right.

Hole	1	2	3	4	5	6	7	8	9	Out	BLUE	Rating 72.0
BLUE	388	499	429	491	184	317	333	149	393	3183		Slope 128
WHITE	377	463	412	468	159	297	318	143	370	3007		
Par	4	5	4	5	3	4	4	3	4	36	WHITE	Rating 70.0
Handicap	11	15	1	9	3	5	17	13	7			Slope 124
RED	333	400	359	437	122	247	292	113	336	2639		
Par	4	5	4	5	3	4	4	3	4	36	RED	Rating 71.4
Handicap	9	5	1	3	13	11	15	17	7			Slope 123
Hole	10	11	12	13	14	15	16	17	18	In		Totals
BLUE	401	399	188	411	548	143	353	475	423	3341	BLUE	6524
WHITE	377	363	175	404	471	117	330	448	398	3083	WHITE	6090
Par	4	4	3	4	5	3	4	5	4	36	Par	72
Handicap	2	8	12	4	14	16	10	18	6			
RED	310	316	148	360	437	98	288	420	338	2715	RED	5354
Par	4	4	3	4	5	3	4	5	4	36	Par	72
Handicap	4	12	16	2	6	18	10	14	8			

Manager: Robert Paquet **Pro**: Ron Jensen, PGA   **Supt**: John Adriance
Architect: William Mitchell 1971

MILLBROOK GOLF & TENNIS CLUB

Route 343 P.O. Box 1096, Millbrook, NY 12545 **(914) 677-3810**

Millbrook is a 9 hole private course open 7 days a week and closed Nov. 1-April 1. Guests play accompanied by a member. Tee time reservations are not necessary.

- •Driving Range
- •Practice Green
- •Power Carts
- •Pull Carts
- •Club Rental
- Caddies
- •Lockers
- •Showers
- •Food
- •Clubhouse
- •Outings
- •Soft Spikes

Course Description: Panoramic views of the Hudson Valley are part of the charm that is Millbrook. Hilly, the many uneven lies lead to greens that are relatively small, tricky and fast. The 5th is rated one of the top ten prettiest holes in Dutchess County. The drive is from an elevated tee over a pond to the landing area; the approach shot is to a green surrounded by bunkers. A stream and a creek may affect play on #s 4 and 6. It is prudent to lay up on the 1st hole to avoid the creek in the middle of the fairway. The signature 9th is a most difficult par 3. The original clubhouse was destroyed by fire in 1931.

Directions: Dutchess County, #17
Take I-684 to end which becomes Rte.22. Continue north on Rte.22 to Dover Plains. Go right onto Rte.343 about 6 miles to course on right. From Taconic, take Rte.343 exit.

Hole	1	2	3	4	5	6	7	8	9	Out	BLUE	Rating
BLUE												Slope
WHITE	497	188	518	289	326	441	155	386	207	3007		
Par	5	3	5	4	4	5	3	4	3	36	WHITE	Rating 69.1
Handicap	11	5	9	15	13	7	17	1	3			Slope 121
RED	455	139	414	243	179	389	109	291	151	2370		
Par	5	3	5	4	4	5	3	4	3	36	RED	Rating 68.3
Handicap	3	15	7	13	17	5	11	1	9			Slope 121

Hole	10	11	12	13	14	15	16	17	18	In		Totals
BLUE											BLUE	
WHITE	485	188	478	320	275	389	145	343	242	2865	WHITE	5872
Par	5	3	5	4	4	5	3	4	3	36	Par	72
Handicap	10	6	12	4	18	2	16	8	14			
RED	485	188	296	145	275	325	145	343	207	2409	RED	4779
Par	5	3	5	4	4	5	3	4	3	36	Par	72
Handicap	2	10	4	18	6	14	8	16	12			

Manager: John Paonessa   **Pro:** Peter Serafimoff, PGA   **Supt:** Dave Vince
Architect: Henry McLane 1903 Geoffrey Cornish 1963

MOREFAR GOLF CLUB

Federal Hill Rd., Brewster, NY 10509   **(914) 279-5086**

Morefar is an 18 hole private club open 7 days a week and closed in the winter. Guests play accompanied by a member. Tee time reservations are not necessary. The driving range is for warmup only. Pull carts are allowed on rainy days.

•**Driving Range**	•**Lockers**
•**Practice Green**	•**Showers**
•**Power Carts**	•**Food**
• **Pull Carts**	•**Clubhouse**
•**Club Rental**	•**Outings**
Caddies	•**Soft Spikes**

Course Description: Morefar is a heavily treed course that has a fair amount of water and thick rough. It has only corporate memberships and thus is busier during the week than on weekends. The back nine is very hilly and somewhat longer than the front. The fairways are narrow.

Directions: Putnam County, #18
Take I-684N and follow signs for and take Rte22.N, Pawling. Watch for Heidi's Motel on right. In about 1 mi. turn right onto Milltown Rd. Take right fork onto Federal Hill Rd. Morefar is ahead on left.

Hole	1	2	3	4	5	6	7	8	9	Out	BLUE	Rating 73.0
BLUE	340	150	533	303	347	368	178	344	612	3175		Slope 133
WHITE	333	137	520	298	337	360	165	318	582	3050		
Par	4	3	5	4	4	4	3	4	5	36	WHITE	Rating 70.7
Handicap	11	17	3	15	5	9	13	7	1			Slope 129
RED	288	100	450	238	322	300	127	315	507	2647		
Par	4	3	5	4	4	4	3	4	5	36	RED	Rating 71.4
Handicap	11	17	3	15	5	9	13	7	1			Slope 127
Hole	10	11	12	13	14	15	16	17	18	In		Totals
BLUE	437	478	607	150	406	410	423	185	477	3573	BLUE	6748
WHITE	392	395	565	133	353	372	335	142	455	3142	WHITE	6192
Par	4	4	5	3	4	4	4	3	5	36	Par	72
Handicap	6	4	2	18	12	10	14	16	8			
RED	310	355	508	100	306	352	305	123	385	2744	RED	5391
Par	4	4	5	3	4	4	4	3	5	36	Par	72
Handicap	6	4	2	18	12	10	14	16	8			

Manager: Ans DeBeus   **Pro:** Tom Kochan, PGA   **Supt:** Mike Maffai
Built:1962

PUTNAM COUNTRY CLUB

PUBLIC

Hill St., Mahopac, NY 10541 **(914) 628-3451**

Putnam is an 18 hole course open to the public 7 days a week all year, weather permitting. Golfers can call up to 1 week in advance for reservations for a $4 per person fee. Driving range is for irons only. Carts mandatory Fri-Sun.

•**Driving Range**	Lockers
•**Practice Green**	•**Showers**
•**Power Carts**	•**Food**
•**Pull Carts**	•**Clubhouse**
•**Club Rental**	•**Outings**

Fees	Weekday	Weekend
Daily	$24	$38
Senior	$22	
Twi	$14	$23
Carts pp	$12	$12

Course Description: Putnam was built in the 1950s as a private club. It is a fairly open, somewhat hilly course with sloping average sized greens that are fast in summer. Water is in play on 2 holes. The deceptively difficult signature par 4 #17 features an elevated tee, a contoured fairway and a slightly rising entrance to a green guarded by bunkers. The ninth is a straight uphill and long par 4.

Directions: Putnam County, #19
Take the Taconic Pkwy to Rte.6 (Mahopac/Shrub Oak exit). Make a right at light onto Rte.6.Go left onto Rte.6N for approx. 3 miles and turn left onto Hill Street. Go 1 mile to club on the left.

Hole	1	2	3	4	5	6	7	8	9	Out	BLUE	Rating 72.4
BLUE	408	347	180	510	393	210	530	470	454	3502		Slope 129
WHITE	392	304	162	493	363	195	513	438	438	3298		
Par	4	4	3	5	4	3	5	4	4	36	WHITE	Rating 70.5
Handicap	7	15	17	9	13	3	11	5	1			Slope 125
RED	374	292	144	452	318	176	470	430	408	3064		
Par	4	4	3	5	4	3	5	5	4	37	RED	Rating 73.7
Handicap	3	13	15	5	11	17	1	9	7			Slope 132
Hole	10	11	12	13	14	15	16	17	18	In		Totals
BLUE	555	424	387	467	160	351	180	375	373	3272	BLUE	6774
WHITE	540	394	345	447	142	321	166	360	359	3074	WHITE	6372
Par	5	4	4	4	3	4	3	4	4	35	Par	71
Handicap	10	4	14	2	16	12	18	8	6			
RED	459	383	307	404	125	289	150	333	285	2735	RED	5799
Par	5	4	4	5	3	4	3	4	4	36	Par	73
Handicap	4	2	10	6	18	12	16	8	14			

Manager: Al Duarte **Pro:** Frank Misarti, PGA **Supt:** Doug George
Architect: William Mitchell 1959

QUAKER HILL COUNTRY CLUB

Quaker Hill Rd., Pawling, NY 12584   **(914) 855-1040**

Quaker Hill is a private 9 hole course. It is open 7 days a week and closed in winter. Guests play accompanied by a member. Tee time reservations are not necessary.

•**Driving Range**	•**Lockers**
•**Practice Green**	•**Showers**
•**Power Carts**	•**Food**
•**Pull Carts**	•**Clubhouse**
Club Rental	Outings
•**Caddies**	•**Soft Spikes**

Course Description: Quaker Hill is a beautifully maintained course with many old trees. It is very hilly and has magnificent views of the mountains in the distance. The greens are fast and well-bunkered. The natural terrain provides many uneven lies. The wind proves to be a factor in course management. Water is in play on some holes. Lowell Thomas and Governor Thomas E. Dewey played here.

Directions: Dutchess County, #20
Take I-684N which becomes Rte.22. Continue north on Rte22 to Pawling. At light, turn right onto Quaker Hill Rd. At 'T' intersection, turn left. Continue approx. 2 miles to club entrance on left.

Hole	1	2	3	4	5	6	7	8	9	Out	BLUE	Rating
BLUE												Slope
WHITE	372	414	502	136	410	164	375	505	164	3042		
Par	4	4	5	3	4	3	4	5	3	35	WHITE	Rating 69.4
Handicap	11	3	5	17	1	13	9	7	15			Slope 123
RED	355	360	430	125	400	137	370	435	117	2729		
Par	4	5	5	3	5	3	4	5	3	37	RED	Rating 72.2
Handicap	11	7	3	17	5	13	9	1	15			Slope 122

Hole	10	11	12	13	14	15	16	17	18	In		Totals
BLUE											BLUE	
WHITE	405	362	440	144	453	196	355	535	135	3025	WHITE	6067
Par	4	4	4	3	5	3	4	5	3	35	Par	70
Handicap	10	6	2	16	8	14	12	4	18			
RED	395	350	425	134	413	186	345	495	125	2868	RED	5597
Par	4	5	5	3	5	3	4	5	3	37	Par	74
Handicap	14	8	6	18	4	12	10	2	16			

Manager/Pro: Craig Smith, PGA **Supt:** Gary Lattrell
Architect: Robert Trent Jones 1939

RED HOOK GOLF CLUB

RD2, Box 131, Red Hook, NY 12571   **(914) 758-8652**

Red Hook is a semi-private 18 hole course open 6 1/2 days a week (closes Mon. AM) from April 1 to Nov. 15, weather permitting. Memberships are available. Members may call for tee times 1 wk. in advance, non-members have 48 hours.

•Driving Range	•Lockers
•Practice Green	•Showers
•Power Carts	•Food
•Pull Carts	•Clubhouse
•Club Rental	•Outings
•Soft Spikes	

Fees	Weekday	Weekend
Daily(18)	$24	$30
Daily (9)	$15	$20
Twi /(3:30)	$20	
Power carts	$22	

Course Description: The original 9 hole Red Hook was private but later became semi-private. Abundant apple orchards block the view of the other holes. The terrain is gently rolling with some contour but no major hills. The fairways are reasonably wide yet they are bounded by trees. The par 5 13th, a sharp dogleg left, could be considered the signature hole; it has a pond that may require a lay up off the tee. The par 4s are long and tough and water comes into play on 3 holes. The medium sized greens are smooth and relatively fast. The course is becoming more popular.

Directions: Dutchess County, #21
Taconic Pkwy. to exit for Red Hook. Take Rte.199 west for 5 miles to light and bear right. It is still Rte.199. Course is 1/2 mile on left.

Hole	1	2	3	4	5	6	7	8	9	Out	BLUE	Rating 70.7
BLUE	396	171	559	407	497	148	436	392	349	3355		Slope 128
WHITE	364	158	519	384	476	138	380	383	336	3138		
Par	4	3	5	4	5	3	4	4	4	36	WHITE	Rating 69.5
Handicap	9	15	1	5	8	17	4	7	11			Slope 126
RED	302	122	347	306	415	115	342	286	316	2551		
Par	4	3	4	4	5	3	4	4	4	35	RED	Rating 72.6
Handicap	11	17	5	8	2	16	6	13	7			Slope 126
Hole	10	11	12	13	14	15	16	17	18	In		Totals
BLUE	360	429	172	480	351	155	338	544	335	3164	BLUE	6519
WHITE	342	412	141	470	331	134	326	525	315	2996	WHITE	6031
Par	4	4	3	5	4	3	4	5	4	36	Par	72
Handicap	10	3	18	6	12	16	14	2	13			
RED	296	380	116	401	278	115	297	455	266	2604	RED	5524
Par	4	4	3	5	4	3	4	5	4	36	Par	71
Handicap	12	3	18	4	9	15	10	1	14			

Manager: Tom Schaad **Pro:** John Mahon, PGA   **Supt:** Craig Burkhardt
Architect: David Horn 1996 **Estab:** 1931

THE SEDGEWOOD CLUB

Route 301, Carmel, NY 10512   **(914) 225-5227**

The Sedgewood Club is a 9 hole private facility. It is open 7 days a week and closed in the winter. Tee time reservations are not necessary.

Driving Range	Lockers
Practice Green	Showers
•**Power Carts**	Food
•**Pull Carts**	•**Clubhouse**
Club Rental	•**Outings**
Caddies	Soft Spikes

Course Description: Sedgewood was originally the Carmel Country Club. It is a somewhat hilly layout situated on a mountaintop in a wooded area near a reservoir. The course is fairly wide open but errant shots are penalized by the deep woods along the edge of the rough. The 6th hole has a 200 foot drop from an elevated tee. It is considered a par 4, although a long and accurate shot could drive the green. The poa and bent grass greens are of moderate to fast speed with considerable break. Water is not in play. From this high point in the county, there are beautiful views of the distant mountains and valleys. Yardages below are the same for back and forward tees. Only pars and handicaps change.

Directions: Putnam County, #22
Take the Taconic Parkway to Exit for Rte.21N in Tompkins Corners. Go northeast on Rte.21. At Kent Cliiffs, make right onto Rte.301 for about 1 mile until club on right.

Hole	1	2	3	4	5	6	7	8	9	Out	BLUE	Rating
BLUE												Slope
WHITE	372	350	117	454	395	259	391	169	498	3005		
Par	4	4	3	4	4	4	4	3	5	35	WHITE	Rating 66.2
Handicap	5	11	17	1	3	13	7	15	9			Slope 108
RED												
Par	4	4	3	5	5	4	5	3	5	38	RED	Rating 71.0
Handicap	3	11	17	7	9	13	5	15	1			Slope 116

Hole	10	11	12	13	14	15	16	17	18	In		Totals
BLUE											BLUE	
WHITE	346	292	98	394	390	193	320	147	464	2644	WHITE	5649
Par	4	4	3	4	4	3	4	3	4	33	Par	68
Handicap	4	12	18	10	6	8	14	16	2			
RED											RED	
Par	4	4	3	5	5	3	4	3	5	36	Par	74
Handicap	4	10	18	12	8	6	10	12	2			

Manager/Pro/Supt: Clarence Fogal, PGA
Architect: William H. Tucker 1920s

SOUTHERN DUTCHESS CC

53 North Ave. Route 9D, Beacon, NY 12508   **(914) 831-0762**

Southern Dutchess is a 9 hole private course open 7 days a week and closed Dec. 1-April 1. Memberships are available. Tee time reservations are necessary for weekends only.

Driving Range	•**Lockers**
•**Practice Green**	•**Showers**
•**Power Carts**	•**Food**
•**Pull Carts**	•**Clubhouse**
•**Club Rental**	•**Outings**
•Caddies	Soft Spikes

Course Description: The beautiful hilly fairways at Southern Dutchess are so lush that there is little roll and the course plays long. The well-irrigated greens are fairly small with some slope. The signature par 5 #9 is a long return to the clubhouse; Mt Beacon can be seen in the distance. The 4th requires a well struck tee shot over a pond to a dogleg left. The 8th is a tough uphill dogleg right. A different set of tees are used for the back nine.

Directions: Dutchess County, #23
Take NY Thruway (Rte.87) to Rte.84 and at Exit 11 go south on Rte.9D. Club is immediately on the right.

Hole	1	2	3	4	5	6	7	8	9	Out	BLUE	Rating
BLUE												Slope
WHITE	389	172	342	505	153	510	156	362	420	3009		
Par	4	3	4	5	3	5	3	4	4	35	WHITE	Rating 68.7
Handicap	3	13	7	11	15	9	17	5	1			Slope 119
RED	380	160	320	460	145	460	150	310	415	2800		
Par	4	3	4	5	3	5	3	4	5	36	RED	Rating 67.3
Handicap	7	13	9	1	15	3	17	11	5			Slope 116

Hole	10	11	12	13	14	15	16	17	18	In		Totals
BLUE											BLUE	
WHITE	395	181	362	512	158	385	162	372	480	3007	WHITE	6016
Par	4	3	4	5	3	5	3	4	4	35	Par	70
Handicap	2	14	6	12	16	8	18	4	10			
RED	389	172	342	505	153	465	156	315	420	2917	RED	5717
Par	4	3	4	5	3	5	3	4	5	36	Par	72
Handicap	8	14	10	2	16	4	18	12	6			

Manager/Pro: Tony De Stefano, PGA   **Supt:** Roy Watters
Estab: 1902

THOMAS CARVEL COUNTRY CLUB

Ferris Road, PO Box 763, Pine Plains, NY 12567   **(914) 266-3377**

Thomas Carvel is an 18 hole course open 7 days a week, and closed between Thanksgiving and April 1. Tee times may be made 1 week in advance by phone. New ownership has taken over in late 1997.

- **Driving Range**
- **Practice Green**
- **Power Carts**
- Pull Carts
- **Club Rental**
- Soft Spikes

- **Lockers**
- **Showers**
- **Food**
- **Clubhouse**
- **Outings**

Fees	Weekday	Weekend
Daily	$34	$40

Power carts included

Course Description: Thomas Carvel is a long open arena type course with large, fast undulating greens many of which are elevated and hard to read. They are considered by many to be the best in the Hudson Valley. There are several small ponds that affect play but the difficulty lies in the fast greens and length of the course (7025 yds. from the blues). The par 3 17th signature hole is downhill and very tight with woods on both sides. Many of the excellently maintained fairways slope left to right or right to left. Scenic views of the Catskills in the distance are part of the attraction here.

Directions: Dutchess County, #24
Taconic Pkwy. North to Exit D-25. Go East on Ferris Rd. to club.

Hole	1	2	3	4	5	6	7	8	9	Out	BLUE	Rating 73.5
BLUE	426	404	409	166	367	533	227	404	588	3524		Slope 127
WHITE	417	385	376	151	292	458	205	396	555	3235		
Par	4	4	4	3	4	5	3	4	5	36	WHITE	Rating 71.6
Handicap	3	11	5	17	9	15	13	7	1			Slope 123
RED	322	285	333	148	216	396	173	287	287	2447		
Par	5	4	5	3	4	5	3	4	4	37	RED	Rating 69.0
Handicap	3	9	1	7	11	17	13	5	15			Slope 115
Hole	10	11	12	13	14	15	16	17	18	In		Totals
BLUE	415	203	388	491	363	389	574	185	493	3501	BLUE	7025
WHITE	401	196	379	458	340	380	558	169	484	3365	WHITE	6600
Par	4	3	4	5	4	4	5	3	5	37	Par	73
Handicap	6	14	8	10	16	4	2	18	2			
RED	335	186	318	408	240	274	361	118	379	2619	RED	5066
Par	5	3	4	5	4	4	5	3	5	38	Par	75
Handicap	8	16	4	10	14	6	12	18	2			

Manager: Joseph Gerentine   **Supt:** George Wade
Architect: William Mitchell 1967

VAILS GROVE GOLF COURSE

R.R.#2 Peach Lake, Brewster, NY 10509   **(914) 669-5721**

Vail's Grove is a 9 hole course that has memberships and is also open to the public. Members only may play up until 1PM on weekends and holidays. It is open 7 days a week and closes between Thanksgiving & April 1. Tee time reservations are not necessary. Memberships include green fees for the season and have varying costs.

Driving Range	•**Lockers**
•**Practice Green**	•**Showers**
•**Power Carts**	•**Food**
•**Pull Carts**	•**Clubhouse**
Club Rental	•**Outings**
Soft Spikes	

Fees	Weekday	Weekend
Daily(18holes)	$10	$20
Twilight		$10
Sr/Jr		$15
Power carts	$20 (18holes)	

Course Description: Vails Grove is well-maintained and has enough variation to make it challenging.   There is no water in play. The relatively fast greens are small. The 2nd hole is a short par 3 and is considered quite difficult. From an elevated tee the golfer encounters traps on the left, a road on the right and a green that slopes front to back. It is hard to recover if the ball doesn't land on the green. The yardages below can be repeated for the second nine.

Directions: Putnam County, #25
Take I-684 towards Brewster to Rte.6 (exit just after I-84 intersection). Turn left onto Rte.6. Go approx. 1 mile & turn right on Rte.121 for 1 mile to club on left.

Hole	1	2	3	4	5	6	7	8	9	Out	BLUE	Rating 61.3
BLUE	302	136	274	306	225	294	225	172	467	2401		Slope 95
WHITE	286	118	262	282	185	272	210	163	450	2228		
Par	4	3	4	4	3	4	3	3	5	33	WHITE	Rating 60.1
Handicap	11	17	13	7	9	5	3	15	1			Slope 93
RED	280	114	256	190	160	268	210	163	425	2066		
Par	4	3	4	4	3	4	4	3	6	35	RED	Rating 61.9
Handicap	11	17	13	7	9	5	3	15	1			Slope 94
Hole	10	11	12	13	14	15	16	17	18	In		Totals
BLUE											BLUE	4802
WHITE											WHITE	4456
Par											Par	66
Handicap												
RED											RED	4132
Par											Par	70
Handicap												

Architect: Marcus Knapp 1929   **Supt:** Tom Farrelly

VASSAR GOLF COURSE

Raymond Ave., Vassar Campus, Poughkeepsie, NY 12603 **(914) 473-1550**

Vassar College Golf Course is a privately owned 9 hole facility open to the public 7 days a week and closed between Nov.15 and April 1. Discounts are available for students of the college. Tee times for foursomes may be made 1 day or more in advance.

Driving Range	Lockers
•**Practice Green**	Showers
•**Power Carts**	Food
•**Pull Carts**	Clubhouse
•**Club Rental**	•**Outings**
Soft Spikes	

Fees	Weekday	Weekend
Daily (9)	$7.50	$8.50
Daily (18)	$14	$15.50
Power carts	$10.50(9)	$17(18)

Course Description: Vassar is a scenic 9 hole course that is relatively flat and easy to walk. There are gently rolling hills with fairly small greens that have slight breaks. Many seniors and beginners play here. There is no water in play on the course. It was originally built for women attending Vassar College, and in the 40's it was leased out and opened to the public as well.

Directions: Dutchess County, #26
Rte.84 to Exit 13; go north on Rte. 9 to Rte.77 (Vassar Rd.)which becomes New Hackensack Rd. & Rte.376. Make a right onto Raymond to the next traffic light; go left onto College View Ave. to end of street and turn right through the Vassar College gate. Course is at the far East side of the campus.

Hole	1	2	3	4	5	6	7	8	9	Out	BLUE	Rating
BLUE												Slope
WHITE	325	298	131	410	350	171	320	395	390	2790		
Par	4	4	3	4	4	3	4	4	4	34	WHITE	Rating
Handicap	9	13	17	1	7	15	11	3	5			Slope
RED												
Par											RED	Rating
Hand icap												Slope

Hole	10	11	12	13	14	15	16	17	18	In		Totals
BLUE											BLUE	
WHITE											WHITE	
Par											Par	
Handicap												
RED											RED	
Par											Par	
Handicap												

Manager: Carol Vinall   **Supt:** Harry Vinall
Built: 1927

WHISPERING PINES GOLF CLUB

Route 9, Poughkeepsie, NY 12601 **(914) 452-4256**

Whispering Pines is on the grounds of the Hudson River Psychiatric Center. It is owned by the State and leased out. It is a 9 hole course open all year (weather permitting), 7 days a week. Tee times may be made 2 days in advance. Season passes are available.

Driving Range	•**Lockers**
•**Practice Green**	•**Showers**
•**Power Carts**	•**Food**
•**Pull Carts**	•**Clubhouse**
•**Club Rental**	•**Outings**
Soft Spikes	

Fees	Weekday	Weekend
Daily(18)	$14	$18
9 holes	$8	$10
Power carts	$18 (18)	

Course Description: Whispering Pines has some of the best views of the mountains of Orange & Ulster Counties as well as Woodstock in the distance. It is somewhat hilly with well trapped greens that are in great condition. There is no water in play. It is rustic; an old trapping cabin built in the 1930s is next to the pro shop. The layout is fairly short (4854 yds.); a great place for practice. The condition of the course is the best it has been in years.

Directions: Dutchess County, #27
Take I-684 North to I-84 West. Go on I-84 West to Taconic St. Pkwy. North to Rte.55 West. Proceed West to Rte. 9 North; make a right onto hospital grounds & bear left to clubhouse.

Hole	1	2	3	4	5	6	7	8	9	Out	BLUE	Rating
BLUE												Slope
WHITE	370	109	253	194	474	334	147	358	188	2427		
Par	4	3	4	3	5	4	3	4	3	33	WHITE	Rating 63.4
Handicap	5	17	9	13	1	7	15	3	11			Slope 102
RED	339	109	253	194	411	292	138	338	171	2245		
Par	4	3	4	3	5	4	3	4	3	33	RED	Rating 65.7
Handicap	5	17	9	13	1	7	15	3	11			Slope 105
Hole	10	11	12	13	14	15	16	17	18	In		Totals
BLUE											BLUE	
WHITE											WHITE	4854
Par											Par	66
Handicap												
RED											RED	4490
Par											Par	66
Handicap												

Manager: Cliff Dunkle   **Pro./Supt:** William Reynolds, PGA
Built: 1938

Golf

It is a test of temper, a trial of honor,

and revealer of character.

It is a contest, a duel or a melee,

calling for courage, skill, strategy and self.

It affords a chance to play the man, and

act the gentleman.

It is a cure for care -- an antidote to worry.

(Vail's Grove)

FAIRFIELD COUNTY

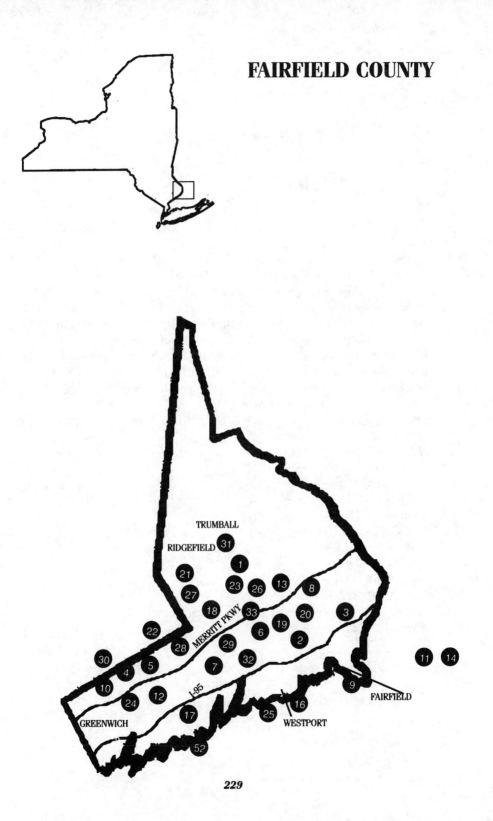

TRUMBALL

RIDGEFIELD 31

21

27

18 MERRITT PKWY

22

28

30 5

4

10

24 12 I-95

17

GREENWICH

52

1

23 26 13 8

33 20 3

6 19

29 2

7 32

9

FAIRFIELD

16

25 WESTPORT

11 14

229

FAIRFIELD COUNTY

Public Courses appear in **_bold italics_**

ASPETUCK VALLEY CC

67 Old Redding Rd., Weston, CT 06883   **(203) 226-9989**

Aspetuck is a private 18 hole course open all year, weather permitting, 6 days a week. Guests play accompanied by a member. Pull carts are allowed when power carts are not available. Tee time reservations are not necessary.

•**Driving Range**	•**Lockers**
•**Practice Green**	•**Showers**
•**Power Carts**	•**Food**
•**Pull Carts**	•**Clubhouse**
•**Club Rental**	•**Outings**
•**Caddies**	•**Soft Spikes**

Course Description: Aspetuck Valley is a very hilly course with tight tree lined fairways and many uneven lies. The fast greens have a great deal of undulation. Water is in play on 12 holes. The signature par 5 #11 is a beautiful downhill with water on the right and left and OB right. Water surrounds the green; a picturesque bridge is nearby. The 7th is long from the blues, a downhill par 4. The clubhouse has recently been rebuilt.

Directions: Fairfield County, #1
Take the Merritt Pkwy to Exit 42. Turn left off the ramp onto Weston Rd. Go diagonally across and left onto Easton Rd (Rte.136). Go north 4 miles and left onto Old Redding. Course is ahead on right.

Hole	1	2	3	4	5	6	7	8	9	Out	BLUE	Rating 73.1
BLUE	381	359	349	566	155	540	421	180	376	3326		Slope 129
WHITE	360	349	332	519	140	523	398	165	361	3147		
Par	4	4	4	5	3	5	4	3	4	36	WHITE	Rating 71.4
Handicap	13	7	11	9	17	13	1	15	5			Slope 126
RED	337	336	293	489	109	404	289	150	240	2647		
Par	4	4	4	5	3	5	4	3	4	36	RED	Rating 71.6
Handicap	7	1	11	3	17	5	13	15	9			Slope 126
Hole	10	11	12	13	14	15	16	17	18	In		Totals
BLUE	409	539	150	341	395	381	445	230	378	3268	BLUE	6594
WHITE	359	518	135	328	372	357	416	205	361	3051	WHITE	6198
Par	4	5	3	4	4	4	4	3	4	35	Par	71
Handicap	12	10	18	6	14	2	4	16	8			
RED	322	487	120	261	358	337	403	177	341	2806	RED	5453
Par	4	5	3	4	4	4	5	3	4	36	Par	72
Handicap	10	6	18	12	8	2	16	14	4			

Manager: Bruce Campbell   **Pro:** John Strevens, PGA   **Supt:** Steve Colangeli
Architect: Hal Purdy 1966

BIRCHWOOD COUNTRY CLUB

25 Kings Highway South, Westport, CT 06880   **(203) 221-3282**

Birchwood is a 9 hole private course open 6 days a week, and closed for Jan. and Feb. Tee time reservations are not necessary. Guests may play accompanied by a member.

- •Driving Range   •Lockers
- •Practice Green   •Showers
- •Power Carts   •Food
- Pull Carts   •Clubhouse
- •Club Rental   Outings
- •Caddies   •Soft Spikes

Course Description: Birchwood was originally an 18 hole course called Westport CC and later reduced to 9 holes with dramatic improvement. The fair sized lush bent grass greens have considerable breaks and are well bunkered. It is a tight layout with some water in play in the form of a creek that affects three holes. The thick rough is punishing and the fairways are narrow and tree lined. Different tee placements for the second nine make it play like a completely different round.

Directions: Fairfield County, #2
Merritt Pkwy.to Exit #41. Proceed South on Wilton Rd. (Rte.33) 1.3 miles to Kings Hwy.(STOP sign). Turn right to STOP light and bear right onto Boston Post Rd. Go over to the left lane & bear left at next light onto Kings Hwy. South to club on left.

Hole	1	2	3	4	5	6	7	8	9	Out	BLUE	Rating
BLUE												Slope
WHITE	373	504	334	135	370	413	183	362	483	3157		
Par	4	5	4	3	4	4	3	4	5	36	WHITE	Rating 71.8
Handicap	11	3	13	17	9	1	15	7	5			Slope 127
RED	365	457	236	128	312	369	160	331	477	2835		
Par	4	5	4	3	4	5	3	4	5	37	RED	Rating 73.7
Handicap	9	13	5	17	3	1	15	11	7			Slope 124
Hole	10	11	12	13	14	15	16	17	18	In		Totals
BLUE											BLUE	
WHITE	399	467	349	165	396	376	189	336	499	3176	WHITE	6333
Par	4	5	4	3	4	4	3	4	5	36	Par	72
Handicap	6	12	10	18	2	8	16	14	4			
RED	389	413	324	124	386	350	177	329	459	2951	RED	5786
Par	4	5	4	3	5	4	3	4	5	37	Par	74
Handicap	8	12	6	18	2	10	16	14	4			

Manager: Daniel Brophy   **Pro:** Michael Breed, PGA   **Supt:** Ed Consolati
Architect: Orrin Smith 1946

BROOKLAWN COUNTRY CLUB

500 Algonquin Rd., Fairfield, CT 06432   **(203) 334-9033**

Brooklawn is a private 18 hole course open 6 days a week and closed in February. Guests play accompanied by a member. Tee time reservations are necessary.

- •**Driving Range** •**Lockers**
- •**Practice Green** •**Showers**
- •**Power Carts** •**Food**
- Pull Carts •**Clubhouse**
- •**Club Rental** •**Outings**
- •**Caddies** •**Soft Spikes**

Course Description: Brooklawn was originally a nine hole course designed by its members in the 19th century. Later, additional property was acquired and A. W. Tillinghast was hired to make this a championship quality course. It is beautiful with tight tree lined fairways and fairly hilly terrain. Water is in play on 5 holes. The rather small greens are severly contoured, fast and guarded by deep bunkers. The 8th could be considered the signature hole. It is scenic and particularly picturesque in the Fall. The 7th is an extremely long par 5 from the Blues (over 600 yards). The Women's Open was held here in 1979.

Directions: Fairfield County, #3
Take the Merritt Pkwy to Exit 46. Take Rte.59South for 3.3 miles to Algonquin Ave. and follow signs to club entrance.

Hole	1	2	3	4	5	6	7	8	9	Out	BLUE	Rating 72.5
BLUE	435	208	370	450	165	386	608	456	382	3460		Slope 135
WHITE	415	200	363	430	160	381	563	448	320	3280		
Par	4	3	4	4	3	4	5	5	4	36	WHITE	Rating 71.4
Handicap	5	15	11	3	17	7	1	9	13			Slope 132
RED	397	159	280	406	131	305	490	357	299	2824		
Par	5	3	4	5	3	4	5	5	4	38	RED	Rating 72.4
Handicap	5	15	13	11	17	7	1	3	9			Slope 125
Hole	10	11	12	13	14	15	16	17	18	In		Totals
BLUE	140	534	390	385	420	135	332	415	406	3157	BLUE	6617
WHITE	135	522	385	373	410	130	320	397	400	3072	WHITE	6352
Par	3	5	4	4	4	3	4	4	4	35	Par	71
Handicap	18	2	12	4	6	16	14	10	18			
RED	119	455	327	312	399	117	288	351	344	2712	RED	5536
Par	3	5	4	4	5	3	4	4	4	36	Par	74
Handicap	18	2	14	4	12	16	8	6	10			

Manager: John Clyne   **Pro:** Brad Worthington, PGA   **Supt:** Peter Bly
Architect: A. W. Tillinghast **Estab:** 1895

BRUCE MEMORIAL GOLF COURSE

1300 King Street, Greenwich, CT 06831   **(203) 531-7261**

Bruce Memorial is an 18 hole public course that is open 7 days a week between April and December. There are memberships open for Greenwich residents. Tee times may be made up to 2 days in advance; 531-7200 for weekends, 531-8253 for weekdays.

•Driving Range	•Lockers
•Practice Green	•Showers
•Power Carts	•Food
•Pull Carts	•Clubhouse
•Club Rental	•Outings
•Soft Spikes	

Fees	Weekday	Weekend
Daily(res mem)	$14	$15
Guest & non-mem	$35	$35
Sr/Res/Mem	$10	
Power carts	$22	

Course Description: Bruce Memorial is moderately hilly and easy to walk. The back nine is tight and cut out of the woods with hardly any water in play. The greens are fairly small, moderately fast and deceptively sloped. The first is a good and difficult starting hole featuring a dogleg, OB on the right and left and traps in the fairway. It is a long walk uphill to the sixteenth tee located on the elevated part of the course. The signature par 5 fourteenth is tight and demanding. Over 50,000 rounds are played here yearly.

Directions: Fairfield County, #4
Hutch.Pkwy. North to Exit #30, King St.(NY/CT border). Go north (toward Armonk) on King St. approx. 2 miles to club on right.

Hole	1	2	3	4	5	6	7	8	9	Out	BLUE	Rating 70.5
BLUE	426	384	521	408	186	451	153	536	343	3408		Slope 120
WHITE	407	365	503	378	169	437	138	519	323	3239		
Par	4	4	5	4	3	4	3	5	4	36	WHITE	Rating 68.6
Handicap	5	7	13	3	15	1	17	9	11			Slope 115
RED	391	350	481	358	152	424	121	490	308	3075		
Par	4	4	5	4	3	5	3	5	4	37	RED	Rating 73.6
Handicap	3	9	5	7	15	11	17	1	13			Slope 128

Hole	10	11	12	13	14	15	16	17	18	In		Totals
BLUE	316	203	329	402	528	165	389	444	328	3104	BLUE	6512
WHITE	291	198	310	380	448	140	351	426	310	2854	WHITE	6093
Par	4	3	4	4	5	3	4	4	4	35	Par	72
Handicap	14	16	10	6	2	18	8	4	12			
RED	271	189	243	367	426	110	331	408	290	2635	RED	5710
Par	4	3	4	4	5	3	4	5	4	36	Par	73
Handicap	16	12	14	2	4	18	6	8	10			

Manager/Supt: Mike Leary   **Pro:** Joe Felder, PGA
Architect: Robert Trent Jones 1965

BURNING TREE COUNTRY CLUB PRIVATE

120 Perkins Road, Greenwich, CT 06830   **(203) 869-9010**

Burning Tree is an 18 hole course open 6 days a week, all year, weather permitting. Guests may play accompanied by a member. Tee time reservations are required.

Driving Range	•Lockers
•Practice Green	•Showers
•Power Carts	•Food
Pull Carts	•Clubhouse
Club Rental	•Outings
•Caddies	•Soft Spikes

Course Description: There is trouble lurking on almost every shot at the challenging Burning Tree golf course. Narrow fairways, water on many holes, and the out of bounds account for the fact that par was only broken here twice. The greens are large with some undulation although the course is basically flat. The signature #4, a long par 5, is considered one of the toughest in CT. It requires an absolutely straight and long tee shot to a dogleg left with water on both sides; a brook crossing the hole near the elevated green makes the approach shot demanding. Often a provisional must be hit for a lost ball that finds itself on the Merritt Parkway.

Directions: Fairfield County, #5
Merritt Pkwy.to Exit #31(North St.-Greenwich) and turn toward Greenwich(South). Go about 1 mile, turn left onto Taconic Rd. 0.5 mi.to Interlacken Rd. & turn right to club.

Hole	1	2	3	4	5	6	7	8	9	Out	BLUE	Rating 73.8
BLUE	427	162	334	590	393	359	510	249	418	3442		Slope 139
WHITE	404	133	302	555	358	330	465	228	394	3169		
Par	4	3	4	5	4	4	5	3	4	36	WHITE	Rating 72.7
Handicap	5	17	15	1	3	9	11	13	7			Slope 137
RED	344	110	261	500	325	311	444	165	349	2809		
Par	4	3	4	5	4	4	5	3	4	36	RED	Rating 74.5
Handicap	11	17	15	1	5	7	3	13	9			Slope 135
Hole	10	11	12	13	14	15	16	17	18	In		Totals
BLUE	437	490	195	452	462	496	353	380	195	3460	BLUE	6902
WHITE	417	471	178	430	447	479	346	362	183	3313	WHITE	6482
Par	4	5	3	4	4	5	4	4	3	36	Par	72
Handicap	6	8	18	4	2	10	14	12	16			
RED	370	446	162	417	342	436	297	339	165	2974	RED	5783
Par	4	5	3	4	4	5	4	4	3	36	Par	72
Handicap	6	2	16	8	10	4	14	12	18			

Manager: Roger Loose   **Pro:** Stan Mosel, PGA   **Supt:** Gary Glazier
Architect: Hal Purdy 1965

COUNTRY CLUB OF DARIEN

PRIVATE

362 Mansfield Avenue, Darien, CT 08620   **(203) 655-7043**

Darien is an 18 hole private course open 6 days a week and closed Jan. & Feb. Guests may play accompanied by a member. Tee time reservations are required on weekends.

- •**Driving Range**
- •**Practice Green**
- •**Power Carts**
- •**Pull Carts**
- •**Club Rental**
- •**Caddies**
- •**Lockers**
- •**Showers**
- •**Food**
- •**Clubhouse**
- •**Outings**
- •**Soft Spikes**

Course Description: Darien offers its members a beautiful well maintained facility. The back nine is longer and far more challenging than the front with long difficult fairways and water in play on 5 holes. The bent grass greens are fast, good sized and have subtle breaks. The signature par 4 3rd hole is long with a sloping dogleg left, and a semi-island two tiered green. Long hitters are tempted to cut corners over the trees. The par 4 #12 is a scenic hole with out of bounds left, a pond on the right and an inverted bowl shaped green.

Directions: Fairfield County, #6
I-95 North (CT. Tpke.) to Exit #12 (Tokeneke Rd.) & turn left. Proceed to STOP light & turn onto Boston Post Rd. Go to light at Mansfield Ave. (Rte.124) & turn left. Club is 1.5 miles on right.

Hole	1	2	3	4	5	6	7	8	9	Out	BLUE	Rating 73.1
BLUE	360	383	424	374	175	564	157	409	510	3356		Slope 132
WHITE	348	357	393	366	148	549	152	393	500	3206		
Par	4	4	4	4	3	5	3	4	5	36	WHITE	Rating 71.5
Handicap	14	10	2	8	18	4	16	6	12			Slope 128
RED	340	297	303	342	117	476	147	306	418	2746		
Par	4	4	4	4	3	5	3	4	5	36	RED	Rating 73.7
Handicap	10	14	6	8	18	2	16	12	4			Slope 128
Hole	10	11	12	13	14	15	16	17	18	In		Totals
BLUE	361	152	425	602	397	412	520	231	422	3522	BLUE	6878
WHITE	352	132	390	555	371	397	508	207	383	3295	WHITE	6501
Par	4	3	4	5	4	4	5	3	4	36	Par	72
Handicap	9	17	5	1	11	7	13	15	3			
RED	319	114	363	505	357	338	483	167	345	2991	RED	5737
Par	4	3	4	5	4	4	5	3	4	36	Par	72
Handicap	11	17	5	1	7	13	3	15	9			

Manager: Ian Fetigan   **Pro:** Ed Nicholson, PGA   **Supt:** Tim O'Neill
Architect: Alfred Tull, 1957

E. GAYNOR BRENNAN GOLF COURSE

451 Stillwater Road, Stamford, CT 06902   **(203) 324-6507**

E.Gaynor Brennan is a municipal 18 hole course open 7 days a week between March 20 and December 1. There is a lottery for tee times on weekends and a 2 day advance for weekdays, (203) 324-4185.

Driving Range	•Lockers
•Practice Green	•Showers
•Power Carts	•Food
•Pull Carts	•Clubhouse
•Club Rental	•Outings
•Soft Spikes	

Fees	Weekday	Weekend
Daily(w/per)	$10	$11
Non-res	$25	$30
Sr.(w/per)	$6	$11
Power carts	$22	

Course Description: Originally called Hubbard's Heights CC, E.Gaynor Brennan is a hilly, relatively short course tucked into 90 acres of land. The bent grass greens are somewhat small and quick, with some break. Ponds or streams affect play on 11 holes. The 220 yard par 3 thirteenth, has a severely sloped back to front small green. There are about 50,000 rounds played here annually though it usually takes no more than 4 hrs. & 15 min. to complete a round at this well maintained course.

Directions: Fairfield County, #7
I-95 North (CT Tpke) to Exit #6. Proceed to 2nd traffic light, turn left onto West Ave. and continue to end. Turn left onto Stillwater Rd.(bears left) to club on right.

Hole	1	2	3	4	5	6	7	8	9	Out	BLUE	Rating
BLUE												Slope
WHITE	361	389	147	433	372	492	378	346	105	3023		
Par	4	4	3	5	4	5	4	4	3	36	WHITE	Rating 67.8
Handicap	7	5	13	9	3	15	1	11	17			Slope 122
RED	284	389	138	433	372	450	378	346	105	2895		
Par	4	5	3	5	4	5	4	4	3	37	RED	Rating 72.3
Handicap	13	11	15	3	1	5	7	9	17			Slope 124
Hole	10	11	12	13	14	15	16	17	18	In		Totals
BLUE											BLUE	
WHITE	354	321	341	225	397	177	279	428	323	2845	WHITE	5868
Par	4	4	4	3	4	3	4	5	4	35	Par	71
Handicap	10	14	2	6	4	8	18	16	12			
RED	354	321	310	225	397	144	279	343	323	2696	RED	5591
Par	4	4	4	4	5	3	4	4	4	36	Par	73
Handicap	4	12	6	16	8	18	14	2	10			

Manager: Mike Dale   **Pro:** Bill Fraioli, PGA   **Supt:** Mike Sullivan
Architect: Maurice McCarthy Sr. 1925

FAIRCHILD WHEELER GOLF COURSE

PUBLIC

2390 Easton Turnpike, Fairfield, CT 06432   (203) 373-5911

D. Fairchild Wheeler has 2 18 hole courses, the Red & the Black owned by the town of Bridgeport and open all year 7 days a week. Residents get discounts. Tee times may be made up to 7 days in advance by calling 373-5917. Club members can come in Thurs. night to reserve time.

•Driving Range	•Lockers
•Practice Green	•Showers
•Power Carts	•Food
•Pull Carts	•Clubhouse
•Club Rental	•Outings
Soft Spikes	

Fees	Weekday	Weekend
Daily(6:30-8AM)	$26	$34
11AM-5PM 2 payers/wcart$50		$70
Twi(5-6PM(2players/wcart $40		$48

Course Description: The Red at Fairchild Wheeleris a links type course characterized by rolling fairways, a stream meandering throughout and large fairly flat greens. Most think the Black course is more difficult, a traditional tree lined layout. Its signature par 3 17th is over a pond to a picturesque green. Although Tillinghast didn't build the course, many of his creative trademarks are apparent. The course is managed by National Fairways and many improvements have been made recently. Julius Boros grew up playing at this facility and his family still plays here. The scorecard below is for the Red course.

Directions: Fairfield County, #8
Hutchinson River/Merritt Pkwy.North to Exit #46. Go right off ramp (at light). Proceed to 1st traffic light and turn left to course on left.

Hole	1	2	3	4	5	6	7	8	9	Out	BLUE	Rating
BLUE												Slope
WHITE	460	415	495	150	330	425	345	190	395	3205		
Par	4	4	5	3	4	4	4	3	4	35	WHITE	Rating 69.7
Handicap	1	7	11	17	15	5	13	9	3			Slope 122
RED	415	350	455	130	310	345	310	160	325	2800		
Par	5	4	5	3	4	4	4	3	4	36	RED	Rating 75.5
Handicap	1	7	11	17	15	5	13	9	3			Slope 122
Hole	10	11	12	13	14	15	16	17	18	In		Totals
BLUE											BLUE	
WHITE	510	425	125	425	355	210	345	515	485	3395	WHITE	6600
Par	5	4	3	4	4	3	4	5	5	37	Par	72
Handicap	2	8	18	10	12	16	14	4	6			
RED	415	365	105	355	295	170	315	465	410	2895	RED	5695
Par	5	4	3	4	4	3	4	5	4	36	Par	72
Handicap	6	16	14	2	4	12	8	18	8			

Manager: Don Carpenter   **Pro:** Jeff Miller, PGA   **Supt:** Jon Festa
Built: 1934

COUNTRY CLUB OF FAIRFIELD

936 Sasco Hill Rd., Fairfield, CT 06420   **(203) 255-3951**

The CC of Fairfield is an 18 hole private course open 6 days a week and closed Dec.1- March 1. Guests play accompanied by a member. Tee time reservations are not necessary.

> - **Driving Range**
> - **Practice Green**
> - **Power Carts**
> - **Pull Carts**
> - **Club Rental**
> - **Caddies**
> - **Lockers**
> - **Showers**
> - **Food**
> - **Clubhouse**
> - **Outings**
> - Soft Spikes

Course Description: With the L.I Sound in view on most holes, the beautifully maintained Country Club of Fairfield is a scenic links type course. It is fairly flat; the clubhouse and the 18th green are the high points. Water, in the form of ponds and wetlands, affects play on 7 holes. The signature 4th hole is a par 3 that features a tee shot over a picturesque lagoon. The small sloped greens are quite fast. With the Sound so close by, wind is often a factor here.

Directions: Fairfield County, #9
Take I-95 to Exit 19 (Rte.1). Turn right onto Post Rd (Rte.1). Go for 1/2 m. and turn right just after small bridge onto Sasco Hill Rd. Proceed 1/2 mile to club on right.

Hole	1	2	3	4	5	6	7	8	9	Out	BLUE	Rating 71.6
BLUE	524	402	353	133	351	419	320	525	198	3225		Slope 133
WHITE	516	396	343	126	340	409	304	514	189	3137		
Par	5	4	4	3	4	4	4	5	3	36	WHITE	Rating 70.7
Handicap	7	5	11	17	9	1	13	3	15			Slope 131
RED	459	337	311	122	320	388	298	450	143	2828		
Par	5	4	4	3	4	4	4	5	3	36	RED	Rating 71.8
Handicap	3	9	11	15	7	1	13	5	17			Slope 126
Hole	10	11	12	13	14	15	16	17	18	In		Totals
BLUE	510	176	429	435	179	433	386	193	392	3133	BLUE	6858
WHITE	499	161	412	423	174	412	369	178	385	3013	WHITE	6150
Par	5	3	4	4	3	4	4	3	4	34	Par	70
Handicap	10	18	6	2	16	4	12	14	8			
RED	445	137	408	326	156	367	335	132	352	2658	RED	5486
Par	5	3	5	4	3	4	4	3	4	35	Par	71
Handicap	2	16	4	12	18	8	10	14	4			

Manager: George Poole   **Pro:** Jack Druga, PGA   **Supt:** Pat Sisk
Architect: Seth Raynor 1914

FAIRVIEW COUNTRY CLUB

1241 King Street, Greenwich, CT 06831 **(203) 531-4283**

Fairview is an 18 hole course open 6 days a week from Mar. 25 to Dec.1. Guests may play accompanied by a member. Tee time reservations are needed on weekends only.

- •Driving Range
- •Practice Green
- •Power Carts
- Pull Carts
- Club Rental
- •Caddies

- •Lockers
- •Showers
- •Food
- •Clubhouse
- •Outings
- •Soft Spikes

Course Description: Fairview's two nines are quite different in nature; the front is relatively short with water in play on 5 holes. The longer back is a scenic tract carved out of the woods. The rolling fairways are narrow and the well bunkered undulating large greens play fast adding to the challenge of the course. The second hole has a sharp drop off the tee into the woods, affecting the drive. There is also a large pond along the final 100 yards of the fairway that constrains the approach shot to the elevated green. A qualifying round for the Met-Am was held here in 1997.

Directions: Fairfield County, #10
Hutchinson Pkwy. North to Exit #30 (King St.) Proceed West on King St. toward Armonk to club on right (approx. 3 miles).

Hole	1	2	3	4	5	6	7	8	9	Out	BLUE	Rating 73.0
BLUE	377	532	174	348	488	432	387	182	317	3237		Slope 131
WHITE	370	482	137	333	452	392	335	156	293	2950		
Par	4	5	3	4	5	4	4	3	4		WHITE	Rating 70.8
Handicap	11	3	17	7	5	1	9	13	15			Slope 127
RED	331	451	117	288	414	355	296	119	262	2633		
Par	4	5	3	4	5	4	4	3	4	36	RED	Rating 72.5
Handicap	5	1	17	13	7	3	9	15	11			Slope 126
Hole	10	11	12	13	14	15	16	17	18	In		Totals
BLUE	404	540	398	574	216	338	186	441	413	3510	BLUE	6747
WHITE	374	523	376	524	190	323	162	409	378	3259	WHITE	6209
Par	4	5	4	5	3	4	3	4	4	36	Par	72
Handicap	10	14	6	2	16	8	18	4	12			
RED	332	473	317	455	135	300	140	388	334	2874	RED	5900
Par	4	5	4	5	3	4	3	4	4	36	Par	72
Handicap	10	8	12	2	18	4	16	6	14			

Manager: Drew Campbell   **Pro:** Walter T. Campbell, PGA   **Supt:** Richard Marcks
Architect: Robert Trent Jones, 1968 **Estab:** 1904

FISHERS ISLAND CLUB

Fishers Island, NY 06390   **(516) 788-7223**

Fisher's Island is an 18 hole private course open 6 days a week from May 15 to October 15. Guests may play accompanied by a member. Tee times are not required.

•**Driving Range**	•**Lockers**
•**Practice Green**	•**Showers**
•**Power Carts**	•**Food**
•**Pull Carts**	•**Clubhouse**
•**Club Rental**	•**Outings**
•**Caddies**	•**Soft Spikes**

Course Description: With spectacular views of the ocean on many holes, Fisher's Island is accessible only by boat or ferry from New London, CT. It is a very private club with a small clubhouse in keeping with its low key atmosphere. With bent grass greens that are often elevated and water in play on about a dozen holes the course offers its members fine, challenging golf in a beautiful setting. The design concept of the layout was originally by Seth Raynor. When he died in 1926, Charles Banks and Ralph Barton completed the work. Scorecard details were unavailable. Course is par 72.

Ratings BLUE 72.9 6544   WHITE 70.9 6103   RED 71.0 5393
Slopes   134   130   118

Directions: Fairfield County, #11
From CT, take the ferry at New London to the island. Club is off Rte. 95.

Manager: Tony Bussmann   **Pro:** Tom O'Brien, PGA   **Supt:** Rich Schock
Architect: Seth Raynor 1925

GREENWICH COUNTRY CLUB

Doubling Road, Greenwich CT 06836   **(203) 869-4222**

Greenwich is an 18 hole course open 6 days a week and closed late Dec. to early March. Guests may play accompanied by a member. Tee time reservations are required on weekends.

•Driving Range	•Lockers
•Practice Green	•Showers
•Power Carts	•Food
Pull Carts	•Clubhouse
•Club Rental	•Outings
•Caddies	•Soft Spikes

Course Description: Greenwich began in other locations first as a five hole layout then later 9 holes. It wasn't until 1908 that a full 18 were laid out. The course has character; many blind drives, deep long rough and small brooks meander throughout. The small well conditioned greens are medium paced and have subtle breaks. On the 7th, the pin isn't visible; a big hill is encountered in front of the green. The eighth, a 422 yard par 4, has a daunting approach shot over a creek. Greenwich is the third oldest club in the U.S.

Directions: Fairfield County, #12
Merritt Pkwy. to Exit #31 (North St., Greenwich). Turn left toward Greenwich (south) 2.7 miles to Doubling Rd. Turn left and bear right to club.

Hole	1	2	3	4	5	6	7	8	9	Out	BLUE	Rating 73.1
BLUE	318	187	385	568	408	417	419	422	420	3544		Slope 135
WHITE	311	180	374	559	371	380	409	405	390	3379		
Par	4	3	4	5	4	4	4	4	4	36	WHITE	Rating 71.6
Handicap	15	17	11	1	13	9	3	5	7			Slope 132
RED	289	159	344	494	364	320	403	323	338	3034		
Par	4	3	4	5	4	4	5	4	4	37	RED	Rating74.5
Handicap	15	17	9	1	3	13	7	5	11			Slope 133

Hole	10	11	12	13	14	15	16	17	18	In		Totals
BLUE	330	374	165	366	516	205	415	378	413	3162	BLUE	6706
WHITE	308	317	148	356	510	193	402	369	403	3006	WHITE	6385
Par	4	4	3	4	5	3	4	4	4	35	Par	71
Handicap	16	12	18	6	2	14	4	10	8			
RED	293	304	127	343	504	124	380	356	386	2817	RED	5851
Par	4	4	3	4	5	3	5	4	5	37	Par	74
Handicap	14	12	18	4	2	16	8	6	10			

Manager: Dan Denehy   **Pro:** Jerry Coats, PGA   **Supt:** Greg Wojick
Architects: Lawrence Van Etten   **Redesign:** Seth Raynor, Donald Ross   **Estab:** 1892

H. SMITH RICHARDSON GC

2425 Moorehouse Highway, Fairfield, CT 06430   **(203) 255-7300**

H.Smith Rlichardson is an 18 hole course that is open 7 days a week all year (weather permitting) with temporary greens in winter. There are special rates for residents of Fairfield Township. Tee times can be made 7 days in advance for weekdays and 3 days for weekends.

•**Driving Range**	•**Lockers**
•**Practice Green**	•**Showers**
•**Power Carts**	•**Food**
•**Pull Carts**	•**Clubhouse**
•**Club Rental**	•**Outings**
•**Soft Spikes**	

Fees	Weekday	Weekend
Daily(Res)	$12	$14
Non Res	$24	$28
Power carts	$21	
9 hole rates are available		

Course Description: H.Smith Richardson is in excellent shape with narrow tree lined fairways and yardage markers clearly visible. The large greens are very undulating and fast; water is in play on 6 holes. The signature 536 yard par 5 #18, is a dogleg left; water on the left affects the approach shot. The 13th and 14th holes have wonderful views of LI Sound. An additional nine holes are planned for the future. It gets quite busy here in season.

Directions: Fairfield County, #13
Hutch. River/Merritt Pkwy. North to Exit#45 (Black Rock Tpke.) Turn back under Pkwy. to 1st right. Go 2 blocks to Moorehouse, turn left to course.

Hole	1	2	3	4	5	6	7	8	9	Out	BLUE	Rating 71.0
BLUE	402	320	185	359	410	517	398	202	503	3296		Slope 127
WHITE	375	310	160	339	397	503	383	180	486	3133		
Par	4	4	3	4	4	5	4	3	5	36	WHITE	Rating 70.2
Handicap	6	14	18	12	2	4	8	16	10			Slope 124
RED	332	285	120	314	362	463	355	137	465	2833		
Par	4	4	3	4	4	5	4	3	5	36	RED	Rating 72.8
Handicap	7	11	17	13	3	1	9	15	5			Slope 129

Hole	10	11	12	13	14	15	16	17	18	In		Totals
BLUE	397	368	203	523	426	368	168	391	536	3380	BLUE	6676
WHITE	373	351	176	502	405	350	140	373	520	3190	WHITE	6323
Par	4	4	3	5	4	4	3	4	5	36	Par	72
Handicap	3	13	15	7	1	11	17	5	9			
RED	356	325	140	465	385	330	112	323	495	2931	RED	5764
Par	4	4	3	5	5	4	3	4	5	37	Par	73
Handicap	2	14	16	4	8	10	18	12	6			

Manager/Pro: Sean Garrity, PGA   **Supt:** Tom Fletcher
Architect: Stephen Kay 1972

HAY HARBOR GOLF CLUB

Fisher's Island, NY 06390   (516) 788-7514

Hay Harbor is a private 9 hole facility that is open 6 days a week in summer. Guests may play accompanied by a member. Tee times are not necessary.

- •Driving Range
- •Practice Green
- •Power Carts
- Pull Carts
- •Club Rental
- •Caddies
- •Lockers
- •Showers
- •Food
- •Clubhouse
- •Outings
- •Soft Spikes

Course Description: Hay Harbor is a resort course that has difficulty on the first two holes; a 425 yard first hole and a 395 yard second with water in play. The scorecard was not available. Rating/White=69, Slope/White=111   Total 6210 Par 68
Rating/Red=72.8, Slope/Red=118   Total 5900 Par 76

Directions: Fairfield County, #14
From CT, take the ferry at New London to the island.

Pro: Dan Calvin, PGA   **Supt:** Allen Barry
Architect: Members   **Estab:** 1898

INNIS ARDEN GOLF CLUB

120 Tomac Ave., Old Greenwich, CT 06870   **(203) 637-3679**

Innis Arden is a private 18 hole course open 6 days a week all year, weather permitting. Guests may play accompanied by a member. Tee time reservations may be made on weekends.

•**Driving Range**	•**Lockers**
•**Practice Green**	•**Showers**
•**Power Carts**	•**Food**
Pull Carts	•**Clubhouse**
•**Club Rental**	Outings
•**Caddies**	•**Soft Spikes**

Course Description: Innis Arden is a short, hilly, tight and well maintained course. The fast well bunkered greens are small and have little break. A creek running through the course affects play on 13 holes. The signature # 1 handicap par 4 15th, 445 yards from an elevated tee, has a lake on the left and is straight uphill to a small green. William Mitchell who was the pro here for many years, died in 1996; the Mitchell Tournament is held here annually.

Directions: Fairfield County, #15
I-95 (NEThruwy-Conn Tpke.) to Exit #5. Turn right onto Boston Post Rd. to Sound Beach Ave.(1st light), turn right. Bear right at rotary then take first left (Forest Ave.) Go to end of road, turn right onto Tomac Ave. and club is 1/2 mile on left.

Hole	1	2	3	4	5	6	7	8	9	Out	BLUE	Rating 70.3
BLUE	402	401	351	408	414	270	138	362	278	3024		Slope 128
WHITE	385	370	340	380	400	260	125	356	270	2886	WHITE	Rating 69.1
Par	4	4	4	4	4	4	3	4	4	35		Slope 125
Handicap	8	6	12	4	2	16	18	10	14			
RED	360	357	325	300	380	236	113	343	252	2666	RED	Rating 72.6
Par	4	4	4	4	5	4	3	4	4	36		Slope 134
Handicap	5	7	1	9	3	11	17	13	15			
Hole	10	11	12	13	14	15	16	17	18	In		Totals
BLUE	310	423	364	167	523	445	187	515	197	3131	BLUE	6155
WHITE	300	410	351	150	495	420	176	495	180	2977	WHITE	5863
Par	4	4	4	3	5	4	3	5	3	35	Par	70
Handicap	11	3	9	17	7	1	15	5	13			
RED	298	400	309	115	453	414	152	477	161	5445	RED	5445
Par	4	5	4	3	5	5	3	5	3	37	Par	73
Handicap	10	8	12	18	2	6	14	4	16			

Manager: Bill Brinkman   **Pro:** Gary Murphy, PGA   **Supt:** Patrick Lucas
Architect: Members, 1899

LONGSHORE CLUB PARK

260 Compo Road South, Westport. CT 06880   (203) 222-7535

Longshore is an 18 hole course that is for town of Westport pass holding residents and their guests only. It is open 7 days a week between April 1 and November 30. Tee time reservations may be made Wed. for Sat.; Thurs. for Sun.; and 3 days in advance for weekdays. (See sheet at course for more details).

•**Driving Range** Lockers	
•**Practice Green** •**Showers**	
•**Power Carts** •**Food**	
•**Pull Carts** •**Clubhouse**	
•**Club Rental** •**Outings**	
•**Soft Spikes**	

Fees	Weekday	Weekend
Daily(with pass)	$11	$13
With $75 permit	$8	$10
See sheet for detailed prices		

Course Description: Originally a nine hole private course Longshore was later expanded to 18 holes and made public in the 1920s. It has a short, flat layout with small well-bunkered greens and open fairways. There is not much water in play although there is water in view; namely the Long Island Sound and Northport Harbor. The signature par 4 17th overlooks this panorama and requires a precision tee shot over water to a bunkered fairway. Both the 11th & 13th are long par 3s with OB on the right and well trapped greens.

Directions: Fairfield County, #16
I-95 to Exit #18 and go left. Make a left at the 2nd light and then at 1st light go left on Compo Rd. to club on right .

Hole	1	2	3	4	5	6	7	8	9	Out	BLUE	Rating 67.3
BLUE	347	151	394	305	301	418	536	130	351	2933		Slope 115
WHITE	341	146	390	287	296	413	520	127	346	2866		
Par	4	3	4	4	4	4	5	3	4	35	WHITE	Rating 66.6
Handicap	9	13	5	15	11	1	3	17	7			Slope 113
RED	335	141	386	251	291	408	414	125	341	2692		
Par	4	3	5	4	4	5	5	3	4	37	RED	Rating 69.9
Handicap	11	15	7	13	9	3	1	17	5			Slope 119
Hole	10	11	12	13	14	15	16	17	18	In		Totals
BLUE	494	201	293	205	404	173	388	344	410	2912	BLUE	5845
WHITE	459	192	289	189	401	166	383	334	397	2810	WHITE	5676
Par	5	3	4	3	4	3	4	4	4	34	Par	69
Handicap	8	14	18	12	4	16	6	10	2			
RED	449	157	262	151	397	132	331	272	384	2535	RED	5227
Par	5	3	4	3	5	3	4	4	5	37	Par	73
Handicap	2	14	10	16	8	18	6	12	4			

Managers: Paul Taylor/Stuart McCarthy   **Pro:** John Cooper, PGA   **Supt:** Dan Rackliffe
Estab: 1920s **Redesigned:** 1956

THE MILBROOK CLUB

61 Woodside Drive, Greenwich, CT 06830   **(203) 869-4684**

Milbrook is a 9 hole private course that is open 6 days a week and closed for Jan. & Feb. Guests may play accompanied by a member. Tee time reservations are required.

- •**Driving Range**   •**Lockers**
- •**Practice Green**   •**Showers**
- •**Power Carts**   •**Food**
-   Pull Carts   •**Clubhouse**
- •**Club Rental**   Outings
- •**Caddies**   •**Soft Spikes**

Course Description: Milbrook has tight tree-lined fairways with unforgiving rough. The medium sized greens are slightly contoured. Elevation changes allow for differing tee positions each time around. The par 3 7th hole is a short iron shot to a well bunkered narrow green with an intimidating tree on the left. The tee shot on the par 4 #3 must carry over a mound about 180 yards out and from then on its entirely uphill to an elevated green that slopes from back to front. Although there is no water on the course, it is surely challenging.

Directions: Fairfield County, #17
I-95 North (NEThruwy-CT Tpk) to Exit #4(Indian Field Rd.)and turn left. Follow to end (Rte.1) and turn left. Go 100 yards downhill, turn left between 2 pillars to club.

Hole	1	2	3	4	5	6	7	8	9	Out	BLUE	
BLUE												
WHITE	493	404	359	380	329	446	124	380	190	3105		
Par	5	4	4	4	4	4	3	4	3	35	WHITE	Rating 70.3
Handicap	10	3	7	11	14	1	18	5	16			Slope 120
RED	475	400	301	380	320	401	124	379	181	2961		
Par	5	5	4	4	4	5	3	4	3	37	RED	Rating 73.5
Handicap	3	7	6	9	14	11	18	1	16			Slope 125

Hole	10	11	12	13	14	15	16	17	18	In		Totals
BLUE											BLUE	
WHITE	509	355	359	416	345	422	137	405	211	3159	WHITE	6264
Par	5	4	4	4	4	4	3	4	3	35	Par	70
Handicap	9	12	8	6	13	4	17	2	15			
RED	500	312	308	416	319	305	131	337	209	2837	RED	5798
Par	5	4	4	5	4	4	3	4	3	36	Par	73
Handicap	2	12	5	8	13	15	17	4	10			

Manager: John Zerega   **Pro:** John Budkins, PGA   **Supt:** Jim Calladio
Built: 1923

COUNTRY CLUB of NEW CANAAN

95 Country Club Road, New Canaan, CT 06840   **(203) 966-3033**

New Canaan is an 18 hole course open 6 days a week and closed for the month of February. Guests may play accompanied by a member. It is necessary to make tee time reservations.

•Driving Range	•Lockers
•Practice Green	•Showers
•Power Carts	•Food
•Pull Carts	•Clubhouse
•Club Rental	Outings
•Caddies	•Soft Spikes

Course Description: New Canaan is not a very long course but requires accurate placement of tee shots to be able to approach the green from the best angle. It has very narrow tree lined fairways; a number of bunkers around the green are not apparent as the golfer hits up toward the putting surface. The small greens are fast with little break. The seventeenth is a short par 4 with a green tough to hold as it slopes front to back and from left to right. Deep pot bunkers can catch a short incoming shot. A US Open local qualifying round was played here in 1997.

Directions: Fairfield County, #18
Merritt Pkwy.to Exit #38 and turn right onto Rte.123North for 3.8 miles to Country Club Rd. Turn left; club is on right.

Hole	1	2	3	4	5	6	7	8	9	Out	BLUE	Rating 71.5
BLUE	339	507	375	379	157	437	181	370	438	3183		Slope 132
WHITE	322	500	372	367	143	430	175	349	431	3089		
Par	4	5	4	4	3	4	3	4	4	35	WHITE	Rating 70.6
Handicap	11	5	9	7	17	1	15	13	3			Slope 129
RED	310	460	365	339	137	408	151	316	427	2913		
Par	4	5	4	4	3	5	3	4	5	37	RED	Rating 74.1
Handicap	13	1	9	7	17	3	15	11	5			Slope 131
Hole	10	11	12	13	14	15	16	17	18	In		Totals
BLUE	438	383	172	565	170	340	506	345	340	3259	BLUE	6442
WHITE	414	370	166	559	163	332	500	340	335	3179	WHITE	6268
Par	4	4	3	5	3	4	5	4	4	36	Par	71
Handicap	2	8	16	4	18	12	6	10	14			
RED	401	320	145	502	156	265	476	324	307	2896	RED	5809
Par	5	4	3	5	3	4	5	4	4	37	Par	74
Handicap	4	10	14	2	8	16	12	18	6			

Manager: John Lippke   **Pro:** Paul Leslie III, PGA   **Supt:** Mike Reeb
Architect: Willie Park   **Redesign:** Alfred Tull, Robert Trent Jones   **Estab:** 1893

OAK HILLS PARK GOLF CLUB

PUBLIC

165 Fillow St., Norwalk, CT 06850   **(203) 853-8400**

Oak Hills is an 18 hole course open 7 days a week, all year, weather permitting. Tee times may be made in person 1 week in advance or a day before by calling 838-1015. Residents obtain season permit.

Driving Range	Lockers
•**Practice Green**	Showers
•**Power Carts**	•**Food**
•**Pull Carts**	Clubhouse
•**Club Rental**	•**Outings**
Soft Spikes	

Fees	Weekday	Weekend
Daily(res w/per) $14		$15
Non-res	$29	$34
Jr/Sr	$8	
Power carts	$23	

Course Description: Oak Hills is a very tight tree-lined course. Its greens are large, relatively flat, and easy to putt. The front nine is hillier than the back. Water is in play on 6 holes. The signature ninth is a long 456 yard par 4 with many trees along the fairway. The 15th, 235 yards from the blues, slopes from back to front and is partially over water. The #11 is a good driving hole to a dogleg left. There are about 55,000 rounds played here each year.

Directions: Fairfield County, #19
I-95 North to Exit #13, Darien. Go right at 2nd light; then go left onto Richards Ave. to end. Make a right to triangle and a sharp right onto Fillow St. Club is ahead on right after the tennis courts.

Hole	1	2	3	4	5	6	7	8	9	Out	BLUE	Rating 70.7
BLUE	382	328	147	345	195	304	355	591	456	3103		Slope 128
WHITE	374	295	109	307	174	284	336	484	440	2803		
Par	4	4	3	4	3	4	4	5	4	35	WHITE	Rating 69.5
Handicap	3	11	17	9	15	13	5	7	1			Slope 126
RED	287	247	92	253	108	264	237	432	425	2345		
Par	4	4	3	4	3	4	4	5	5	36	RED	Rating 72.6
Handicap	8	10	18	12	16	6	14	2	4			Slope 126
Hole	10	11	12	13	14	15	16	17	18	In		Totals
BLUE	547	367	516	165	406	235	366	361	341	3304	BLUE	6407
WHITE	528	365	501	154	386	205	342	336	300	3117	WHITE	5920
Par	5	4	5	3	4	3	4	4	4	36	Par	71
Handicap	4	14	8	18	2	12	10	6	16			
RED	502	347	466	138	356	178	315	312	262	2876	RED	5221
Par	5	4	5	3	4	3	4	4	4	36	Par	72
Handicap	6	16	14	2	4	12	8	18	10			

Manager: Vincent Grillo, Jr.   **Pro:** Vincent Grillo,Sr., PGA   **Supt:** Harry Ward
Architect: Alfred Tull, 1969

THE PATTERSON CLUB

PRIVATE

1118 Cross Highway, Fairfield, CT 06430   **(203) 255-2121**

The Patterson Club is an 18 hole private course open 6 days a week all year, weather permitting.   Guests may play accompanied by a member. Tee time reservations are not necessary.

Driving Range	•Lockers
•Practice Green	•Showers
•Power Carts	•Food
•Pull Carts	•Clubhouse
Club Rental	•Outings
•Caddies	•Soft Spikes

Course Description: The Patterson Club, a beautifully maintained 18 hole course was constructed on a former horse farm. A number of stone boulders were left as support for tees, greens and mounds adding to its charming surroundings. Wildlife can be found in abundance. The small greens are fast, undulating and well bunkered. The signature par 3 3rd is over water with a lateral hazard on the left side to a green with a bunker on the right. The US Senior Amateur Qualifying Round, and an Assistant Pro tournament have been held here as well as the Connecticut Open in 1996.

Directions: Fairfield County, #20
Merritt Pkwy.North to Exit #42 (Weston Rd.) Turn left at bottom of ramp. Go straight thru blinking light at fork to end of road, and turn left on Cross Hwy. to club on left.

Hole	1	2	3	4	5	6	7	8	9	Out	BLUE	Rating 72.5
BLUE	427	440	206	400	552	175	284	376	501	3361		Slope 134
WHITE	419	430	156	378	515	156	271	348	493	3166		
Par	4	4	3	4	5	3	4	4	5	36	WHITE	Rating 71.2
Handicap	3	1	13	7	5	15	17	9	11			Slope 130
RED	410	358	126	356	427	143	260	310	485	2875		
Par	5	4	3	4	5	3	4	4	5	37	RED	Rating 73.0
Handicap	9	3	17	1	5	15	11	13	7			Slope 122

Hole	10	11	12	13	14	15	16	17	18	In		Totals
BLUE	398	534	213	395	192	404	425	414	459	3434	BLUE	6795
WHITE	388	519	197	378	155	383	405	396	442	3263	WHITE	6429
Par	4	5	3	4	3	4	4	4	4	35	Par	71
Handicap	4	12	16	8	18	10	2	14	6			
RED	322	466	177	297	125	334	314	348	425	2808	RED	5683
Par	4	5	3	4	3	4	4	4	5	36	Par	73
Handicap	4	8	14	12	18	2	6	10	16			

Manager: David Beaman   **Pro:** Brenda Walsh, PGA   **Supt:** Jonathan Jennings
Architect: Robert Trent Jones 1946 **Estab:** 1929

RIDGEFIELD GOLF COURSE

545 Ridgebury Rd., Ridgefield, CT 06877 **(203) 748-7008**

Ridgefield is an 18 hole course open to the public 7 days a week and closed 12/15-4/1. Prepaid starting times for foursomes on Fri., Mon-Thurs no reservations needed. Ridgefield res: lottery for wkends and holidays. Irons only for driving range.

•Driving Range	•Lockers
•Practice Green	•Showers
•Power Carts	•Food
•Pull Carts	•Clubhouse
•Club Rental	•Outings

Fees	Weekday	Weekend
Resident	$12	$12
Non-res	$35	$35
Twi/Res (4)	$10	
Non-res	$18	

Course Description: At Ridgefield the front nine plays shorter, the back tighter and more hilly. At this busy course, the fairways are of medium width and traps can be encountered on most holes. The greens are average size, relatively fast and have little break. Water is in play on 5 holes on the back. The par 3 12th requires a shot over a pond to a green with trouble behind it. The signature par 4 15th features an elevated tee to a relatively narrow fairway that has a deep drop on the left and a water hazard all along the right.

Directions: Fairfield County, #21

Take I-684North in Westchester to Rte.84East to Exit 1 toward Danbury. Take Saw Mill Rd South for 2 and1/2 miles to STOP and road becomes Ridgebury. Course on right.

Hole	1	2	3	4	5	6	7	8	9	Out	BLUE	Rating 70.9
BLUE	408	411	163	344	147	542	412	411	378	3216		Slope 123
WHITE	391	367	150	320	139	518	338	381	371	2975		
Par	4	4	3	4	3	5	4	4	4	35	WHITE	Rating 68.9
Handicap	12	8	16	14	18	2	10	4	6			Slope 120
RED	348	291	132	223	112	483	274	323	297	2483		
Par	4	4	3	4	3	5	4	4	4	35	RED	Rating 70.6
Handicap	8	10	16	14	18	2	12	6	4			Slope 119
Hole	10	11	12	13	14	15	16	17	18	In		Totals
BLUE	564	336	163	377	493	414	324	140	400	3216	BLUE	6427
WHITE	533	311	147	351	459	395	311	127	386	2975	WHITE	5995
Par	5	4	3	4	5	4	4	3	4	36	Par	71
Handicap	3	11	15	9	7	1	13	17	5			
RED	485	260	116	328	369	360	282	113	334	2647	RED	5130
Par	5	4	3	4	5	5	4	3	5	38	Par	73
Handicap	3	11	15	5	1	9	13	17	7			

Manager/Pro: Vincent Adams, PGA   **Supt:** Anton Steger
Architect: Tom Fazio 1974

ROCKRIMMON COUNTRY CLUB

2949 Long Ridge Road, Stamford, CT 06903   **(203) 322-2850**

Rockrimmon is an 18 hole course open 6 days a week and closed between Nov. 15 & Apr. 1. Guests may play accompanied by a member. Tee time reservations are required on weekends.

•Driving Range	•Lockers
•Practice Green	•Showers
•Power Carts	•Food
Pull Carts	•Clubhouse
•Club Rental	•Outings
•Caddies	•Soft Spikes

Course Description: Rockrimmon straddles the border of NY and CT. An uphill tram crosses the state line from the 9th to the 10th hole making it the shortest interstate RR in the country. Originally 9 holes, the 2nd nine was built in 1953. A difficult course with tree lined fairways and picturesque vistas overlooking NYState, there are many blind shots and elevated greens. The 574 yard par 5 3rd has a descending fairway and needs a downhill shot to an elevated green surrounded by traps and woods behind it. The 8th is the toughest par 4; a severely sloped fairway and a punchbowl green gives even the most adept golfer a challenge. The 15th is a short tight par 5 needing an approach shot over a stream to land on the green.

Directions: Fairfield County, #22
Merritt Pkwy. to Exit #34 (Long Ridge Rd.-Rte.104) Proceed North 4.5 miles to club on right.

Hole	1	2	3	4	5	6	7	8	9	Out	BLUE	Rating 73.8
BLUE	477	388	574	394	433	435	124	454	187	3466		Slope 128
WHITE	471	377	561	366	398	405	117	413	167	3275		
Par	5	4	5	4	4	4	3	4	3	36	WHITE	Rating 72.7
Handicap	9	13	1	11	7	3	17	5	15			Slope 126
RED	342	310	476	336	347	385	106	404	121	2827		
Par	4	4	5	4	4	5	3	5	3	37	RED	Rating 73.6
Handicap	3	11	1	5	7	9	17	13	15			Slope 130
Hole	10	11	12	13	14	15	16	17	18	In		Totals
BLUE	413	158	430	438	568	514	337	137	481	3476	BLUE	6942
WHITE	406	152	422	405	562	508	335	130	413	3333	WHITE	6608
Par	4	3	4	4	5	5	4	3	4	36	Par	72
Handicap	4	18	10	2	6	12	14	16	8			
RED	338	137	345	398	460	479	265	126	403	2951	RED	5778
Par	4	3	4	5	5	5	4	3	5	38	Par	72
Handicap	8	18	10	6	2	4	14	16	12			

Manager: Bob Musich   **Pro:** Jerry Yochum, PGA   **Supt:** Tony Girardi
Architect: Robert Trent Jones, 1949

ROLLING HILLS COUNTRY CLUB

333 Hurlbutt St., Wilton, CT 06897   **(203) 762-5147**

Rolling Hills is an 18 hole course open 6 days a week and closed Dec. 1 to April 1. Guests may play accompanied by a member. Tee time reservations are necessary on weekends.

•**Driving Range**	•**Lockers**
•**Practice Green**	•**Showers**
•**Power Carts**	•**Food**
Pull Carts	•**Clubhouse**
Club Rental	•**Outings**
•**Caddies**	•**Soft Spikes**

Course Description: Rolling Hills has a tight hilly layout with many uneven lies and moderately wide yet forgiving fairways. A number of greens are elevated small, fast and sloping. Water is in play on several par threes. The 7th & 8th are tough back to back par 4s; the former a 420 yd. uphill dogleg right and the latter a 439 yd. hole featuring a 2 tiered fairway, both giving golfers quite a challenge. From the elevated tee on the signature fourth, the valley below provides a sight particularly spectacular in the Fall. The par 3 fifteenth hole has a large pond to traverse and a lovely flower bed behind the green.

Directions: Fairfield County, #23
Merritt Pkwy. to Exit #41and turn right onto Rte.33. Proceed 1.3 miles to light at Chestnut Hill Rd, (Rte.53), and turn right. Go 1.3 miles, bear left at fork, then continue straight for 2 miles to club on left.

Hole	1	2	3	4	5	6	7	8	9	Out	BLUE	Rating 72.7
BLUE	526	371	197	376	333	199	455	456	518	3431		Slope 134
WHITE	509	353	177	362	308	186	420	439	493	3247		
Par	5	4	3	4	4	3	4	4	5	36	WHITE	Rating 71.0
Handicap	5	9	15	11	13	17	3	1	7			Slope 130
RED	466	306	111	330	294	127	381	386	467	2868		
Par	5	4	3	4	4	3	5	4	5	37	RED	Rating 72.2
Handicap	5	13	15	11	9	17	7	3	1			Slope 122
Hole	10	11	12	13	14	15	16	17	18	In		Totals
BLUE	485	449	365	240	380	172	335	369	466	3261	BLUE	6692
WHITE	465	423	328	212	362	156	330	345	436	3057	WHITE	6304
Par	5	4	4	3	4	3	4	4	4	35	Par	71
Handicap	16	4	8	14	6	18	12	10	2			
RED	417	395	316	177	272	123	272	307	408	2687	RED	5555
Par	5	4	4	3	4	3	4	4	5	36	Par	73
Handicap	10	2	6	14	12	18	16	8	4			

Manager: John O'Brien   **Pro:** Joe Bostic, PGA   **Supt:** Greg Moore
Architect: Alfred Tull 1965

ROUND HILL CLUB

33 Round Hill Club Rd., Greenwich, CT 06831   **(203) 661-1648**

Round Hill is an 18 hole course open 6 days a week, all year weather permitting. Guests may play accompanied by a member. Tee time reservations are not necessary.

> - **Driving Range**
> - **Practice Green**
> - **Power Carts**
> - **Pull Carts**
> - **Club Rental**
> - **Caddies**
> - **Lockers**
> - **Showers**
> - **Food**
> - **Clubhouse**
> - Outings
> - **Soft Spikes**

Course Description: Round Hill is hilly and nestled among beautiful homes set in the woods. The meticulously maintained course is elegant, understated and tasteful. Its terrain has dramatic changes in elevation and the greens are quite contoured. The eleventh is a par 3 over a lake that reaches from tee to green and is surrounded by lovely willow trees. Billie Burke was the pro here for three years (1930-1932) during which he won the US Open in 1931. Many USGA Senior tournaments have been played here.

Directions: Fairfield County, #24
Merritt Pkwy. North to Exit #28, Round Hill Rd. Turn right toward Greenwich. Proceed 1.2 miles to Round Hill Club Rd. & turn right to club.

Hole	1	2	3	4	5	6	7	8	9	Out	BLUE	Rating 73.8
BLUE	351	525	217	432	413	179	335	430	419	3301		Slope 139
WHITE	346	507	213	409	403	172	328	413	401	3192		
Par	4	5	3	4	4	3	4	4	4	35	WHITE	Rating 72.7
Handicap	13	9	15	1	7	17	11	3	5			Slope 137
RED	331	476	154	341	346	166	302	407	389	2912		
Par	4	5	3	4	4	3	4	5	5	37	RED	Rating 74.5
Handicap	9	1	17	11	3	15	13	7	5			Slope 135

Hole	10	11	12	13	14	15	16	17	18	In		Totals
BLUE	307	152	332	342	442	513	542	188	406	3224	BLUE	6525
WHITE	296	142	307	332	434	504	523	182	400	3120	WHITE	6312
Par	4	3	4	4	4	5	5	3	4	36	Par	71
Handicap	16	18	10	12	2	8	4	14	6			
RED	286	110	272	298	424	472	447	147	353	2809	RED	5721
Par	4	3	4	4	5	5	5	3	4	37	Par	74
Handicap	14	18	10	12	8	2	4	16	6			

Manager: Dennis Meermans   **Pro:** Tom Henderson, PGA   **Supt:** Bill Gaydosh
Architect: Walter Travis 1924   **Redesign:** Robert Trent Jones 1965

SHOREHAVEN GOLF CLUB

14 Canfield Avenue, E. Norwalk, CT 06855   **(203) 838-8717**

Shorehaven is an 18 hole course open 6 days a week, and closed for Jan. & Feb. Guests may play accompanied by a member. Tee time reservations are not necessary.

```
•Driving Range   •Lockers
•Practice Green  •Showers
•Power Carts     •Food
 Pull Carts      •Clubhouse
•Club Rental     •Outings
•Caddies         •Soft Spikes
```

Course Description: Shorehaven has a flat layout and is designed for the average golfer. However, the par 3s are very tough with some forced carries. Wind is a major factor here since it is so near the Sound. The par 3 17th has water behind the green and is 200 yards from the blues. The greens are relatively small and have a back to front slope. The tree lined fairways are tight and the rough is heavy; it is important to stay in the fairway. There are great views of LI Sound from several holes and from the clubhouse. Met tournaments have been held here as well as the "Ike" qualifying round.

Directions: Fairfield County, #25
I-95 North to Exit #16; go right onto East Ave. Continue on East (under RR trestle) & turn left onto Cemetery Rd. which changes to Gregory Blvd. Proceed to monument in center of rd., turn left & go **uphill** to Marvin Ave. (sharp turn to right) to club on left.

Hole	1	2	3	4	5	6	7	8	9	Out	BLUE	Rating 72.4
BLUE	490	150	449	385	245	335	395	390	425	3264		Slope 134
WHITE	475	140	395	375	195	325	375	370	415	3065		
Par	5	3	4	4	3	4	4	4	4	35	WHITE	Rating 71.0
Handicap	7	13	5	3	17	11	1	15	9			Slope 131
RED	444	111	378	287	135	215	357	250	399	2576		
Par	5	3	4	4	3	4	4	4	5	36	RED	Rating 72.9
Handicap	4	16	6	8	18	12	2	14	10			Slope 132

Hole	10	11	12	13	14	15	16	17	18	In		Totals
BLUE	430	500	505	240	335	160	555	200	410	3335	BLUE	6599
WHITE	420	490	495	230	325	145	545	195	350	3195	WHITE	6260
Par	4	5	5	3	4	3	5	3	4	36	Par	71
Handicap	6	4	10	16	12	14	2	18	8			
RED	410	425	430	217	318	125	478	163	303	2879	RED	5455
Par	5	5	5	4	4	3	5	3	4	38	Par	74
Handicap	9	3	7	13	5	17	1	15	11			

Manager: Bill Boulay   **Pro:** Dale Kahlden, PGA   **Supt:** Jim Weiland
Architect: Willie Park Jr., 1923

SILVERMINE GOLF CLUB

95 North Seir Hill Road, Norwalk, CT 06850 **(203) 846-2552**

Silvermine is a 27 hole golf facility open 6 days a week all year weather permitting. Guests may play accompanied by a member. Tee time reservations are required on weekends only.

Driving Range	Lockers
•**Practice Green**	Showers
•**Power Carts**	•**Food**
•**Pull Carts**	•**Clubhouse**
•**Club Rental**	•**Outings**
Caddies	•**Soft Spikes**

Course Description: Silvermine is made up of 18 regulation (Grey Hollow) and 9 executive type holes. Grey Hollow is short, hilly and treacherous; the rough is deep, the fairways narrow. The small greens are hard to hold and elevated. Water is in play on 8 holes including the signature par 5 #17 which has a lake on the approach shot and a severe drop if the ball goes over the green. Views of scenic Long Island can be seen as the course is situated in the highest part of Norwalk. Silvermine members are fortunate to have a separate 9 holer on the premises to practice on or play when time is limited.

Directions: Fairfield County, #26
Merritt Pkwy.North to Exit #39B. Proceed north on Rte.7 to Glover Ave. (Shell Sta. on corner), turn left. Go 1/2 mile to Seir Hill Rd. and turn left. Club is 1 mile on left.

Hole	1	2	3	4	5	6	7	8	9	Out	BLUE	Rating 65.0
BLUE												Slope 107
WHITE	383	306	141	278	240	144	246	251	446	2435		
Par	4	4	3	4	4	3	4	4	5	35	WHITE	Rating 66.3
Handicap	1	7	15	5	13	17	11	9	3			Slope 112
RED	368	289	120	261	228	131	238	243	423	2301		
Par	4	4	4	3	4	5	3	4	4	35	RED	Rating 68.9
Handicap	1	13	17	9	11	15	5	7	3			Slope 120
Hole	10	11	12	13	14	15	16	17	18	In		Totals
BLUE											BLUE	
WHITE	472	280	168	339	150	338	289	475	141	2652	WHITE	5087
Par	5	4	3	4	3	4	4	5	3	35	Par	70
Handicap	8	10	12	4	16	2	14	6	18			
RED	450	272	160	275	113	331	274	470	137	2480	RED	4781
Par	5	4	3	4	3	4	4	5	3	35	Par	70
Handicap	4	10	16	8	18	6	12	2	14			

Manager: Bill Warner   **Pro:** Michael Silver, PGA   **Supt:** Al Goodwin
Architect: Jack Warner, Sr. 1951

SILVER SPRING COUNTRY CLUB   PRIVATE

439 Silver Spring Rd., Ridgefield, CT 06877   (203) 438-0100

Silver Spring is a private 18 hole course open 6 days a week all year weather permitting. Guests play accompanied by a member. Tee time reservations are not necessary.

- •Driving Range
- •Practice Green
- •Power Carts
- Pull Carts
- Club Rental
- •Caddies

- •Lockers
- •Showers
- •Food
- •Clubhouse
- Outings
- •Soft Spikes

Course Description: At Silver Spring, the golfer finds gently rolling hills, narrow fairways, some elevated tees and tight doglegs. The front is more heavily treed, the back more wide open. The members refer to it as a "small club in the country". Simplicity, quality and character are its essence. No water is in play but many bunkers add to the difficulty. The rather small greens are very fast and undulating. Considered a shot maker's course, it is harder for higher handicap players.

Directions: Fairfield County, #27
Take the Merritt Pkwy to Exit 38. Proceed north on Rte.123 for about 10 miles to Rte. 35 and turn right. Go for about 1 and 1/2 miles and turn right on Silver Spring Rd. Bear left immediately and proceed to club entrance on the right.

Hole	1	2	3	4	5	6	7	8	9	Out	BLUE	Rating 72.1
BLUE	342	535	185	325	356	420	403	218	395	3179		Slope 132
WHITE	331	512	171	312	343	408	390	202	380	3049		
Par	4	5	3	4	4	4	4	3	4	35	WHITE	Rating 70.8
Handicap	17	5	13	15	9	3	1	11	7			Slope 129
RED	326	427	167	309	340	404	385	167	351	2876		
Par	4	5	3	4	4	5	5	3	4	37	RED	Rating 73.0
Handicap	11	1	15	13	9	7	5	17	3			Slope 121
Hole	10	11	12	13	14	15	16	17	18	In		Totals
BLUE	165	483	437	530	394	132	419	381	398	3339	BLUE	6518
WHITE	156	473	421	500	350	127	404	370	371	3172	WHITE	6221
Par	3	5	4	5	4	3	4	4	4	36	Par	71
Handicap	16	12	2	6	14	18	4	10	8			
RED	153	408	336	425	345	119	320	364	311	2781	RED	5657
Par	3	5	4	5	4	3	4	4	4	36	Par	73
Handicap	16	2	8	6	10	18	12	4	14			

Manager: Bob Sommer   **Pro:** Stan Garrett, PGA   **Supt:** Peter Rappocchio
Architect: Robert White 1929   **Redesign:** Alfred Tull

THE STANWICH CLUB

North Street, Greenwich, CT 06830   **(203) 869-2072**

The Stanwich Club is a private 18 hole course open 6 days a week between April 1 and Dec.1. Guests may play accompanied by a member. Tee time reservations are required.

•Driving Range	•Lockers
•Practice Green	•Showers
•Power Carts	•Food
Pull Carts	•Clubhouse
•Club Rental	•Outings
•Caddies	•Soft Spikes

Course Description: The Stanwich layout is long, tight and relatively flat with trees lining all the carpet-like fairways. The hard, fast undulating greens are a true test of a golfer's skill. Water comes into play on 8 holes in the form of lakes and streams. The signature par 3 13th must carry over a lake to an elevated deeply trapped green. A change in pin placement makes the golfer think twice about what club to use to get close. The MET Open was held here in 1996.

Directions: Fairfield County, #28
Merritt Pkwy.to Exit #31 (North St.) Turn toward Banksville, proceed 2.2 miles to club on right. (Entrance is hidden; look carefully).

Hole	1	2	3	4	5	6	7	8	9	Out	BLUE	Rating 76.0
BLUE	373	415	376	254	534	430	401	203	577	3563		Slope 144
WHITE	343	390	359	193	512	397	373	191	545	3303		
Par	4	4	4	3	5	4	4	3	5	36	WHITE	Rating 73.1
Handicap	13	7	5	15	1	9	11	17	3			Slope 139
RED	329	370	352	141	440	358	355	142	468	2955		
Par	4	4	4	3	5	4	4	3	5	36	RED	Rating 76.2
Handicap	11	7	3	17	5	13	9	15	1			Slope 139
Hole	10	11	12	13	14	15	16	17	18	In		Totals
BLUE	397	424	452	198	520	445	172	568	394	3570	BLUE	7133
WHITE	364	406	417	163	488	393	150	540	364	3285	WHITE	6588
Par	4	4	4	3	5	4	3	5	4	36	Par	72
Handicap	10	8	4	16	12	6	18	2	14			
RED	347	385	371	145	438	385	117	464	301	2953	RED	5908
Par	4	5	4	3	5	5	3	5	4	38	Par	74
Handicap	6	14	8	12	4	16	18	2	10			

Manager: Peter Tuniley   **Pro:** Billy Farrell, PGA   **Supt:** Scott Niven
Architect: William Gordon 1963

STERLING FARMS GOLF COURSE

1349 Newfield Road, Stamford, CT 06905   (203) 329-7888

Sterling Farms is an 18 hole course open 7 days a week and closed in Jan. & Feb. and on Thursdays for outings. There is no non-res. play on weekends until 2PM. A lottery is held for reserving tee times; call 461-9090 up to a week in advance.

			Fees	Weekday	Weekend
•**Driving Range**	Lockers		Daily(Res)	$12	$13
•**Practice Green**	Showers		Non-res	$35	$40
•**Power Carts**	•**Food**		Sr/Jr/Twi	$9	
•**Pull Carts**	•**Clubhouse**		Power carts	$20	
•**Club Rental**	•**Outings**				
•**Soft Spikes**					

Course Description: The immaculately maintained Sterling Farms is easily walkable, well bunkered and moderately hilly. Views of LI Sound, New Canaan, Darien and Stamford abound and a camp-like atmosphere prevails. Water comes into play on 8 holes in the form of streams and ponds. The contoured greens are larger than average with some break. The signature par 4 14th has water in play on the approach shot; making good placement imperative. A new irrigation system has been installed which accounts for the great condition of the course. Over 50,000 rounds are played here annually.

Directions: Fairfield County, #29
Merritt Pkwy. to Exit #35; turn right and proceed 1/2 mile to light at Vine Rd. Turn left for 1 mi. to end of road. Turn left onto Newfield Ave. for 1/2 mi. to club on right.

Hole	1	2	3	4	5	6	7	8	9	Out	BLUE	Rating 71.1
BLUE	359	524	327	352	221	438	398	179	348	3146		Slope 118
WHITE	337	499	310	333	198	415	372	174	335	2973		
Par	4	5	4	4	3	5	4	3	4	36	WHITE	Rating 69.3
Handicap	17	9	15	5	3	7	1	13	11			Slope 115
RED	313	459	293	292	171	396	352	166	321	2763		
Par	4	5	4	4	3	5	4	3	4	36	RED	Rating 72.8
Handicap	15	3	11	5	17	1	7	13	9			Slope 125
Hole	10	11	12	13	14	15	16	17	18	In		Totals
BLUE	411	304	353	508	404	154	309	232	487	3162	BLUE	6308
WHITE	381	274	332	480	365	140	295	217	465	2949	WHITE	5922
Par	4	4	4	5	4	3	4	3	5	36	Par	72
Handicap	6	14	4	10	2	18	12	8	16			
RED	359	252	320	412	340	131	234	250	434	2732	RED	5495
Par	4	4	4	5	4	3	4	4	5	37	Par	73
Handicap	6	16	14	2	4	12	8	18	10			

Manager: Paul Grillo **Pro:** Angela Aulenti, PGA **Supt:** Tracey Holiday
Architects: Geoffrey Cornish & Wlilliam Robinson 1971

TAMARACK COUNTRY CLUB

PRIVATE

55 Locust Road, Greenwich, CT 06831   **(203) 531-7364**

Tamarack is an 18 hole course open 6 days a week all year, weather permitting. Guests may play accompanied by a member. Tee time reservations are required on weekends.

•**Driving Range**	•**Lockers**
•**Practice Green**	•**Showers**
•**Power Carts**	•**Food**
Pull Carts	•**Clubhouse**
•**Club Rental**	•**Outings**
•**Caddies**	•**Soft Spikes**

Course Description: Tamarack is a course that plays long and is characterized by generously treed fairways, deep bunkers (typical of architect Charles Banks) and large greens. The latter are subtlely contoured and difficult to read. The signature 14th, a long par 4, has OB on the right and water on the left; the golfer must bear right on the tee shot or be blocked on the 2nd shot. As if that isn't enough, it has the most undulating green on the course. The well known MET area "IKE" tournament was begun at Tamarack in 1953. Former President Eisenhower had given permission to use his nickname. It continued to be held here for a number of years.

Directions: Fairfield County, #30
I-684 to Exit #2, turn left at light onto Rte.120(North). At 2nd road on right, turn right. At STOP sign turn left onto King St.(120A.) Proceed North (King becomes Locust Rd.) to club on left.

Hole	1	2	3	4	5	6	7	8	9	Out	BLUE	Rating 72.9
BLUE	446	367	171	463	587	399	196	431	376	3436		Slope 126
WHITE	438	348	157	453	577	387	183	417	367	3327		
Par	4	4	3	4	5	4	3	4	4	35	WHITE	Rating 71.7
Handicap	5	11	17	1	3	9	15	7	13			Slope 124
RED	428	337	145	338	470	298	175	403	283	2877		
Par	5	4	3	4	5	4	3	5	4	37	RED	Rating 71.8
Handicap	5	3	17	9	1	11	15	7	13			Slope 120

Hole	10	11	12	13	14	15	16	17	18	In		Totals
BLUE	366	443	214	491	452	156	370	508	398	3398	BLUE	6834
WHITE	352	432	197	473	443	143	325	488	387	3240	WHITE	6567
Par	4	4	3	5	4	3	4	5	4	36	Par	71
Handicap	14	4	10	12	2	18	16	8	6			
RED	284	421	156	407	352	130	308	402	306	2766	RED	5643
Par	4	5	3	5	4	3	4	5	4	37	Par	74
Handicap	18	4	16	6	2	14	10	8	12			

Manager: Tom Tutthill   **Pro:** Paul Miner, PGA   **Supt:** Jeff Scott
Architect: Charles Banks 1929

TASHUA KNOLLS GOLF CLUB

Tashua Knolls Lane, Trumbull, CT 06611   (203) 261-5989

Tashua Knolls is an 18 hole course open 7 days a week and closed from Dec. to March. There are memberships available. Tee times may be made 1 day ahead for weekdays and Wed. mornings for weekends.

•**Driving Range**	•**Lockers**
•**Practice Green**	•**Showers**
•**Power Carts**	•**Food**
•**Pull Carts**	•**Clubhouse**
•**Club Rental**	•**Outings**
•**Soft Spikes**	

Fees	Weekday	Weekend
Daily(Res)	$12	$14
Non Res	$24	$27
Sr/Res	$6	$9
Power carts	$22	

Course Description: Tashua Knolls is a hilly New England type course with picturesque views particularly on the back nine. The large greens have some slight break. It is built on what was formerly 3 farms and many of the stone walls were kept for their natural beauty. The golfer encounters up and down terrain as he progresses along the open fairways. The par 5 14th signature hole has an elevated tee with a slight dogleg left and ponds on the left and right.

Directions: Fairfield County, #31
Merritt Pkwy. to Exit #49. Take Rte.25 North to end. Take the second left onto Tashua Rd. to course on left.

Hole	1	2	3	4	5	6	7	8	9	Out	BLUE	Rating 70.8
BLUE	561	375	167	391	370	211	501	366	378	3320		Slope 118
WHITE	532	317	151	342	353	192	480	354	356	3077		
Par	5	4	3	4	4	3	5	4	4	36	WHITE	Rating 69.3
Handicap	3	9	15	5	11	17	1	13	7			Slope 122
RED	489	270	146	308	316	149	436	308	295	2717		
Par	5	4	3	4	4	3	5	4	4	36	RED	Rating 71.3
Handicap	3	15	13	5	7	17	1	9	11			Slope 112
Hole	10	11	12	13	14	15	16	17	18	In		Totals
BLUE	373	385	163	303	506	394	527	162	407	3220	BLUE	6540
WHITE	349	367	154	262	495	373	506	145	391	3042	WHITE	6119
Par	4	4	3	4	5	4	5	3	4	36	Par	72
Handicap	8	12	18	14	6	2	4	16	10			
RED	321	304	142	243	480	326	454	132	335	2737	RED	5454
Par	4	4	3	4	5	4	5	3	4	36	Par	72
Handicap	10	12	18	2	4	12	8	18	10			

Manager/Pro: Walter Bogues, PGA   **Supt:** Ed Zenisky
Architect: Al Zikorus 1976

WEE BURN COUNTRY CLUB

PRIVATE

410 Hollow Tree Ridge Road., Darien, CT 06820   **(203) 655-2929**

Wee Burn is an 18 hole course open 6 days a week, all year, weather permitting. Guests may play accompanied by a member. Tee time reservations are needed only on Sundays.

> • **Driving Range** • **Lockers**
> • **Practice Green** • **Showers**
> • **Power Carts** • **Food**
> • **Pull Carts** • **Clubhouse**
> • **Club Rental** Outings
> • **Caddies** • **Soft Spikes**

Course Description: Wee Burn is a challenging yet easily walkable course, so many members choose to walk using a caddie. The greens are small and relatively fast with a fair amount of break and since they are also tightly bunkered, accurate iron shots are needed. The 5th is considered by many to be the toughest hole; trees line both sides of the fairway from the tee to an uphill green which has a swale in the middle and mounds protecting it. The Wee Burn Stream winds through the course both across and along the holes. Wind is also a factor here.

Directions: Fairfield County, #32
Merritt Pkwy. to Exit #37; turn right onto Mansfield Ave.(Rte.124). Proceed 1.3 miles to Middlesex Rd. & turn right. Go 0.2 mi. to Stop sign, turn left to Hanson Rd. & then turn right. Proceed to club at top of hill on right.

Hole	1	2	3	4	5	6	7	8	9	Out	BLUE	Rating 73.8
BLUE	422	363	422	160	435	588	172	383	371	3316		Slope 139
WHITE	409	338	415	148	423	578	153	375	352	3191		
Par	4	4	4	3	4	5	3	4	4	35	WHITE	Rating 72.7
Handicap	5	13	7	15	1	3	17	9	11			Slope 137
RED	355	281	375	110	378	512	137	338	326	2812		
Par	4	4	4	3	4	5	3	4	4	35	RED	Rating 74.5
Handicap	9	13	5	17	3	1	15	11	7			Slope 135

Hole	10	11	12	13	14	15	16	17	18	In		Totals
BLUE	509	391	390	419	395	212	336	371	488	3511	BLUE	6827
WHITE	504	375	370	414	377	190	326	352	470	3378	WHITE	6569
Par	5	4	4	4	4	3	4	4	5	37	Par	72
Handicap	16	6	14	2	4	12	8	18	10			
RED	430	329	324	360	333	162	276	319	385	2918	RED	5730
Par	5	4	4	4	4	3	4	4	5	37	Par	72
Handicap	4	10	14	2	8	16	12	18	6			

Manager: Steve McVey   **Pro:** Roy Pace, PGA   **Supt:** Rich Schock
Architect: Devereux Emmet 1925   **Estab:** 1896

WOODWAY COUNTRY CLUB

412 Hoyt St., Darien, CT 06820   **(203) 322-1298**

Woodway is an 18 hole private course open 6 days a week, all year, weather permitting.   Tee time reservations may be made up to one week in advance. Guests may play accompanied by a member.

•Driving Range	•Lockers
•Practice Green	•Showers
•Power Carts	•Food
•Pull Carts	•Clubhouse
•Club Rental	•Outings
•Caddies	•Soft Spikes

Course Description: At Woodway the fairways are thickly tree lined. The greens are of average size, relatively fast with a great deal of undulation. Streams and ponds affect play on 16 of the holes. A slope of 139 means a challenging course; at Woodway position is everything. The signature 4th requires a shot over a pond, then an approach shot uphill to a two-tiered green. The intimidating 1st hole, a 428 yard par 4, has a long second shot to an elevated green surrounded by trees and traps. The Connecticut Open was hosted here.

Directions: Fairfield County, #33
Hutchinson to Merritt Pkwy. North to Exit #36. Turn right off exit ramp onto Hoyt St.towards Stamford-Darien. Proceed 1 mile to club on right.

Hole	1	2	3	4	5	6	7	8	9	Out	BLUE	Rating 72.8
BLUE	428	358	378	384	401	373	189	377	450	3338		Slope 139
WHITE	413	349	371	374	392	367	179	357	430	3232		
Par	4	4	4	4	4	4	3	4	4	35	WHITE	Rating 71.5
Handicap	5	13	9	1	7	11	17	15	3			Slope 136
RED	395	312	318	303	383	350	168	322	398	2949		
Par	5	4	4	4	4	4	3	4	5	37	RED	Rating 74.1
Handicap	11	9	3	7	1	5	15	17	13			Slope 131
Hole	10	11	12	13	14	15	16	17	18	In		Totals
BLUE	213	382	575	420	365	168	327	570	358	3378	BLUE	6716
WHITE	193	357	552	401	346	133	317	560	334	3193	WHITE	6425
Par	3	4	5	4	4	3	4	5	4	36	Par	71
Handicap	14	8	6	2	16	18	12	4	10			
RED	156	306	506	391	339	125	292	481	284	2880	RED	5829
Par	3	4	5	5	4	3	4	5	4	37	Par	74
Handicap	16	12	2	6	10	18	8	4	14			

Manager: John Schuler   **Pro:** Mike Gallo, PGA   **Supt:** Larry Pakkala
Architect: Willie Park, 1916

A golfer is more than a ball-driving brute

He is more than a mug-hunting Czar.

To be known as a golfer, you don't have to shoot

The course of your home club in par.

But you do have to love every blade of the grass,

Every inch of the fairway and greens.

If you don't take care of the course as you pass,

You're not what a "good golfer" means.

(Vail's Grove)

ORANGE AND ROCKLAND COUNTIES

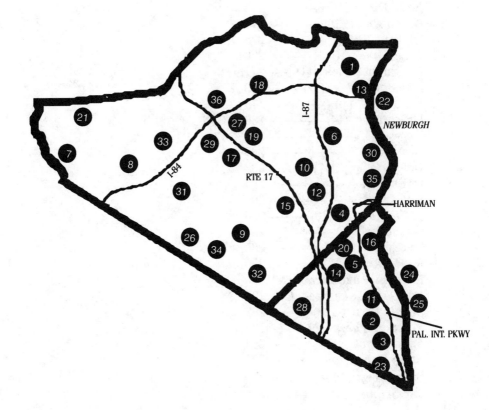

ORANGE and ROCKLAND COUNTIES

Public Courses appear in *bold italics*

APPLE GREENS GOLF COURSE

161 South St., Highland, NY 12528   **(914) 883-5500**

Apple Greens is an 18 hole course open to the public 7 days a week and closed 11/30-4/1. Limited memberships are available. Tee time reservations may be made up to 1 week in advance.

- **Driving Range**   Lockers
- **Practice Green** **•Soft Spikes**
- **Power Carts**   **•Food**
- **Pull Carts**   Clubhouse
- **Club Rental**   **•Outings**

Fees	Weekday	Weekend
Daily	$22	$27
9 holes/2PM	$15 4PM/	$18
Carts	$24/18	$14/9

Course Description: Apple Greens was built through an apple orchard and many of the trees are still standing. In the Fall, golfers are allowed to pick apples off the trees. Amidst the spectacular views of the Shawangunk Mountains, lies this challenging course of moderate length and well maintained fairways, a fair test of golfing skills. The signature par 4 10th has a green, in the center of the golf course shaped like an apple as viewed from above, and the bunkers give the effect of leaves and a stem. The putting surface is crown shaped, sloping to the sides. The putts can be fast, depending upon pin placement. One par 3 has an island green. Water is in play on 11 holes.

Directions: Orange County, #1
Take I-87N to Exit 18 (New Paltz). Go right on Rte.299. At blinking light, make right onto South St. Go 1& 1/2 miles to club on right.

Hole	1	2	3	4	5	6	7	8	9	Out	BLUE	Rating 70.4
BLUE	401	360	172	610	156	538	350	364	445	3396		Slope 124
WHITE	340	350	159	540	138	511	328	358	405	3129		
Par	4	4	3	5	3	5	4	4	4	36	WHITE	Rating 68.4
Handicap	7	17	9	3	15	5	13	11	1			Slope 120
RED	295	305	108	465	101	436	257	315	302	2584		
Par	4	4	3	5	3	5	4	4	4	36	RED	Rating 67.6
Handicap	5	11	13	1	17	3	7	9	15			Slope 122

Hole	10	11	12	13	14	15	16	17	18	In		Totals
BLUE	310	201	341	354	365	452	510	226	355	3114	BLUE	6510
WHITE	281	190	331	329	348	402	490	206	343	2920	WHITE	6049
Par	4	3	4	4	4	4	5	3	4	35	Par	71
Handicap	12	14	10	18	6	2	8	4	16			
RED	236	133	284	264	259	342	443	155	259	2375	RED	4959
Par	4	3	4	4	4	4	5	3	4	35	Par	71
Handicap	16	18	8	12	10	2	4	6	14			

Manager: Richard Gibbons   **Pro:** John Magaletta, PGA **Supt:** Don Shambo
Architect: John Magaletta 1996

BLUE HILL GOLF CLUB

285 Blue Hill Road, Pearl River, NY 10965   **(914) 735-2094**

Blue Hill is a 27 hole golf course open to the public 7 days a week all year, weather permitting. Memberships for Orangetown residents with reduced fees & preferred tee time privileges on weekends are available. 1 day advance for tee times.

Driving Range	•**Lockers**
•**Practice Green**	•**Showers**
•**Power Carts**	•**Food**
•**Pull Carts**	•**Clubhouse**
Club Rental	•**Outings**
•**Soft Spikes**	

Fees	Weekday	Weekend
Daily(non-res)	$29	$35
Daily (res)	$14	$18
Sr/Jr	Discounts available	
Power carts	$26	$26

Course Description: An extremely playable course for the average golfer, Blue Hill is made up of three nines, Woodland (built in 1996), Pines & Lakeside. The roughs are well-trimmed, and all three nines are par 36. With some water in play and four tee placements, the golfer has a variety of options. The greens are of medium speed and have been remodeled. The unique par 3 #3 signature hole on Woodlands has a tee shot from a cliff to a target below. This busy course, carved out of a forest, is hilly and quite picturesque. The scorecard below is for the Pines and Woodland Courses.

Directions: Rockland County, #2
Take the Palisades Pkwy. to Exit 6W.   Take Orangeburg Rd. going West.   At the third traffic light, turn right. Course is 1/2 mile on right.

Hole	1	2	3	4	5	6	7	8	9	Out	BLUE	Rating 70.0
BLUE	469	495	305	375	188	480	325	190	425	3252		Slope 116
WHITE	446	475	288	357	155	465	300	175	415	3076		
Par	4	5	4	4	3	5	4	3	4	36	WHITE	Rating 68.6
Handicap	1	5	8	4	9	3	7	6	2			Slope 114
RED	411	440	275	316	115	419	264	135	374	2749		
Par	4	5	4	4	3	5	4	3	4	36	RED	Rating 70.6
Handicap	4	4	15	4	13	4	5	5	14			Slope 117
Hole	10	11	12	13	14	15	16	17	18	In		Totals
BLUE	374	487	109	320	305	435	524	166	385	3105	BLUE	6357
WHITE	353	471	102	307	290	406	513	153	376	2971	WHITE	6047
Par	4	5	3	4	4	4	5	3	4	36	Par	72
Handicap	3	4	9	6	7	1	2	8	5			
RED	246	375	81	217	240	330	392	146	335	2362	RED	5111
Par	4	5	3	4	4	4	5	3	4	36	Par	72
Handicap	4	4	15	4	13	4	5	5	14			

Manager/Pro: James Stewart, PGA
Architect: Stephen Kay   **Estab:** 1924

BROADACRES GOLF CLUB

 PUBLIC

140 Old Orangeburg Rd., Orangeburg, NY10962   (914) 359-8218

Broadacres is a 9 hole semi-private course that is on the grounds of the Rockland Psych. Center. It is open to the public 6 days a week and closed fromDec. 1 to Mar. 15. Yearly memberships are available. Tee times: Weekdays up to 48 hours in advance Weekends: reserve no later than 3PM the Thurs. before.

Driving Range	•Lockers
•Practice Green	•Showers
•Power Carts	•Food
•Pull Carts	Clubhouse
Club Rental	Outings
•Soft Spikes	

Fees	Weekday	Weekend
Daily(guest)	$19	$24
(non-mem)	$22	$27
Power carts	$22	$22

Course Description: Broadacres was built with the help of patients at the Rockland Psychiatric Center and was originally used by hospital staff only. Later, afterbeing leased from NY State, it became semi-private and open to members, guests and the public. This well-maintained regulation 9 hole course has narrow fairways with greens in excellent condition. It is said that the third hole is the most difficult par 3 in Rockland County. A membership here is $1025 yearly including green fees.

Directions: Rockland County, #3
Palisades Pkwy. North to Exit 6W. Go past light, make 2nd right onto Orangeburg Rd., follow signs to Rockland Psychiatric Ctr. Stay on main road to 1st stop and turn right. Course is on left. Sign says "Golf Parking".

Hole	1	2	3	4	5	6	7	8	9	Out	BLUE	Rating 70.4
BLUE	365	360	228	460	509	158	319	374	365	3138		Slope 126
WHITE	357	351	221	449	503	143	304	362	357	3047	WHITE	Rating 69.6
Par	4	4	3	4	5	3	4	4	4	35		Slope 124
Handicap	7	13	5	1	3	17	15	11	9			
RED	339	249	151	363	407	127	297	346	345	2624		
Par	4	4	3	4	5	3	4	4	4	35	RED	Rating 70.4
Handicap	7	13	5	1	3	17	15	11	9			Slope 121

Hole	10	11	12	13	14	15	16	17	18	In		Totals
BLUE											BLUE	3138
WHITE											WHITE	3047
Par											Par	35
Handicap												
RED											RED	2624
Par											Par	35
Handicap												

Manager: Nancy Finnegan   **Supt:** Mike Caravella
Architects: H. Blaisdell & V. Margiotta 1962

CENTRAL VALLEY GOLF COURSE

PUBLIC

266 Smith Clove Rd., Central Valley, NY 10917   (914) 928-6924

Central Valley is an 18 hole semi-private course. It is open 7 days a week and closed 12/1-3/15. There are memberships that cover annual greens fees and for guaranteed starting times. Phone reservations may be made up to 7 days in advance for tee times.

Driving Range	• Lockers
• **Practice Green**	• **Showers**
• **Power Carts**	• **Food**
• **Pull Carts**	• **Clubhouse**
• **Club Rental**	• **Outings**

Fees	Weekday	Weekend
Daily	$23	$33
9 holes 2PM	$12	$18
Power Carts	$24	

Course Description: Central Valley plays longer than the scorecard indicates because of the hilly terrain. This very scenic layout has narrow fairways and small greens. Due to the mountainside topography, there are many blind shots to the elevated greens. The most challenging is the very narrow and tree-lined #6, a par 4 from the regular tees, and rated a par 5 from the forward tees. It is a long slight dogleg left with out of bounds on the left side. There is not much water in play on this course (just some drainage ditches). Corporate outings are a specialty here.

Directions: Orange County, #4
Take I-87N to Exit 16. Go right on Rte.32N for 1 mile to Smith Clove Rd. Turn right and club is 1 mile ahead on right.

Hole	1	2	3	4	5	6	7	8	9	Out	BLUE	Rating
BLUE												Slope
WHITE	455	360	405	150	243	433	320	125	485	2976		
Par	5	4	4	3	4	4	4	3	5	36	WHITE	Rating 67.7
Handicap	5	8	2	17	14	1	10	18	6			Slope 116
RED	440	330	390	133	216	408	300	113	440	2770		
Par	5	4	5	3	4	5	4	3	5	38	RED	Rating 70.9
Handicap	3	8	2	17	13	1	10	18	4			Slope 116

Hole	10	11	12	13	14	15	16	17	18	In		Totals
BLUE											BLUE	
WHITE	407	150	285	308	300	318	335	198	367	2668	WHITE	5644
Par	4	3	4	4	4	4	4	3	4	34	Par	70
Handicap	3	16	13	9	11	12	4	15	7			
RED	401	140	263	300	279	298	329	178	359	2547	RED	5317
Par	5	3	4	4	4	4	4	3	4	35	Par	73
Handicap	5	16	14	9	11	12	6	15	7			

Manager: Wendy Lewis   **Pro:** John Banse   **Supt:** Peter Schmidt
Architect: Hal Purdy 1968 (Redesign)   **Estab:** 1922

DELLWOOD COUNTRY CLUB

PRIVATE

60 Zukor Road, New City, NY 10956　　　**(914) 634-4626**

Dellwood is an 18 hole course open 6 days a week and closed for the month of January. Guests may play accompanied by a member. Tee time reservations are required.

•Driving Range	•Lockers
•Practice Green	•Showers
•Power Carts	•Food
Pull Carts	•Clubhouse
•Club Rental	•Outings
•Caddies	•Soft Spikes

Course Description: Dellwood's championship 18 hole golf course, built on property that was originally the Adolph Zukor estate, is situated in the rolling hills of Rockland County. The course is heavily treed with greens that are particularly challenging when recently rolled. The par 3 3rd hole has a double tiered target area. With the ongoing upgrade, including new sand traps, the course is better than ever. The fifth hole is most scenic, featuring an elevated tee and a splendid view toward the west. In June of 1996, a qualifying round for the USGA Seniors took place here.

Directions: Rockland County #5
Palisades Pky. to Exit 11. (New Hempstead Rd., New City) Turn right on N. Hempstead Rd. for 1.7 miles to end of rd. (Main St.) and turn left. Continue North for 2 miles to Dellwood's gates.

Hole	1	2	3	4	5	6	7	8	9	Out	BLUE	Rating 73.0
BLUE	372	586	134	381	408	381	536	432	167	3397		Slope 129
WHITE	361	577	127	370	400	363	509	419	153	3279		
Par	4	5	3	4	4	4	5	4	3	36	WHITE	Rating 71.8
Handicap	1	3	17	7	9	11	13	5	15			Slope 126
RED	317	507	102	300	380	335	476	316	136	2869		
Par	4	5	3	4	4	4	5	4	3	36	RED	Rating 72.4
Handicap	1	3	17	11	5	9	7	13	15			Slope 127
Hole	10	11	12	13	14	15	16	17	18	In		Totals
BLUE	422	370	393	239	350	431	427	504	193	3329	BLUE	6726
WHITE	403	337	378	214	323	413	410	493	183	3154	WHITE	6433
Par	4	4	4	3	4	4	4	5	3	35	Par	71
Handicap	8	12	4	18	10	6	2	14	16			
RED	329	319	352	198	308	384	281	383	132	2686	RED	5555
Par	4	4	5	3	4	5	4	5	3	37	Par	73
Handicap	16	4	10	12	2	14	8	6	18			

Manager: Kurt Kombert　　**Pro:** Christopher Walsh, PGA　　**Supt:** Dave Roule
Architect: A.W. Tillinghast

DUFFERS PAR 3

Mt. Airy Rd., New Windsor, NY 12553   **(914) 567-1711**

Duffers is a regulation par 3 golf course open 7 days a week and closed Nov. 1-April 1. Tee time reservations are not necessary.

Driving Range	Lockers
•**Practice Green**	Showers
Power Carts	•**Food**
•**Pull Carts**	Clubhouse
Club Rental	•**Outings**

Fees	Weekday	Weekend
Daily/9	$5	$5
18 holes	$9	$9

Course Description: This practice facility, used as a teaching center, is connected with a driving range on Windsor Highway in Newburgh which has miniature golf and a full pro shop. Many young children and families come here as it is easily walkable. Somewhat contoured, it has small, fairly fast greens that have some break. The new golfer can get great chipping opportunities here. A round can be played very quickly.

Directions: Orange County, #6
I-87 North to Exit 17. Then go South on Rte.32. Turn right on Rte.207 past Stewart. Make a left onto the 1st road after the airfield. The course is 1 mile ahead on the right.

Hole	1	2	3	4	5	6	7	8	9	Out	BLUE	Rating
BLUE												Slope
WHITE	70	75	65	100	150	110	71	66	75	782		
Par	3	3	3	3	3	3	3	3	3	27	WHITE	Rating
Handicap												Slope
RED	70	75	65	55	80	55	71	66	75	612		
Par	3	3	3	3	3	3	3	3	3	27	RED	Rating
Handicap												Slope

Hole	10	11	12	13	14	15	16	17	18	In		Totals
BLUE											BLUE	
WHITE											WHITE	
Par											Par	
Handicap												
RED											RED	
Par											Par	
Handicap												

Manager/Pro: Jerry Impellittiere, PGA
Built: 1960s

EDDY FARM RESORT & GOLF COURSE

Eddy Farm Road, Sparrow Bush, NY 12780   **(914) 858-4333**

Eddy Farm has two 9 hole courses; one is a par 3 Executive (Blue) and the other is a regulation course (Red).   It is part of a resort but opens to the public when available. (Call ahead to check). It is open 7 days a week from April 1 through Nov. 30.

Driving Range	Lockers
•**Practice Green**	Showers
•**Power Carts**	•**Food**
•**Pull Carts**	Clubhouse
•**Club Rental**	•**Outings**
Soft Spikes	

Fees   Weekday & Weekend

Daily(Red)	$18	Twi.$8
Daily(Blue)	$6	Twi $4
(Twi. = after 4PM)		
Carts	$20	

Course Description: This is a picturesque course that runs along the Delaware River which can often catch a slice on the 7th and 8th holes. Carefully maintained, it has several hills and well treed fairways of varying widths. A stream crosses some holes affecting play. The Bermuda grass greens are of average size. The par three Blue course is useful for practice and family play. In the Fall, the view of the mountains and the foliage is spectacular. The Golf Card is accepted here. The scorecard below is for the Red Course.

Directions: Orange County, #7
From the GWBridge: Rte 80 West to Rte. 23 North at Wayne to Port Jervis. Take Rte.6 through Port Jervis to Rte. 97/42 West to Eddy Farm Road (on left in Sparrowbush).

Hole	1	2	3	4	5	6	7	8	9	Out	BLUE	
BLUE												
WHITE	172	275	277	160	445	130	490	316	320	2585		
Par	3	4	4	3	5	3	5	4	4	35	WHITE	
Handicap	7	6	5	8	2	9	1	4	3			
RED	172	275	277	160	445	130	490	316	320	2585		
Par	4	5	5	3	5	3	6	4	5	40	RED	
Handicap	7	6	5	8	2	9	1	4	3			

Hole	10	11	12	13	14	15	16	17	18	In		Totals
BLUE											BLUE	
WHITE											WHITE	5170
Par											Par	70
Handicap												
RED											RED	5170
Par											Par	80
Handicap												

Manager: Thomas Patterson   **Pro:** Herb De Young   **Supt:** John Patterson
Built: 1928

GREEN RIDGE GOLF CLUB

Gregory Road, Johnson, NY 10933 **(914) 355-1317**

Green Ridge is a 9 hole course open 7 days a week all year, weather permitting. Tee time reservations are not necessary.

Driving Range	Lockers
Practice Green	Showers
•**Power Carts**	•**Food**
•**Pull Carts**	Clubhouse
•**Club Rental**	•**Outings**
Soft Spikes	

Fees	Weekday	Weekend
Daily	$12	$16
Twi	$9(5PM)	$13(2PM)
Power carts	$22	

Course Description: Originally called Johnson CC, Green Ridge GC is a friendly 9 hole course where the wait to play is usually short or not at all. The old farmhouse, built in 1888, adds charm and contains a collection of antique golf memorabilia. There are three ponds on the course and a stream runs alongside. The bent grass greens are moderate in size and have little break. It is a relatively flat course with several elevated tees. There are plans to expand to 18 holes.

Directions: Orange County, #8
NYThruway to Exit #16 (Harriman)to Rte.17 to Rte.84 West to Exit #3. Turn West on Rte. 6, proceed to Rte. 284 & go South for 3 miles; then turn right. Follow signs for city of Johnson & golf course.

Hole	1	2	3	4	5	6	7	8	9	Out	BLUE	Rating
BLUE												Slope
WHITE	515	320	185	450	285	265	300	165	265	2750		
Par	5	4	3	5	4	4	4	3	4	36	WHITE	Rating
Handicap	1	7	8	3	6	4	2	9	5			Slope
RED	495	280	165	410	240	200	250	120	225	2385		
Par	5	4	3	5	4	4	4	3	4	36	RED	Rating
Handicap	1	7	8	3	6	4	2	9	5			Slope

Hole	10	11	12	13	14	15	16	17	18	In		Totals
BLUE											BLUE	
WHITE											WHITE	5500
Par											Par	72
Handicap												
RED											RED	4770
Par											Par	72
Handicap												

Manager: Jeannine **Pro/Supt.:** Lance Enholm
Architect: Harvey Izeo, 1965

HICKORY HILL GOLF COURSE

156 Route 17A, Warwick, NY 10990   **(914) 986-7100**

Hickory Hill is an Orange County 18 hole course operating 7 days a week and stays open in winter according to weather conditions. Memberships are available. Tee time reservations may be made 1 week in advance in person or Wed. by phone.

•Driving Range	•Lockers
•Practice Green	•Showers
•Power Carts	•Food
•Pull Carts	•Clubhouse
•Club Rental	•Outings
•Soft Spikes	

Fees	Weekday	Weekend
Daily(member)	$11	$13
Cty. res.non mem.	$13	$15
Non-cty mbr.	$22	$26
Non-cty res.non mbr	$26	$30

Course Description: A sister course to Stony Ford, Hickory Hill is relatively new and already in excellent condition as it begins to mature. The hilly terrain abounds with uneven lies, and along with the wind, makes the course interesting. The elevated greens are of average size and can be quite fast as the season progresses. Hal Purdy put an apple tree on #13 (Purdy has a big tree on every one of his courses) and it gets bigger every year making it very difficult to get by. Hickory Hill gets very busy on weekends in season.

Directions: Orange County, #9
Tappan Zee Br. to I-87 North to Exit #15A. Turn left at light onto Rte. 17N. Pass thru Sloatsburg & Tuxedo, turn left at STOP onto Rte. 17A (sign reads Greenwood Lake/Sterling Forest). Go 12.5 miles to club on left.

Hole	1	2	3	4	5	6	7	8	9	Out	BLUE	Rating 72.8
BLUE	432	320	218	340	529	143	386	297	537	3202		Slope 123
WHITE	416	308	193	304	515	133	370	290	504	3033		
Par	4	4	3	4	5	3	4	4	5	36	WHITE	Rating 70.9
Handicap	7	13	5	11	3	17	9	15	1			Slope 119
RED	386	290	174	258	473	98	354	277	471	2781		
Par	4	4	3	4	5	3	4	4	5	36	RED	Rating 74.2
Handicap	7	13	5	11	3	17	9	15	1			Slope 125

Hole	10	11	12	13	14	15	16	17	18	In		Totals
BLUE	328	560	250	386	460	206	595	409	401	3595	BLUE	6257
WHITE	305	530	196	372	452	187	551	369	379	3341	WHITE	6031
Par	4	5	3	4	4	3	5	4	4	36	Par	72
Handicap	18	14	12	4	2	6	10	16	8			
RED	289	491	173	360	397	171	531	351	354	3117	RED	5524
Par	4	5	3	4	4	3	5	4	4	36	Par	73
Handicap	18	14	12	4	2	6	10	16	8			

Manager: David Killin   **Pro:** Rudy Napora, PGA   **Supt:** John Fagan
Architect: Hal Purdy 1992

LAKE ANNE COUNTRY CLUB

Clove Road, Monroe, NY 10950   **(914) 783-6575**

Lake Anne is a 9 hole course open to the public 7 days a week and closed in winter. Tee time reservations are not necessary; players come on a first come first serve basis.

•**Driving Range**	Lockers
•**Practice Green**	Showers
•**Power Carts**	•**Food**
•**Pull Carts**	•**Clubhouse**
•**Club Rental**	•**Outings**
Soft Spikes	

Fees	Weekday	Weekend
Daily	$12	$12

Course Description: Lake Anne is in the process of being refurbished. The course was closed for 10 years and is in need of modernization. The plan is for homes to be built around the course. Special attention is being made to improve the greens. There are 20 sand traps and four holes affected by water adding to the challenge. A par 39 course with a par 6 hole of 630 yards, one of the longest in the NY area, makes Lake Anne quite unusual. While Alfred Tull was working on the Nevele he designed Lake Anne as well.

Directions: Orange County, #10
Take I-87 to Exit#16 (Harriman). Pay toll & go to and turn left on Rte. 32 for 1.2 mi. Make sharp right onto Rte.17M West to Rte. 208North to Rte.27(Clove Rd.). Bear right; club is on the right.

Hole	1	2	3	4	5	6	7	8	9	Out	BLUE	
BLUE												
WHITE	480	385	365	495	270	160	425	630	290	3500		
Par	5	4	4	5	4	3	4	6	4	37	WHITE	
Handicap	9	5	7	11	17	13	1	3	15			
RED	460	365	345	475	250	140	405	490	270	3200		
Par	5	4	4	5	4	3	4	6	4	37	RED	
Handicap	9	5	7	11	17	13	1	3	15			

Hole	10	11	12	13	14	15	16	17	18	In		Totals
BLUE											BLUE	
WHITE											WHITE	7000
Par											Par	74
Handicap												
RED											RED	6400
Par											Par	74
Handicap												

Manager: Marvin Greene   **Architect:** Alfred Tull 1970s

MANHATTAN WOODS

1 Ahlmayer Dr., W. Nyack, NY 10994   (914) 627-2222

Manhattan Woods is an 18 hole private club opening in July 1998. It is open 6 days a week all year. Guests play accompanied by a member. A new clubhouse will be ready in September 1998. Course ratings, slope and handicaps will be done later as well.

•Driving Range	•Lockers
•Practice Green	•Showers
•Power Carts	•Food
Pull Carts	•Clubhouse
•Club Rental	•Outings
•Caddies	•Soft Spikes

Course Description: In late 1997, this new course was nearly completed. The grass is growing in for the Summer 1998 opening. The Gary Player influence can be seen in the utilization of the natural terrain and in the design function of the holes. The course is wooded and hilly. The average size greens have subtle breaks with mounding and contouring to add interest. Wetlands are crossed numerous times; in some cases substantial carries are necessary. The rough has blue rye fescue in the primary and fescue in the second cut. Multiple tee boxes for all levels of players are provided. The facility will include a David Leadbetter Golf Academy.

Directions: Rockland County, #11

Take the Palisades ParkwayN to Exit 7. Cross under parkway and enter southbound entrance ramp. Stay straight on that road (do not bear left onto pkwy.) to course entrance.

Hole	1	2	3	4	5	6	7	8	9	Out	BLUE	Rating
BLUE	426	400	504	198	423	347	187	535	464	3484		Slope
WHITE	403	391	498	182	414	343	180	502	444	3357		
Par	4	4	5	3	4	4	3	5	4	36	WHITE	Rating
Handicap												Slope
RED	374	312	445	134	348	282	148	439	387	2869		
Par	4	4	5	3	4	4	3	5	4	36	RED	Rating
Handicap												Slope
Hole	10	11	12	13	14	15	16	17	18	In		Totals
BLUE	458	415	154	550	460	491	453	198	386	3563	BLUE	7047
WHITE	425	381	141	540	431	479	434	187	379	3397	WHITE	6754
Par	4	4	3	5	4	5	4	3	4	36	Par	72
Handicap												
RED	370	304	105	479	391	428	365	125	280	2847	RED	5716
Par	4	4	3	5	4	5	4	3	4	36	Par	72
Handicap												

Supt: Barry Anes
Gary Player Signature Golf Design /Project **Architect:** Stephen Kay 1998

MANSION RIDGE COUNTRY CLUB

1292 Orange Turnpike, Monroe, NY 10950   **(914) 774-3377**

Mansion Ridge is a new 18 hole semi-private club opening in 1998. It is a Nicklaus design with a limited membership for residents and open to the public. It will be open 7 days a week all year, weather permitting.

•**Driving Range**	•**Lockers**
•**Practice Green**	•**Showers**
•**Power Carts**	•**Food**
•**Pull Carts**	•**Clubhouse**
•**Club Rental**	•**Outings**
Soft Spikes	

Fees	Weekday	Weekend
Daily	$75	$85

Course Description: There are 5 sets of tees on each hole of this brand new par 72 course. Five holes are in the wetlands and woods. On a clear day one can see spectacular views of the Catskill Mountains and up to 100 miles to the North. A large mansion in the center of the complex will be used as a conference hall; the clubhouse is a renovated existing stone barn. Plans are in motion for new homes to be built around the course. The scorecard below shows appproximate figures.

Directions: Orange County, #12
I-87North to Exit #16 (Harriman). Pay toll & just after toll booths, exit for Rte.17 (right lane). At end of ramp, go straight thru light for 2 mi. to "T". Go left at this intersection & stay on this rd. Pass 1 light: now called Orange Tpke. for 1 & 1/2 mi. to "Fairway Estates" on left. Go uphill past intersection of Mambasha Rd. to stone gateway on left to club.

Hole	1	2	3	4	5	6	7	8	9	Out	BLACK	Rating
BLACK	356	150	408	356	184	406	508	357	553	3276		Slope
WHITE	289	112	345	288	132	315	471	288	506	2746		
Par	4	3	4	4	3	4	5	4	5	36	WHITE	Rating
Handicap												Slope
RED	262	299	326	238	113	231	440	249	463	2421		
Par	4	3	4	4	3	4	5	4	5	36	RED	Rating
Handicap												Slope

Hole	10	11	12	13	14	15	16	17	18	In		Totals
BLACK	350	527	161	427	422	523	389	225	467	3489	BLACK	6764
WHITE	304	476	101	357	334	485	331	159	413	2960	WHITE	5706
Par	4	5	3	4	4	5	4	3	4	36	Par	72
Handicap												
RED	237	415	78	256	320	424	204	137	374	2445	RED	5524
Par	4	5	3	4	4	5	4	3	4	36	Par	72
Handicap												

Manager: American Golf   **Supt:** Ed Walsh
Architect: Nicklaus Design Group 1997

MILLCREEK GOLF COURSE

Route 9W North Newburgh, NY 12550 **(914) 236-3160**

Millcreek is a 9 hole course open to the public 7 days a week and closed in winter. Tee time reservations are necessary on weekends. There is a special annual greens fee card. It is 6 miles north of the Newburgh-Beacon bridge.

•Driving Range	•Lockers
•Practice Green	•Showers
•Power Carts	•Food
•Pull Carts	•Clubhouse
•Club Rental	•Outings

Fees	Weekday	Weekend
Daily/18	$16	$20
9 holes	$11	$14
Power carts	$22	
9 holes "	$12	

Course Description: Millcreek is a regulation par 36 course. The property is mostly flat with some fairways uphill to the greens. A creek runs through 7 of the holes and affects the golfer's strategy or whether to lay up or try to hit a good shot to carry the water. The course was opened in 1996 and is still maturing. There is irrigation on the tees, greens and fairways. The 4th hole is the longest, a dogleg left par 5. It has a target landing area that penalizes an errant shot.

Directions: Orange County, #13
Take I-87 to Exit 17. Take Rte.84 east to Exit 10. Then take Rte.9W 5 miles north to course on right.

Hole	1	2	3	4	5	6	7	8	9	Out	BLUE	Rating
BLUE	341	320	360	480	100	465	317	290	218	2891		Slope
WHITE	328	317	348	462	90	460	310	280	208	2803		
Par	4	4	4	5	3	5	4	4	3	36	WHITE	Rating
Handicap	7	15	1	5	17	9	13	11	3			Slope 117
RED	296	315	310	421	85	430	305	274	155	2585		
Par	4	4	4	5	3	5	4	4	3	36	RED	Rating
Handicap	7	15	1	5	17	9	13	11	3			Slope 120
Hole	10	11	12	13	14	15	16	17	18	In		Totals
BLUE											BLUE	5782
WHITE											WHITE	5606
Par											Par	72
Handicap												
RED											RED	5170
Par											Par	72
Handicap												

Manager: Gene Weed   **Supt:** Glenn Joergle
Architect: Steve Esposito 1996

MINISCEONGO GOLF CLUB

110 Pomona Road, Pomona, NY 10970   (914) 362-8348

Minisceongo Golf Club is a private club open 6 days a week and closed for Jan. & Feb. Guests may play accompanied by a member. Advance tee times are recommended on weekends.

•Driving Range	•Lockers
•Practice Green	•Showers
•Power Carts	•Food
Pull Carts	•Clubhouse
•Club Rental	•Outings
•Caddies	•Soft Spikes

Course Description: The large rolling fairways surrounded by fescue grass make this golf course special indeed. Hilly and challenging, water comes into play from the Minisceongo creek and marshland is everywhere. Golfers must play target golf on the manicured turf, truly a shotmaker's course. There are old stone towers, a cemetary dating back to the 1700's, and arrowheads displayed, reminding us that this course has history dating back to 7,000 BC. The course was developed with great environmental sensitivity to the expanses of wetland. There are breathtaking views from many of the multi-tiered elevated tees along the naturally contoured layout.

Directions: Rockland County, #14
Pal. Pkwy. North to Exit 12. Make a left off exit ramp to 1st traffic light. Go left onto Rte.45 South. At 2nd light on Rte.45 make a right onto Pomona Rd. Go 1/2 mile to club on right.

Hole	1	2	3	4	5	6	7	8	9	Out	BLUE	Rating 72.3
BLUE	341	166	422	531	375	545	344	186	374	3284		Slope 135
WHITE	331	147	416	522	369	529	335	174	367	3190		
Par	4	3	4	5	4	5	4	3	4	36	WHITE	Rating 70.2
Handicap	14	16	4	2	8	6	12	18	10			Slope 125
RED	248	100	343	430	278	438	213	115	288	2453		
Par	4	3	4	5	4	5	4	3	4	36	RED	Rating 72.6
Handicap	14	16	4	2	8	6	12	18	10			Slope 121
Hole	10	11	12	13	14	15	16	17	18	In		Totals
BLUE	405	193	344	402	163	545	414	455	504	3425	BLUE	6709
WHITE	393	182	332	389	145	452	394	437	496	3220	WHITE	6410
Par	4	3	4	4	3	5	4	4	5	36	Par	72
Handicap	7	15	13	3	17	1	11	5	9			
RED	297	101	228	305	102	373	279	320	424	2429	RED	5475
Par	4	3	4	4	3	5	4	4	5	36	Par	72
Handicap	7	15	13	3	17	1	11	5	9			

Manager: John Napier   **Pro:** Mark Beran, PGA   **Supt:** Bobby DiPalma
Architect: Roy Case, 1994

MONROE COUNTRY CLUB

Still Road, Monroe, NY 10950　　　　　(914) 783-9045

Monroe is a semi-private 9 hole course with memberships available. On weekends, the public may play only after 2 PM. It is open 7 days a week all year, weather permitting. Tee time reservations are not necessary.

Driving Range	•Lockers
•Practice Green	•Showers
•Power Carts	•Food
•Pull Carts	•Clubhouse
•Club Rental	•Outings
•Soft Spikes	

Fees	Weekday	Weekend
Daily (9)	$14	
Daily (18)	$20	$25
Sr.	$17	$23
Power carts	$15 (9)	$30 (18)

Course Description: A well maintained course, Monroe has undulating tough greens which are very fast with lots of break. There are no "gimme" putts. The fairways are open and gently sloped. A stream runs through the middle of the course and affects play on 4 out of nine holes. The 8th, a 298 yard par 4, has a very difficult approach shot to an extremely right-to-left sloped green.

Directions: Orange County, #15
Take I-87 to Exit #16 (Harriman). Pay toll and go to and turn left on Rte.#32 for 1.2 miles. Make a sharp right onto Rte.17M; proceed 2.2 miles to Still Rd. Turn left to club.

Hole	1	2	3	4	5	6	7	8	9	Out	BLUE	Rating
BLUE												Slope
WHITE	268	185	475	189	463	175	435	298	311	2799		
Par	4	3	5	3	5	3	4	4	4	35	WHITE	Rating 65.5
Handicap	11	7	5	17	3	15	1	9	13			Slope 114
RED												
Par	4	3	5	3	5	3	5	4	4	36	RED	Rating 70.3
Handicap												Slope 121
Hole	10	11	12	13	14	15	16	17	18	In		Totals
BLUE											BLUE	
WHITE	238	185	475	135	400	125	462	298	311	2629	WHITE	5428
Par	4	3	5	3	4	3	5	4	4	35	Par	70
Handicap	12	8	6	18	2	16	4	10	14			
RED											RED	
Par	4	3	5	3	5	3	5	4	4	36	Par	72
Handicap												

Manager: Bernie Modder　**Pro:** Julie De Maio　**Supt:** Carol Oakley
Built: 1924

NEW YORK COUNTRY CLUB

103 Brick Church Rd., NewHempstead, NY10977   **(914) 362-2196**

New York Country Club is a private 18 hole golf course open 6 days a week, all year, weather permitting. Guests may play accompanied by a member. There will be a health club on the premises. The course will be open to the public in 1998 as an introduction.

•**Driving Range**	•**Lockers**
•**Practice Green**	•**Showers**
•**Power Carts**	•**Food**
Pull Carts	•**Clubhouse**
•**Club Rental**	•**Outings**
•**Caddies**	•**Soft Spikes**

Course Description: New York Country Club, one of the newest golf clubs in Rockland County, is characterized by dog-legs, water holes and large bent grass greens, tees and fairways. Challenging, with many severely sloped fairways and spectacular views, one would never get tired of playing here. Hardly any water is in play, but the bunker placement and course slope will keep the low handicap golfer alert. This course is a welcome addition to the Rockland County golfing community.

Directions: Rockland County, #16

Take the Pal. Pkwy. North to Exit 11. Go left on New Hempstead Rd.; at 3rd traffic light go left onto Hempstead Rd. Make first right onto Brick Church Rd. Entrance is after crest of hill on left (across from school playground).

Hole	1	2	3	4	5	6	7	8	9	Out	BLUE	Rating
BLUE	534	387	131	427	401	400	540	202	350	3372		Slope
WHITE	509	372	124	400	385	377	520	187	327	3201		
Par	5	4	3	4	4	4	5	3	4	36	WHITE	Rating
Handicap	15	5	17	1	9	11	3	13	7			Slope
RED	437	311	92	325	275	302	457	140	259	2598		
Par	5	4	3	4	4	4	5	3	4	36	RED	Rating
Handicap	15	5	17	1	9	11	3	13	7			Slope

Hole	10	11	12	13	14	15	16	17	18	In		Totals
BLUE	310	324	144	540	384	440	382	161	498	3183	BLUE	6555
WHITE	300	312	134	507	367	411	372	151	450	3004	WHITE	6205
Par	4	4	3	5	4	4	4	3	5	36	Par	72
Handicap	18	12	16	2	10	4	6	14	8			
RED	275	272	97	425	339	316	290	127	403	2544	RED	5142
Par	4	4	3	5	4	4	4	3	5	36	Par	72
Handicap	18	12	16	2	10	4	6	14	8			

Pro: Bill Osetek, PGA   **Supt:** John Kavanaugh
Architect: Stephen Kay 1996

ORANGE COUNTY GOLF CLUB

Golf Links Road, Middletown, NY 10940   **(914) 343-1284**

Orange County is an 18 hole course open 7 days a week and closed Dec. 1 to April 1. Guests may play accompanied by a member. Tee time reservations are required for weekends.

•**Driving Range**	•**Lockers**
•**Practice Green**	•**Showers**
•**Power Carts**	•**Food**
•**Pull Carts**	•**Clubhouse**
Club Rental	•**Outings**
Caddies	•**Soft Spikes**

Course Description: The beautifully maintained Orange County Golf Club is a wide open, relatively flat tree lined course with a back nine more hilly than the front. The greens are moderate in size, not overly fast and several have severe breaks. Golfers must cross a bridge over the Wallkill River (which flows South to North throughout the course) twice during play. Holes 8 through 11 are the toughest stretch of the course; #s 9 & 10, long par 4s are considered the most challenging.

Directions: Orange County, #17
NYThruway to Exit#16 Harriman. Go north on Rte.17 to Exit#122 (Middletown Rd.) At STOP sign turn right crossing over Rte.17. Go 0.6 miles to Golf Links Rd. & turn left to Orange County Golf Club on right.

Hole	1	2	3	4	5	6	7	8	9	Out	BLUE	Rating 72.6
BLUE	337	401	384	537	354	222	578	367	436	3616		Slope 129
WHITE	337	376	370	521	343	203	578	322	382	3432		
Par	4	4	4	5	4	3	5	4	4	37	WHITE	Rating 71.4
Handicap	11	5	9	13	15	7	3	17	1			Slope 127
RED	328	362	345	445	291	178	516	291	371	3127		
Par	4	4	4	5	4	3	5	4	4	37	RED	Rating 74.6
Handicap	13	6	9	7	15	17	1	11	3			Slope 130
Hole	10	11	12	13	14	15	16	17	18	In		Totals
BLUE	450	389	173	325	486	537	145	346	197	3048	BLUE	6664
WHITE	450	383	161	314	486	525	130	338	182	2969	WHITE	6401
Par	4	4	3	4	5	5	3	4	3	35	Par	72
Handicap	2	4	10	8	14	6	18	12	16			
RED	447	364	130	305	481	494	117	282	180	2800	RED	5927
Par	5	4	3	4	5	5	3	4	3	36	Par	73
Handicap	5	8	14	10	2	4	18	12	16			

Manager: Paul Hayes   **Pro:** Geoff Walsh, PGA   **Supt.:** Darren Batisky
Architect: Robert White 1925   **Estab:** 1899 (Member organized)

OSIRIS COUNTRY CLUB

PRIVATE

Lake Osiris Rd., Walden, NY 12586   **(914) 778-5795**

Osiris is an 18 hole private course, open 7 days a week and closed Nov.1-Apr.1. Guests play accompanied by a member. Tee time reservations are not necessary.

•Driving Range	•Lockers
•Practice Green	•Showers
•Power Carts	•Food
• Pull Carts	•Clubhouse
•Club Rental	•Outings
Caddies	•Soft Spikes

Course Description: The front nine at Osiris is shorter and flatter than the longer and more hilly back. The former offers more level putting on smaller surfaces. The second nine has larger well bunkered greens, all of medium speed. The course is relatively tight with some doglegs and some 2 tiered greens. The signature hole is the par 4 #15, a dogleg left with a lake in front of the green. Steve Esposito did some redesign work here recently. Osiris is a golfing club in excellent condition.

Directions: Orange County, #18
Take I-87North (NY Thruway) to Exit 17. Take I-84 West to Exit 5. Go north on Rte.208 toward Walden. Continue on 208 (a right turn in Walden) now Ulster Ave. Continue about 1mile. At fork, bear right onto Osiris Rd. 1 mile to club on left.

Hole	1	2	3	4	5	6	7	8	9	Out	BLUE	Rating 70.1
BLUE	520	376	326	199	306	460	310	118	378	2993		Slope 128
WHITE	490	376	312	189	292	460	301	114	368	2902		
Par	5	4	4	3	4	5	4	3	4	36	WHITE	Rating 68.7
Handicap	2	8	12	4	14	10	16	18	6			Slope 125
RED	450	370	286	143	220	421	245	110	368	2613		
Par	5	4	4	3	4	5	4	3	4	36	RED	Rating 71.8
Handicap	4	2	10	12	14	8	16	18	6			Slope 121
Hole	10	11	12	13	14	15	16	17	18	In		Totals
BLUE	368	170	540	442	383	363	546	165	345	3324	BLUE	6317
WHITE	345	157	513	415	358	349	505	153	322	3117	WHITE	6019
Par	4	3	5	4	4	4	5	3	4	36	Par	72
Handicap	7	15	3	1	9	5	13	17	11			
RED	322	137	486	388	341	274	464	139	299	2850	RED	5463
Par	4	3	5	4	4	4	5	3	4	36	Par	72
Handicap	7	15	1	3	5	11	9	17	13			

Manager: Bill Hughes   **Pro:** Jim Dwyer, PGA   **Supt:** Jim Smart
Estab: 1927   Frank Duane 1960s 2nd nine

OTTERKILL GOLF & CC

Otter Rd., Campbell Hall, NY 10916   **(914) 437-2301**

Otterkill is an 18 hole private course open 7 days a week and closed Nov. 15 to Apr.1. Guests play accompanied by a member. Tee time reservations are necessary for weekends.

•Driving Range	•Lockers
•Practice Green	•Showers
•Power Carts	•Food
•Pull Carts	•Clubhouse
•Club Rental	•Outings
Caddies	•Soft Spikes

Course Description: Otterkill terrain is gently rolling farmland, a great walking course. Harder than rated, it plays long and is very challenging. Where water affects play, it is a significant obstacle to negotiate. Although the greens are average size and medium fast, they are deceiving. Golfers tend to overread them; they have less break than it appears. A number of MGA events are held here.

Directions: Orange County, #19
Take I-87N (NYThruway) to Exit 17. Go west on Rte.84 to Exit 5. Take Rte.208 South and just after Maybrook turn right onto Otter Rd to club on left.

Hole	1	2	3	4	5	6	7	8	9	Out	BLUE	Rating 72.9
BLUE	553	424	192	382	424	336	562	380	192	3445		Slope 129
WHITE	537	403	178	352	412	323	552	373	189	3319		
Par	5	4	3	4	4	4	5	4	3	36	WHITE	Rating 71.8
Handicap	3	5	15	9	7	11	1	13	17			Slope 126
RED	440	370	138	323	356	283	456	341	156	2863		
Par	5	4	3	4	4	4	5	4	3	36	RED	Rating 72.2
Handicap	5	3	17	7	9	11	1	13	15			Slope 124

Hole	10	11	12	13	14	15	16	17	18	In		Totals
BLUE	428	380	483	177	528	414	310	181	415	3316	BLUE	6761
WHITE	380	372	475	170	521	403	304	168	398	3319	WHITE	6510
Par	4	4	5	3	5	4	4	3	4	36	Par	72
Handicap	4	12	10	16	8	2	14	18	16			
RED	328	350	417	141	442	353	233	97	327	2688	RED	5551
Par	4	4	5	3	5	4	4	3	4	36	Par	72
Handicap	6	12	2	16	8	4	14	18	10			

Manager: Bob Wasserman   **Pro:** Bill Glancey, PGA   **Supt:** Thomas Lambert
Architect: William Mitchell 1957

PHILIP J. ROTELLA GOLF COURSE

Thiells-Mt. Ivy Rd., Haverstraw, NY 10927 **(914) 354-1616**

Philip J. Rotella is an 18 hole municipal course with special rates for residents. It is open 7 days a week from 3/15 to 12/15 or longer, weather permitting. Residents have pre-booked times, non-res.- Wed. for weekends. Walk-ons during the week.

•**Driving Range**	Lockers
•**Practice Green**	Showers
•**Power Carts**	•**Food**
•**Pull Carts**	•**Clubhouse**
•**Club Rental**	•**Outings**

Fees	Weekday	Weekend
Daily(Res)	$9	$14
Non-res	$22	$29
Sr/Jr	Discounts	available
Power carts	$20	$20

Course Description: Hilly and difficult to walk, Rotella is kept in good condition with a fairly good drainage system. The front nine is tough with little water in play. The back has water on 4 holes, and both have narrow fairways and elevated tees. The greens are fast, relatively large and somewhat flat with little break. The 604 yard par 5 eleventh features a dogleg and a two tiered green. This Hal Purdy municipal course is challenging for golfers of every level.

Directions: Rockland #20
Take the Palisades Pkwy. North to Exit #13 (Thiells Mt. Ivy Rd.) Go left off ramp and proceed 1 mile to course on left.

Hole	1	2	3	4	5	6	7	8	9	Out	BLUE	Rating 71.4
BLUE	335	393	215	198	526	200	468	336	174	3207		Slope 126
WHITE	295	371	198	526	200	468	336	174	438	3006		
Par	4	4	3	5	3	5	4	3	5	36	WHITE	Rating 69.4
Handicap	17	3	11	5	13	1	9	15	7			Slope 122
RED	271	271	108	454	160	329	291	138	324	2346		
Par	4	4	3	5	3	5	4	3	5	36	RED	Rating 71.7
Handicap	17	3	7	5	13	1	9	15	11			Slope 123

Hole	10	11	12	13	14	15	16	17	18	In		Totals
BLUE	337	604	190	523	362	211	545	149	374	3295	BLUE	6502
WHITE	309	562	163	506	343	196	507	133	343	3062	WHITE	6068
Par	4	5	3	5	4	3	5	3	4	36	Par	72
Handicap	14	2	16	8	10	12	4	18	6			
RED	294	482	143	417	253	150	346	110	315	2510	RED	4856
Par	4	5	3	5	4	3	5	3	4	36	Par	72
Handicap	14	2	16	12	10	8	4	18	6			

Pro: Dave Fusco, PGA   **Supt:** Cal Fowx
Architect: Hal Purdy 1984

PORT JERVIS COUNTRY CLUB

Box 103, Neversink Drive, PortJervis,NY12771   **(914) 856-5391**

Port Jervis is an 18 hole private course open 7 days a week between April 1 and November 1. Guests may play accompanied by a member. Tee time reservations are generally not necessary.

Driving Range	•Lockers
•Practice Green	•Showers
•Power Carts	•Food
•Pull Carts	•Clubhouse
Club Rental	•Outings
Caddies	•Soft Spikes

Course Description: Port Jervis is a relatively flat course with several tricky holes on the front nine. The greens are small with subtle breaks. Water is in play on several holes. The 580 yard signature 18th, is a long par 5 and considered very difficult. The picturesque views of the mountains as a backdrop on the 7th and the cornfields in the distance on the 3rd add to an enjoyable round of golf. An Assistant Pro PGA event was held here in Sept. 1997.

Directions: Orange County, #21
Take the NYThruwy. to Exit #16 (Harriman). Then take Rte.17 North to Rte.17M going West and North to Rte.6 West to Neversink Rd. to club.

Hole	1	2	3	4	5	6	7	8	9	Out	BLUE	Rating
BLUE												Slope
WHITE	439	378	372	315	379	145	337	355	174	2894		
Par	4	4	4	4	4	3	4	4	3	34	WHITE	Rating 69.8
Handicap	1	5	7	11	3	17	13	9	15			Slope 121
RED	407	274	307	247	315	118	284	283	128	2363		
Par	5	4	4	4	4	3	4	4	3	35	RED	Rating 67.3
Handicap	3	9	5	13	1	15	11	7	17			Slope 110

Hole	10	11	12	13	14	15	16	17	18	In		Totals
BLUE											BLUE	
WHITE	395	383	163	362	123	325	505	375	573	3204	WHITE	6098
Par	4	4	3	4	3	4	5	4	5	36	Par	70
Handicap	4	10	14	6	18	16	8	12	2			
RED	313	280	125	315	101	288	387	331	485	2625	RED	4988
Par	4	4	3	4	3	4	4	4	5	35	Par	70
Handicap	10	14	16	8	18	12	4	6	2			

Manager: Dave Eberhard   **Pro:** Todd Batchelder, PGA   **Supt:** James Masuck
Architects: A. W. Tillinghast, Harry Spears, Fred Conrad 1918

POWELTON CLUB

PRIVATE

26 Balmville Rd., Newburgh, NY 12553   **(914) 561-7409**

Powelton is an 18 hole private course open 7 days a week and closed Nov. 30-Apr. 1.
Guests play accompanied by a member. Tee time reservations are only necessary for
weekend mornings.

Driving Range	•**Lockers**
•**Practice Green**	•**Showers**
•**Power Carts**	•**Food**
Pull Carts	•**Clubhouse**
Club Rental	•**Outings**
Caddies	•**Soft Spikes**

Course Description: Powelton is the oldest golf course in Newburgh and celebrated
its centennial in 1992. It is narrow, with small greens that are fast in summer and
tough to read. The sand traps have been redone recently. Water comes into play in a
significant way on 3 holes. The signature par three 7th requires an accurate shot to the
putting surface because trouble lurks in the form of trees to the left and right of the
very small green as well as a pond on the left.

Directions: Orange County, #22
Take the Thruway (I-87)to Exit 17. Take Rte.84 East to Exit 10. Go north on 9W. Turn
right on North St. and left on Balmville to club.

Hole	1	2	3	4	5	6	7	8	9	Out	BLUE	Rating
BLUE												Slope
WHITE	370	258	193	454	397	350	180	335	419	2956		
Par	4	4	3	5	4	4	3	4	4	35	WHITE	Rating 69.3
Handicap	4	18	14	16	10	6	8	12	2			Slope 127
RED	370	214	143	454	319	304	149	335	419	2707		
Par	4	4	3	5	4	4	3	4	5	36	RED	Rating 72.2
Handicap	3	15	17	1	13	11	9	5	7			Slope 120
Hole	10	11	12	13	14	15	16	17	18	In		Totals
BLUE											BLUE	
WHITE	366	490	416	423	165	375	140	406	300	3081	WHITE	6037
Par	4	5	4	4	3	4	3	4	4	35	Par	70
Handicap	76	11	1	3	15	9	17	5	13			
RED	366	430	381	356	165	352	117	352	272	2791	RED	5498
Par	4	5	5	4	3	4	3	4	4	36	Par	72
Handicap	2	8	10	12	16	4	18	6	14			

Manager: Rex James   **Pro:** Bob Minicozzi, PGA   **Supt:** Bob De Marco
Architects: Devereux Emmet, Geoffrey Cornish (Redesign) **Estab:** 1882

ROCKLAND COUNTRY CLUB

Route 9W, Sparkill, NY   **(914) 359-9702**

Rockland Country Club is an 18 hole private golf course that is 15 miles north of the GWBridge. It is open 6 days a week from March through December. Guests may play accompanied by a member. Tee times are not required.

- •**Driving Range**
- •**Practice Green**
- •**Power Carts**
- Pull Carts
- •**Club Rental**
- •**Caddies**
- •**Lockers**
- •**Showers**
- •**Food**
- •**Clubhouse**
- •**Outings**
- •**Soft Spikes**

Course Description: Robert White took this 9 hole golf course and in 1928 redesigned it as 18 holes using the additional property purchased for that purpose. Rockland CC has small multi-tiered greens, many blind shots and some elevated tees. The par 4 12th is long and difficult dropping into a valley then ascending to a two tiered green. The course is well maintained and plays long because of the uphills. It is in the process of renovation, with John Harvey from the Robert Trent Jones group upgrading by improving the bunkers and installing 2 new greens. Also being added are new tee boxes, a large pond and a few creeks that will affect play. Stephen Kay created the master plan for the current renovation.

Directions: Rockland County #23
Pal. Pkwy. North to Exit #4 (Rte.9W). Go north on 9W approx. 3 miles (shortly after crossing the NJ, NY border) to club on left.

Hole	1	2	3	4	5	6	7	8	9	Out	BLUE	Rating 71.7
BLUE	386	216	348	358	443	416	411	166	351	3095		Slope 128
WHITE	375	200	342	349	434	410	403	160	345	3018		
Par	4	3	4	4	4	4	4	3	4	34	WHITE	Rating 70.9
Handicap	9	13	15	5	1	3	7	17	11			Slope 125
RED	368	179	248	301	424	400	392	150	294	2756		
Par	4	3	4	4	5	5	4	3	4	36	RED	Rating 73.5
Handicap	7	13	15	11	5	3	1	17	9			Slope 126

Hole	10	11	12	13	14	15	16	17	18	In		Totals
BLUE	178	507	427	517	416	152	395	336	515	3443	BLUE	6538
WHITE	172	500	417	500	405	140	384	329	503	3350	WHITE	6368
Par	3	5	4	5	4	3	4	4	5	37	Par	71
Handicap	16	8	2	12	4	18	10	6	14			
RED	159	455	356	428	346	128	370	256	409	2907	RED	5663
Par	3	5	4	5	4	3	4	4	5	37	Par	73
Handicap	16	4	2	8	14	18	6	10	12			

Manager: Al Cavalluzzo   **Pro:** Keith Larsen, PGA   **Supt:** Matt Ceplo
Architects: Harry Stark 1906, Alfred Tull 1963

ROCKLAND LAKE STATE PARK

Route 9W, Congers, NY 10920   (914) 268-7275

Rockland Lake is an 18 hole regulation course open 7 days a week from April 1 through Dec. 21. Tee time reservations: 1 week in advance for card holders, 1 day ahead all others. Computerized tee times are available by calling (914) 267-2323.

- •Driving Range
- •Practice Green
- •Power Carts
- •Pull Carts
- •Club Rental
- •Soft Spikes
- •Lockers
- •Showers
- •Food
- •Clubhouse
- Outings

Fees	Weekday	Weekend
Daily	$20	$24
Twilight	$11	$13
Sr/Jr(res.)	$12	
Power carts	$24	$24

Course Description: Hilly and challenging, Rockland Lake offers panoramic views of the countryside. The long fast elevated greens break toward the lake with hardly a flat lie on the tree lined fairways. Walking is permitted but not recommended. The par 4 # 1 handicap 4th hole is long with a severely sloping green. Water is in play on the 16th hole and a brook runs across the 3rd. It gets quite busy in season. The State Park also offers an executive course that is accessed from another entrance.

Directions: Rockland County #24
Palisades Pkwy. North to Exit #4. At the first light go left onto Rte. 9W and go 12 miles to course on right.

Hole	1	2	3	4	5	6	7	8	9	Out	BLUE	Rating 72.2
BLUE	371	439	515	431	368	217	553	405	182	3481		Slope 121
WHITE	343	401	468	402	350	188	503	380	166	3201		
Par	4	4	5	4	4	3	5	4	3	36	WHITE	Rating 70.2
Handicap	13	5	11	1	15	9	3	7	17			Slope 116
RED	319	333	411	343	330	169	429	352	149	2835		
Par	4	4	5	4	4	3	5	4	3	36	RED	Rating 67.4
Handicap	13	5	11	1	15	9	3	7	17			Slope 108

Hole	10	11	12	13	14	15	16	17	18	In		Totals
BLUE	358	485	226	415	542	431	171	389	366	3383	BLUE	6864
WHITE	341	466	200	386	501	395	157	367	333	3146	WHITE	6347
Par	4	5	3	4	5	4	3	4	4	36	Par	72
Handicap	16	6	8	4	2	10	18	12	14			
RED	320	407	161	365	444	336	140	347	308	2828	RED	5663
Par	4	5	3	4	5	4	3	4	4	36	Par	72
Handicap	16	6	8	4	2	10	18	12	14			

Manager/Supt. Sam D'Auria   **Pro:** Jim McCann, PGA
Architect: David Gordon 1969

ROCKLAND LAKE STATE PARK

Rte. 9W, Congers, NY 10920 (South entrance)   (914) 268-7930

Rockland Lake is an executive 18 hole course (all par 3s), open to the public 7 days a week from April 1 through the first Sunday in Nov. Tee time reservations: 1 week in advance for card holders and 1 day for all others. Computerized tee times may be made by calling (914) 267-2323.

Driving Range	•Lockers
•Practice Green	•Showers
•Power Carts	•Food
•Pull Carts	•Clubhouse
•Club Rental	•Outings

Fees	Weekday	Weekend
Daily	$11	$13
Sr/Jr (NYS res) $6		
PowerCarts	$19/(18)	$13/9

Course Description: Scenic Rockland Lake Executive is excellent for learning and practicing. Great views of the lake, a brook running through the fairway on 2 holes and ponds on the 7th & 14th holes add to the interest of the course. It boasts one of the toughest par 3's on the East Coast. There is a hiking trail next to the course, which leads up a mountain and overlooks the Hudson River. In addition to golf, the area is great for bird- watching and you might spot an occasional deer, raccoon or fox. The staff is friendly and encouraging.

Directions: Rockland County, #25
Palisades Pkwy. North to Exit #4. Take Rte. 9W North for 12 miles to park on right. Follow signs to golf course.

Hole	1	2	3	4	5	6	7	8	9	Out	BLUE	Rating
BLUE												Slope
WHITE	180	150	110	185	136	133	120	149	212	1375		
Par	3	3	3	3	3	3	3	3	3	27	WHITE	Rating
Handicap												Slope
RED												
Par											RED	Rating
Handicap												Slope
Hole	10	11	12	13	14	15	16	17	18	In		Totals
BLUE											BLUE	
WHITE	140	120	160	206	133	196	182	108	160	1405	WHITE	2780
Par	3	3	3	3	3	3	3	3	3	27	Par	54
Handicap												
RED												
Par												
Handicap												

Manager: Thomas Walsh   **Pro:** Jim McCann, PGA
Architect: Mr. Pugh, 1966

SCENIC FARMS GOLF COURSE

525 Glenwood Rd., Pine Island, NY 10969   **(914) 258-4455**

Scenic Farms is a 9 hole executive golf course open 7 days a week and closes with heavy snow (approximately 11/30-4/1). Season passes are available. Reservations for tee times are necessary on weekends. The driving range is all turf.

•**Driving Range**	Lockers
•**Practice Green**	Showers
Power Carts	Food
•**Pull Carts**	Clubhouse
•**Club Rental**	•**Outings**
•**Soft Spikes**	

Fees	Weekday	Weekend
9 holes	$9	$11
18 holes	$14	$16

Course Description: With the greens fee at Scenic Farms, the golfer is offered a complimentary bucket of 20 balls to hit at the driving range. The emphasis is on improving your game, either by a playing lesson with the pro or just using the facility for sharpening your skills.. This well manicured course has fairly flat, open fairways and is great for walking. The bent grass greens are fast, medium size and have some contour. The "water traps" are in the form of irrigation ditches. The yardages are the same for the back nine from the Red tees.

Directions: Orange County, #26
I-87 to Exit 16. Take Rte.17 to Goshen-Fla. exit. At light, make left. Go 1& 1/2 miles and right onto Pulaski Hwy. Proceed 9 miles, continue after STOP to club 1/2 m. on right. From Sussex Cty, NJ: Rte.517 becomes Glenwood in NY. Go 7 miles to course.

Hole	1	2	3	4	5	6	7	8	9	Out	BLUE	Rating
BLUE												Slope
WHITE	145	322	94	308	160	106	150	115	108	1508		
Par	3	4	3	4	3	3	5	3	3	29	WHITE	Rating
Handicap	9	3	13	4	6	17	7	11	15			Slope
RED	130	230	90	284	150	98	140	108	98	1324		
Par	3	4	3	4	3	3	5	3	3	29	RED	Rating
Handicap												Slope

Hole	10	11	12	13	14	15	16	17	18	In		Totals
BLUE											BLUE	
WHITE	145	332	94	308	180	106	150	115	108	1538	WHITE	3046
Par	3	4	3	4	3	3	3	3	3	29	Par	58
Handicap	10	1	14	5	2	18	8	12	16			
RED											RED	2648
Par											Par	58
Handicap												

Manager/Supt: Helene Reinsma   **Pro:** Lee Serrec
Architect: Stephen Kay 1994

SCOTTS CORNERS GOLF COURSE

Route 208, Montgomery, NY 12549　　(914) 457-9141

Scotts Corners is a 9 hole course open to the public 7 days a week and closed in winter. Tee time reservations are not ncessary.

Driving Range	Lockers
•Practice Green	Showers
•Power Carts	•Food
•Pull Carts	Clubhouse
•Club Rental	•Outings
•Soft Spikes	

Fees	Weekday	Weekend
Daily	$12	$15
Twi (5PM)	$7.50	$9.50
Sr.	$8	
Power carts	$12/9	$21/18

Course Description: Scotts Corners was originally called Tilson's, then later Walden Country Club. The new ownership took over in 1989. The course is relatively flat and easily walkable. There are 18 separate tees to give variety. The fairways are fairly open with water on 2 holes. The drainage here is good and the greens are in great condition. The par 4 8th hole necessitates a drive over a pond: a moat is located in front of the green to catch the approach shot.

Directions: Orange County, #27
From either I-684N or Rte.87 North (Exit 17), go West on Rte.84 to Exit 5. Then take Rte.208 north 2.5 miles to golf course on left.

Hole	1	2	3	4	5	6	7	8	9	Out	BLUE	Rating
BLUE												Slope
WHITE	350	465	198	419	137	384	308	282	468	3011		
Par	4	5	3	4	3	4	4	4	5	36	WHITE	Rating 67.4
Handicap	9	7	11	1	18	3	5	15	13			Slope 107
RED	350	465	198	419	137	384	262	282	468	2965		
Par	4	5	3	5	3	4	4	4	5	37	RED	Rating 71.3
Handicap	9	7	11	1	18	3	5	15	13			Slope 115
Hole	10	11	12	13	14	15	16	17	18	In		Totals
BLUE											BLUE	
WHITE	339	401	160	533	165	473	262	328	405	3068	WHITE	6079
Par	4	4	3	5	3	5	4	4	4	36	Par	72
Handicap	8	4	17	2	16	10	14	12	6			
RED	339	401	160	533	165	473	262	282	468	3083	RED	6048
Par	4	4	3	5	3	4	4	4	5	36	Par	73
Handicap	8	4	17	2	16	10	14	12	6			

Manager: Peg Di Martino　　**Pro:** John Di Martino　**Supt:** John Di Martino, Jr.
Architect: Tilson 1930s

SPOOK ROCK GOLF COURSE

Spook Rock Road, Suffern, NY, 10901   **(914) 357-6466**

Spook Rock is an 18 hole public course open 7 days a week and closed Nov. 30 to Mar. 1. Memberships are available for Town of Ramapo residents with discounted rates. Weekend drawings for tee times are on Monday nights for ID card holders. Others Thurs. mornings at 7AM.

•Driving Range	•Lockers
•Practice Green	•Showers
•Power Carts	•Food
•Pull Carts	•Clubhouse
•Club Rental	•Outings

Fees	Weekday	Weekend
Daily(Res)	$14	$16
Non-res	$31	$41
Sr/Jr	$9.50	$16
Power carts $25(Dbl)		$25

Course Description: Spook Rock has been rated by Golf Digest in 1996 & 97 as one of the top 75 affordable courses in the US. A five year renovation was completed in 1996 making it more challenging than ever. It is a relatively flat course with water in play on 3 holes; the par 3 13th signature hole has a pond in play. The 18th is a long, tight somewhat uphill par 4 leading to a difficult well-bunkered green. Well maintained, it has tree-lined fairways adding to the scenic ambience in all seasons.

Directions: Rockland County, #28
NYThruway (I-87)to Exit 14B (Airmont Rd.) Turn right heading North. Go approx. 1 mile to light at Spook Rock Rd. & turn left. Bear left at fork to course on left.

Hole	1	2	3	4	5	6	7	8	9	Out	BLUE	Rating 72.7
BLUE	400	520	378	196	392	538	426	210	372	3432		Slope 129
WHITE	385	468	337	166	370	484	407	179	352	3148		
Par	4	5	4	3	4	5	4	3	4	36	WHITE	Rating 70.3
Handicap	11	5	13	15	1	9	7	17	3			Slope 125
RED	313	381	243	104	286	400	327	101	264	2419		
Par	4	5	4	3	4	5	4	3	4	36	RED	Rating 73.4
Handicap	11	5	13	15	1	9	7	17	3			Slope 128
Hole	10	11	12	13	14	15	16	17	18	In		Totals
BLUE	374	511	360	202	432	539	361	179	417	3375	BLUE	6807
WHITE	345	480	331	164	410	505	342	160	386	3123	WHITE	6271
Par	4	5	4	3	4	5	4	3	4	36	Par	72
Handicap	4	6	10	16	8	2	14	18	12			
RED	265	382	255	90	369	433	273	107	297	2471	RED	4890
Par	4	5	4	3	4	5	4	3	4	36	Par	72
Handicap	4	6	10	16	8	2	14	18	12			

Manager: Dan Covert   **Pro:** Marty Bohen, PGA   **Supt:** Dan Madar
Architect: Frank Duane 1969   **Redesign:** Stephen Kay

STONY FORD GOLF COURSE

550 Route 416, Montgomery, NY 12549   **(914) 457-4949**

Stony Ford is an 18 hole course open 7 days a week Nov.30-Apr.1 and run by Orange County. Memberships are available. Tee time reservations may be made 1 week in advance in person & after 12 noon on Wednesdays, by phone. Walkons are allowed.

•**Driving Range**	•**Lockers**
•**Practice Green**	•**Showers**
•**Power Carts**	•**Food**
•**Pull Carts**	•**Clubhouse**
•**Club Rental**	•**Outings**
	•**Soft Spikes**

Fees	Weekday	Weekend
Resident	$17	$24
Non-res	$30	$30
Twi	$11	$11
Power carts	$23.75	

Course Description: Stony Ford is a traditional course, hilly, with wide open rolling fairways. The large greens are gently sloped and become faster in summer. The property originally housed a farm and later a county park and picnic grove. Eventually, Hal Purdy landscaped a section for golf. Water affects play on 7 holes. The 9th and 18th ascend toward the clubhouse. The signature par four 15th has an impressive view from the elevated tee. The hole is long and tree lined uphill to an elevated green. Some say this is"a big hitters' course".

Directions: Orange County, #29
Take I-87(NYThruway) to Exit 16. Go West on Rte.17 to Exit 124(Goshen). Then take Rte.207N and then left on Rte.416. Go 1 mile and course is on the left.

Hole	1	2	3	4	5	6	7	8	9	Out	BLUE	Rating 72.4
BLUE	497	363	417	245	385	404	203	368	497	3379		Slope 128
WHITE	478	338	392	206	356	368	177	349	474	3138		
Par	5	4	4	3	4	4	3	4	5	36	WHITE	Rating 70.3
Handicap	11	5	1	7	9	13	3	17	15			Slope 124
RED	471	321	370	175	336	348	154	328	455	2958		
Par	5	4	4	3	4	4	3	4	5	36	RED	Rating 74.0
Handicap	11	5	1	7	9	13	3	17	15			Slope 128
Hole	10	11	12	13	14	15	16	17	18	In		Totals
BLUE	367	512	164	386	392	469	489	173	320	3272	BLUE	6651
WHITE	351	486	132	358	358	449	466	151	293	3044	WHITE	6182
Par	4	5	3	4	4	4	5	3	4	36	Par	72
Handicap	14	4	12	8	6	2	10	16	18			
RED	343	460	124	334	341	448	444	131	273	2898	RED	5856
Par	4	5	3	4	4	5	5	3	4	37	Par	73
Handicap	14	4	12	8	6	2	10	16	18			

Manager: Tom Quinlisk   **Pro:** John Healy, PGA   **Supt:** Joe Schoen
Architect: Hal Purdy 1968

STORM KING GOLF CLUB

Ridge Rd., Cornwall, NY 12518

(914) 534-3844

Storm King is a 9 hole private course open 7 days a week and closed November through March. Guests play accompanied by a member. Tee time reservations are not necessary.

Driving Range	•**Lockers**
•**Practice Green**	•**Showers**
•**Power Carts**	•**Food**
Pull Carts	•**Clubhouse**
Club Rental	•**Outings**
Caddies	•**Soft Spikes**

Course Description: Storm King celebrated its 100th anniversary in 1994 with a gala party. A time capsule was buried to be uncovered in 50 years. This course features tight fairways and small target greens. The tee shot on #7 must carry a huge ravine. The second shot is a layup for many on this par 5 with the approach shot over water. The last two holes have steep hills. The course is not far from West Point to the south. On the scorecard below, only one set of yardages is shown.

Directions: Orange County, #30
Take Palisades Pkwy north to Bear Mtn Circle. Take Rte.9W North toward Cornwall. Bear right onto Angola Rd. At circle, make 2nd right onto Hasbrouke Ave. Go left onto Ridge to club.

Hole	1	2	3	4	5	6	7	8	9	Out	BLUE	Rating
BLUE												Slope
WHITE	388	364	215	340	355	406	503	141	285	2997		
Par	4	4	3	4	4	4	5	3	4	35	WHITE	Rating 70.4
Handicap	11	7	9	13	5	3	1	15	17			Slope 124
RED												
Par	4	4	3	4	4	5	5	3	4	36	RED	Rating
Handicap	5	3	7	11	9	13	1	17	15			Slope
Hole	10	11	12	13	14	15	16	17	18	In		Totals
BLUE											BLUE	
WHITE	356	364	368	392	408	395	488	107	334	3212	WHITE	6209
Par	4	4	4	4	4	4	5	3	4	36	Par	71
Handicap	16	10	12	6	2	8	4	18	14			
RED											RED	
Par	4	4	4	4	4	4	5	3	4	36	Par	72
Handicap	16	8	12	6	2	10	4	18	14			

Manager: Peter Raso   **Supt:** George Urbich
Estab: 1894

TAMACQUA GOLF COURSE

Ford Lea Rd., Westtown, NY 10998   **(914) 726-3660**

Tamacqua is a 9 hole par 3 course. It is open from Memorial Day until Labor Day 7 days a week. Tee time reservations are not necessary.

•**Driving Range**	Lockers
•**Practice Green**	Showers
Power Carts	•**Food**
•**Pull Carts**	Clubhouse
•**Club Rental**	•**Outings**

Fees Weekday & Weekend

9 holes	$5pp
All day	$7

Course Description: This short par 3 course is flat and easy to walk. No water is in play. It is a facility particularly good for practice or for just a short enjoyable visit.

Directions: Orange County, #31
Rte17.W to Rte.84W to Exit 3East (Middletown). Go to 1st light and make right onto Rte.6. Then make right onto Rte.284. Course is 7 miles ahead on right.

Manager: Kirk Butryn
Built: 1950s

THE TUXEDO CLUB

West Lake Rd., Tuxedo, NY 10987   **(914) 351-4543**

Tuxedo is an 18 hole private club open 6 days a week and closed in winter. Guests play accompanied by a member. Tee times are necessary on weekends.

•**Driving Range**	•**Lockers**
•**Practice Green**	•**Showers**
•**Power Carts**	•**Food**
Pull Carts	•**Clubhouse**
Club Rental	•**Outings**
•**Caddies**	•**Soft Spikes**

Course Description: The Tuxedo Club was originally established in 1886. The Tudor clubhouse, now some distance from the playing area, is impressive. In 1892, the 6 hole layout was converted to nine holes and later that decade expanded to 18. In the 1950s the present course was designed by Robert Trent Jones. It is beautifully maintained and contoured, a part of Sterling Forest Reserve. Water is in play on several holes; the golf property is surrounded by deep woods. In 1992, Tuxedo hosted the Westchester PGA Championship. A new golfers' clubhouse will be constructed in 1998.

Directions: Orange County, #32

Take I-87 to Exit 15A. At light, turn left onto Rte.17N and then left onto Sterling Mine Rd(approx 2 miles). Go right on Eagle Valley Rd, then onto South Gate Rd. to club entrance.

Hole	1	2	3	4	5	6	7	8	9	Out	BLUE	Rating 72.7
BLUE	417	422	182	401	362	166	382	531	440	3303		Slope 136
WHITE	401	372	164	351	347	138	367	505	425	3070		
Par	4	4	3	4	4	3	4	5	4	35	WHITE	Rating 70.7
Handicap	5	13	17	9	7	15	11	1	3			Slope 132
RED	374	300	128	303	300	127	358	408	317	2615		
Par	5	4	3	4	4	3	4	5	4	36	RED	Rating 70.9
Handicap	3	15	17	9	1	13	7	5	11			Slope 118
Hole	10	11	12	13	14	15	16	17	18	In		Totals
BLUE	538	413	432	392	361	184	374	178	518	3390	BLUE	6693
WHITE	518	388	416	372	342	161	344	148	478	3167	WHITE	6237
Par	5	4	4	4	4	3	4	3	5	36	Par	71
Handicap	4	10	2	14	6	18	12	16	8			
RED	450	330	393	354	265	132	296	110	423	2753	RED	5368
Par	5	4	5	4	4	3	4	3	5	37	Par	73
Handicap	2	4	12	10	14	16	8	18	6			

Manager: Robert Josey   **Pro:** Dave Carazo, PGA   **Supt:** Tim Garceau
Architect Robert Trent Jones 1956 **Estab:** 1886

WALLKILL GOLF CLUB

40 Sands Road, Middletown, NY 10941   **(914) 361-1022**

Wallkill is an 18 hole municipally owned course that is open 7 days a week from April through December. Reservations for weekdays call Sat. of preceding week, weekends begin Mon. for town residents and Tues. for others.

•**Driving Range**	•**Lockers**
•**Practice Green**	•**Showers**
•**Power Carts**	•**Food**
•**Pull Carts**	•**Clubhouse**
•**Club Rental**	•**Outings**
•**Soft Spikes**	

Fees	Weekday	Weekend
Daily(res)	$11	$15
Non-res.	$23	$35
Sr.	$10	
Power carts	$24	$24

Course Description: Carved out of the woods, Wallkill has a New England type lay-out. The golfer encounters rolling terrain and many elevated tees and greens. The tree lined fairways make it difficult to see the nearby holes. The back nine is somewhat hilly; offering many sharp dog legs and several blind shots. With water coming into play on 11 holes, knowledge of the course is essential for shot placement. The par 4 13th has an approach shot over a large pond to an island green.

Directions: Orange County, #33
I-87 North (NYThruway) to Exit #16, Harriman. Proceed North on Rte.17 to Rte. 302 (Wallkill, Exit 119). Proceed West on **Old Rte. 17,** take 1st right onto Sands Rd. 0.5 miles to club.

Hole	1	2	3	4	5	6	7	8	9	Out	BLUE	Rating 70.7
BLUE	302	424	178	430	505	355	157	565	422	3338		Slope 128
WHITE	291	412	163	384	483	340	147	550	402	3172		
Par	4	4	3	4	5	4	3	5	4	36	WHITE	Rating 69.5
Handicap	15	1	13	9	7	11	17	3	5			Slope 126
RED	253	277	135	369	460	305	111	428	335	2673		
Par	4	4	3	4	5	4	3	5	4	36	RED	Rating 72.6
Handicap	15	1	11	7	3	13	17	9	5			Slope 126

Hole	10	11	12	13	14	15	16	17	18	In		Totals
BLUE	317	142	476	368	349	148	574	385	340	3099	BLUE	6437
WHITE	300	126	451	353	311	137	562	369	323	2932	WHITE	6104
Par	4	3	5	4	4	3	5	4	4	36	Par	72
Handicap	14	18	8	6	12	16	2	4	10			
RED	275	115	376	301	299	100	450	325	257	2498	RED	5171
Par	4	3	5	4	4	3	5	4	4	36	Par	73
Handicap	10	18	16	4	8	14	6	2	12			

Manager: David J. Vernooy   **Pro:** Willie Carter   **Supt:** Richard Evans
Architect: Steve Esposito 1991

WARWICK VALLEY COUNTRY CLUB

PRIVATE

46 Oakland Avenue, Warwick, NY 10990   (914) 986-9609

Warwick Valley is a 9 hole private course open 7 days a week and closed in the winter. Guests may play accompanied by a member. Tee time reservations are not necessary.

```
Driving Range    •Lockers
•Practice Green  •Showers
•Power Carts     •Food
•Pull Carts      •Clubhouse
•Club Rental     •Outings
•Caddies         •Soft Spikes
```

Course Description: Warwick Valley CC, formerly the Red Swan Inn, a hotel with a golf course, was redesigned into a par 36, and the hotel was razed. Babe Ruth had played here back in those early days. The beautifully conditioned well treed course is fairly hilly, with small well bunkered greens and several ponds. The course looks easier than it plays. In the 1930s the local high school played football here.

Directions: Orange County, #34
Tappan Zee Br. to I-87 North to Exit #15A. Left at light onto Rte.17North. Go thru Tuxedo & Sloatsburg. Turn left at light onto Rte.17A (sign reads Greenwood Lake Sterling Forest) to end; club straight ahead.

Hole	1	2	3	4	5	6	7	8	9	Out	BLUE	Rating
BLUE												Slope
WHITE	303	225	432	377	126	565	289	315	219	2851		
Par	4	3	5	4	3	5	4	4	3	35	WHITE	Rating 68.5
Handicap	15	11	5	3	17	1	9	7	13			Slope 122
RED	303	120	432	322	126	376	289	280	219	2467		
Par	4	3	5	4	3	5	4	4	4	36	RED	Rating 68.6
Handicap	5	17	1	9	15	3	7	11	13			Slope 118

Hole	10	11	12	13	14	15	16	17	18	In		Totals
BLUE											BLUE	
WHITE	331	200	477	377	166	535	311	315	280	2992	WHITE	5843
Par	4	3	5	4	3	5	4	4	4	36	Par	71
Handicap	12	14	4	6	16	2	8	10	18			
RED	331	225	369	351	84	345	177	315	268	2465	RED	4932
Par	4	4	5	4	3	5	4	4	4	37	Par	73
Handicap	6	14	2	8	18	4	16	10	12			

Manager: Bruce Etheridge   **Supt:** Jim Laroe
Built: 1915

WEST POINT GOLF COURSE

Bldg. 1230 Rte 218, West Point, NY 10996   **(914) 938-2435**

West Point is an 18 hole course, formerly only for military & Defense personnel. It is now open to the public 7 days a week and closed 11/30-4/1. Tee times: 8 days in advance for active duty & cadets, 5 days other military, 24 hrs for the general public.

Driving Range	•**Lockers**
•**Practice Green**	•**Showers**
•**Power Carts**	•**Food**
•**Pull Carts**	•**Clubhouse**
•**Club Rental**	•**Outings**
•**Soft Spikes**	

Fees	Weekday	Weekend
Cadets	$8	$10
E1-E6	$8	$10
Public	$30	$40
Power carts	$20	

Course Description: 9 holes were built during World War II and the second nine was designed later by Robert Trent Jones. New greens, tees, fairways and an irrigation system were recently installed. West Point has a very mountainous layout, heavily treed, with many blind shots to the greens. The first hole features an elevated tee and a stream in front of a severely elevated green. The 11th is a beautiful par 3 with a pond to carry and a stream in back. Throughout the course there are breathtaking views of the surrounding mountains, an enjoyable and memorable experience.

Directions: Orange County, #35
Take Pal. Int. Pkwy.N to end. At circle, continue north on 9W, do not make right into West Point at sign. After passing under pedestrian and golf cart overpass on 9W, make right onto Rte.218 and an immediate right into course entrance.

Hole	1	2	3	4	5	6	7	8	9	Out	BLUE	Rating 70.0
BLUE	372	175	360	495	400	191	509	380	201	3083		Slope 127
WHITE	323	151	342	472	365	186	498	359	185	2881		
Par	4	3	4	5	4	3	5	4	3	35	WHITE	Rating 67.8
Handicap	7	17	11	5	3	16	1	9	13			Slope 123
RED	313	127	285	374	283	169	390	337	153	2431		
Par	4	3	4	5	4	4	5	4	3	36	RED	Rating 67.5
Handicap	5	16	11	3	7	17	1	9	13			Slope 117

Hole	10	11	12	13	14	15	16	17	18	In		Totals
BLUE	326	175	389	154	418	350	382	485	493	3172	BLUE	6255
WHITE	309	155	365	132	377	303	360	429	474	2904	WHITE	5785
Par	4	3	4	3	4	4	4	5	5	36	Par	71
Handicap	12	15	10	18	6	14	8	2	4			
RED	269	121	300	120	331	220	279	361	377	2378	RED	4809
Par	4	3	4	3	4	4	4	5	5	36	Par	72
Handicap	12	15	6	18	8	14	10	2	4			

Manager/Pro: Michael Ernst, PGA   **Supt:** James Shapiro
Built: 1940s   **Architect:** Robert Trent Jones - Redesign

WINDING HILL GOLF COURSE

Route 17K P.O. Box 194, Montgomery, NY 12549   **(914) 457-3187**

Winding Hill began operations in 1997 as an 18 hole executive course. It is open to the public 7 days a week and closed Nov.1-Apr. 1. Tee time reservations are necessary on weekends.

Driving Range	Lockers
•Practice Green	Showers
•Power Carts	•Food
•Pull Carts	•Clubhouse
•Club Rental	•Outings
	•Soft Spikes

Fees	Weekday	Weekend
Daily	$15	$18
Srs	$12	
Power carts	$10pp	
Srs. carts $6 weekdays		

Course Description: Winding Hill is a heavily treed, very tight layout cut through forest and intentionally preserved wetlands. An unusual feature here are stone walls, rebuilt during construction, that lend character to the hilly terrain. The very narrow fairways demand accuracy; strategic shot placement will be rewarded. This short course is in excellent condition with water in play on one hole. The greens have gentle slopes. All the cart paths are paved. From some locations, there are beautiful vistas and houses are being built around the property. Ratings and slopes are not yet available.

Directions: Orange County, #36
From I-87 at Exit 17, take Rte.84 West to Exit 5 in Walden. Take Rte.208 North to Rte.17K in Maybrook. Go west 7 miles through Montgomery. Course is on left.

Hole	1	2	3	4	5	6	7	8	9	Out	BLUE	Rating
BLUE												Slope
WHITE	127	126	258	151	137	274	90	95	207	1465		
Par	3	3	4	3	3	4	3	3	3	29	WHITE	Rating
Handicap	9	11	1	15	5	13	7	17	3			Slope
RED	106	88	232	119	110	262	63	77	182	1239		
Par	3	3	4	3	3	4	3	3	3	29	RED	Rating
Handicap	9	11	1	15	5	13	7	17	3			Slope

Hole	10	11	12	13	14	15	16	17	18	In		Totals
BLUE											BLUE	
WHITE	94	109	135	256	112	119	86	76	143	1130	WHITE	2595
Par	3	3	3	4	3	3	3	3	3	28	Par	57
Handicap	10	14	4	2	8	12	18	16	6			
RED	79	83	108	233	76	103	66	61	112	921	RED	2160
Par	3	3	3	4	3	3	3	3	3	28	Par	57
Handicap	10	14	4	2	8	12	18	16	6			

Manager/Pro: Neil Richards, PGA   **Supt:** Gina Gatto
Architect: Steve Esposito 1997

ULSTER COUNTY

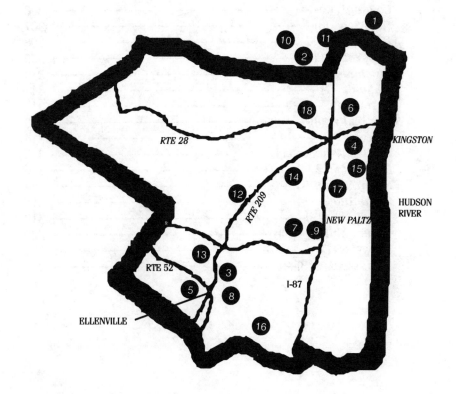

ULSTER COUNTY

Public Courses appear in *bold italics*

CATSKILL GOLF CLUB

27 Brooks Lane, Catskill, NY 12414   (518) 943-0302

Catskill Golf Club is a semi-private 9 hole course open to the public 7 days a week, between April 1 & October 31. There are memberships available that give tee time privileges for weekend mornings. Reservations may be made 24 hrs. in advance.

Driving Range	•**Lockers**
•**Practice Green**	•**Showers**
•**Power Carts**	•**Food**
•**Pull Carts**	•**Clubhouse**
•**Club Rental**	•**Outings**
Soft Spikes	

Fees	Weekday	Weekend
Daily (18)	$20	$30 inc cart
Daily (9)	$12	
Power carts Mandatory wkds.		

Course Description: Catskill Golf Club offers scenic mountain views from the elevated tees and greens. Much of the challenge here is from the uneven lies characteristic of this type of hilly course. The fairways are quite narrow; on some holes the greens are small and undulating. The difficult 560 yard par 5 3rd, has two water hazards and most golfers lay up before the approach shot. This course, although it is 9 holes, plays like an 18 holer with 2 distinct sets of tees as shown in the scorecard below.

Directions: Greene County, #1
NYThruway to Exit #21. Take Jefferson Hts. Rd. toward Catskill. Turn left approx. 1 mile onto Brooks Lane to course on left.

Hole	1	2	3	4	5	6	7	8	9	Out	BLUE	Rating
BLUE												Slope
WHITE	312	382	560	353	279	378	197	380	297	3138		
Par	4	4	5	4	4	4	3	4	4	36	WHITE	Rating 68.7
Handicap	15	3	1	11	17	9	5	7	13			Slope 117
RED	310	263	475	270	275	318	179	378	295	2763		
Par	4	4	5	4	4	4	3	4	4	36	RED	Rating 70.6
Handicap	9	15	1	5	17	7	13	3	11			Slope 119

Hole	10	11	12	13	14	15	16	17	18	In		Totals
BLUE											BLUE	
WHITE	320	385	430	388	184	360	150	504	297	3018	WHITE	6156
Par	4	4	4	4	3	4	3	5	4	35	Par	71
Handicap	14	6	2	4	16	10	18	8	12			
RED	318	263	420	270	182	358	150	445	295	2701	RED	5464
Par	4	4	5	4	3	4	3	5	4	36	Par	72
Handicap	10	14	2	8	16	6	18	4	12			

Manager: Roberta Penchina   **Pro:** Brian Lowe, PGA   **Supt:** Chuck Santanani
Architect: Jim Thompson, 1929

COLONIAL COUNTRY CLUB

Route 23A, Tannersville, NY 12485   (518) 589-9807

Colonial is a 9 hole course open 7 days a week and closed 11/1-4/15. Tee time reservations may be made up to 1 week in advance for weekends.

Driving Range	Lockers
Practice Green	Showers
•Power Carts	•Food
•Pull Carts	Clubhouse
•Club Rental	•Outings

Fees	Weekday	Weekend
Resident	$13	$16
Twi	$9	$12
Power carts	$12/18	$6/9

Course Description: About one half of the holes at Colonial are flat; the other half are up and down mountain type. To score well, the golfer needs to place the ball accurately. A pond in front of the 3rd hole is in play on the approach shot. The greens are small and undulating, the fairways narrow. The signature par 3 8th is downhill over a stream to the green. Most people play 18 holes here. As can be seen in the scorecard below, only some holes have differing yardages for the forward tees.

Directions: Greene County, #2
Take I-87 (NYThruway) to Exit 20. Go left at light onto Rte.32N (then right to continue on 32N). Take Rte.32A and bear left. Make left on Rte.23A through Tannersville to course on left.

Hole	1	2	3	4	5	6	7	8	9	Out	BLUE	Rating
BLUE												Slope
WHITE	208	252	343	295	282	281	313	134	573	2681		
Par	3	4	4	4	4	4	4	3	5	35	WHITE	Rating 65.8
Handicap	9	15	5	3	13	11	7	17	1			Slope 107
RED	153			237	196		215		388	2199		
Par											RED	Rating 64.8
Handicap												Slope 103

Hole	10	11	12	13	14	15	16	17	18	In		Totals
BLUE											BLUE	
WHITE											WHITE	5362
Par											Par	70
Handicap												
RED											RED	4398
Par											Par	70
Handicap												

Manager/Pro: Tim Leach, PGA   **Supt:** Richard Legg
Built: Unknown

FALLSVIEW RESORT & CC

Nevele Rd., Ellenville, NY 12428   **(914) 647-4960**

Fallsview has a 9 hole course on the grounds of the resort hotel. It is open 7 days a week and closed from Thanksgiving to Apr. 1. There are discounts for hotel guests. Tee time reservations are necessary on weekends in summer.

•Driving Range	•Lockers
•Practice Green	•Showers
•Power Carts	•Food
•Pull Carts	•Clubhouse
•Club Rental	•Outings

Fees	Weekday	Weekend
Guest	$12/9	$18/18
non-g	$13/9	$15/9
non-g	$20/18	$23/18
Power carts	$14/9	$26/18

Course Description: Fallsview has been highly rated by Golf World as one of the best nine hole courses in New York State. There are beautiful views of the nearby mountains, particularly from the tees on the 8th and 9th. The personnel here have great pride in the course. The immaculate bent and poana greens are fast with considerable break. Water is in play on the 1st, 3rd, 6th and 7th. The signature is the long and difficult par 5 606 yard #6. The Head Pro Championship for the MGA in 1997 gave the participants a chance to rave about this course.

Directions: Ulster County, #3
NY Thruway (I-87) to Exit 16. Take Rte.17West to Exit 113. Take Rte.209North to Ellenville. At entrance to Nevele, bear left into Fallsview.

Hole	1	2	3	4	5	6	7	8	9	Out	BLUE	Rating 72.5
BLUE	401	173	509	433	204	606	211	417	478	3432		Slope 126
WHITE	384	157	475	404	172	560	181	392	448	3173		
Par	4	3	5	4	3	5	3	4	4	35	WHITE	Rating 70.4
Handicap	11	17	9	7	15	1	13	5	3			Slope 121
RED	330	134	332	402	139	511	146	319	415	2728		
Par	4	3	4	5	3	5	3	4	5	36	RED	Rating 72.7
Handicap	11	17	9	7	15	1	13	5	3			Slope 123
Hole	10	11	12	13	14	15	16	17	18	In		Totals
BLUE											BLUE	6864
WHITE											WHITE	6346
Par											Par	70
Handicap												
RED											RED	5456
Par											Par	72
Handicap												

Manager/Pro: Werner Teichmann, PGA   **Supt:** Jay O'Donnell
Architect: Robert Trent Jones 1962

GREEN ACRES GOLF COURSE

Harwich St., Kingston, NY 12401   **(914) 331-2283**

Green Acres is a 9 hole course open to the public 7 days a week and closed Dec. 1-April 1. Tee time reservations are not necessary.

•**Driving Range**	Lockers
Practice Green	Showers
•**Power Carts**	Food
•**Pull Carts**	Clubhouse
•**Club Rental**	Outings

Fees	Weekday	Weekend
9 hole	$7.50	$9
All day	$10.50	$13

Course Description: Green Acres is a fairly flat, easy to walk course. Well maintained, it offers an excellent opportunity for learning the game. No water or sand traps confound the golfer. The greens are medium size with some undulations. It is a convenient and inexpensive 2774 yard facility.

White   Rating 68.2   Slope 101
Red   Rating 70.6   Slope 105

Directions: Ulster County, #4
I-87 to Exit 19. Take 3rd exit off traffic circle onto Rte.587. Go to light and bear left for 1 mile and then left onto Harwich to course.

Proprietor/ Supt: Durrell Vigna
Built: 1963

HOMOWACK GOLF COURSE

Route 209, Spring Glen, NY 12483 **(914) 647-6800**

Homowack is a 9 hole course open to the public and guests of the hotel. Memberships are available. It is open 7 days a week and closed in the winter. Tee time reservations are not necessary.

•**Driving Range**	Lockers
•**Practice Green**	Showers
•**Power Carts**	•**Food**
•**Pull Carts**	Clubhouse
•**Club Rental**	•**Outings**

Fees	Weekday	Weekend
All Day	$10	$11
Hotel guests	$9	
Power carts	$12/9	$18/18

Course Description: Homowack is a challenging, scenic and somewhat hilly course. A stream affects play on the 8th, a pond and stream on the 1st and 9th as well. The 3rd hole is a par 3 with a tiny green. In general, the greens are excellent; some have considerable contour. Four holes are open in a valley and five are in the woods with narrow fairways giving variety to the layout.

Directions: Ulster County, #5
NY thruway (I-87) to Exit 16. Take Rte.17West to Exit 113. Go north on Rte.209 7.5 miles to hotel in Spring Glen just over the border in Ulster County.

Hole	1	2	3	4	5	6	7	8	9	Out	BLUE	Rating
BLUE												Slope
WHITE	252	310	121	350	400	128	300	395	235	2441		
Par	4	4	3	4	5	3	4	4	4	35	WHITE	Rating
Handicap	7	8	3	5	1	6	4	2	9			Slope
RED	157	180	111	210	285	128	250	290	152	1763		
Par	4	4	3	4	5	3	4	4	4	35	RED	Rating
Handicap	7	2	6	4	1	8	5	3	9			Slope
Hole	10	11	12	13	14	15	16	17	18	In		Totals
BLUE											BLUE	
WHITE											WHITE	
Par											Par	
Handicap												
RED											RED	
Par											Par	
Handicap												

Manager: Patty Gray **Pro:** Eddie Gray, PGA **Supt:** Ray MacNamara
Built: 1940s, expanded to regulation 1971

KATSBAAN GOLF CLUB

1754 Old Kings Highway, Saugerties, NY 12477   **(914) 246-8182**

Katsbaan is a 9 hole course open to the public 7 days a week and closed Dec. 1-Mar. 15. Memberships are available. Tee times are necessary for weekends.

Driving Range	Lockers
•Practice Green	Showers
•Power Carts	•Food
•Pull Carts	•Clubhouse
•Club Rental	•Outings

Fees	Weekday	Weekend
Daily	$10 (all day)	$15
Twi (4:30)		$10
Power carts	$25/18	$15/9

Course Description: Katsbaan is appreciated for its diversity. Some holes are open, others are tight but no two holes are similar. The course is safe, well laid out and designed to walk. The greens vary in size, are medium fast and have some break. The par 5s are flat and ther is only one major hill on this course. Three ponds affect play. Katsbaan is not far from the Thruway exit and popular with all levels of players.

Directions: Ulster County, #6
Take NY thruway (I-87) to Exit 20. Make a left at light onto Rte.32 and then turn right following signs to 32N. Proceed for 1 and 1/2 miles for Katsbaan signs and course on right.

Hole	1	2	3	4	5	6	7	8	9	Out	BLUE	Rating
BLUE												Slope
WHITE	160	363	535	155	333	340	135	525	410	3005		
Par	3	4	5	3	4	4	3	5	4	35	WHITE	Rating 68.5
Handicap	14	7	1	11	15	10	17	5	3			Slope
RED	160	333	480	125	225	295	120	485	342	2590		
Par											RED	Rating
Handicap												Slope

Hole	10	11	12	13	14	15	16	17	18	In		Totals
BLUE											BLUE	
WHITE											WHITE	6010
Par											Par	70
Handicap												
RED											RED	5180
Par											Par	70
Handicap												

Manager: John Dooley   **Pro:** Cary Davis, PGA   **Supt:** John Espey
Architect: Hal Purdy 1990

MOHONK MOUNTAIN HOUSE

100 Mountain Rest Rd., New Paltz, NY 12561   **(914) 256-2154**

Mohonk Mountain House has a 9 hole golf course open to the public 7 days a week and closed 11/15-4/1. Memberships are available. Tee time reservations may be made up to 1 week in advance. Mohonk hotel guests get complimentary greens fees (midweek).

Driving Range	Lockers
•**Practice Green**	Showers
•**Power Carts**	•**Food**
•**Pull Carts**	Clubhouse
•**Club Rental**	•**Outings**

Fees	**Weekday**	**Weekend**
Daily/9	$10	$13
18	$15	$19
Power Carts	$12/9	$20/18

Course Description: Mohonk is extremely challenging for golfers new to the course. It is of Scottish design featuring many blind shots, uneven lies and elevated greens and tees. The original clubhouse is situated at the 2nd hole. It was built in 1903, and is now used as a guest cottage for the hotel. The postage stamp greens are of moderate speed with severe breaks. Thickly treed, the course has no water in play and offers scenic views of the surrounding valleys. The 1st hole is a signature par 3 that plays uphill to a green flanked by bunkers and the old clubhouse as a backdrop. The course was redesigned in 1911 maintaining its old style.

Directions: Ulster County, #7
I-87(Thruway) to Exit 18. Go left at light onto Rte.299W through town, over bridge and right on Springtown Rd. At fork, bear left onto Mountain Rest Rd. 2 mi. to club on left.

Hole	1	2	3	4	5	6	7	8	9	Out	BLUE	Rating
BLUE												Slope
WHITE	185	316	375	375	116	306	226	261	470	2630		
Par	3	4	4	4	3	4	4	4	5	35	WHITE	Rating 64.6
Handicap	2	5	1	3	9	4	8	6	7			Slope 107
RED	120	285	365	345	106	300	205	250	410	2451		
Par	3	4	5	4	3	4	4	4	5	36	RED	Rating 66.7
Handicap	7	6	3	1	9	2	8	5	4			Slope 109

Hole	10	11	12	13	14	15	16	17	18	In		Totals
BLUE											BLUE	
WHITE											WHITE	
Par											Par	70
Handicap												
RED											RED	
Par											Par	72
Handicap												

Manager: Eric Loheide   **Supt:** Tom Wright
Architects: R.D. Pryde, A. K. Smiley   **Estab:** 1897

NEVELE COUNTRY CLUB

Route 209, Ellenville, NY 12428 **(914) 647-6000**

The 18 hole golf course at the Nevele is open 7 days a week from 3/1-12/15. The resort offers slightly reduced fees for guests and special golf packages. Reservations for tee times may be made up to 3 weeks in advance.

| • Driving Range • Lockers |
| • Practice Green • Showers |
| • Power Carts • Food |
| • Pull Carts • Clubhouse |
| • Club Rental • Outings |

Fees	Weekday	Weekend
Hotel guests	$40	$45
Non-guests	$45	$55
Twi/4PM	$30	$30
Rates include elec. cart		

Course Description: The Nevele redesign makes the layout more challenging than ever. Water is in play on more than half of the 18. The well maintained course plays long from the blues. The fairly large greens in perfect shape are of above average speed and have some break. The signature par 4 #16 features a tee shot over water to a narrow fairway and includes a daunting approach to a green with traps in front, a pond on the left and a lake on the right. The mountains in the distance add to the beauty of the course.

Directions: Ulster County, #8
Take NY thruway (I-87) to Exit 16. Take Rte.17West to Exit 113. Take Rte.209N to Ellenville and hotel entrance.

Hole	1	2	3	4	5	6	7	8	9	Out	BLUE	Rating 71.9
BLUE	415	505	406	241	373	434	443	208	366	3391		Slope 128
WHITE	375	467	386	190	364	367	408	165	328	3050		
Par	4	5	4	3	4	4	4	3	4	35	WHITE	Rating 69.4
Handicap	4	13	7	9	11	5	1	17	15			Slope 123
RED	315	360	291	131	264	339	326	118	273	2417		
Par	4	5	4	3	4	4	4	3	4	35	RED	Rating 71.1
Handicap	4	13	7	9	11	5	1	17	15			Slope 125.5
Hole	10	11	12	13	14	15	16	17	18	In		Totals
BLUE	426	214	499	331	393	297	362	214	405	3141	BLUE	6532
WHITE	395	154	493	325	342	285	330	137	378	2839	WHITE	5889
Par	4	3	5	4	4	4	4	3	4	35	Par	70
Handicap	8	16	6	12	2	14	10	18	4			
RED	270	130	385	240	290	260	228	103	247	2153	RED	4570
Par	4	3	5	4	4	4	4	3	4	35	Par	70
Handicap	8	16	6	12	2	14	10	18	4			

Manager/Pro: Jack Breno, PGA   **Supt:** Ernie Steinhofer
Architect: Alfred Tull   **Redesign:** Tom Fazio 1980s

NEW PALTZ GOLF COURSE

215 Huguenot St., New Paltz, NY 12561   **(914) 255-8282**

New Paltz is a 9 hole course open to the public 7 days a week and closed Nov. 1-April 1. There are memberships available. Tee time reservations are not necessary. The practice area includes a chipping green.

•Driving Range	Lockers
•Practice Green	Showers
•Power Carts	**•Food**
•Pull Carts	Clubhouse
•Club Rental	**•Outings**

Fees	Weekday	Weekend
Daily (9)	$11	$13
18 holes	$15	$19
Power carts	$12/9	$24/18

Course Description: Scenic New Paltz is a challenging, fairly long and wooded golf course with large, sloping greens that are in excellent shape. Deer, ducks and swans flourish here. The Walkill River, one of the three rivers in the world that runs away from the Equator, and three ponds on the course affect play. The 6th hole has a peninsula tee. The par 3 8th requires a tee shot over water with a tree looming to the left. The ninth is one of the most difficult holes in Ulster County. Mohonk Mountain can be seen in the distance. The property was formerly the Briarwood Riding School.

Directions: Ulster County, #9
NY Thruway (I-87) to Exit 18. Go west on Rte.299. Go through village of New Paltz and turn right onto Huguenot St. before crossing bridge over Walkill River and go 1.3 miles to club on left.

Hole	1	2	3	4	5	6	7	8	9	Out	BLUE	Rating 73.0
BLUE	555	430	405	160	345	540	370	200	445	3450		Slope 129
WHITE	535	410	385	140	325	520	365	195	425	3300		
Par	5	4	4	3	4	5	4	3	4	36	WHITE	Rating 71.7
Handicap	1	7	9	17	13	3	11	15	5			Slope 126
RED	410	363	270	130	305	400	330	125	325	2658		
Par	5	4	4	3	4	5	4	3	4	36	RED	Rating 70.4
Handicap	1	7	9	17	13	3	11	15	5			Slope 120
Hole	10	11	12	13	14	15	16	17	18	In		Totals
BLUE											BLUE	
WHITE											WHITE	
Par											Par	72
Handicap												
RED											RED	
Par											Par	72
Handicap												

Pro: Larry Furey, PGA   **Supt:** Stephen Dodge
Architect: Hal Purdy 1970

ONTEORA CLUB

Route 23C, Tannersville, NY 12485

(518) 587-5310

Onteora is a 9 hole private club open 7 days a week and closed 11/1 to 4/15. Guests play accompanied by a member. Most members use pull carts but power carts are available for outings. Tee time reservations are not necessary.

Driving Range	•Lockers
•Practice Green	•Showers
•Power Carts	•Food
•Pull Carts	•Clubhouse
Club Rental	•Outings
Caddies	Soft Spikes

Course Description: Onteora is a family oriented club situated in a secluded camp like atmosphere. Many members own summer homes in close proximity to the club. It is a walker's course with magnificent views. The layout goes downhill on the 2nd and 5th holes and uphill on the 9th. The 6th has a lake along the side. This is listed as one of the oldest courses in the U.S. and part of Onteora Park, one of 3 sister parks, the others being Twilight and Elks. Different tee placements are offered for the second nine.

Directions: Greene County, #10
Take the Thruway(I-87) to Exit 20. Take Rte.32N to Rte.32A and make left in Palenville to Rte23.A. In Tannersville, turn right on Rte.23C to course on left. Watch for sign 'Onteora Club'.

Hole	1	2	3	4	5	6	7	8	9	Out	BLUE	Rating
BLUE												Slope
WHITE	251	371	389	456	169	441	221	326	315	2939		
Par	4	5	4	5	3	4	3	4	4	35	WHITE	Rating
Handicap	13	5	1	7	17	3	11	15	9			Slope 121
RED	215	308	353	398	169	341	180	258	310	2532		
Par	4	5	4	5	3	4	3	4	4	35	RED	Rating
Handicap	13	7	1	3	15	5	17	11	9			Slope 118

Hole	10	11	12	13	14	15	16	17	18	In		Totals
BLUE											BLUE	
WHITE	214	323	353	466	195	496	180	343	315	2885	WHITE	5824
Par	4	5	4	5	3	4	3	4	4	35	Par	70
Handicap	10	12	6	4	18	2	16	14	8			
RED	165	323	281	398	150	430	154	258	300	2459	RED	4991
Par	4	5	4	5	3	4	3	4	4	35	Par	70
Handicap	18	6	8	4	16	2	14	12	10			

Pro: Jim Hutchins, PGA **Supt:** Fred Kappel
Built: 1887

RIP VAN WINKLE COUNTRY CLUB   PUBLIC

Route 23A, Palenville, NY 12463   **(518) 678-9779**

Rip Van Winkle is a 9 hole course open to the public 7 days a week and closed Nov. 15-April 1. Memberships are available. Tee times are necessary on weekends.

Driving Range	Lockers
•**Practice Green**	Showers
•**Power Carts**	•**Food**
•**Pull Carts**	•**Clubhouse**
•**Club Rental**	•**Outings**

Fees	**Weekday**	**Weekend**
9 holes	$10	$10
18 "	$14	$17
Power carts	$26/18	$20/9

Course Description: The family owned Rip Van Winkle is considerably flat for a course in the mountains, but it provides wonderful scenic views of the nearby Catskills. With separate tee locations for the second round, the course offers variety with different yardages and pars. The greens are of average size and not severely contoured. Ponds are in play on the 5th and the 8th. The fairways are generally open. The holes are named in keeping with the legend, i.e. Young Rip, Rip's Awakening, Hudson's Crew, etc.

Directions: Greene County, #11
Take I-87 (Thruway) to Exit 20. Go left at light onto Rte.32N, make right (follow sign) to continue on 32N. Then take Rte.32A and make right at light onto Rte.23A. Course ahead on left.

Hole	1	2	3	4	5	6	7	8	9	Out	BLUE	Rating
BLUE												Slope
WHITE	318	303	131	430	300	474	393	185	471	3005		
Par	4	4	3	4	4	5	4	3	5	36	WHITE	Rating 68.5
Handicap	17	15	11	1	5	7	3	13	9			Slope 115
RED	318	303	131	401	272	402	332	185	354	2698		
Par	4	4	3	5	4	5	4	3	4	36	RED	Rating 70.1
Handicap	17	15	11	1	9	7	5	13	3			Slope 118
Hole	10	11	12	13	14	15	16	17	18	In		Totals
BLUE											BLUE	
WHITE	328	327	105	480	161	490	438	182	490	3001	WHITE	6006
Par	4	4	3	5	3	5	4	3	5	36	Par	72
Handicap	18	16	12	10	8	4	2	14	6			
RED	328	327	105	401	161	402	332	182	414	2652	RED	5350
Par	4	4	3	5	3	5	4	3	5	36	Par	72
Handicap	18	16	12	2	10	4	8	14	6			

Manager: Raymond Smith   **Supt:** Jack Washburn
Architect: Donald Ross 1919

RONDOUT COUNTRY CLUB

Box 194 Whitfield Rd., Accord, NY 12404 **(914) 626-2513**

Rondout is an 18 hole course open to the public 7 days a week and closed 11/1-4/1. Memberships are available. Tee times may be made up to 5 days in advance, 7 days for members.

- •Driving Range •Lockers
- •Practice Green •Showers
- •Power Carts •Food
- •Pull Carts •Clubhouse
- •Club Rental •Outings

Fees	Weekday	Weekend
Daily	$28/18	$38/18
9 hole	$16	$22
Fee includes cart		

Course Description: Rondout golf course utilizes all the clubs in your bag. This well maintained target layout requires play to position. This course is known for its greens which are sometimes elevated, generally undulating and usually fast. The putts are smooth as the surface is true. There are ponds and a creek runs along the left side of #2 and through #4. The signature par 4 #5 has a tee shot over water to a green guarded by a rock wall in front and to the right and three sand traps. The golfer is treated to scenic views of the mountains of the lower Catskills.

Directions: Ulster County, #12
NY Thruway (I-87) to Exit 19 (Kingston).Take Rte.209S 15 & 1/2 miles and go right onto Whitfield. OR take Rte.17 To Exit 113(Rte.209) and go north approx. 20 miles and left onto Whitfield.

Hole	1	2	3	4	5	6	7	8	9	Out	BLUE	Rating 72.7
BLUE	448	429	140	554	330	519	180	460	401	3461		Slope 128
WHITE	438	386	125	475	300	487	179	454	388	3232		
Par	4	4	3	5	4	5	3	5	4	37	WHITE	Rating 70.0
Handicap	5	13	17	1	15	3	5	11	7			Slope 123
RED	350	249	103	404	220	397	115	386	327	2551		
Par	4	4	3	5	4	5	3	5	4	37	RED	Rating 68.4
Handicap	7	17	13	3	9	1	15	11	5			Slope 116

Hole	10	11	12	13	14	15	16	17	18	In		Totals
BLUE	413	475	165	515	178	370	168	350	373	3007	BLUE	6468
WHITE	399	460	157	496	145	362	160	327	352	2858	WHITE	6090
Par	4	5	3	5	3	4	3	4	4	35	Par	72
Handicap	4	12	14	2	10	8	18	16	6			
RED	360	328	140	420	85	253	150	264	271	2271	RED	4822
Par	4	5	3	5	3	4	3	4	4	35	Par	72
Handicap	6	10	16	2	18	14	12	8	4			

Manager: Steve Ellsworth   **Pro:** John De Forest, PGA **Supt:** Paul Jordan
Architect: Hal Purdy 1st nine 1969; 2nd nine 1989

SHAWANGUNK COUNTRY CLUB

PUBLIC

Country Club Rd., Ellenville, NY 12428   (914) 647-6090

Shawangunk is a 9 hole course open 7 days a week from 3/20-10/31, weather permitting. Members get preferred tee times. Generally, tee time reservations are not necessary.

Driving Range	•Lockers
•Practice Green	•Showers
•Power Carts	•Food
•Pull Carts	•Clubhouse
•Club Rental	•Outings

Fees	Weekday	Weekend
Daily/9	$10	$12
18	$15	$18
Power carts	$12/9	$21/18

Course Description: Formerly hilly farmland, Shawangunk has elevated tees and greens and scenic mountain vistas. The rolling contours along the fairways of the course are well maintained. The hand mown, sloping medium fast greens are fairly small. Creeks and a pond affect play. The par 3 #5 is the prettiest hole with a view of the mountains straight ahead.

Directions: Ulster County, #13
NY Thruway to Exit 16. Take Rte.17 West to Exit 113. Then take Rte.209N to Ellenville. At Nevele Hotel, do not turn right. Continue up hill to course.

Hole	1	2	3	4	5	6	7	8	9	Out	BLUE	Rating
BLUE												Slope
WHITE	286	176	407	492	178	362	132	326	381	2740		
Par	4	3	4	5	3	4	3	4	4	34	WHITE	Rating 67.6
Handicap	13	14	1	4	16	9	18	11	6			Slope 118
RED	283	141	427	431	125	251	216	306	301	2481		
Par	4	3	5	5	3	4	4	4	4	36	RED	Rating 69.3
Handicap	9	17	3	1	18	10	13	6	8			Slope 121
Hole	10	11	12	13	14	15	16	17	18	In		Totals
BLUE											BLUE	
WHITE	296	192	427	492	178	365	203	343	381	2877	WHITE	5617
Par	4	3	4	5	3	4	3	4	4	34	Par	68
Handicap	12	15	2	5	17	8	3	10	7			
RED	240	176	427	431	178	211	132	326	381	2502	RED	4983
Par	4	3	5	5	3	4	3	4	5	36	Par	72
Handicap	12	15	4	2	14	11	16	7	5			

Manager/Pro: John Duncan, PGA   **Supt:** Dave Irwin
Built: 1924

STONE DOCK GOLF CLUB

Stone Dock Rd., High Falls, NY 12440   **(914) 687-9944**

Stone Dock is a semi-private 9 hole course open 7 days a week and closed 12/1-4/1. Memberships are available. Tee time reservations are not necessary.

Driving Range	Lockers
•**Practice Green**	Showers
•**Power Carts**	•**Food**
•**Pull Carts**	Clubhouse
•**Club Rental**	•**Outings**

Fees	**Weekday**	**Weekend**
Daily/9	$9.50	$10.50
18	$13	$15
Power carts	$11/9	$21/18

Course Description: Stone Dock is a challenging par 36 9 hole track. Ponds and creeks affect play on five holes. The small, medium speed greens are in good condition. The course has wide, tree-lined fairways and some elevated greens and tees. The signature par 4 4th, although short, is a severe dogleg left over water with a big tree in the center of the fairway. The second nine will have the same yardages.

Directions: Ulster County, #14
Take NY Thruway (I-87) to Exit 19. Then take Rte.209S to Rte.213E over bridge and turn right on Berme Rd. Go 1 & 1/4 m. to club on right.

Hole	1	2	3	4	5	6	7	8	9	Out	BLUE	Rating 71.0
BLUE	385	415	165	330	570	165	530	340	415	3315		Slope 120
WHITE	370	400	150	295	555	150	520	330	400	3170		
Par	4	4	3	4	5	3	5	4	4	36	WHITE	Rating 69.0
Handicap	10	12	14	8	2	18	6	16	4			Slope 116
RED	270	300	105	180	455	110	420	270	300	2410		
Par	4	4	3	4	5	3	5	4	4	36	RED	Rating 66.5
Handicap												Slope 109

Hole	10	11	12	13	14	15	16	17	18	In		Totals
BLUE											BLUE	6630
WHITE											WHITE	6340
Par											Par	72
Handicap												
RED											RED	4820
Par											Par	72
Handicap												

Manager/Pro: Frank Distel   **Supt:** Eric Toggle
Architect: Tom Davenport 1969

TWAALFSKILL GOLF CLUB

282 W. O'Reilly St., Kingston, NY 12401   (914) 331-5577

Twaalfskill is a private 9 hole course open all year 7 days a week, weather permitting. Guests play accompanied by a member. Out of town memberships are offered at reduced rates. Tee time reservations are not necessary.

•Driving Range	•Lockers
•Practice Green	•Showers
•Power Carts	•Food
Pull Carts	•Clubhouse
•Club Rental	•Outings
Caddies	Soft Spikes

Course Description: Originally established in 1873 as Marsfield, an all male club, this hilly course is designed in a links style following the contours of the land. Well seasoned small greens are fast with lots of break. Water is in play on 3 holes. The signature par 3 # 3 is the "toughest in Ulster". The green is severely sloped back to front and traps are positioned on both sides. There are 2 sets of tees on 6 holes to provide variety. The course is fairly narrow and has many uneven lies. Twaalfskill means twelve brooks. Gene Sarazen played here and Joe Lewis as well during his training.

Directions: Ulster County, #15
Take I-87 (NY Thruway) to Exit 19. Take Rte.587West to Broadway going straight. Make a right on W. O'Reilly to club on left.

Hole	1	2	3	4	5	6	7	8	9	Out	BLUE	Rating
BLUE												Slope
WHITE	332	125	220	236	578	170	424	316	391	2792		
Par	4	3	3	4	5	3	5	4	4	35	WHITE	Rating 67.9
Handicap	8	18	5	17	2	15	13	11	4			Slope 115
RED	315	125	195	212	514	137	294	255	386	2433		
Par	4	3	4	4	5	3	4	4	5	36	RED	Rating 72.8
Handicap	7	17	10	13	1	15	5	11	3			Slope 121

Hole	10	11	12	13	14	15	16	17	18	In		Totals
BLUE											BLUE	
WHITE	345	170	195	240	583	185	440	325	401	2884	WHITE	5676
Par	4	3	3	4	5	3	5	4	4	35	Par	70
Handicap	7	9	6	16	1	14	12	10	3			
RED	263	121	157	212	429	128	294	308	380	2292	RED	4725
Par	4	3	3	4	5	3	5	4	4	35	Par	71
Handicap	12	18	11	14	2	16	6	9	4			

Manager: Andrew Connors **Pro:** Rob Gutkin **Supt:** Rich Worth
Estab: 1873 **Redesign:** 1902

WALKER VALLEY GOLF CLUB

Route 52, PO Box169, Walker Valley, NY 12588   **(914) 744-2714**

Walker Valley is a 9 hole executive course open to the public 7 days a week and closed in the winter. Memberships are available. Tee time reservations are not necessary.

Driving Range	Lockers
Practice Green	Showers
Power Carts	•**Food**
•**Pull Carts**	Clubhouse
•**Club Rental**	•**Outings**

Fees	Weekday	Weekend
Daily	$8	$10
Seniors	$7	$10

Course Description: Walker Valley is a short executive course. It has 3 holes where water affects play. The greens were renovated by the present owners. They are fast with some break. The course is very flat and easy to walk and therefore popular with beginners and seniors. It is an excellent facility for working on your short game.

Directions: Ulster County, #16
Take Route 17 to Exit 119. Go right on Rte.302 for 10 miles and then left on Rte.52 for 4 miles to club on left. The course is 20 miles west of Newburgh.

Hole	1	2	3	4	5	6	7	8	9	Out	BLUE	Rating
BLUE												Slope
WHITE	237	251	171	198	108	106	100	238	250	1659		
Par	4	4	3	4	3	3	3	4	4	32	WHITE	Rating
Handicap												Slope
RED												
Par	5	5	4	5	4	3	3	5	5	39	RED	Rating
Handicap												Slope

Hole	10	11	12	13	14	15	16	17	18	In		Totals
BLUE											BLUE	
WHITE											WHITE	
Par											Par	
Handicap												
RED											RED	
Par											Par	
Handicap												

Manager/Pro: Rita and George Rhein **Supt:** George Rhein
Built: 1920s

WILTWYCK GOLF CLUB

404 Stewart Lane, Kingston, NY 12401   (914) 331-7878

Wiltwyck is an 18 hole private club open 7 days a week and closed 11/15-4/1. Guests play accompanied by a member. Tee time reservations are not necessary.

•Driving Range	•Lockers
•Practice Green	•Showers
•Power Carts	•Food
•Pull Carts	•Clubhouse
Club Rental	•Outings
Caddies	•Soft Spikes

Course Description: Before the NY Thruway took the property, Wiltwyck was a 9 hole course on the other side of the road. In 1955, Robert Trent Jones designed the new layout with a risk-reward philosophy. Mounding around the greens make the approach shot key to good scores. Water is in play on 5 holes. The greens are small, undulating and fast. Gently rolling hills and narrow fairways characterize this course. The par 4 #9, the signature hole, is a 429 dogleg right with OB left, water on the right and a pond in front of the green.

Directions: Ulster County, #17
Take NY Thruway(I-87) to Exit 19. Bear left at traffic circle and onto Washington Ave. Go 4 lights and turn right onto Lucas Ave. Club is 1 & 1/4 mile on left on Stewart Lane.

Hole	1	2	3	4	5	6	7	8	9	Out	BLUE	Rating 72.9
BLUE	420	498	392	401	197	362	569	182	429	3450		Slope 130
WHITE	407	488	377	390	190	345	553	168	426	3344		
Par	4	5	4	4	3	4	5	3	4	36	WHITE	Rating 71.6
Handicap	11	9	7	5	13	15	3	17	1			Slope 128
RED	340	479	362	349	150	286	469	149	411	2995		
Par	4	5	4	4	3	4	5	3	5	37	RED	Rating 72.7
Handicap	7	1	9	6	2	5	8	4	3			Slope 126
Hole	10	11	12	13	14	15	16	17	18	In		Totals
BLUE	427	153	508	349	400	425	182	545	413	3402	BLUE	6852
WHITE	413	143	500	334	389	380	168	512	392	3231	WHITE	6575
Par	4	3	5	4	4	4	3	5	4	36	Par	72
Handicap	4	18	6	16	2	10	14	8	12			
RED	396	105	390	317	287	326	157	485	260	2723	RED	5718
Par	5	3	5	4	4	4	3	5	4	37	Par	74
Handicap	4	18	6	8	10	12	16	2	14			

Manager: Jack Ruddick   **Pro:** Harvey Bostic, PGA   **Supt:** Paul Pritchard
Architect: Robert Trent Jones 1955   **Estab:** 1920s

WOODSTOCK GOLF CLUB

PRIVATE

Corner Rtes. 212 & 375, Woodstock, NY 12498 **(914) 679-2914**

Woodstock is a private 9 hole course open 7 days a week from April 1 to October 31. Tee times should be made for weekends & holidays. Guests may play accompanied by a member.

Driving Range	•**Lockers**
•**Practice Green**	•**Showers**
•**Power Carts**	•**Food**
•**Pull Carts**	•**Clubhouse**
•**Club Rental**	•**Outings**
Caddies	•**Soft Spikes**

Course Description: A challenging nine hole layout nestled in the heart of the Catskills, Woodstock is well watered and maintained. Narrow contoured fairways and an abundance of trees characterize this picturesque course. A stream and pond affect play on 5 holes. The bent grass greens are normal in size and speed and have some undulation. The Woodstock Open for pros and amateurs has been held here annually for the last 62 years. The scorecard below indicates "forward" and "back" tees.

Directions: Ulster County, #18
NYState Thruway to Exit #19; then take Rte. 28 North towards Pine Bush to Rte. 375 Woodstock. Go right for 2 miles to club at junction of Rtes. 375 & 212.

Hole	1	2	3	4	5	6	7	8	9	Out	BLUE	Rating
BLUE												Slope
WHITE	318	359	366	140	472	353	327	283	201	2819		
Par	4	4	4	3	5	4	4	4	3	35	WHITE	Rating 66.2
Handicap	13	1	7	17	9	11	3	15	5			Slope 115
RED	292	358	348	110	432	315	322	262	140	2579		
Par	4	4	4	3	5	4	4	4	3	35	RED	Rating 70.1
Handicap	17	1	13	11	3	7	5	15	9			Slope 122
Hole	10	11	12	13	14	15	16	17	18	In		Totals
BLUE											BLUE	
WHITE	301	310	350	172	453	335	340	266	191	2718	WHITE	5537
Par	4	4	4	3	5	4	4	4	3	35	Par	70
Handicap	16	10	8	6	14	12	2	16	18			
RED	292	306	348	110	432	315	322	262	135	2522	RED	5101
Par	4	4	4	3	5	4	4	4	3	35	Par	70
Handicap	8	4	14	12	6	10	2	16	18			

Manager/Supt: Elizabeth Spinelli   **Pro:** Ken LaFave, PGA
Architect: Ralph Twitchell 1929

SULLIVAN COUNTY

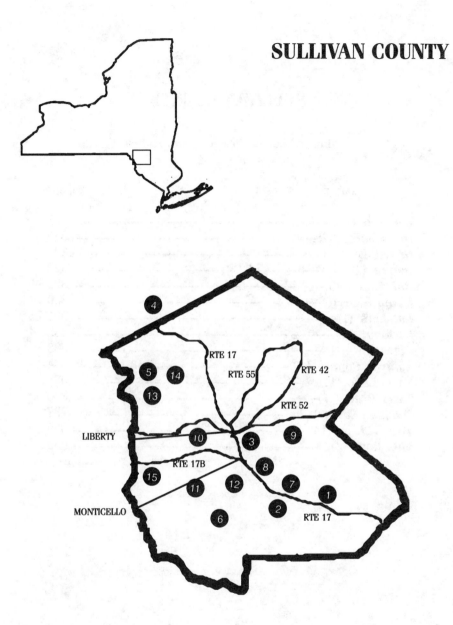

RTE 17
RTE 55
RTE 42
RTE 52
LIBERTY
RTE 17B
MONTICELLO
RTE 17

SULLIVAN COUNTY

Public Courses appear in *bold italics*

CONCORD GOLF CLUB

Concord Rd., Kiamesha Lake, NY 12751

(914) 794-4000
Ext. 3324

The Concord Resort has two 18 hole courses and the 9 hole Challenger, all open 7 days a week and closed 11/1-4/1. There are twilight packages during midweek. Tee times may be made in advance with credit card to hold reservations. Cart req'd on Monster.

- •Driving Range
- •Practice Green
- •Power Carts
- •Pull Carts
- •Club Rental
- •Lockers
- •Showers
- •Food
- •Clubhouse
- •Outings

Fees	Weekday	Weekend
Monster	$80	$90
Intnl.	$50	$55
Challenger	$20	$20

Course Description: Playing the "Monster", built to be a championship course, is a most memorable experience. It is famous for its length, beauty and difficult drives. The large greens are undulating and somewhat fast. The 4th is a long par 5 dogleg uphill with a lake in play. The International, an enjoyable inland mountain layout, has fast bent grass greens in excellent condition. The signature #11 features an elevated tee with a magnificent panoramic view. The contour of the sloping greens dictates that a prudent approach shot land below the hole. The scorecard below is for the "Monster."

Directions: Sullivan County, #1
Take Route 17North to Exit 105B in Monticello. Make right onto Rte. 42North and follow signs to Resort.

Hole	1	2	3	4	5	6	7	8	9	Out	BLUE	Rating 76.4
BLUE	555	458	467	610	224	380	231	443	442	3810		Slope 142
WHITE	522	421	427	585	207	361	216	423	428	3590		
Par	5	4	4	5	3	4	3	4	4	36	WHITE	Rating 74.1
Handicap	13	3	1	9	15	17	5	11	7			Slope 137
RED	386	306	281	396	160	283	149	335	347	2643		
Par	5	4	4	5	3	4	3	4	4	36	RED	Rating 78.5
Handicap												Slope 144

Hole	10	11	12	13	14	15	16	17	18	In		Totals
BLUE	416	198	529	392	177	481	572	420	476	3661	BLUE	7471
WHITE	352	160	515	364	159	440	555	405	449	3399	WHITE	6989
Par	4	3	5	4	3	4	5	4	4	36	Par	72
Handicap	10	16	8	14	18	6	12	2	4			
RED	286	112	374	312	135	302	416	321	300	2558	RED	5201
Par	4	3	5	4	3	4	5	4	4	36	Par	72
Handicap												

Dir. of Golf: Jim Parker   **Pro:** Jan Urso, PGA   **Supt:** Arthur Chandler
Architects: Joe Finger 1962 Alfred Tull 1949

FORESTBURGH COUNTRY CLUB

Tannery Rd., Forestburgh, NY 12777   **(914) 794-6542**

Forestburgh is an 18 hole semi-private course open 7 days a week and closed 12/1-4/1. Memberships are available. Tee time reservations may be made several days in advance.

• Driving Range	• Lockers
• Practice Green	• Showers
• Power Carts	• Food
• Pull Carts	• Clubhouse
• Club Rental	• Outings
• Soft Spikes	

Fees	M-Thurs	Fri-Sun
Daily	$44	$52
Sr/Jr	$36	$30
9 holes	$28	$34
Cart	$22	$22

Course Description: Forestburgh is cut through the woods and rock to conform to USGA specifications for an 18 hole layout. With 3-5 sets of tees, many elevated, all levels of golfers are challenged here. 7 ponds and 2 streams affect play on this recently completed heavily treed golf course. The greens are large and undulating. The first hole has a daunting tee shot over water. The driving range allows for 350 yard drives. When visiting the course, we were informed that the rating for Blue was the same for the other tees as well.

Directions: Sullivan County, #2
Rte.17 to Exit 105A. Take Rte.42 South for 7 miles. 1 block before the firehouse turn right on Tannery Rd. to club.

Hole	1	2	3	4	5	6	7	8	9	Out	BLUE	Rating 72.3
BLUE	350	500	144	350	190	405	500	347	495	3281		Slope 140
WHITE	334	476	138	329	179	389	485	326	477	3133		
Par	4	5	3	4	3	4	5	4	4	36	WHITE	Rating
Handicap	8	4	18	3	10	6	11	12	1			Slope
RED	298	359	133	297	119	283	444	285	432	2650		
Par	4	4	3	4	3	4	5	4	5	36	RED	Rating
Handicap												Slope
Hole	10	11	12	13	14	15	16	17	18	In		Totals
BLUE	500	390	187	470	433	310	250	370	490	3400	BLUE	6681
WHITE	480	370	162	444	373	285	230	345	410	3099	WHITE	6232
Par	5	4	3	4	4	4	3	4	5	36	Par	72
Handicap	14	5	16	9	7	17	2	15	13			
RED	365	350	137	435	329	200	180	303	384	2683	RED	5333
Par	5	4	3	5	4	4	3	4	4	36	Par	72
Handicap												

Manager/Supt: Paul Han   **Pro:** John Yeong, PGA
Architect: William Mitchell 1996

GROSSINGERS COUNTRY CLUB

26 Route 52 East, Liberty, NY 12754   **(914) 292-9002**

Grossingers has 27 holes, a championship 18 hole course, Lake & Valley, and the 9 hole Vista, where pull carts are allowed. It is open 7 days a week and closed 11/1-4/17. Tee time reservations may be made up to 30 days in advance.

- **Driving Range**
- **Practice Green**
- **Power Carts**
- **Pull Carts**
- **Club Rental**
- **Lockers**
- **Showers**
- **Food**
- **Clubhouse**
- **Outings**

Fees	Weekday	Weekend
Daily	$45	$60
Twi (4PM)	$40	$50
Power carts	$15	$15

Course Description: The plush conditions make it a pleasure to play this magnificent championship course, built in 1970. The steep rolling fairways on the Valley and Lake nines offer variety and challenge as well as beautiful views. The Vista course was part of the original hotel. On Lake and Valley, the medium to large greens are fairly fast with slight breaks; it is important to land below the hole. The signature par 5 13th features an elevated tee and a lake along the left to essentially an island green. The NY State Open was held here from 1978-1988. The scorecard below is for the Valley and Lake nines.

Directions: Sullivan County, #3
Rte.17West to Exit 100, Liberty. Go left off exit ramp and proceed through light to Country Club straight ahead.

Hole	1	2	3	4	5	6	7	8	9	Out	BLUE	Rating 73.5
BLUE	441	392	472	529	185	418	219	383	443	3482		Slope 134
WHITE	428	360	455	485	170	397	192	360	412	3259		
Par	4	4	5	5	3	4	3	4	4	36	WHITE	Rating 71.7
Handicap	4	8	5	3	9	2	7	7	1			Slope 133
RED	415	330	424	454	152	380	165	348	390	3058		
Par	5	4	5	5	3	4	3	4	5	38	RED	Rating 74.3
Handicap	3	7	2	1	9	4	8	6	5			Slope 133

Hole	10	11	12	13	14	15	16	17	18	In		Totals
BLUE	368	164	470	512	432	406	502	171	332	3357	BLUE	6839
WHITE	362	143	445	495	412	386	485	152	317	3197	WHITE	6456
Par	4	3	4	5	4	4	5	3	4	36	Par	72
Handicap	7	9	1	4	2	3	5	8	6			
RED	330	128	365	380	377	356	465	131	285	2817	RED	5875
Par	4	3	4	5	5	4	5	3	4	37	Par	75
Handicap	6	9	1	3	2	4	5	8	7			

Supt: Mike McNamara
Architects: *Vista* Andrew Salerno 1928 Joe Finger, William Mitchell 1970

HANAH COUNTRY CLUB

Route 30, Margaretville, NY 12455　　　**(914) 586-4849**

Hanah is an 18 hole course open to the public 7 days a week and closed 11/15 to 4/15. It is located in a Spa Resort. Many golf packages are available. Tee time reservations may be made up to 2 weeks in advance. Pull carts are allowed after 3:30PM.

•Driving Range	•Lockers
•Practice Green	•Showers
•Power Carts	•Food
•Pull Carts	•Clubhouse
•Club Rental	•Outings
•Soft Spikes	

Fees	Weekday	Weekend
18 holes	$40	$50
9 hole	$25	$30
Twi (3:30)	$30	$35
Power carts / included		

Course Description: Formerly Kass's Inn, Hanah CC is called the home of the "Terminator" referring to the last 5 holes. The 14th is a very long par 5, the 15th has a narrow fairway with a river on the left and a pond on the right. The par 4 signature 17th requires a tee shot over a pond to a small landing area; too long a drive can find another pond, a hook encounters a creek. The new ownership has redesigned this course to make it much longer and are adding 9 holes. Bent grass from tee to green, the front is somewhat wide open; the 10th through 13th are up and down doglegs with pretty scenery. In addition, the entire lodging operation is being redone. A major practice facility and Golf School are part of the upgraded Hanah CC.

Directions: Delaware County, #4
Take Rte.87 to Exit 19(Kingston). Then take Rte.28W to Margaretville. Go right onto Rte.30N to hotel and club on left.

Hole	1	2	3	4	5	6	7	8	9	Out	BLUE	Rating 73.5
BLUE	429	470	199	511	380	391	257	587	479	3703		Slope 133
WHITE	346	349	168	485	341	351	169	570	450	3229		
Par	4	4	3	5	4	4	3	5	4	36	WHITE	Rating 70.0
Handicap	17	7	5	9	11	15	13	3	1			Slope 126
RED	291	291	107	440	275	288	160	482	385	2719		
Par	4	4	3	5	4	4	3	5	4	36	RED	Rating 69.7
Handicap	17	7	5	9	11	15	13	3	1			Slope 123
Hole	10	11	12	13	14	15	16	17	18	In		Totals
BLUE	145	341	330	347	598	446	186	414	523	3330	BLUE	7033
WHITE	140	330	324	321	561	329	176	390	513	3084	WHITE	6313
Par	3	4	4	4	5	4	3	4	5	36	Par	72
Handicap	18	10	16	14	4	6	12	2	8			
RED	96	200	267	258	460	301	100	283	441	2406	RED	5125
Par	3	4	4	4	5	4	3	4	5	36	Par	72
Handicap	18	10	16	14	4	6	12	2	8			

Manager: Hide Kiyono　　**Pros:** Bill Barkley, Mike Granick, PGA　**Supt:** Bill Ross
Architect: Redesign: Fred Garvin 1992

HUFF HOUSE

100 Lake Anawanda Rd., Roscoe, NY 12776 **(607) 498-9953**

Huff House is a 9 hole course open to the public 7 days a week from 5/1-11/1. The complex includes a New England style inn built in 1889 and cottages. Although busy on weekends, tee time reservations are not necessary.

•**Driving Range**	Lockers
•**Practice Green**	Showers
•**Power Carts**	•**Food**
•**Pull Carts**	Clubhouse
•**Club Rental**	Outings

Fees	Weekday	Weekend
Daily	$10	$12
Power carts	$7/9	$12/18

Course Description: Huff House is an executive type short course, easy to walk. It is excellent for short game practice and for improving finesse. The emphasis here is on the golf school. The PGA recognizes the hotel as a par 3 learning center. The teaching facility includes a 60 ft. rain shield at the driving range, one flat putting green and another with sand traps for chipping and flop shot practice. There are packages for 3 day, 5 day, mid-week and weekend schools with a stay at this charming well restored Victorian Inn where the food quality is highly reputed.

Directions: Sullivan County, #5
NY thruway (I-87) to Exit 16. Take Rte.17West to Exit 94, Roscoe. Turn left at STOP, then turn left at light. Turn right at STOP and follow signs for Huff House about 6 miles.

Hole	1	2	3	4	5	6	7	8	9	Out	BLUE	Rating
BLUE												Slope
WHITE	95	110	115	130	100	110	95	85	165	1005		
Par	3	3	3	3	3	3	3	3	3	27	WHITE	Rating
Handicap	9	3	5	2	6	4	7	8	1			Slope
RED												
Par	3	3	3	4	4	3	3	3	4	30	RED	Rating
Handicap												Slope
Hole	10	11	12	13	14	15	16	17	18	In		Totals
BLUE											BLUE	
WHITE											WHITE	2010
Par											Par	54
Handicap												
RED											RED	2010
Par											Par	60
Handicap												

Manager/Supt: Joe Forness   **Dir. of Golf:** Steve Eisenberg, PGA
Architect: Joe Forness 1955

ISLAND GLEN COUNTRY CLUB

Box 4, Route 17B, Bethel, NY 12720   **(914) 583-1010**

Island Glen is a regulation 9 hole course open to the public 7 days a week and closed 10/31-5/1. Memberships are available. Tee times may be made 24 hours in advance.

Driving Range	• Lockers
• Practice Green	• Showers
• Power Carts	• Food
• Pull Carts	• Clubhouse
• Club Rental	• Outings

Fees	Weekday	Weekend
9 holes	$7	$11
18 "	$11	$15
Power carts	$6/9	$10/18

Course Description: Island Glen is known as the "Barn Course". The signature par 4 4th requires a hit over a barn in the fairway to land in the middle of the green. This facility is popular with beginner and intermediate players as a good place for practice and for youngsters trying to improve their game. The recently renovated greens are in good condition; they are fast, of average size and sloped. New bunkers on fairways and around greens were installed in 1997. Streams and ponds on the course affect play.

Directions: Sullivan County, #6
Take Rte17W to Exit 104. Go west on 17B approximately 11 miles to course on right.

Hole	1	2	3	4	5	6	7	8	9	Out	BLUE	Rating
BLUE												Slope
WHITE	345	465	165	350	340	420	300	460	155	3000		
Par	4	5	3	4	4	4	4	5	3	36	WHITE	Rating
Handicap	5	1	8	4	6	3	7	2	9			Slope 113
RED												
Par											RED	Rating
Handicap												Slope

Hole	10	11	12	13	14	15	16	17	18	In		Totals
BLUE											BLUE	
WHITE											WHITE	3000
Par											Par	72
Handicap												
RED											RED	
Par											Par	72
Handicap												

Manager: Ed McCormick   **Pro:** Alfred De Gaetano, PGA   **Supt:** Lee Willard
Built: 1972

KUTSHERS COUNTRY CLUB

Kutshers Rd., Monticello, NY 12701   **(914) 794-6000**

Kutshers is a resort hotel with an 18 hole course open 7 days a week and closed from 10/15-4/15. Hotel guests may make tee times well in advance, non-guests 3 days. The fees are discounted for guests and golf packages are available.

•**Driving Range**	•**Lockers**
•**Practice Green**	•**Showers**
•**Power Carts**	•**Food**
Pull Carts	•**Clubhouse**
•**Club Rental**	•**Outings**

Fees	Weekday	Weekend
Daily	$25	$30
Power carts	$30	$30

Course Description: Golfers never get tired of playing this mountainous challenging course. It is moderately long with large ponds in play on five holes. With many elevated greens and tees, sloping tree-lined fairways, and many uneven lies, every club in your bag will probably be used. The average size greens are fast in summer, have subtle undulations and are true. The second hole plays very long with a slope to the right into the woods. The par 4 13th signature features an elevated tee and a large body of water on the left culminating in a narrow fairway to an uphill green guarded by several traps.

Directions: Sullivan County, #7
Rte.17 to Exit 105B. At first light make left. Go 3 miles to Kutsher Rd and make a left. Course and hotel are 1/4 mile up on the right.

Hole	1	2	3	4	5	6	7	8	9	Out	BLUE	Rating 74.3
BLUE	415	460	168	415	425	575	220	415	520	3613		Slope 126
WHITE	395	440	148	385	405	545	200	390	495	3403		
Par	4	4	3	4	4	5	3	4	5	36	WHITE	Rating 72.0
Handicap	13	1	17	9	5	3	15	7	11			Slope 122
RED	360	385	103	340	360	495	140	370	435	2986		
Par	4	4	3	4	4	5	3	4	5	36	RED	Rating 73.3
Handicap												Slope 124
Hole	10	11	12	13	14	15	16	17	18	In		Totals
BLUE	362	378	535	455	188	455	220	370	425	3388	BLUE	7001
WHITE	345	340	490	412	158	425	175	357	405	3107	WHITE	6510
Par	4	4	5	4	3	4	3	4	4	36	Par	72
Handicap	10	8	12	2	18	4	16	14	6			
RED	305	303	445	360	120	360	135	300	360	2688	RED	5676
Par	4	4	5	4	3	4	3	4	4	36	Par	72
Handicap												

Manager: Harry Sperling   **Pro:** Terence Hughes, PGA   **Supt:** Pat McNamara
Architect: William Mitchell 1958

LOCHMOR GOLF COURSE

Route 104, Loch Sheldrake, NY 12759   **(914) 434-9079**

Lochmor is a Town of Fallsburg 18 hole course open 7 days a week and closed 11/1-4/1. In Oct., weekends only. Memberships are available. For tee times, call Wed. for Sat. and Thurs. for Sun. Mon-Thurs $22 with cart after 1PM.

•**Driving Range**	Lockers
•**Practice Green**	Showers
•**Power Carts**	•**Food**
•**Pull Carts**	Clubhouse
•**Club Rental**	•**Outings**

Fees	Weekday	Weekend
18 holes	$18	$23
9 holes	$11	$15
Twi	$9	$12
Power carts	$26	$26

Course Description: Lochmor is a somewhat hilly course that is easily walkable. The classic front nine has open approaches to the small greens. The back plays longer and is more difficult requiring more carry to the greens which are small with some break. Water is in play on a few holes. The picturesque par 5 #15 signature borders the lake on the left with a forced carry to the green.

Directions: Sullivan County, #8
Take NY Thruway (I-87) to Exit 16. then take Rte.17 to Exit 105B. Go left at light. Follow signs for 8 miles towards Loch Sheldrake to course.

Hole	1	2	3	4	5	6	7	8	9	Out	BLUE	Rating 69.4
BLUE	325	361	381	210	445	450	378	387	165	3102		Slope 117
WHITE	310	354	375	203	430	440	370	380	158	3020		
Par	4	4	4	3	4	5	4	4	3	35	WHITE	Rating 68.3
Handicap	17	11	13	5	3	7	9	1	15			Slope 115
RED	222	300	317	138	402	315	300	340	128	2462		
Par	4	4	4	3	4	5	4	4	3	35	RED	Rating 69.6
Handicap	16	12	6	18	14	2	8	4	10			Slope 116
Hole	10	11	12	13	14	15	16	17	18	In		Totals
BLUE	279	211	578	157	415	473	406	415	390	3324	BLUE	6426
WHITE	274	203	522	147	409	465	397	395	335	3147	WHITE	6167
Par	4	3	5	3	4	5	4	4	4	36	Par	71
Handicap	18	10	4	16	6	12	8	2	14			
RED	247	154	446	118	309	341	367	365	320	2667	RED	5129
Par	4	3	5	3	4	5	4	4	4	36	Par	71
Handicap	13	15	1	17	5	7	9	3	11			

Manager/Pro: Glenn Sonnenschein, PGA   **Supt:** Billy Hannole
Architect: William Mitchell 1958

THE PINES GOLF COURSE

PUBLIC

Laurel Ave., So. Fallsburg, NY 12779 **(914) 434-6000**

The Pines Hotel course is 9 holes and open 7 days a week from 4/15-11/15. Memberships are available. Hotel guests get a discount. Tee times may be made up to 3 days in advance at extension 1584.

Driving Range	Lockers
•Practice Green	Showers
•Power Carts	•Food
•Pull Carts	Clubhouse
•Club Rental	•Outings

Fees	Weekday	Weekend
Daily	$10	$12
Guests	$8	$8
Twi 3PM	$7	$7
Power carts	$12/9	$24/18

Course Description: This rather wide open Robert Trent Jones design is well bunkered with fairly large fast greens that are tough to read. The course is tree-lined along the left side; the fairways are semi hilly resulting in many uneven lies. Water is in play on 2 holes. The par 4 6th is the most difficult featuring a dogleg left and a severely sloped fairway that causes trouble. The approach shot must find its target, a well-bunkered green.

Directions: Sullivan County, #9
Rte.17 To Exit 107. Go to 2nd blinker & turn right onto Rte.42. At 2nd light(theatre) turn left. Golf course is 1/2 mile on right after the hotel.

Hole	1	2	3	4	5	6	7	8	9	Out	BLUE	Rating
BLUE												Slope
WHITE	340	135	410	280	115	375	275	210	190	2330		
Par	4	3	4	4	3	4	4	3	3	32	WHITE	Rating 30.1
Handicap	5	17	1	11	15	3	9	7	13			Slope 102
RED	324	103	310	240	87	269	250	178	164	1925		
Par	4	3	4	4	3	4	4	3	3	32	RED	Rating
Handicap	5	17	1	11	15	3	9	7	13			Slope 101

Hole	10	11	12	13	14	15	16	17	18	In		Totals
BLUE											BLUE	
WHITE											WHITE	4660
Par											Par	64
Handicap												
RED											RED	3850
Par											Par	64
Handicap												

Manager/Pro: Tom Duplessis, PGA   **Supt:** Terry McNamara
Architect: Robert Trent Jones

SULLIVAN COUNTY GOLF & CC

Route 52, Liberty , NY 12754   **(914) 292-9584**

The 9 hole Sullivan County course is open to the public 7 days a week and closed 11/1-4/15. Memberships are available. Tee time reservations are not necessary.

Driving Range	•**Lockers**
•**Practice Green**	Showers
•**Power Carts**	•**Food**
•**Pull Carts**	•**Clubhouse**
•**Club Rental**	•**Outings**

Fees	Weekday	Weekend
Daily	$12	$20
Twi (5PM)	$7	(2PM) $12
Power carts	$12/9	$20/18

Course Description: With views of the mountains in the distance, Sullivan County has generally wide open fairways. It is hilly enough so that many choose to ride but it is walkable. The greens are fairly small with some break. Water is in play on five holes. The most difficult is the par 4 #3 with a right to left sloping fairway. In dry months, it is important to bear right skirting the trees to stay in the fairway when the ball finally comes to rest.

Directions: Sullivan County, #10
Take Rte.17West to Exit 100 (Liberty). Make left off ramp and go straight on Route 52. In Liberty, make left at light on Chestnut to club on right.

Hole	1	2	3	4	5	6	7	8	9	Out	BLUE	Rating
BLUE												Slope
WHITE	315	295	400	152	280	275	422	545	395	3079		
Par	4	4	4	3	4	4	4	5	4	36	WHITE	Rating 69.5
Handicap	9	11	1	15	13	17	7	5	3			Slope 120
RED	315	295	400	152	280	275	422	397	395	2931		
Par	4	4	5	3	4	4	5	5	5	39	RED	Rating 73.5
Handicap	9	11	3	17	13	15	7	1	5			Slope 125T
Hole	**10**	**11**	**12**	**13**	**14**	**15**	**16**	**17**	**18**	**In**		**Totals**
BLUE											BLUE	
WHITE	305	280	515	152	285	275	402	397	395	3006	WHITE	6085
Par	4	4	4	3	4	4	4	5	4	36	Par	72
Handicap	10	12	2	16	14	18	8	6	4			
RED	305	280	400	152	285	275	402	397	395	2891	RED	5822
Par	4	4	5	3	4	4	5	5	5	39	Par	78
Handicap	10	12	4	18	14	16	8	2	6			

Manager/Pro: Greg Rohrback, PGA   **Supt:** Gene Eck
Architect: A. W. Tillinghast 1925

SWAN LAKE GOLF & CC

Mt. Hope Rd., Swan Lake, NY 12783   **(914) 292-0748**

Swan Lake is an 18 hole course open to the public 7 days a week and closed Nov. 1-
Apr. 1. Memberships are available. Tee times may be made up to 2 weeks in advance.

•**Driving Range**	•**Lockers**
•**Practice Green**	•**Showers**
•**Power Carts**	•**Food**
•**Pull Carts**	•**Clubhouse**
•**Club Rental**	•**Outings**
•**Soft Spikes**	

Fees	Weekday	Weekend
Daily 9	$15	$20
18	$20	$30
Twi (4PM)	$20	$30/cart
Power carts	$15/9	$20/18

Course Description: Swan Lake is nestled in the Catskill Mountains and is hilly and scenic. This well maintained course has open fairways characterized by uneven lies. Water is in play on 2 holes. The large greens are undulating; a few are two tiered and require careful approach shots so that you avoid landing above the hole. Some tees and greens are elevated.

Directions: Sullivan County, #11
NY Thruway(I-87) to Exit 16. Take Rte.17West to Exit 101. Take Rte.55 to Mt. Hope Rd. and turn right to course.

Hole	1	2	3	4	5	6	7	8	9	Out	BLUE	Rating 71.8
BLUE	412	398	477	403	385	209	512	409	180	3385		Slope 132
WHITE	383	370	441	378	348	174	479	371	150	3094		
Par	4	4	5	4	4	3	5	4	3	36	WHITE	Rating 69.0
Handicap	5	11	1	15	9	13	7	3	17			Slope 122
RED	356	318	374	316	315	138	419	334	115	2685		
Par	4	4	5	4	4	3	5	4	3	36	RED	Rating 70.2
Handicap												Slope 118
Hole	10	11	12	13	14	15	16	17	18	In		Totals
BLUE	418	182	516	400	375	399	196	537	412	3435	BLUE	6820
WHITE	391	148	489	356	343	369	179	472	380	3127	WHITE	6221
Par	4	3	5	4	4	4	3	5	4	36	Par	72
Handicap	6	18	12	2	14	4	16	8	10			
RED	343	106	444	310	298	310	123	396	324	2654	RED	5339
Par	4	3	5	4	4	4	3	5	4	36	Par	72
Handicap												

Manager: Song Cha Gallo   **Supt**: John Sundholm
Built: 1950s

TARRY BRAE GOLF COURSE

Pleasant Valley Rd., So. Fallsburg, NY 12779   (914) 434-2620

Tarry Brae is an 18 hole town course open 7 days a week and closed in winter. There are memberships available and special discounts for residents. Tee time reservations may be made Wed. for Sat. and Thurs. for Sun. Carts mandatory weekends until 1PM.

•Driving Range	Lockers
•Practice Green	Showers
•Power Carts	•Food
•Pull Carts	Clubhouse
•Club Rental	•Outings

Fees	Weekday	Weekend
18 holes	$18	$25
9 holes	$11	$16
Twi	$9	$12
Power carts	$26	$26

Course Description: Tarry Brae is a scenic hilly course with narrow tree-lined fairways and many uneven lies. It features well bunkered greens that are difficult to read, and some have considerable break. Water is in play on 2 holes. The par 4s provide variety, a need to use all your clubs. The par 3s are very challenging. The signature par 4 #8 is narrow with sand traps on both sides of the landing area. The golfer then faces a difficult uphill approach to a sloped green. The 18th hole is a long, tough and memorable finishing hole. After 1PM Mon-Thurs., the price is $22 per person with a cart.

Directions: Sullivan County, #12
Take Thruway (I-87) to Exit 16. Take Rte.17W to Exit 107. Go about 4 miles and make right onto Rte.42 to So. Fallsburg (about 2 miles). Turn left onto Pleasant Valley Rd. Proceed about 2 miles to course on left.

Hole	1	2	3	4	5	6	7	8	9	Out	BLUE	Rating 73.4
BLUE	412	396	441	206	391	477	184	415	525	3447		Slope 129
WHITE	380	353	387	188	337	445	167	368	474	3099		
Par	4	4	4	3	4	5	3	4	5	36	WHITE	Rating 70.3
Handicap	6	4	12	8	11	18	14	1	10			Slope 126
RED	337	335	359	155	310	397	154	345	448	2840		
Par	4	5	4	3	4	5	3	5	5	38	RED	Rating 72.2
Handicap	6	4	12	8	11	18	14	1	10			Slope 126
Hole	10	11	12	13	14	15	16	17	18	In		Totals
BLUE	496	200	382	430	380	383	419	217	534	3441	BLUE	6888
WHITE	435	177	365	402	351	360	387	194	500	3171	WHITE	6270
Par	5	3	4	4	4	4	4	3	5	36	Par	72
Handicap	17	7	15	2	9	13	3	16	5			
RED	416	144	330	343	327	329	349	148	384	2768	RED	5610
Par	5	3	4	5	4	4	5	3	5	38	Par	76
Handicap	17	7	15	2	9	13	3	16	5			

Manager/Pro: Glenn Sonnenschein, PGA   **Supt:** Richie Farquhar
Architect: William Mitchell 1958

TENNANAH LAKE GOLF CLUB

PUBLIC

100 Belle Rd., Roscoe, NY 12776

(914) 794-2900
(607) 498-5502

Known as Tennanah Lake Golf & Tennis Club, this is an 18 hole semi-private facility open 7 days a week and closed 11/15-4/15. Resort memberships and golf packages for motel guests are available. Tee times may be made up to 3 weeks in advance.

• Driving Range	Lockers
• Practice Green	Showers
• Power Carts	• Food
• Pull Carts	• Clubhouse
• Club Rental	• Outings
• Soft Spikes	

Fees	M-Thurs	Fri-Sun
Resident	$28	$32
Sr/Motel	$24	$28
Twi (5)/cart	$28	$28
Power carts	$28/2	$18/1

Course Description: The redesign by Sam Snead at Tennanah Lake made the yardages longer and added 9 more holes. The undulating greens are postage stamp sized and moderately fast. The fairways are narrow with differing topography and many doglegs. Woods separate each hole. The signature par 4 6th features a narrow chute tee shot, a huge tree on the right guarding the landing area and bunkers on either side of the fairway. A stream running across and up and down the terrain give challenge with the difficulty continuing due to a troubling hazard over the green. The John Jacobs Golf School has a separate teaching facility here as well.

Directions: Sullivan County, #13
Rte.17 West to Exit 94. Left at STOP. Proceed 200 yards to light &: make left for 1000 yds and at T, turn right. Then go about 4 miles and course is ahead on the right.

Hole	1	2	3	4	5	6	7	8	9	Out	BLUE	Rating 73.7
BLUE	355	554	386	200	362	416	485	340	190	3288		Slope 132
WHITE	345	544	365	192	355	400	446	328	181	3156		
Par	4	5	4	3	4	4	5	4	3	36	WHITE	Rating 71.9
Handicap	16	8	6	12	4	2	14	10	18			Slope 128
RED	333	517	336	172	335	344	406	293	135	2871		
Par	4	5	4	3	4	4	5	4	3	36	RED	Rating 74.9
Handicap	16	8	6	12	4	2	14	10	18			Slope 131
Hole	10	11	12	13	14	15	16	17	18	In		Totals
BLUE	392	195	505	332	557	433	432	205	430	3481	BLUE	6769
WHITE	382	154	485	300	494	402	403	174	420	3214	WHITE	6370
Par	4	3	5	4	5	4	4	3	4	36	Par	72
Handicap	5	15	9	17	13	1	7	11	3			
RED	359	115	476	271	455	383	355	129	383	2926	RED	5797
Par	4	3	5	4	5	4	4	3	4	36	Par	72
Handicap	7	17	9	15	11	1	3	13	5			

Manager/Pro: Gregory Smith, PGA   **Supt:** Bruce Petrelli
Architect: Sam Snead 1952 **Estab:** 1912

TWIN VILLAGE GOLF CLUB

Rockland Rd., Roscoe, NY 12776 **(607) 498-9983**

Twin Village is a semi-private 9 hole course open to the public 7 days a week and closed in the winter. Memberships are available. Tee time reservations are not necessary.

Driving Range	•Lockers
Practice Green	Showers
•Power Carts	•Food
•Pull Carts	Clubhouse
•Club Rental	Outings

Fees	Weekday	Weekend
Resident	$11	$16
Twi (4PM)	$5.50	$8
Power carts	$9/9	$18/18

Course Description: Twin Village is a short, walkable course although somewhat hilly. The 4th is known as "heart attack hill." It is considered the signature, a par 3 with an elevated green. A brook crosses through the course and water is in play on several holes. The 9th is narrow off the tee to a fairway that has rough on one side and the brook on the other. The green is surrounded by sand traps. Twin Village has a very active Ladies League.

Directions: Sullivan County, #14
Take Rte.17W to Exit 94 and make left. Go straight on Rockland Rd (Rte.206) to course on right.

Hole	1	2	3	4	5	6	7	8	9	Out	BLUE	Rating
BLUE												Slope
WHITE	241	222	210	133	252	168	297	173	349	2045		
Par	4	4	3	3	4	3	4	3	4	32	WHITE	Rating 59.6
Handicap	15	17	1	5	13	7	11	9	3			Slope 94
RED	203	222	210	133	202	168	275	173	284	1870		
Par	4	4	4	3	4	3	4	3	4	33	RED	Rating 63.0
Handicap	9	7	17	3	15	13	5	11	1			Slope 96

Hole	10	11	12	13	14	15	16	17	18	In		Totals
BLUE											BLUE	
WHITE											WHITE	4090
Par											Par	64
Handicap												
RED											RED	3740
Par											Par	66
Handicap												

Manager: Casey Tallman **Supt:** Francis Temple
Built: 1925

VILLA ROMA RESORT

340 Villa Roma Rd., Callicoon, NY 12723   **(914) 887-5097**

Villa Roma is an 18 hole resort course open 7 days a week and closed 11/30-4/1. In addition to guests from the hotel, there is also a golf school and special golf packages. Non-guests may make tee times 24 hrs in advance. 9 hole & Sr. rates available.

•**Driving Range**	•**Lockers**
•**Practice Green**	•**Showers**
•**Power Carts**	•**Food**
Pull Carts	•**Clubhouse**
•**Club Rental**	•**Outings**
•**Soft Spikes**	

Fees	Weekday	Weekend
Guest	$44	$44
Non-guest	$48	$54
Twi (4PM)	$29	$10/9
Carts included		

Course Description: Villa Roma is a well maintained challenging course. Many very uneven lies confront the golfer as well as doglegs, elevated tees and greens. Water is in play with ponds and streams running throughout the hilly layout. New ponds have just been installed on the 8th and 10th. The greens are large, undulating and fast, making this 18 interesting and enjoyable. A straight shot off the tee is imperative here as the rough is very thick and lush. The surrounding mountains provide the back-drop for the beautiful scenic views, especially in the Fall. It has bent grass from tee to green.

Directions: Sullivan County, #15
Take the NY thruway (I-87) to Exit 16. Take Rte.17West to Exit 104. Follow Rte.17B for about 20 miles. Then follow signs to course.

Hole	1	2	3	4	5	6	7	8	9	Out	BLUE	Rating 70.6
BLUE	365	178	533	408	395	400	171	495	203	3148		Slope 125
WHITE	365	174	506	408	395	339	147	490	175	3000		
Par	4	3	5	4	4	4	3	5	3	35	WHITE	Rating 66.9
Handicap	11	15	1	7	3	5	17	9	13			Slope 118
RED	349	142	420	359	329	332	136	430	143	2640		
Par	4	3	5	4	4	4	3	5	3	35	RED	Rating 68.3
Handicap	9	15	1	5	3	11	17	7	13			Slope 117
Hole	10	11	12	13	14	15	16	17	18	In		Totals
BLUE	385	545	357	174	332	513	430	180	415	3331	BLUE	6479
WHITE	368	520	318	158	310	455	412	164	310	3015	WHITE	6015
Par	4	5	4	3	4	5	4	3	4	36	Par	71
Handicap	8	6	12	18	10	14	4	16	2			
RED	325	413	265	118	230	418	362	143	415	2689	RED	5329
Par	4	5	4	3	4	5	4	3	5	37	Par	72
Handicap	8	6	12	18	10	14	4	16	2			

Manager/Pro: Matt Kleiner, PGA   **Supt:** Steve Luty
Architect: David Postlethwaite 1988

Swan Lake Weather Report

If the rock is wet, it is raining

If the rock is hot, it is sunny

If the rock is white, it is snowing

If the rock is moving, it is windy

If the rock is cool, it is overcast

If the rock is gone, it is a tornado.

The meek may inherit the earth

But they'll never reach the green in two!

(Swan Lake)

NEW JERSEY UPDATE

THE NEWEST COURSES

NEW JERSEY UPDATE

Public Courses appear in **bold italics**

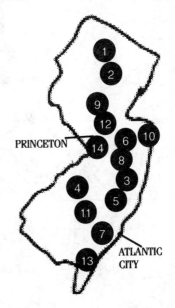

PRINCETON

ATLANTIC CITY

BALLYOWEN

Wheatsworth Rd., Hamburg, NJ 07419   **(973) 827-5996**

Ballyowen is a new 18 hole semi-private course open 7 days a week and closed in winter. Memberships are available that include playing privileges at Black Bear, Crystal Springs and the Spa. Tee time reservations are accepted up to 10 days in advance.

•Driving Range	•Lockers
•Practice Green	•Showers
•Power Carts	•Food
Pull Carts	•Clubhouse
•Club Rental	•Outings
•Soft Spikes	

Fees	Weekday	Weekend
Daily	$75	$100
Twi	$45	$65
Fees include power cart		

Course Description: With panoramic views of the Great Gorge area and the Appalachian Mountains, Ballyowen takes advantage of the unique natural landscape. The property was reclaimed from a former sand and gravel mine and is virtually treeless. Multiple tee locations give golfers of all skill levels a chance to enjoy this links-style layout. The architect specializes in environmentally sensitive design. The broad verdant rolling fairways, the bent grass greens, the wind shifts, and the wheat-like native grasses in the rough, make this new facility a unique and challenging attraction for the up-scale metropolitan area public golfer.

Directions: Sussex County, #1
Rte.80 West to Exit 53B. Take Rte.23N to Hamburg. Go left on Rte.94S for 2 mi to Wheatsworth Rd. Turn left and proceed 1 mi. to course on right.

Manager: Art Walton   **Pro:** Dave Glenz, PGA   **Supt:** Rich La Bar
Architect: Roger Rulewich 1998

BLACK BEAR GOLF & CC

138 Route 23 North, Franklin, NJ 07416   **(973) 209-2226**

Black Bear is a semi-private 18 hole golf course open the the public 7 days a week from March 1 to December 31. Bruin Club Memberships are available featuring reciprocity with Crystal Springs, The Spa and the new Ballyowen and all its practice facilities. Tee time reservations are required.

•**Driving Range**	•**Lockers**
•**Practice Green**	•**Showers**
•**Power Carts**	•**Food**
Pull Carts	•**Clubhouse**
•**Club Rental**	•**Outings**
•**Soft Spikes**	

Fees	Weekday	Weekend
Daily	$50	$65
Twilight	$29	$39
Power carts inc. in price		

Course Description: The 6,673 yard layout of Black Bear combines the spectacular beauty of the Great Gorge area with an array of amenities that rivals any golf facility in the Metropolitan area. There is a diversity of topography, an abundance of wildlife and remarkable scenery. It serves as the headquarters for the well known David Glenz Golf Academy which utilizes 100,000 square feet for instruction. With two distinct nines on 280 acres of a former farm, the front weaves in and out of forests and sloping terrain, while the back offers interesting mounding. The 11th and 16th cross over a large pond stocked with a variety of fish. Sussex County is becoming a mecca for golfers from near and far.

Directions: Sussex County, #2
Take Rte.80 West or East to Rte.23 North. Course is on the right 1/4 mile after the intersection of Rte. 631 in Franklin.

Hole	1	2	3	4	5	6	7	8	9	Out	BLUE	Rating 72.5
BLUE	369	484	422	396	185	535	193	311	420	3315		Slope 134
WHITE	349	451	394	386	158	500	142	295	400	3075		
Par	4	5	4	4	3	5	3	4	4	36	WHITE	Rating 69.7
Handicap	9	11	1	5	17	13	7	15	3			Slope 128
RED	240	382	329	310	120	437	122	251	305	2496		
Par	4	5	4	4	3	5	3	4	4	36	RED	Rating 68.9
Handicap	11	5	1	7	17	9	13	15	3			Slope 119
Hole	10	11	12	13	14	15	16	17	18	In		Totals
BLUE	360	143	370	528	154	255	480	357	372	3019	BLUE	6324
WHITE	335	123	350	496	137	230	455	340	342	2808	WHITE	5873
Par	4	3	4	5	3	4	5	4	4	36	Par	72
Handicap	8	18	4	2	16	14	12	6	10			
RED	266	103	335	366	111	164	380	267	297	2260	RED	4756
Par	4	3	4	5	3	4	5	4	4	36	Par	72
Handicap	12	18	4	2	16	14	6	10	8			

Manager/Pro: Jeffrey Miller, PGA   **Pro:** David Glenz, PGA   **Supt:** Eric Tomzic
Architects: Jack Kurlander, David Glenz 1996

CHARLESTON SPRINGS GOLF COURSE PUBLIC

Route. 527, Millstone Township, NJ 08535   (732) 842-4000

Charleston Springs will have 2 18 hole courses, a part of the Monmouth County Park System. The courses will be open 7 days a week and closed in winter. Residents may obtain Golf ID card for reduced rates and access to the automated tee time service.

•Driving Range	Lockers
•Practice Green	Showers
•Power Carts	•Food
•Pull Carts	•Clubhouse
•Club Rental	Outings

Fees	Weekday	Weekend
Res/ID	$18	$21
Non-res	$36	$41
Fees are approximate		

Course Description: Monmouth County is answering the golf needs of the community by building two new courses. In addition, they have recently purchased Bel-Aire, a 27 hole facility in Allenwood, to increase golfing opportunities. The North course at Charleston Springs is targeted to open in the Spring of 1999. It will be links-style, wide open with few trees and a variety of grasses. The South, for which ground has yet to be broken will be a more traditional, park style course. Non-county residents must purchase a Reservation Service Card to access automated tee time.

Directions: Monmouth County, #3
From Freehold, Take Rte.537 west to Smithburg Rd. (Rte. 527) and turn right. Proceed a mile to course on left.

Supt: Ron Luepke   **Architects:** Cornish, Silver & Mungeaum 1999

DEERWOOD COUNTRY CLUB

18 Deerwood Dr., Westhampton, NJ 08060   **(609) 265-1800**

Deerwood is an 18 hole semi-private course open 7 days a week, all year. Opened in 1996, it has memberships available. Tee times may be made up to 1 week in advance for members, 1 day for non-members.

- •**Driving Range**
- •**Practice Green**
- •**Power Carts**
- Pull Carts
- •**Club Rental**
- •**Soft Spikes**
- •**Lockers**
- •**Showers**
- •**Food**
- •**Clubhouse**
- •**Outings**

Fees	Weekday	Weekend
Daily	$63	$73
Fees include power cart		

Course Description: Deerwood can be deceptively difficult. This flat, intriguing course is generally wide open and features sculpted fairways with some minor mounding. A few holes on the back are in the woods where the drives necessitate more careful target positioning. Natural wild growth and fescue grass abound in the rough; an errant shot will either be lost or require a skillful short game in order to avoid a penalty. The excellently maintained greens are tricky and undulating, but true. The course is quite mature for its youth and provides a real private club atmosphere.

Directions: Burlington County, #4
Take NJTpke to Exit 5. Go right onto Rte.541S. At next light turn left onto Woodlane Rd. Club is 1/2 mile up on the left.

Hole	1	2	3	4	5	6	7	8	9	Out	BLUE	Rating 69.4
BLUE	380	383	365	136	465	350	513	209	334	3135		Slope 126
WHITE	371	369	349	130	436	325	481	197	323	2981		
Par	4	4	4	3	4	4	5	3	4	35	WHITE	Rating 67.9
Handicap	7	11	9	17	1	13	5	3	15			Slope 124
RED	316	273	294	114	367	294	405	131	267	2461		
Par	4	4	4	3	4	4	5	3	4	35	RED	Rating 67.2
Handicap	7	11	9	17	1	13	5	3	15			Slope 111
Hole	10	11	12	13	14	15	16	17	18	In		Totals
BLUE	375	368	176	139	398	310	398	556	376	3096	BLUE	6231
WHITE	364	330	164	130	380	287	383	546	363	2947	WHITE	5928
Par	4	4	3	3	4	4	4	5	4	35	Par	70
Handicap	10	12	16	18	4	14	8	2	6			
RED	300	303	137	118	221	224	311	441	291	2346	RED	4807
Par	4	4	3	3	4	4	4	5	4	35	Par	70
Handicap	10	12	16	18	4	14	8	2	6			

Manager: Steve Pasalaqua **Pro:** Greg Farrow, PGA **Supt:** Joel Collura
Architects: Dick Alaimo, Jim Blaukovitch 1996

FOUR SEASONS SPA & CC

1600 Spring Meadow Dr., Lakewood, NJ 08701   **(732) 477-8222**

Four Seasons is a 9 hole executive course within a private adult community. It is only available to residents and open 7 days a week in season. Tee time reservations are not necessary. Homes are situated along the fairways.

Driving Range	Lockers
•**Practice Green**	Showers
•**Power Carts**	Food
•**Pull Carts**	•**Clubhouse**
Club Rental	Outings
Caddies	Soft Spikes

Course Description: The par 30 executive course at Four Seasons will have a golf cart path winding throughout. The layout is shaped to suit the natural terrain, utilizing waste areas and sand and water as hazards confrontingthe golfer. The large bentgrass greens have some undulation. The 3rd gives the golfer the opportunity to use a driver for this 360 yard hole. The signature par 3 4th has an island-type green mostly surrounded by a lake. A short game practice area is available for the homeowners to enjoy.

Directions: Ocean County, #5
Take GSPkwy to Exit 88. Go East on Rte.70 and make a right on Shorrock. Pass Lions Head Woods and make a right on Four Seasons Dr. to Spring Meadow Dr. and Four Seasons Spa and Country Club.

Hole	1	2	3	4	5	6	7	8	9	Out	BLUE	Rating
BLUE												Slope
WHITE	140	135	320	130	266	146	120	300	92	1649		
Par	3	3	4	3	4	3	3	4	3	30	WHITE	Rating
Handicap	15	13	3	5	7	9	11	1	17			Slope
RED	114	95	283	120	223	120	100	256	82	1393		
Par	3	3	4	3	4	3	3	5	3	31	RED	Rating
Handicap												Slope

Hole	10	11	12	13	14	15	16	17	18	In		Totals
BLUE											BLUE	
WHITE											WHITE	
Par											Par	30
Handicap												
RED											RED	
Par											Par	31
Handicap												

Supt: Harry Leonard   **Built:** 1997

GREENBRIAR at WHITTINGHAM GC | PRIVATE

101 Whittingham Drive, Monroe Township 08831   **(609) 860-6621**

Greenbriar is a 9 hole private course open 7 days a week and closed in Jan. & Feb. Guests may play when accompanied by a member. It is necessary to make tee time reservations in advance.

Driving Range	•**Lockers**
•**Practice Green**	•**Showers**
•**Power Carts**	•**Food**
•**Pull Carts**	•**Clubhouse**
•**Club Rental**	Outings
Caddies	•**Soft Spikes**

Course Description: As part of an adult community, Greenbriar at Whittingham is a welcome addition to New Jersey golf. The lovely homes surrounding the course give it a character all its own. This well bunkered and mounded walkable layout is a good test of golf for the intermediate player. Water is in play on three holes. The par 5 eighth is 485 yards from the blues and goes through heavily wooded terrain. Busy in season, lucky are the residents who can play in their own backyard.

Directions: Middlesex County, #6
Take the NJ Tpke. to Exit #8A. Then go on Rte.32East (Forsgate Drive) to light. On Half Acre Road, turn right; entrance is on left and reads "Greenbriar at Whittingham."

Hole	1	2	3	4	5	6	7	8	9	Out	BLUE	Rating 68.2
BLUE	350	390	190	135	525	380	200	485	345	3000		Slope 118
WHITE	305	360	145	120	475	355	180	475	300	2715		
Par	4	4	4	3	5	4	3	5	4	35	WHITE	Rating 64.8
Handicap	13	1	11	17	5	3	9	7	15			Slope 108
RED	225	340	125	105	420	325	170	430	275	2415		
Par	4	4	4	3	5	4	3	5	4	35	RED	Rating 66.8
Handicap	13	5	15	17	3	7	9	1	11			Slope 110

Hole	10	11	12	13	14	15	16	17	18	In		Totals
BLUE											BLUE	6000
WHITE											WHITE	5430
Par											Par	70
Handicap												
RED											RED	4830
Par											Par	70
Handicap												

Manage/Pro: Pete Wyndorf, PGA   **Supt:** Harry Harsin
Architect: Brian Ault 1996

HARBOR PINES GOLF CLUB

500 St. Andrews Dr., Egg Harbor Twnshp., NJ 01234 **(609) 927-0006**

Harbor Pines is a semi-private 18 hole course open 7 days a week all year. Associate and corporate memberships are available. Tee times may be reserved up to 8 days in advance. Fees below include power cart. Twilight rates and timing vary with season.

- •Driving Range
- •Practice Green
- •Power Carts
- Pull Carts
- •Club Rental
- •Soft Spikes
- •Lockers
- •Showers
- •Food
- •Clubhouse
- •Outings

Fees	Weekday	Fri-Sun
5/2-10/12	$83	$95
3/17-5/1	$65	$75
12/1-12/31	$52	$52
Rest of year varies accordingly		

Course Description: Opened in the Spring of 1997, Harbor Pines is a relatively flat excellently maintained course that takes advantage of the surrounding beauty and landscape to provide an interesting experience for all levels of golfers. Set in a parkland, five sets of tees, strategically placed bunkers and 12 holes affected by water illustrate the variety of challenge offered here. The large greens are fast; the grass is tightly mown so that even the rough is short. The 9th fairway, sloping on both sides, has water on the left and woods on the right. The course is in the midst of an upscale development. The well stocked Pro Shop is a feature of the contemporary clubhouse.

Directions: Atlantic County, #7
Take GSPKwy South to Exit 29 and follow Rte.9North. At 6th light, about 3 miles, turn left onto Ocean Heights Ave. Proceed 1.6 miles to Harbor Pines.

Hole	1	2	3	4	5	6	7	8	9	Out	BLUE	Rating 72.3
BLUE	505	380	170	400	452	394	526	215	460	3502		Slope 129
WHITE	465	340	143	370	402	345	474	170	419	3128		
Par	5	4	3	4	4	4	5	3	4	36	WHITE	Rating 69.1
Handicap	15	9	17	5	3	7	13	11	1			Slope 122
RED	412	271	123	296	360	263	418	137	346	2626		
Par	5	4	3	4	4	4	5	3	4	36	RED	Rating 68.8
Handicap	9	11	17	7	1	13	5	15	3			Slope 118

Hole	10	11	12	13	14	15	16	17	18	In		Totals
BLUE	540	182	339	400	335	179	402	461	487	3325	BLUE	6827
WHITE	511	162	291	351	315	150	367	409	458	3014	WHITE	6142
Par	5	3	4	4	4	3	4	4	5	36	Par	72
Handicap	8	10	14	6	16	18	4	2	12			
RED	419	130	233	296	252	108	298	335	402	2473	RED	5099
Par	5	3	4	4	4	3	4	4	5	36	Par	72
Handicap	4	16	14	8	12	18	6	2	10			

Manager: Dick Grant   **Pro:** Joe Cieri, PGA   **Supt:** Rick Broome
Architect: Stephen Kay 1996

KNOB HILL COUNTRY CLUB

PUBLIC

360 Route 33, Manalapan, NJ 07726   **(732) 792-7722**

Knob Hill CC is an 18 hole semi-private course open 7 days a week all year, weather permitting. Memberships are available. Tee time reservations must be made in advance.

- **Driving Range**
- **Practice Green**
- **Power Carts**
- **Pull Carts**
- **Club Rental**
- **Soft Spikes**
- **Lockers**
- **Showers**
- **Food**
- **Clubhouse**
- **Outings**

Fees	Weekday	Weekend
Not available at press time		

Course Description: The total redesign of the 140 acre layout at Knob Hill promises to be one of the wonderful new courses in New Jersey. Great care is being taken to protect the environment by keeping the original trees intact. Playing a round will surely be referred to as a "four hour vacation". A completely automated double line irrigation system guarantees exceptional course conditioning. In addition to the scenic views, there will be a variety of fine grass fairways, 15 ponds, lakes and elevation changes to make this a very challenging course indeed.

Directions: Monmouth County, #8
NJTpke. to Exit #8. Take Rte.33 East for approx. 6 miles and make a "U" turn at Woodward Rd. Golf course can be seen from road on the right.

       Manager/Owner: Isaac Kantor   **Architect:** Mark McCumber 1998

NEW JERSEY NATIONAL GOLF CLUB

579 Allen Rd., Basking Ridge, NJ 07920   **(908) 781-2575**

NJ National is an 18 hole semi-private course open 7 days a week all year. Temporary greens are utilized in winter. Memberships are available with 14 day advanced tee times. Non-members can reserve 7 days in advance.

- •Driving Range
- •Practice Green
- •Power Carts
- Pull Carts
- •Club Rental
- •Soft Spikes
- •Lockers
- •Showers
- •Food
- •Clubhouse
- •Outings

Fees	M-Thurs	Fri-Sun
Daily	$65	$80
Members	$40	$47.50
Carts included in above fees		

Course Description: New Jersey National is carved out of heavily treed terrain and natural wetlands but with a European flavor. It is an impressive and beautiful course having virtually no parallel fairways. The holes are each memorable; differing lengths, unique topography and level changes add interest. The large bent grass greens are fast and well trapped. The signature par 4 #17 requires a long carry over a catch basin from the back tees. The 8th is a double dogleg with a lengthy carry over a ditch. The 5 sets of tees make the course playable for golfers of every skill level.

Directions: Morris County, #9
Take Rte.287South to Exit 22. Bear right at exit and then make an immediate U turn onto Rtes.202-206South. Get in left lane, go under Rte.287 and turn left onto Schley Mt. Rd. Proceed through Hills development. Course is about 2 miles ahead on left.

Hole	1	2	3	4	5	6	7	8	9	Out	BLUE	Rating 73.7
BLUE	425	522	396	182	405	398	152	549	385	3414		Slope 137
WHITE	365	471	367	145	380	371	131	515	361	3106		
Par	4	5	4	3	4	4	3	5	4	36	WHITE	Rating 70.6
Handicap	8	4	10	16	14	6	18	2	12			Slope 131
RED	298	412	281	118	257	288	107	405	235	1234		
Par	4	5	4	3	4	4	3	5	4	36	RED	Rating 68.8
Handicap	10	2	8	16	12	6	18	4	14			Slope 121
Hole	10	11	12	13	14	15	16	17	18	In		Totals
BLUE	484	220	392	560	446	201	366	396	577	3642	BLUE	7056
WHITE	423	184	355	521	409	170	335	335	535	3267	WHITE	6373
Par	4	3	4	5	4	3	4	4	5	36	Par	72
Handicap	1	13	9	7	5	15	17	11	3			
RED	325	130	310	468	345	122	270	219	429	2618	RED	5019
Par	4	3	4	5	4	3	4	4	5	36	Par	72
Handicap	7	17	9	3	5	15	13	11	1			

Manager/Pro: Charles Kilkenny, PGA   **Supt:** Steve Frich
Architect: Roy Case 1997

PEBBLE CREEK GOLF CLUB

40 Route 537, Colt's Neck, NJ 07722   **(732) 303-9090**

Pebble Creek is an 18 hole course open all year 7 days a week, weather permitting. Tee time reservations may be made 5 days in advance. Power carts are mandatory till 1PM.

Driving Range   Lockers
- **Practice Green**   Showers
- **Power Carts**
- Pull Carts   **•Food**
- **Club Rental**   **•Clubhouse**
- **Soft Spikes**   **•Outings**

Fees	Weekday	Weekend
Daily	$30	$40
Twi	$20	$30
Srs	$20	
Power carts $15pp		

Course Description: The picturesque natural atmosphere makes the recently opened Pebble Creek a welcome addition to the world of New Jersey golf. Several holes are surrounded by mature woods; others are links type. Water is in play on six holes of the more difficult back nine. The greens are large, undulating and true. The par 4 16th, a 340 yard dogleg with water in play on both shots has birdie potential. Maintained well, golfers have quite a challenge here.

Directions: Monmouth County, #10
Garden State Pkwy. South to Exit #109. Take Rte.520 West approx. 6 miles to Rte.34 South for 3 miles to Rte.347 East. Club is on right.

Hole	1	2	3	4	5	6	7	8	9	Out	BLUE	Rating 69.3
BLUE	330	405	177	411	197	341	290	540	352	3043		Slope 116
WHITE	322	387	162	394	172	325	274	530	345	2911		
Par	4	4	3	4	3	4	4	5	4	35	WHITE	Rating 68.1
Handicap	9	5	17	3	15	7	13	1	11			Slope 114
RED	230	365	126	370	157	297	245	480	305	2575		
Par	4	4	3	4	3	4	4	5	4	35	RED	Rating 71.0
Handicap	9	5	17	3	15	7	13	1	11			Slope 119

Hole	10	11	12	13	14	15	16	17	18	In		Totals
BLUE	380	218	320	298	585	366	344	527	184	3222	BLUE	6265
WHITE	370	200	301	291	570	361	329	502	167	3091	WHITE	6002
Par	4	3	4	4	5	4	4	5	3	36	Par	71
Handicap	12	14	8	16	2	6	10	4	18			
RED	334	182	263	251	540	341	295	442	133	2781	RED	5356
Par	4	3	4	4	5	4	4	5	3	36	Par	71
Handicap	12	14	8	16	2	6	10	4	18			

Manager/Pro: David Melody, PGA   **Supt:** Rick Krok
Architect: Hal Purdy 1996

RENAISSANCE AT MANCHESTER

3130 Ridgeway Rd., Lakehurst, NJ 08733   1(888) 55ADULT

Renaissance by Calton Homes is a new adult community which will include a 4200 yard 18 hole executive course. The first nine will open in late 1998. It is private, open 7 days a week and closed in winter. Guests will play accompanied by a member.

•Driving Range	•Lockers
•Practice Green	•Showers
•Power Carts	•Food
Pull Carts	•Clubhouse
•Club Rental	•Outings
•Caddies	•Soft Spikes

Course Description: With a 25,000 sq. ft. clubhouse and many recreational opportunities, Renaissance will take its place with other up scale adult communities. The very pretty setting is surrounded by forest. Water is in play if the golfer takes up the challenge. The tees are arranged with one set requiring a carry over water and others further down the tee box that aim directly toward the fairway. The layout wends its way through lots for single family residences many of which will have golf course home sites. For a modest membership fee, residents will have a fine quality golf experience playing on this new course.

Directions: Ocean County, #11
Take the GSPkwy to Exit 88. Go west on Rte.70 for 5.9 miles and turn right on Rte. 571. Proceed 4/10 mile to signs on right for Renaissance.

Architect: Chris Cummins 1998

ROYCEBROOK GOLF CLUB

201 Hamilton Rd., Somerville, NJ 08876   (908) 904-0333

Roycebrook is a semi-private 36 hole golf club open to the public 7 days a week all year, weather permitting. Corporate memberships are available. Reservations may be made up to 14 days in advance. On the scorecard below "T" means temporary.

- •**Driving Range**   •**Lockers**
- •**Practice Green**   •**Showers**
- •**Power Carts**   •**Food**
- Pull Carts   •**Clubhouse**
- •**Club Rental**   •**Outings**

Fees	Weekday	Weekend
Daily	$55	$75
Includes cart		

Course Description: The East course at Roycebrook is fairly open and meanders through the trees. The average size greens have some undulation and strategically placed bunkers add interest. Accuracy of the approach shot is the key to scoring well here. The somewhat longer West course is more of a links style where the bunkers are deep and more prevalent. Both courses have bent grass pockets around and behind the greens so that over-shooting makes the ball roll off severely. Little water comes into play. Roycebrook offers an excellent practice facility and teaching area. These 36 holes will be a welcome addition to the upscale quality courses offered in New Jersey.

Directions: Somerset County, #12
Take Rte. 287South to Rte.22 West. From Somerville circle, go about 5 mi. south on Rte.206. Take jughandle at Hamilton Rd. and go 1.9 mi to course on left. North from Princeton on Rte.206, right at Ham. Rd.

Hole	1	2	3	4	5	6	7	8	9	Out	BLUE	Rating 74.0T
BLUE	401	441	536	418	219	461	553	177	461	3667		Slope 132T
WHITE	351	376	491	378	190	420	495	135	391	3227		
Par	4	4	5	4	3	4	5	3	4	36	WHITE	Rating 69.9T
Handicap	17	5	7	15	11	3	13	9	1			Slope 124T
RED	304	335	433	308	95	337	461	113	354	2740		
Par	4	4	5	4	3	4	5	3	4	36	RED	Rating 70.6T
Handicap	17	5	7	15	11	3	13	9	1			Slope 119T

Hole	10	11	12	13	14	15	16	17	18	In		Totals
BLUE	417	512	213	419	464	445	310	170	541	3491	BLUE	7158
WHITE	375	475	170	362	386	366	278	141	489	3042	WHITE	6269
Par	4	5	3	4	4	4	4	3	5	36	Par	72
Handicap	8	6	12	14	2	10	16	18	4			
RED	308	438	108	329	345	352	204	120	422	2626	RED	5366
Par	4	5	3	4	4	4	4	3	5	36	Par	72
Handicap	8	6	12	14	2	10	16	18	4			

Architect: Steve Smyers 1998

SAND BARRENS GOLF CLUB

1765 Route 9 North, Swainton, NJ 08210   **(609) 465-3555**

Sand Barrens is a semi-private 27 hole course open to the public 7 days a week all year weather permitting. Memberships are available with discounted rates and preferred reservation privileges. Tee times: up to 7 days in advance. New clubhouse in 1998.

•**Driving Range**	Lockers
•**Practice Green**	Showers
•**Power Carts**	•**Food**
Pull Carts	•**Clubhouse**
•**Club Rental**	•**Outings**
• **Soft Spikes**	

Fees	Weekday	Weekend
Daily	$65	$75
Twi/4PM	$45	$45
Reduced rates off season		
Power carts included		

Course Description: The first 18 holes had their grand opening in June of 1997 with the other nine expected to be ready for the 1999 season. Sand Barrens has wide gently rolling fairways and large relatively fast contoured greens, all of bent grass. Unique are huge waste areas of sand in play on every hole where the golfer may ground his club. Also, two holes, the 2nd and 13th, share the same green. The environment has been treated with respect leaving wetlands, native grasses and bayberry vegetation in the rough. This beautifully maintained course with a "Pine Valley"" flavor is a welcome addition to New Jersey golf.

Directions: Cape May County, #13
Take the GSP to Exit 13. Go right to Route 9 and turn right. Course is 1/2 mile north on the left.

Hole	1	2	3	4	5	6	7	8	9	Out	BLUE	Rating 72.5
BLUE	401	411	401	391	161	580	442	595	201	3583		Slope 134
WHITE	355	377	365	345	140	539	416	545	171	3253		
Par	4	4	4	4	3	5	4	5	3	36	WHITE	Rating 69.7
Handicap	7	9	11	15	17	3	5	1	13			Slope 128
RED	266	282	273	255	90	425	308	479	85	2463		
Par	4	4	4	4	3	5	4	5	3	36	RED	Rating 68.9
Handicap	7	9	11	15	17	3	5	1	13			Slope 119
Hole	10	11	12	13	14	15	16	17	18	In		Totals
BLUE	386	561	175	398	295	440	365	188	511	3319	BLUE	6902
WHITE	362	530	141	356	276	409	329	163	485	3051	WHITE	6304
Par	4	5	3	4	4	4	4	3	5	36	Par	72
Handicap	8	4	18	6	16	2	12	14	10			
RED	250	448	113	279	210	308	254	105	387	2354	RED	4817
Par	4	5	3	4	4	4	4	3	5	36	Par	72
Handicap	8	4	18	6	16	2	12	14	10			

Manager: Mike Gaffney   **Pro:** Alden Richards, Jr. PGA   **Supt:** Steve Malikowski
Architects: Dr. Mike Hurdzan, Dana Fry 1997

TPC AT JASNA POLANA

8 Lawrenceville Rd., Princeton, NJ 08540   **(609) 683-9305**

This TPC is a private 18 hole course open 6 days a week all year. Members may make tee times 14-30 days in advance. Guests play accompanied by a member. Motorized pull carts permitted for walkers.

•Driving Range	•Lockers
•Practice Green	•Showers
•Power Carts	•Food
Pull Carts	•Clubhouse
•Club Rental	•Outings
Caddies	Soft Spikes

Course Description: On the impressive Johnson estate, the Gary Player designed golf course has taken the most innovative advantage of this unusual tract of land. The natural topography, preserved by Player's design style, provides interesting elevation changes, adding drama and beauty to the layout. TPC at Jasna Polana offers bent grass tees, fairways and greens, gently rolling terrain and strategically placed bunkers. The elegant Jasna Polana, the neoclassical villa home of the late Seward Johnson, is part of the property that his widow, Barbara, made available to the TPC, a unique and attractive clubhouse indeed. The yardages below are from a preliminary scorecard. At press time, the course had not been rated.

Directions: Mercer County, #14
Take Rte. 287S to Rte.22west. From Somerville circle take Rte.206S, the Princeton Lawrenceville Rd, make right onto Province Line Rd and entrance to club on right.

Hole	1	2	3	4	5	6	7	8	9	Out	BLUE	Rating
BLUE	400	153	522	322	382	438	580	210	477	3484		Slope
WHITE	373	110	452	290	339	390	518	151	415	3038		
Par	4	3	5	4	4	4	5	3	4	36	WHITE	Rating
Handicap												Slope
RED	306	58	405	255	310	333	403	84	239	2393		
Par											RED	Rating
Handicap												Slope

Hole	10	11	12	13	14	15	16	17	18	In		Totals
BLUE	429	196	536	450	428	442	320	207	538	3546	BLUE	7030
WHITE	397	157	479	360	370	369	292	173	504	3101	WHITE	6139
Par	4	3	5	4	4	4	4	3	5	36	Par	72
Handicap												
RED	245	120	401	290	292	265	240	122	433	2408	RED	4801
Par											Par	72
Handicap												

Manager: Billy Dettlaff   **Supt:** Roger Stewart
Architect: Gary Player 1998

INDEX

Key: Names of golf clubs or golf courses are in **bold**.

Names of architects are in *italics*.

Towns indexed are locations of the courses.

Head golf pros are listed by name.

GOLF GUIDES

by
Weathervane Press

If you play golf in the
Metropolitan Area
complete your **"Golf Guide"** library

with

GARDEN STATE GOLF GUIDE

for a set of reference books
covering **every course** within a
75 mile radius of NYC

**See the following page for direct ordering,
or book may be purchased at book stores,
driving ranges, golf stores and golf courses.**

TO ORDER THIS BOOK

Telephone: (201) 569-6605
(201) 461-7960

Postal Orders: **Weathervane Press**
44 Bliss Avenue
Tenafly, NJ 07670

THE GREATER NY GOLF GUIDE
Send check or money order for $18.95, add your local tax, plus shipping and handling ($3.00).

THE GARDEN STATE GOLF GUIDE
Send check or money order for $15.95 plus tax, shipping and handling.

Shipping and handling: $3.00 per book.

For quantity orders, please call Weathervane Press at telephone numbers above.